WITHDRAWN

FINANCE AND STRATEGY

ADVANCES IN STRATEGIC MANAGEMENT

Series Editor: Brian S. Silverman

Recent Volumes:

Volume 21: Business Strategy over the Industry Lifecycle
Edited by: Joel A. C. Baum and Anita M. Mcgahan

Volume 22: Strategy Process
Edited by: Gabriel Szulanski, Joe Porac and Yves Doz

Volume 23: Ecology and Strategy
Edited by: Joel A. C. Baum, Stanislav D. Dobrev and Arjen van Witteloostuijn

Volume 24: Real Options Theory
Edited by: Jeffrey J. Reuer and Tony W. Tong

Volume 25: Network Strategy
Edited by: Joel A. C. Baum and Tim J. Rowley

Volume 26: Economic Institutions of Strategy
Edited by: Jackson A. Nickerson and Brian S. Silverman

Volume 27: Globalization of Strategy Research
Edited by: Joel A. C. Baum and Joseph Lampel

Volume 28: Project-Based Organizing and Strategic Management
Edited by: Gino Cattani, Simone Ferriani, Lars Frederiksen and Florian Taube

Volume 29: History and Strategy
Edited by: Steven J. Kahl, Brian S. Silverman and Michael A. Cusumano

Volume 30: Collaboration and Competition in Business Ecosystems
Edited by: Ron Adner, Joanne E. Oxley and Brian S. Silverman

ADVANCES IN STRATEGIC MANAGEMENT VOLUME 31

FINANCE AND STRATEGY

EDITED BY

BELÉN VILLALONGA

*Leonard N. Stern School of Business,
New York University, New York, NY, USA*

United Kingdom – North America – Japan
India – Malaysia – China

Emerald Group Publishing Limited
Howard House, Wagon Lane, Bingley BD16 1WA, UK

First edition 2014

Copyright © 2014 Emerald Group Publishing Limited

Reprints and permission service
Contact: permissions@emeraldinsight.com

No part of this book may be reproduced, stored in a retrieval system, transmitted in any form or by any means electronic, mechanical, photocopying, recording or otherwise without either the prior written permission of the publisher or a licence permitting restricted copying issued in the UK by The Copyright Licensing Agency and in the USA by The Copyright Clearance Center. Any opinions expressed in the chapters are those of the authors. Whilst Emerald makes every effort to ensure the quality and accuracy of its content, Emerald makes no representation implied or otherwise, as to the chapters' suitability and application and disclaims any warranties, express or implied, to their use.

British Library Cataloguing in Publication Data
A catalogue record for this book is available from the British Library

ISBN: 978-1-78350-493-0
ISSN: 0742-3322 (Series)

ISOQAR certified Management System, awarded to Emerald for adherence to Environmental standard ISO 14001:2004.

Certificate Number 1985
ISO 14001

INVESTOR IN PEOPLE

CONTENTS

LIST OF CONTRIBUTORS — vii

INTRODUCTION: CORPORATE FINANCE AND STRATEGY — ix

PART I: HOW EXTERNAL MARKETS SHAPE CORPORATE DECISIONS AT THE INTERSECTION OF FINANCE AND STRATEGY

INVESTMENTS IN RECESSIONS
Eirik Sjåholm Knudsen and Lasse B. Lien — 3

THE EFFECT OF INSTITUTIONAL FACTORS ON THE VALUE OF CORPORATE DIVERSIFICATION
Venkat Kuppuswamy, George Serafeim and Belén Villalonga — 37

TERMINATION PAYMENT PROVISIONS IN ACQUISITIONS: AN INFORMATION ECONOMICS PERSPECTIVE
Cheng-Wei Wu and Jeffrey J. Reuer — 69

CAN YOU BELIEVE IT? MANAGERIAL DISCRETION AND FINANCIAL ANALYSTS' RESPONSES TO MANAGEMENT EARNINGS FORECASTS
Guoli Chen and Craig Crossland — 103

PART II: HOW CAPITAL AND OWNERSHIP STRUCTURES SHAPE STRATEGY

FINANCIAL HEALTH AND PARTNER ATTRACTIVENESS IN THE MARKET FOR INTER-FIRM COLLABORATION
Fabio Zambuto, M. V. Shyam Kumar and Jonathan P. O'Brien   147

ACTIVE INVOLVEMENT OF PRIVATE EQUITY FIRMS IN PORTFOLIO COMPANIES AND ITS PERFORMANCE EFFECTS
Christian Landau   185

WHEN DO VENTURE CAPITALISTS BECOME BOARD MEMBERS IN NEW VENTURES?
Haemin Dennis Park and H. Kevin Steensma   231

OWNERSHIP EFFECTS ON UNRELATED DIVERSIFICATION: AN INSTITUTIONS' PERSPECTIVE
Nikolaos Kavadis and Xavier Castañer   253

PART III: HOW STRATEGY SHAPES CAPITAL AND OWNERSHIP STRUCTURES

HOW INNOVATION CAN AFFECT OWNERSHIP STRUCTURE: THE CASE OF TRANSIENT AND DEDICATED INSTITUTIONAL INVESTORS
Abdullah A. Alshwer and Edward Levitas   291

HOW INNOVATION SHAPES A FIRM'S SURVIVAL PROFILE: TAKEOVERS, REGULATORY AND VOLUNTARY DELISTINGS
Silvio Vismara and Andrea Signori   321

THE ROLE OF R&D IN ENTREPRENEURIAL FINANCE AND PERFORMANCE
Alicia Robb and Robert Seamans   341

LIST OF CONTRIBUTORS

Abdullah A. Alshwer	Department of Finance, College of Business Administration King Saud University, Riyadh, Saudi Arabia
Xavier Castañer	Department of Strategy, Globalization and Society, Faculty of Business and Economics, University of Lausanne, Lausanne, Switzerland
Guoli Chen	INSEAD, Singapore
Craig Crossland	Mendoza College of Business, University of Notre Dame, Notre Dame, IN, USA
Nikolaos Kavadis	Department of Business Administration, University Carlos III Madrid, Madrid, Spain
Eirik Sjåholm Knudsen	NHH Norwegian School of Economics, Bergen, Norway
M. V. Shyam Kumar	Lally School of Management, Rensselaer Polytechnic Institute, Troy, NY, USA
Venkat Kuppuswamy	Kenan-Flagler Business School, University of North Carolina at Chapel Hill, Chapel Hill, NC, USA
Christian Landau	EBS Universität für Wirtschaft und Recht, EBS Business School, Oestrich-Winkel, Germany
Edward Levitas	Sheldon B. Lubar School of Business, University of Wisconsin − Milwaukee, Milwaukee, WI, USA
Lasse B. Lien	NHH Norwegian School of Economics, Bergen, Norway

Jonathan P. O'Brien	Lally School of Management, Rensselaer Polytechnic Institute, Troy, NY, USA
Haemin Dennis Park	LeBow College of Business, Drexel University, Philadelphia, PA, USA
Jeffrey J. Reuer	Krannert School of Management, Purdue University, West Lafayette, IN, USA
Alicia Robb	Ewing Marion Kauffman Foundation, Kansas City, MD, USA; University of California, Berkeley, Berkeley, CA, USA
Robert Seamans	Department of Management, Stern School of Business, New York University, New York, NY, USA
George Serafeim	Harvard Business School, Cambridge, MA, USA
Andrea Signori	Department of Economics and Technology Management, University of Bergamo, Bergamo, Italy
H. Kevin Steensma	Foster School of Business, University of Washington, Seattle, WA, USA
Belén Villalonga	Leonard N. Stern School of Business, New York University, New York, NY, USA
Silvio Vismara	Department of Economics and Technology Management, University of Bergamo, Bergamo, Italy
Cheng-Wei Wu	Faculty of Business and Economics, The University of Hong Kong, Hong Kong
Fabio Zambuto	Dipartimento di Ingegneria Chimica, Gestionale, Informatica e Meccanica, Università degli Studi di Palermo, Palermo, Italy

INTRODUCTION: CORPORATE FINANCE AND STRATEGY

Strategy and finance are closely interrelated in the practice of management and have become even more so over the past decade. With the increased informational demands resulting from regulatory changes like Sarbanes Oxley and Regulation Fair Disclosure ("Reg FD"), the boundary between the roles of the CEO of the CFO has become increasingly blurred. Moreover, the global financial crisis has made painfully salient the need to incorporate financial considerations into managerial decisions about firm strategy.

In academic research, however, the two fields have by and large developed independently of each other, even on research topics that have received much attention from both fields, such as mergers and acquisitions, corporate diversification, or corporate governance (Amit & Villalonga, 2006).

This volume seeks to fill this gap by offering a collection of studies at the intersection of finance and strategy. The studies cover a wide range of strategic and financial decisions and research methodologies and showcase how research that bridges both fields of inquiry can contribute new insights of relevance for academics in both fields as well as for practitioners.

HOW EXTERNAL MARKETS SHAPE CORPORATE DECISIONS AT THE INTERSECTION OF FINANCE AND STRATEGY

The first four chapters in this volume analyze how external markets (for capital, labor, products, etc.) shape decisions that lie at the intersection of strategy and corporate finance, or rather, corporate investment — also a major subject of enquiry within the finance field.

In "Investments in Recessions," Knudsen and Lien model how reductions in demand and/or credit availability affect three different types of investments: physical capital, R&D and innovation, and human and organizational capital. Their model builds on the recent and growing finance literature that examines the impact of economic and financial crises on physical capital investment (Campello, Giambona, Graham, & Harvey, 2011; Campello, Graham, & Harvey, 2010; Dimitrov & Tice, 2006; Duchin, Ozbas, & Sensoy, B., 2010), as well as on a much smaller economics literature that looks at the cyclicality of investments in R&D (Aghion, Askenazy, Berman, Cette, & Eymard, 2012; Bloom, 2007) or of human and organizational capital (DeJong & Ingram, 2001). However, by extending prior investment models to multiple types of assets, and in situations like a recession, where the decision to invest in one asset may come at the expense of reduced investment in another, the authors are able to provide a much more comprehensive theory of investment. Indeed, their results critically suggest that recessions affect not only the level but also the composition of investments, sometimes in rather counterintuitive ways. For example, investments in R&D are both more and less sensitive to credit constraints than physical capital is, depending on available internal finance. Investments in human capital grow as demand falls, and both R&D and human capital investments show important nonlinearities with respect to changes in demand.

Moreover, given the well-established finding in the field of strategy that knowledge stocks critically determine competitive outcomes (Barney, 1991; Dierickx & Cool, 1989), this chapter offers an important contribution to strategy by deepening our understanding of how recessions affect knowledge stocks via changes in corporate investment behavior.

The Knudsen and Lien chapter also points to a potentially fruitful avenue for empirical research at the intersection of strategy and finance: exploiting exogenous variation in economic and financial conditions to analyze firms' strategic responses to the availability of resources in capital and product markets. In this vein, Kuppuswamy and Villalonga (2010) analyze how the "diversification discount" evolved during the 2007–2009 global economic and financial crisis and show that value of corporate diversification increased during this period as a result of the financing and investment advantages that diversified firms enjoyed.

In a related chapter included in this volume, "The Effect of Institutional Factors on the Value of Corporate Diversification," Kuppuswamy, Serafeim, and Villalonga exploit a different source of external variation — institutional development across 38 countries — to analyze when corporate diversification is most and least valuable. They test whether frictions in a country's capital, labor, and/or product markets affect the diversification discount or premium. Consistent with the arguments and single-country evidence provided by Khanna and Palepu (2000), Kuppuswamy et al. find that the excess value of diversified firms relative to their focused peers is higher in countries with less efficient capital and labor markets. However, they find no evidence that product market efficiency affects the relative value of diversification.

The next two chapters in the volume focus on the role of information in the relation between external markets and managerial decision-making within firms.

In "Termination Payment Provisions in Acquisitions: An Information Economics Perspective," Wu and Reuer argue that the termination payment provisions (TPP) often imposed by acquirers on target firms at the time of a merger or acquisition are a response to contracting problems in M&A markets. Specifically, when targets are able to wait for a better offer and possibly sell to an alternative bidder, acquirers run the risk of being expropriated of the value of any investments they may make in due diligence, negotiations, and post-acquisition planning – a classic hold-up problem that is exacerbated when the information available on targets' resources and prospects creates better outside options for them. In these situations, TPPs such as termination fees and lockup options compensate the acquirer for the loss of deal-specific investments.

The authors test their hypotheses on a sample of newly public firms – a context where the dissemination of substantial information about the target (during the IPO process) is recent and, to a large degree, exogenous to the acquirer's deal-specific investments.

In "Can You Believe It? Managerial Discretion and Financial Analysts' Responses to Management Earnings Forecasts," Chen and Crossland focus on the critical role played by financial analysts as information intermediaries between corporations and capital markets.

Their study shows that the credibility attributed by financial analysts to management disclosures relative to their own forecasts, to the extent that they two differ, is positively related to the level of managerial discretion. Namely, in high-discretion contexts, characterized by few firm-level constraints, rapid and dynamic industry change, and greater ambiguity about means and ends, analysts place more weight on CEOs' guidance and less on their own original predictions, which are largely based on prior performance.

HOW CAPITAL AND OWNERSHIP STRUCTURES SHAPE STRATEGY

A small but influential literature stream in corporate finance has analyzed the impact of capital structure on product market competition, that is, how firms' financing decisions shape their competitive strategy decisions (see Maksimovic, 1995 for a review). This literature has dealt with issues such as how changes in leverage affect firms' incentives and value in an oligopoly (Brander & Lewis, 1986); how debt influences the firm's ability to enter into implicit and explicit contracts with competitors and customers (Titman, 1984); how competitors' investment choices affect the firm's capital structure and its own investment choices (Maksimovic & Zechner, 1991); and how competitors can exploit conflicts of interest caused by the firm's need for external finance (Bolton & Scharfstein, 1990; Chevalier, 1995).

Three possible extensions to this line of research can evolve into potentially fruitful avenues at the intersection of strategy and finance. The first one is the analysis of the impact of capital structure on more complex competitive and corporate strategies, beyond pricing decisions and the level of capital expenditures as considered within the literature referenced above.

Zambuto, Kumar, and O'Brien's chapter, "Financial Health and Partner Attractiveness in the Market for Inter-Firm Collaboration" (this volume) is an excellent example of this type of extension. The authors argue that a firm's capital structure and financial health can be an important determinant of its attractiveness as an alliance partner in the market for inter-firm collaboration. Other things being equal, high leverage makes firms less desirable partners because the risk of their financial distress makes it more likely that the alliance will be involuntarily terminated, thereby imposing a cost on the partner(s) who may have made relationship-specific investments. In support of this proposition, Zambuto et al. find that leverage is negatively related to the intensity of alliance activity, and that firms are more likely to partner with each other when their levels of leverage are similar. They also show that alliances with highly leveraged firms are more likely to involve equity participation as a form of ex-post protection, especially when the partner has relatively lower leverage.

The chapter offers an important contribution to the strategy literature on alliances, which has emphasized the importance of firms' resources and capabilities as well as risk reduction as a frequent motive for collaboration, yet has fallen short of incorporating firms' ex-ante financial conditions. But perhaps its contribution is even greater to the field of corporate finance, where research on strategic alliances has been egregiously scant.

The second potentially fruitful extension to the literature on capital structure and business strategy lies in focusing on the equity component of capital structure to analyze the impact of corporate ownership on strategy. Thus, while the first extension suggested above can be seen as broadening the "dependent variable" (strategy), the second one can be seen as a refinement of the "independent variable" (capital structure).

The refinement is particularly timely because the study of ownership structure and its impact on performance has received a great deal of attention from the corporate finance field over the last two decades (see, for instance, Demsetz & Villalonga, 2001, and the reviews of the finance literature on corporate governance by Shleifer & Vishny, 1997 and Becht, Bolton, & Röell, 2004). Yet little is known about *how* ownership impacts performance, particularly through the strategy channel.

One of the most revolutionary "discoveries" of this literature, which calls into question the focus of much corporate finance research (and even U.S. securities regulation) on the agency problem between owners and managers, has been that the Berle and Means (1932) model of a corporation as one with a dispersed base of shareholders in which control is exercised by management is more the exception than the rule around the world (La Porta, De Silanes, & Shleifer, 1999) and even in the United States (Holderness, 2009; Villalonga & Amit, 2009). Rather, most firms have a controlling shareholder, for the most part individuals or families, but also states, banks, and other institutions (Claessens, Djankov, & Lang, 2000; Faccio & Lang, 2002; Villalonga & Amit, 2006, 2010). Accordingly, there is increasing recognition of the importance of ownership *identity* and not just structure: Who are these controlling owners? What is their objective function? And how do these owners' goals and preferences shape firms' strategies and ultimately, their performance?

A burgeoning literature in finance and strategy has begun to look at these questions for the most prevalent type of controlling shareholders: founders and their families (see Gómez-Mejía, Cruz, Berrone, & De Castro's, 2011 review of the research on strategies used by family firm owners to preserve their socioemotional wealth, as well as Astrachan, 2010 and all papers subsequently published in the Journal of Family Business Strategy).

Several of the chapters in this volume explore the nature and performance impact of the active involvement of other controlling or, at least, significantly influential owners, like private equity firms, venture capitalists, and institutional investors.

Landau's chapter, "Active Involvement of Private Equity Firms in Portfolio Companies and Its Performance Effects," is particularly valuable in this regard since research about (later-stage) private equity investments is scarce and has largely been circumscribed to the fund level of analysis, rather than at the portfolio company level, which is critical for understanding how private equity owners add value to the businesses they invest in.

Using a unique survey data set from 267 European buyouts, Landau shows that private equity firms play an active ownership role as board members by becoming directly involved in strategic and operational decisions at their investees, and by not simply monitoring, but also supporting the top management team through the provision of both financial and strategic resources, such as networks and management expertise. He also finds that private equity firms' financial and strategic involvement, but not their operational involvement, are associated with significant increases in the financial performance and competitive prospects of portfolio companies.

In addition to the novel empirical findings of this chapter about how private equity owners add value to their investees, this chapter enriches the extant literature on the subject by bringing a resource-based view to bear on a discussion that, like many other areas of corporate finance research, has been dominated almost exclusively by an agency theory perspective.

Complementing the evidence in the previous chapter, Park and Steensma ask the research question "When do Venture Capitalists Become Board Members in New Ventures?" (the title of their chapter in this volume). Using dyadic data on venture capitalists (VCs) and the entrepreneurial ventures they help finance, the authors find that VCs' board membership in these ventures is the outcome of a bargaining process between VCs and entrepreneurs. Specifically, VCs have greater bargaining power and are more likely to gain board membership when their reputation is enhanced by the success of their prior ventures, while entrepreneurs have the upper hand (making VCs board membership less likely) when their own reputation is enhanced by superior innovation or marketing track records.

In "Ownership Effects on Unrelated Diversification: An Institutions' Perspective," Kavadis and Castañer use a sample of French firms with a diversity of institutional shareholders to study how different owners' preferences shape corporate strategy. They specifically focus on shareholders' willingness to protect their value-maximization goals when CEOs fail to do so in the pursuit of their own interests, and on unrelated diversification, which they find to be value-destroying in their sample and hence a valid example of a strategy driven by managerial self-interest. They find that the presence of Anglo-American banks and insurance companies in a firm's shareholder base leads to subsequent reductions in the firm's degree of unrelated diversification, whereas the presence of domestic institutional shareholders leads to subsequent increases.

HOW STRATEGY SHAPES CAPITAL AND OWNERSHIP STRUCTURES

The third potentially fruitful avenue for extending earlier research about the relation between financing decisions and competitive strategy decisions is to analyze the reverse causal direction in this relationship. The last three chapters in this volume push the research frontier in this direction. Namely, instead of examining how capital structure shapes strategy, their focus is on how strategy shapes capital and ownership structures.

Understanding how strategy shapes ownership structure is again critical for understanding the relation between ownership structure and corporate performance that has spawned so much research in corporate finance. It is in fact in the context of this relation that Demsetz (1983) and Demsetz and Lehn (1985) pioneered the concerns about endogeneity and causal inference that have only begun to receive the attention they deserve from researchers in both strategy and corporate finance 25 years later. Thus, this line of research can yield valuable insights about the drivers of the demand for different types of owner and the way in which a firm's ownership is structured.

Alshwer and Levitas' chapter, "How Innovation Can Affect Ownership Structure: The Case of Transient and Dedicated Institutional Investors," provides an interesting juxtaposition to the previous chapter in the volume, as it, too, focuses on the heterogeneity of preferences across different institutional investors. However, Alshwer and Levitas' focus is on a different aspect of owners' preferences (the length of their investment horizon), a different strategic choice (innovation) and as noted above, a different causal direction in the relation between the two (how a firm's innovation strategy can attract investment from one type of shareholder or another).

Using the innovation-intensive U.S. biopharmaceutical industry as their empirical setting and Bushee's (1998) categorization of institutional investors into dedicated versus transient owners, they find that dedicated owners (those with long investment horizons) increase their holdings of a firm's equity as the firm increases the number of products it has in the first two phases of FDA clinical trials (where uncertainty is at its highest).

Their findings provide evidence of reverse causation in the relation between the long-term orientation of shareholders and their choices for R&D and innovation strategies that has been documented in earlier research (Brickley, Lease, & Smith, 1988; Bushee, 1998; Kochhar & David, 1996).

The theme of innovation and its impact on ownership and capital structure decisions continues in the following chapter, by Vismara and Signori, "How Innovation Shapes a Firm's Survival Profile: Takeovers, Regulatory and Voluntary Delistings." As the title suggests, the authors study how publicly listed firms' innovation activity determines whether, when, and how they will be delisted. Using a sample of high-tech newly public firms in Europe, they find that more innovative firms have a higher probability of being taken over. The propensity of firms to delist for other reasons is also affected by firms' innovation decisions, but the sign of the relationship is contingent on the reason for delisting as well as on the measure of innovative activity used: While firms with a rich portfolio of patents are less likely to voluntarily delist, R&D investment increases a firm's likelihood of being delisted due to compliance failure.

The last chapter, "The Role of R&D in Entrepreneurial Finance and Performance," by Robb and Seamans, weaves together several of the themes in the volume to deepen further our understanding of how firms' innovation strategies shape their capital structure. In it, the authors bring different economic theories of the firm (Transaction Cost Economics and information economics) to bear on an entrepreneurial finance setting and argue that R&D-focused start-up firms will have a greater likelihood of financing themselves with equity rather than debt. Using a large representative data set of U.S. start-up firms, they find support for their argument. They also show that mechanisms that reduce information asymmetry, including owner work experience and financier reputation, will increase the probability of funding with more debt. Finally, they show that startups that correctly align their financing mix to their R&D focus will perform better than firms that are misaligned.

The chapters in this volume show that there is as much to learn from bringing financial factors into the study of strategy as there is from bringing strategic considerations into the study of corporate finance. But they are only the tip of the iceberg in terms of the potential gains from integrating research across both fields. We therefore hope that this volume will be a source of encouragement and inspiration for future research at the confluence of finance and strategy.

Belén Villalonga
Editor

REFERENCES

Aghion, P., Askenazy, P., Berman, N., Cette, G., & Eymard, L. (2012). Credit constraints and the cyclicality of R&D investment: Evidence from France. *Journal of the European Economic Association*, *10*, 1001–1024.

Amit, R., & Villalonga, B. (2006). Strategy and corporate finance: Can the interface lead to new insights? Paper presented at Academy of Management Association Annual Meeting, Atlanta.

Astrachan, J. (2010). Strategy in family business: Toward a multidimensional research agenda. *Journal of Family Business Strategy*, *1*, 6–14.

Barney, J. (1991). Firm resources and sustained competitive advantage. *Journal of Management*, *17*, 99–120.

Becht, M., Bolton, P., & Röell, A. (2004). Corporate governance and control. In G. M. Constantinides, M. Harris, & R. M. Stulz (Eds.), *Handbook of the economics of finance* (Vol. 1A, pp. 1–109). Corporate Finance. Amsterdam: Elsevier North-Holland.

Berle, A., & Means, G. (1932). *The modern corporation and private property*. New York, NY: Harcourt, Brace, & World.

Bloom, N. (2007). Uncertainty and the dynamics of R&D. *American Economic Review*, *97*, 250–255.

Bolton, P., & Scharfstein, D. (1990). A theory of predation based on agency problems in financial contracting. *The American Economic Review*, *80*, 93–106.

Brander, J., & Lewis, T. (1986). Oligopoly and financial structure: The limited liability effect. *The American Economic Review*, *76*, 956–970.

Brickley, J., Lease, R., & Smith, C. (1988). Ownership structure and voting on antitakeover amendments. *Journal of Financial Economics*, *20*, 267–291.

Bushee, B. (1998). The influence of institutional investors on myopic R&D investment behavior. *The Accounting Review*, *73*, 305–333.

Campello, M., Giambona, E., Graham, J., & Harvey, C. (2008). *Liquidity management and corporate investment during a financial crisis*. NBER Working Paper.

Campello, M., Giambona, E., Graham, J., & Harvey, R. (2011). Liquidity management and corporate investment during a financial crisis. *Review of Financial Studies*, *24*, 1944–1979.

Campello, M., Graham, J., & Harvey, C. (2008). The real effects of financial constraints: Evidence from a financial crisis. *Journal of Financial Economics*, *97*, 470–487.

Campello, M., Graham, J., & Harvey, R. (2010). The real effects of financial constraints: Evidence from a financial crisis. *Journal of Financial Economics*, *97*, 470–487.

Chevalier, J. (1995). Capital structure and product-market competition: Empirical evidence from the supermarket industry. *The American Economic Review*, *85*, 415–435.

Claessens, S., Djankov, S., & Lang, L. (2000). Separation of ownership from control of East Asian firms. *Journal of Financial Economics*, *58*, 81–112.

DeJong, D., & Ingram, B. (2001). The cyclical behavior of skill acquisition. *Review of Economic Dynamics*, *4*, 536–561.

Demsetz, H. (1983). The structure of ownership and the theory of the firm. *Journal of Law and Economics*, *26*, 375–390.

Demsetz, H., & Lehn, K. (1985). The structure of corporate ownership: Causes and consequences. *Journal of Political Economy*, *93*, 1155–1177.

Demsetz, H., & Villalonga, B. (2001). Ownership structure and corporate performance. *Journal of Corporate Finance, 7*, 209–233.

Dierickx, I., & Cool, K. (1989). Asset stock accumulation and sustainability of competitive advantage. *Management Science, 35*, 1504–1511.

Dimitrov, V., & Tice, S. (2006). Corporate diversification and credit constraints: Real effects across the business cycle. *Review of Financial Studies, 19*, 1465–1498.

Duchin, R., Ozbas, O., & Sensoy, B. (2008). Costly external finance, corporate investment, and the subprime mortgage credit crisis. *Journal of Financial Economics, 97*, 418–435.

Duchin, R., Ozbas, O., & Sensoy, B. (2010). Costly external finance, corporate investment, and the subprime mortgage credit crisis. *Journal of Financial Economics, 97*, 418–435.

Faccio, M., & Lang, L. (2002). The ultimate ownership of Western European corporations. *Journal of Financial Economics, 65*, 365–395.

Gómez-Mejía, L., Cruz, C., Berrone, P., & De Castro, J. (2011). The bind that ties: Socioemotional wealth preservation in family firms. *The Academy of Management Annals, 5*, 653–707.

Holderness, C. (2009). The myth of diffuse ownership in the United States. *Review of Financial Studies, 22*, 1377–1408.

Khanna, T., & Palepu, K. (2000). Is group affiliation profitable in emerging markets? An analysis of diversified Indian business groups. *The Journal of Finance, 55*, 867–891.

Kochhar, R., & David, P. (1996). Institutional investors and firm innovation: A test of competing hypotheses. *Strategic Management Journal, 17*, 73–84.

Kuppuswamy, V., & Villalonga, B. (2010). *Does diversification create value in the presence of external financing constraints? Evidence from the 2007–2009 financial crisis*. Working Paper No. 10 101. Harvard Business School.

La Porta, R., De Silanes, F. L., & Shleifer, A. (1999). Corporate ownership around the world. *Journal of Finance, 54*, 471–517.

Maksimovic, V. (1995). Financial structure and product-market competition. In R. Jarrow, V. Maksimovic, & W. Ziemba (Eds.), *Handbook in operations research and management science* (Vol. 9, pp. 887–920). Finance. Amsterdam: Elsevier North-Holland.

Maksimovic, V., & Zechner, J. (1991). Debt, agency costs, and industry equilibrium. *Journal of Finance, 46*, 1619–1644.

Shleifer, A., & Vishny, R. (1997). A survey of corporate governance. *Journal of Finance, 52*, 737–783.

Titman S. (1984). The effect of capital structure on a firm's liquidation decision. *Journal of Financial Economics, 13*, 137–151.

Villalonga, B., & Amit, R. (2006). How do family ownership, control, and management affect firm value? *Journal of Financial Economics, 80*, 385–417.

Villalonga, B., & Amit, R. (2009). How are U.S. family firms controlled? *Review of Financial Studies, 22*, 3047–3091.

Villalonga, B., & Amit, R. (2010). Family control of firms and industries. *Financial Management, 39*, 863–904.

PART I
HOW EXTERNAL MARKETS SHAPE CORPORATE DECISIONS AT THE INTERSECTION OF FINANCE AND STRATEGY

INVESTMENTS IN RECESSIONS

Eirik Sjåholm Knudsen and Lasse B. Lien

ABSTRACT

The relevance of finance for strategy is probably never greater than during a recession. We argue that the strategy literature has been virtually silent on the issue of recessions, and that this constitutes a regrettable sin of omission. Recessions are also periods when the commonly held view of financial markets in the strategy literature — efficient, and therefore strategically irrelevant — is particularly misplaced. A key route to rectify this omission is to focus on how recessions affect investment behavior, and thereby firms' stocks of assets and capabilities which ultimately will affect competitive outcomes. In the present chapter, we aim to contribute by analyzing how two key aspects of recessions, demand reductions and reductions in credit availability, affect three different types of investments: physical capital, R&D and innovation, and human- and organizational capital. We synthesize and conceptualize insights from finance- and macroeconomics about how recessions affect different types of investments and find that recessions not only affect the level of investment, but also the composition of investments. Some of these effects are quite counterintuitive. For example, investments in R&D are both more and less sensitive to credit constraints than physical capital is, depending on available internal finance. Investments in human capital grow as demand falls, and both R&D and human capital investments show important nonlinearities with respect to changes in demand.

Keywords: Investment; recessions; knowledge; human capital; organizational capital; R&D

INTRODUCTION

This chapter attempts to address two "sins of omission" in the strategy literature. The first is the tendency to brush aside finance and financial resources as strategically uninteresting, because financial markets are considered to be too efficient to have much potential to explain performance differences between firms (Barney, 1986; Peteraf, 1993). The standard view in strategy is that if a firm or an investment project has attractive expected profitability, financing will be made available. So if financing is a real constraint it must be because some other resources/capabilities are missing, keeping expected profitability down. These other resources/capabilities are then the strategically important ones, and they must be associated with significantly less efficient markets, or the absence of a factor market altogether (Dierickx & Cool, 1989). We believe this view is overly simplistic, especially in the context of recessions where financial markets are particularly far from the efficient market ideal. This brings us to the second "sin of omission" of the strategy literature.

A surprising realization that came out of the financial crisis of 2008–2009 was that the strategy literature has very little to say on the subject of recessions and business cycles (Agarwal, Barney, Foss, & Klein, 2009; Bromiley, Navarro, & Sottile, 2008; Latham & Braun, 2011; Mascarenhas & Aaker, 1989). We can only speculate why this is the case. One possible reason is that the coming of age of the strategy field occurred in an unusually stable period, so it did perhaps not seem as important as exploring the opportunities opened up by the resource and capabilities view, the knowledge based view of the firm, NK-landscapes, etc. In addition, the empirical findings of a small year effect in the variance decomposition literature (e.g., McGahan & Porter, 2002) may further have strengthened the notion that research opportunities were greater elsewhere. Since then events have shown us that recessions are not always mild, not always far between, and can have profound impact on the competitive process and its outcomes. Recessions therefore seem to be too important to ignore for a field that purports to understand competitive behavior and competitive outcomes. It is also in our opinion reasonably clear that developing theory that links recessions and strategy involves dispensing with the background assumption of efficient financial markets. Given the interest the field of strategy has devoted to understanding competitive behavior – and how competitive behavior is influenced by forces in firms' external environment – the strategy literature would seem a natural place to look for insights into how recessions affect firm behavior. But since the strategy literature has very little to say on the subject, we need to look to other fields for relevant insights.

The strategy literature has since the 1990s placed accumulation and acquisition of resources and capabilities at center stage in terms of understanding competitive behavior and outcomes. Recessions will affect these processes via changes in firms' investment behavior. Indeed, the hallmark of recessions (and more generally business cycles) is changes in investment levels and investment behavior. Therefore, it seems logical to make changes in investment behavior the starting point for studying firm behavior in recessions.

Finance and macroeconomics, in particular, have devoted considerable attention to both investment behavior and recessions, and to the interaction between the two. For example, there is a broad range of studies in economics about how aggregate investment volumes change over the business cycle (e.g., Aghion, Askenazy, Berman, Cette, & Eymard, 2012; Bernanke, 1983; Petersen & Strongin, 1996). There is also a considerable number of studies in the finance literature on how financing constraints affect investment in general (e.g., Almeida & Campello, 2007; Fazzari, Hubbard, & Petersen, 1988; Hovakimian & Hovakimian, 2009; Hubbard, 1997; Myers & Majluf, 1984), and how it affects investments during recessions (e.g., Campello, Giambona, Graham, & Harvey, 2010; Campello, Graham, & Harvey, 2010; Dimitrov & Tice, 2006; Duchin, Ozbas, & Sensoy, 2010; Kuppuswamy & Villalonga, 2010). Moreover there are literatures that focus on particular types of investment, rather than investment in general. While most papers in economics and finance mainly seem to have physical investment in mind, there is a notable literature on R&D investment during recessions (e.g., Aghion et al., 2012; Bloom, 2007; Bougheas, Görg, & Strobl, 2003) and a significantly smaller literature on human- and organizational capital investment (DeJong & Ingram, 2001; López-García, Montero, & Moral-Benito, 2013).

However, what these literatures rarely do is to combine and contrast the different main categories of investment: physical-, R&D and innovation, and human and organizational capital. We aim to offer such a contrast in the following. Note that this distinction roughly coincides with the distinction between tradable (physical-) and non-tradable (R&D and human capital-) assets, a distinction that is important in the strategy field (e.g., Dierickx & Cool, 1989). Another thing that is largely absent in existing business cycle literature is the recognition that the two main effects of a recession; a decline in demand and reduced credit availability, will have different effects on the different types of investment. Some papers focus on demand. Others focus on credit. We combine and contrast both demand- and credit effects, and how the different types of investment are affected differently by them.

Our goal here falls short of developing a complete theory of strategy for recessions and business cycles. Instead our more modest aim is to contribute by laying some of the groundwork for such a theory by synthesizing and conceptualizing a crucial piece of the knowledge that would need to go into such a theory. We devote special attention to knowledge investments due to the almost universally accepted primary importance of knowledge stocks in determining competitive outcomes (Barney, 1991; Dierickx & Cool, 1989; Wernerfelt, 1984). Understanding how recessions affect knowledge stocks via changes in investment behavior, is presumably of particular value to strategy researchers.

We split knowledge investments into different types of knowledge stocks, specifically investments in R&D and innovation, and investments in human- and organizational capital. To simplify terminology we will refer to the former as R&D and the latter as human capital investments. A key distinction between the two is that R&D and innovation is primarily oriented at creating new knowledge, while investments in human- and organizational capital primarily deals with acquiring, disseminating, and exploiting existing knowledge. As we elaborate below there are important differences between how these two categories of knowledge investments are affected by recessions. We also examine investments in physical assets, partly to form a contrast to knowledge assets, but also because giving prominence to non-tradable assets does not imply that we believe tradable assets can safely be ignored.

Our analysis generates a number of interesting insights about the effects of demand- and credit shocks on different types of investment. For example, R&D investments will be less sensitive to demand reductions than physical investments, and both more and less sensitive to credit constraints than physical capital – depending on available internal finance. Furthermore, human capital investments are actually stimulated by mild demand reductions, but for strong demand reductions they decrease, and notably, they also decrease for firms that experience increases in demand. This implies that there are important nonlinearities in the relationship between demand and human capital investments.

The rest of the chapter is structured as follows: First we present a general theory of how firms' investments are affected by changes in demand and credit, and apply this to physical investments. With this as the standard apparatus we then contrast physical investments with investments in R&D and innovation, and subsequently with investments in human- and organizational capital. In each section, we formulate propositions about the different effects of recessions on investments, and also about differences across asset types with respect to these effects. We close the chapter with conclusions and implications.

INVESTMENTS IN RECESSIONS: A GENERAL APPROACH

While recessions differ in their specific causes, intensity and duration, some common features are present in most recessions, in particular reductions in demand and reductions in access to credit. Both are relevant in most recessions, but firms may experience them in different degrees and in different combinations (Tong & Wei, 2008). They affect firms' investment opportunities (Bernanke, 1983; Ghemawat, 2009), cash flow from operations available to finance investments (Bhagat & Obreja, 2013; Bond, Harhoff, & Reenen, 2005), and the availability of finance (Ivashina & Scharfstein, 2010). For example, the bank channel has been designated as important in depressing investments (Bernanke & Gertler, 1989, 1990) causing firms and industries that are particularly dependent on credit to cut deeper in investments than those that are less dependent, even controlling for investment opportunities (Braun & Larrain, 2005; Campello, 2003). Similarly, Petersen and Strongin (1996) and Geroski and Gregg (1997) show that shocks to investment opportunities and cash flows vary considerably across firms and industries.

The business cycle literature in economics and finance provide ample evidence of the strength of the aggregate effects of recessions. Gilchrist and Sim (2007) estimate that 50–80% of the drop in investment during a recession is due to financial factors that constrain firms' ability fund investments. In sum, then, recessions may cause serious distortions in both the level and composition of investment – factors that are important to competitive behavior and ultimately competitive outcomes.

To illustrate the general effect of reductions in demand and reductions in access to credit on investments, we draw on Hubbard (1997) and Gertler and Hubbard (1988). The most immediate and instinctive association when the term investment is brought up, is investment in physical capital. We therefore let physical capital serve as the vehicle for presenting the general framework for investments in recessions. However, there will be differences between different asset types. These differences will affect the placement and shape of the demand and supply curves in the general model, and also the way the curves shift in a recession. After presenting the general framework, we therefore contrast investments in physical assets with other investment categories, using physical capital as our benchmark.

Fig. 1 shows the relationship between a firm's demand for capital and the supply of capital it faces. The horizontal axis shows the quantity of investments while the cost of capital is on the vertical axis. The demand curve, D, illustrates demand for capital by the firm, and is downward sloping since lower capital costs increases the desired level of investments. The location of the demand curve is determined by the expected future profits of the investments. The supply curve, S, illustrate the supply of capital to the firm. Since firms will finance some (or all) of their investments using internal funds, the supply curve is horizontal to the point CF, which is the firms' cash flow (hence: CF). From here on, external capital is needed to

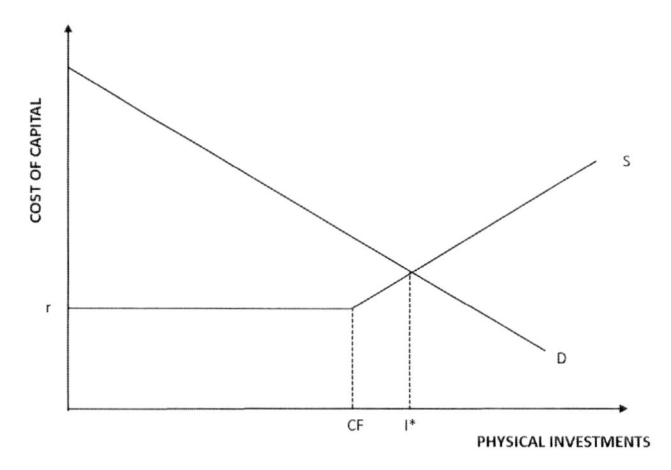

Fig. 1. Basic Framework.

fund further investments.[1] The cost of internal funds is depicted as r, the risk adjusted market rate of return (which is the opportunity cost of internal funds).[2] The slope of the curve of external capital (the S-curve from CF and onward) depends on how much the creditors must be compensated for risk, and will be upward sloping since increasing debt increases the risk to credit suppliers. The equilibrium investments are I^* where the expected marginal profitability of capital equals the marginal interest rate.

Changes in demand can affect firms' investments in two ways, one is by changing the investment opportunities, and the other is by reducing profits and thus access to internal funding. We start with the former.

Investment Opportunities

A reduction in the expected profit of investments causes the demand for capital curve to shift inward, while an increase in expected profit makes it shift outward. The rather unsurprising result of a reduction in investment opportunities is a new equilibrium with reduced investment and reduced demand for credit. Conversely, an increase in investment opportunities will make firms increase their investments. Fig. 2 shows how a reduction in investment opportunities causes firms to reduce their investments.

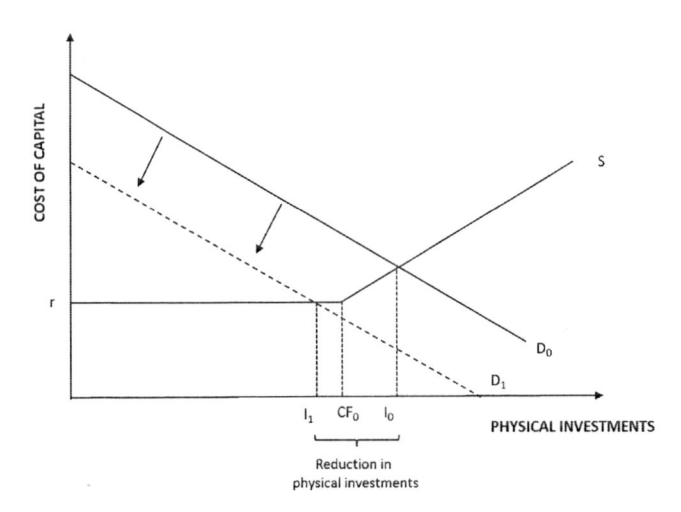

Fig. 2. Reductions in Investment Opportunities for Physical Investments.

Particularly two things drive down investment opportunities for physical capital. First, a firm experiencing a fall in demand is likely to have low capacity utilization, driving down the expected profitability of physical investments. If existing capacity is underutilized, both adding to- and replacing worn out physical capital become less attractive. This means that investment opportunities are reduced, the demand for capital curve (D) will shift inward – and investment will be reduced.

The second effect that reduces investment is the option value associated with postponing investments during times of uncertainty (Bernanke, 1983). Bernanke (1983) argues that the option value of waiting for new information increases when uncertainty temporarily grows. This happens when investment is associated with some degree of irreversibility – *and* new information relevant to assess the long-run returns arrives over time. Firms are better off waiting for new information if improved information is more valuable than the short-term return from undertaking the investments immediately.

Internal Funding

Changes in demand conditions can also affect firms' physical investments via their access to internal funding, that is, their cash flow. A reduction in available internal funding will, as long as internal funds cannot be costlessly replaced by other sources of finance, imply an inward shift in the supply of capital curve (S) and a negative effect on physical investments. This effect is illustrated in Fig. 3 as a shift in the cash flow from CF_0 to CF_1, which causes the supply curve, S, to shift inward. After this shift external sources are needed to fund a larger portion of investments. The upward slope of the external part of the supply curve means that the cost of investments are now higher, and this reduces the desired level of investments as illustrated in Fig. 3. Obviously, an increase in the cost of internal capital (r), for example because of an increase of the risk free rate of return, and/or an increase in the risk premium, will cause an upward shift in the S-curve and also reduce investment.

Reductions in cash flow may also affect the slope of the S-curve. If a firm's cash flow is reduced, the firm has less internal funding for its investments, and supposedly also less collateral that can be used to access external finance. Fazzari et al. (1988) study the tradeoff between internal and external funding of investments during recessions, and find that investments become more sensitive to internal finance (cash flow) as firms have

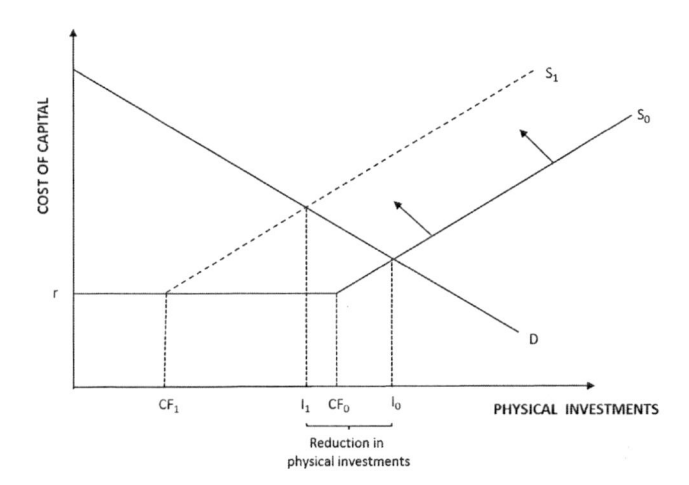

Fig. 3. Reductions in Access to Internal Finance for Physical Investments.

greater difficulties in accessing external finance. A negative shift in access to internal finance may therefore have severe effects on investment as firms both have to substitute internal funds with more costly external finance, and the external finance becomes more costly as the reduction in cash flow increases in magnitude.

Access to Credit

Next we turn to the effect of reduced credit availability. This makes the S-curve steeper, as credit providers demand larger compensation for providing funds. The marginal cost of credit is upward sloping, and the steepness of the curve depends on (a) the value of collateral (Almeida & Campello, 2007) and (b) lenders perceived risk (Fazzari et al., 1988). Both (a) and (b) may cause the S-curve to become steeper in recessions. When lenders experience an adverse shock or a mounting fear of future losses, they reduce lending and raise interest rates (Chava & Purnanandam, 2011). Collateral becomes less valuable because assets are expected to generate less profit (Bernanke & Gertler, 1990), and perceived risk increases due to the general spike in uncertainty in recessions (Bloom, 2007). As a quantitative illustration Ivashina and Scharfstein (2010) find that during the financial crisis of 2008 (in the United States), new loans to large borrowers fell by 79% relative to the peak of the boom, and the volume of loans for real investments fell by 72% relative to the peak level in 2007. Liquidity in capital markets is thus procyclical with the cost and scarcity of capital increasing in recessions (e.g., Acharya & Viswanathan, 2011; Bernanke & Gertler, 1989; Bernanke, Gertler, & Gilchrist, 1996; Eisfeldt, 2004; Eisfeldt & Rampini, 2006; Shleifer & Vishny, 1992). Following the rotation of the supply curve, the firm has to pay a higher price for its external funds, and the desired level of investments decline. This is illustrated in Fig. 4.

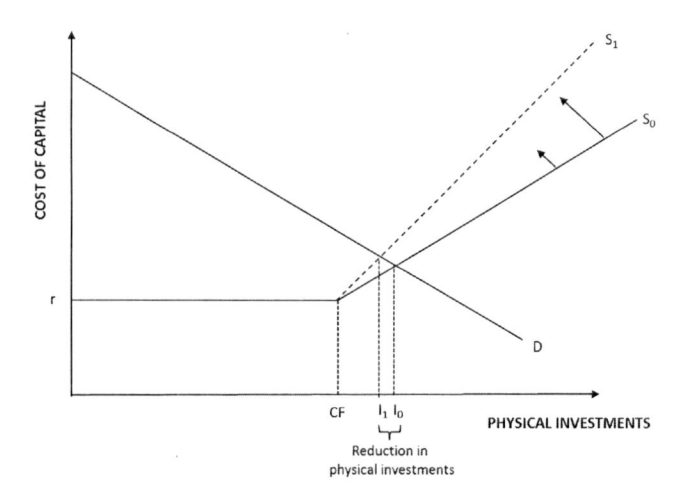

Fig. 4. Reductions in Access to Credit for Physical Investments.

Net Effects

As seen, the three effects all work in the same direction for physical capital. Demand fall in recessions will reduce investment opportunities and thus lower the *incentives* for firms to invest in new capacity, while financing constraints will lower firms' *ability* to finance new physical investments. In sum this implies that physical investments should be strongly procyclical, as indeed they are (Aghion et al., 2012; Petersen & Strongin, 1996). This negative relationship between the severity of demand- and credit shocks and investments in physical capital is shown in Fig. 5.

In terms of the relative size of these effects, the *ability* to access finance will only affect investments for firms with *incentives* to invest, which implies that demand reductions are likely to have a larger effect on physical investments than reductions in access to internal finance or credit.

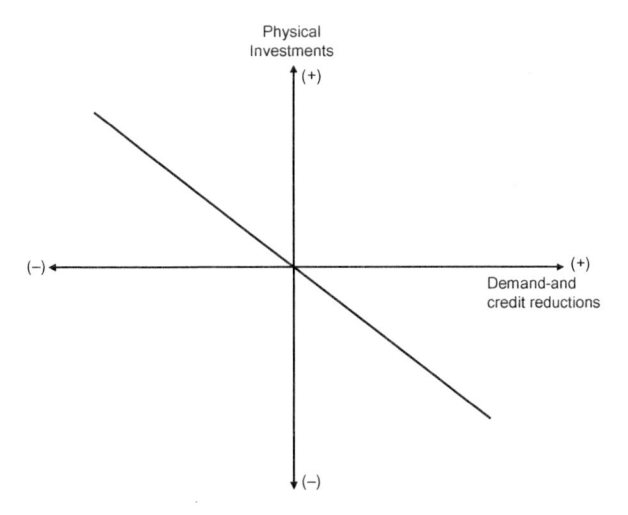

Fig. 5. Net Effects Physical Investments.

So far, we have only looked at physical investments. However, as mentioned above, differences across asset types will affect the placement and shape of the demand- and supply curves in the general model, and also the way the curves shift in a recession. In the following, we therefore examine investments in two additional categories; investments in R&D and human capital.

R&D

In the following, R&D investment refers to any investment related to process- and/or product innovation. As with physical investments, recessions will have three distinct effects. One is changes in investment opportunities, another is reductions in firms' cash flow, and the third is reduced access to credit.

Changes in Investment Opportunities

An important mechanism that may in fact stimulate investment opportunities in R&D during recessions can be derived from the so-called pit-stop view of recessions (Aghion & Saint-Paul, 1998; Davis & Haltiwanger, 1990;

Gali & Hammour, 1993; Hall, 1991). This view claims that the opportunity costs of using idle labor resources in R&D are much lower in periods of low capacity utilization, and that this cost reduction in turn stimulates investment. Investments in R&D have a two component cost structure where one component is out-of-pocket-costs, and the other is the opportunity cost of personnel and other resources involved. Under low capacity utilization this opportunity cost can drop to zero. Under high capacity utilization, the opportunity cost of using production personnel in R&D is the value of the output they could have produced if they were assigned to production. The upshot from this is that R&D becomes more attractive during recessions (D-curve shifts outward, see Fig. 6). Note that there is no equivalent pit-stop effect for physical capital.

Furthermore, there are important mechanisms that make firms conservative about cutting R&D investments. First, investments in R&D are long-term investments that are more difficult to scale up and down than investments in physical capital. If you cut R&D, you are unlikely to be able to scale investments back up again quickly (Li, 2011). A large portion of investments in R&D is related to paying scientists and engineers, and a considerable share of the new knowledge will exist in the form of tacit, highly specialized and firm specific knowledge carried by these workers, or embedded in teams (Hall, 2010). Laying off this type of personnel is costly, because valuable knowledge investments will be lost, and because R&D productivity cannot easily be restored by hiring replacements when demand

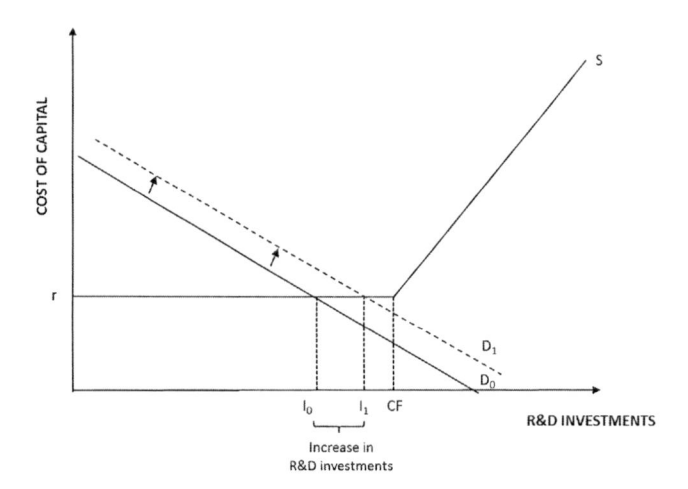

Fig. 6. Increase in Investment Opportunities for R&D Investments.

picks up. As a direct result of these high adjustment costs, firms smooth their R&D investments over time (Hall, 2010).

Another argument is the option value discussed above (Bernanke, 1983). The option value will be inversely related to the time span needed to activate the investment. Since the time span for R&D projects is relatively long (four to six years on average, according to Ghemawat (2009)), the option value of waiting is relatively low for R&D investments. This also reduces their sensitivity to transitory fluctuations in demand.

In sum, the discussion above shows how the absolute effect of demand reductions on investment opportunities in R&D is flat or weakly positive. This makes us suggest the following proposition:

Proposition 1. Reductions in demand will have zero- or a weakly positive effect on investment opportunities in R&D.

If we compare the investment opportunities in R&D with that of physical capital, we see that the former will be less depressed by recessions than the latter. The reasons are that there is no pit-stop effect for physical capital (Aghion & Saint-Paul, 1998; Bean, 1990; Bloom, 2007; Gali & Hammour, 1993), the adjustment costs are higher for R&D investment than for physical capital (Aghion, Angeletos, Banerjee, & Manova, 2010; Hall, Blanchard, & Hubbard, 1986), and finally, the option value of postponing investment is lower for R&D (Bernanke, 1983). This gives us the following proposition:

Proposition 2. Reductions in demand will have a smaller effect on investment opportunities in R&D than on investment opportunities in physical capital.

Changes in Access to Internal Finance

The second effect of reduced demand on R&D is by reducing firms' cash flows, and thereby their access to internal funding (S-curve shifts inward, see Fig. 7). R&D investments are costly to finance externally, and such investments will therefore primarily be financed internally (Bertoni, Colombo, & Croce, 2010; Bougheas et al., 2003; Carpenter & Petersen, 2002; Czarnitzki & Hottenrott, 2011; Müller & Zimmermann, 2009; Myers & Majluf, 1984; Ughetto, 2008). This means that the intersection between the supply- and demand for capital curves is located to the left of the CF-mark. There are several reasons for this. First, there is considerable

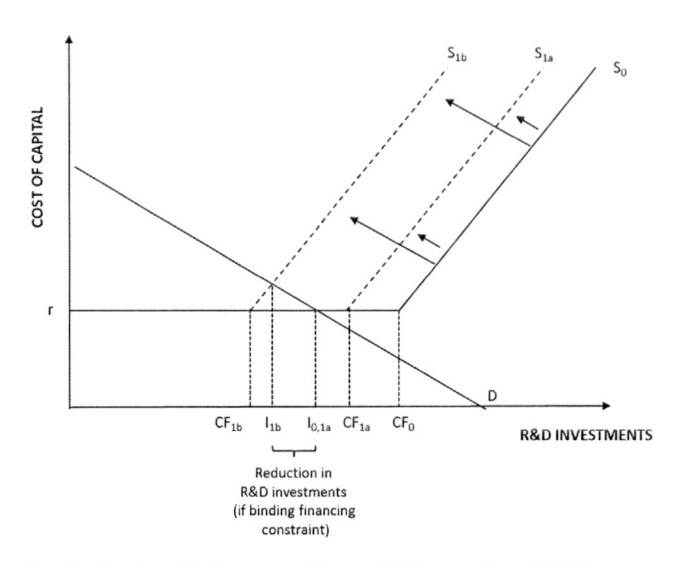

Fig. 7. Reductions in Access to Internal Finance for R&D Investments.

uncertainty related to the output of R&D investments (Hall, 2010), and more uncertain projects are less attractive to credit providers. This is because lenders cannot benefit from the upside of the projects, while equity investors can. So while lenders lack the upside potential, they are confronted with the full downside of R&D projects. Second, the output from R&D investments is usually both intangible and characterized by high specificity, making the salvage value low if the project should fail (Gugler, 2001). Third, the information asymmetries associated with investments in new knowledge are larger than for other types of investment (Hall, 2002), and forth, the low initial cash flow from the innovation projects may be insufficient to cover interest rates on a loan (Gugler, 2001).

All the above implies that (i) the demand curve for capital intersects the supply curve either to the left of the CF-mark or close to it on the right (high share of internal finance), (ii) that the capital supply curve (for external capital) is steep for R&D investments, and (iii) that the steepness will increase in recessions as uncertainty increases. For these reasons R&D investments will be negatively affected by the reduced availability of internal finance if the new intersection between the supply and demand for capital curve is relocated to the right of the CF-mark. If, however, this is not the case, then R&D investments will be insensitive to changes in access to internal finance. Several empirical studies have found support for a relationship between access to internal finance and R&D investments (e.g., Bertoni et al., 2010; Bhagat & Obreja, 2013; Bhagat & Welch, 1995; Brown, Fazzari, & Petersen, 2009; Hall, 1992; Harhoff, 1998; Himmelberg & Petersen, 1994; Rafferty, 2003).

> **Proposition 3.** The relationship between internal finance and R&D investment is a kinked function. Up until the point where internal finance suffices to fully fund R&D, the investment levels are insensitive to small changes in internal finance. Beyond this point reductions in internal finance will reduce R&D-investment.

Next we compare the relative effects of internal finance for R&D with those of our contrast category, physical capital. We can illustrate the difference between the two by comparing the general model of both investment categories under "normal market conditions". As mentioned, R&D investments are usually financed internally, which implies that for this category of capital, the intersection between the demand- and supply curve will be located to the left of the CF-point (or to the right, close to it). In contrast, physical capital investments are usually financed with both internal- and external capital, which in turn implies that the intersection of the demand- and supply curves for physical investments will be located to the right of the CF-mark. Now, imagine that a recession hits and reduces the firms' access to internal finance (an inward shift the supply curve). For physical capital, such a shift has an immediate detrimental effect on investments as the firm is forced to fund a larger share of its investments externally. In contrast, an inward shift in the supply curve will not affect R&D investments if the new intersection between the supply- and demand curve is located to the left of the CF-mark. At this point, the firm still has the ability to finance all of its R&D investments using only internal funds, and the reduced access to internal finance will have no apparent effect. If, however, the negative shift in the supply of capital curve means that the new equilibrium is located to the right of the CF-mark, investments will be reduced as the firm has to turn to costly external credit to fund a portion of its investments. For such large drops in access to internal finance (beyond the CF-point), R&D investments will be more sensitive to internal finance than physical capital. The reason for this is simply that the supply curve for credit for R&D is mainly the supply curve for unused debt capacity in existing physical assets (elaborated below), which in turn means that the supply curve will be steeper for R&D after the CF-point, than is the supply curve for physical capital.

Proposition 4. Compared to physical capital, R&D investments are less sensitive to changes in internal finance when the firm is able to fully fund R&D from internal finance, but more sensitive to changes in internal finance if it is not.

Changes in Access to Credit

As noted, when a negative demand shock occurs, firms that are able to finance R&D and innovation internally will tend to maintain these investments, while firms that are unable to do so must either cut investment and/or increase borrowing (see Fig. 8). Due to the high adjustment costs of R&D investments, firms will prefer increasing debt to cutting investments in R&D and innovation. The reason why firms would rather increase debt, even if credit is costly, is that loans can be repaid, refinanced or substituted with new equity when conditions allow it. A crippled R&D department, on the other hand, may take years to rebuild. There is in other words an essential difference in reversibility between the two options, leading firms to prefer an increase in debt.[3]

How can changes in access to credit be relevant for a category of investment that seems so notoriously difficult to finance by credit? The reason is

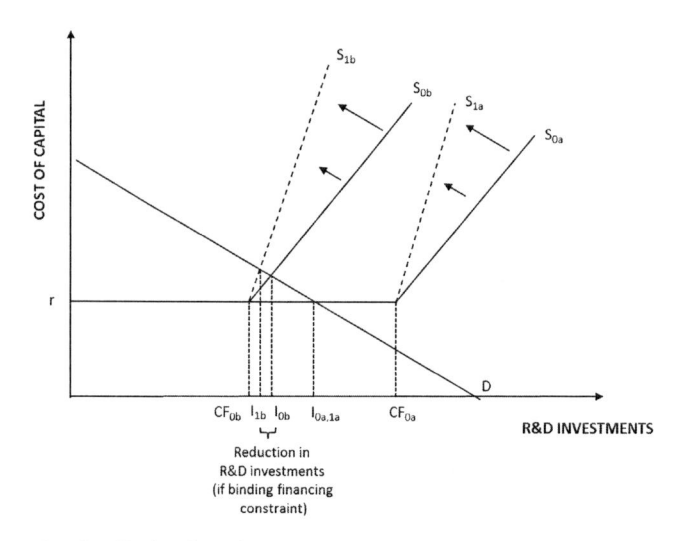

Fig. 8. Reductions in Access to Credit for R&D Investments.

simply that firms do not lend on their R&D assets. Instead they utilize unused borrowing capacity in physical assets to get credit to fund R&D when internal finance is insufficient. So our claim is that the pecking order for R&D funding is the following: First, firms will use internal finance (from operations or reserves). Second, if internal finance is insufficient, firms with unused borrowing capacity in physical assets will use credit to maintain R&D. Third, if they do not have unused borrowing capacity, they will cut. From this it follows that credit constrained firms will be the ones that cut these investments most, while unconstrained firms will borrow to maintain them (Aghion et al., 2012). Credit constraints will mainly be determined by unused borrowing capacity in physical assets (Almeida & Campello, 2007). Note here that during recessions, the unused borrowing capacity in physical assets tends to decline as banks become more restrictive, and collateral values are adjusted downward.

Paradoxically, then, even though R&D investments are not usually financed by credit, these investments are quite sensitive to increasing credit constraints during a recession. Many studies have investigated this empirically and found that credit constraints do indeed affect R&D investments negatively (e.g., Canepa & Stoneman, 2008; Gorodnichenko & Schnitzer, 2010; Mancusi & Vezzulli, 2010; Mohnen, Palm, van der Loeff, & Tiwari, 2008; Paunov, 2012; Savignac, 2008; Schneider & Veugelers, 2010).

Proposition 5. The relationship between access to credit and R&D investment is a kinked function. Up until the point where internal finance suffices to fully fund R&D, the investment levels are insensitive to changes in access to credit. Beyond this point reductions in access to credit will reduce R&D-investment.

The supply curve for credit for R&D is, as we have argued above, mainly the supply curve for unused debt capacity in existing physical assets. Debt will generally be more expensive the larger the share of debt capacity a firm uses. The unused debt capacity in existing physical assets will on the margin be more expensive than the debt capacity used to finance new physical assets under recessions. It will also be more expensive than the unused debt capacity for new physical assets under normal market conditions. This means that (i) the supply curve for external finance will be steeper for R&D investments than for physical investments and (ii) that the steepness will increase relatively more for R&D investments in periods of recessions. The counterintuitive conclusion from this is that credit constraints will actually have a lager negative impact on R&D investments than on physical investments, given that the firm cannot fully fund its R&D internally.

Proposition 6. Compared to physical capital, R&D investments are less sensitive to changes in access to credit when the firm is able to fully fund R&D from internal finance, but more sensitive if not.

Net Effects

The opportunity costs argument implies that firms should be more willing to invest in R&D during recessions, the adjustment cost argument implies that firms will be more reluctant to cut R&D, while the financial constraints (both internal- and external) argument states that intangible investments should be more difficult to finance during recessions. So, which of them dominates?

The above discussion implies that the relationship between demand reduction and R&D investments is non-linear. Regarding the form of this linearity, we reason as follows: For mild reductions in demand, the opportunity costs of investing in R&D will fall, stimulating R&D investments. The strength of this effect will depend on the value of utilizing non-R&D personnel in R&D activities. However, at a certain level of demand reduction, the cash flow of the firm is so diminished that it needs external finance to fund its investments. From this point on, the effect of financing constraints (both internal and external) will dominate the opportunity cost effect, and demand reductions will have an increasingly negative impact on R&D investments. The above discussion can be summarized as tracing out a negative cubic function as illustrated in Fig. 9.

There is considerable empirical (macro-level) evidence that the absolute level of R&D investments is procyclical (e.g., Barlevy, 2007; Comin & Gertler, 2006; Fatas, 2000; Filippetti & Archibugi, 2011; Geroski & Walters, 1995; Ouyang, 2011; Wälde & Woitek, 2004), implying that the financing effects dominate the pit-stop effect. Another set of studies have investigated the relative sizes of the opportunity cost- and the financial constraints effect on R&D investments. Aghion et al. (2012) use a panel of French firms in the period 1993−2004 to analyze the relationship between financial constraints and firms' investments in R&D over the business cycle. Their main findings are that R&D investments as a share of total investments are countercyclical for firms that do not face financial constraints, while they become more procyclical as credit constraints increase. They also find that the latter result is magnified in sectors that rely heavily on external finance. These results further indicate that financial constraints dominate the opportunity costs effect. López-García et al. (2013) and

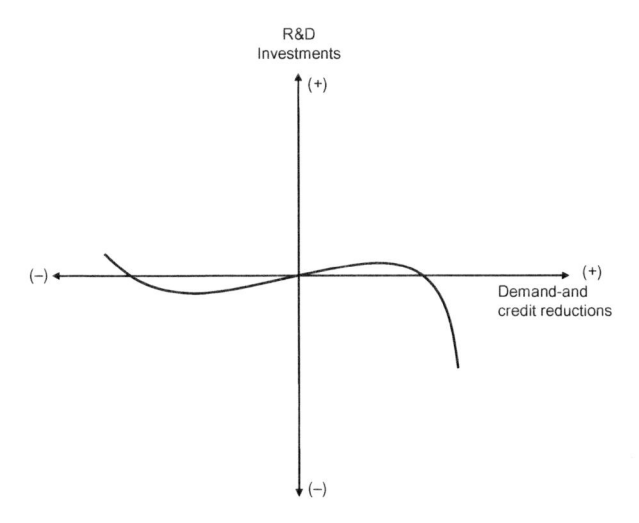

Fig. 9. Net Effects R&D Investments.

Bovha Padilla, Damijan, and Konings (2009) also find that R&D investments are countercyclical for firms without credit constraints and procyclical for constrained firms (for Spanish- and Slovenian firms, respectively).

Summing up, financial constraints (internal and external) have a stronger negative effect on R&D investments than the positive effect of reduced opportunity costs. The above studies suggest that this can explain the observed procyclical behavior of the absolute level of R&D investments on the macro-level. Similarly, R&D investments are less sensitive to changes in investment opportunities than physical investments, due to the higher adjustment cost and the opportunity cost effect.

Proposition 7. The relationship between reductions in demand and -credit, and R&D investments is a negative cubic function.

HUMAN CAPITAL

In the following, human capital investments refer to training of employees and investments in organizational development programs. As before, we'll examine the effects of recessions on human capital investments via changes in investment opportunities, internal funding, and credit availability, and we'll use physical investment as a contrast.

Changes in Investment Opportunities

When demand falls, some human capital is likely to become underutilized. Firms have two options regarding this excess human capacity. One option is to reduce the number of employees to compensate for the excess capacity created. This will cut costs in the short run. However, if the demand fall is expected to be temporary, firms will have to rehire employees to scale their capacity back up, which in turn implies new costs related to searching, hiring, and training the new employees. This implies that firms will not lay off employees until the savings from doing so exceeds the costs of firing/(re)hiring.

The other option is to hoard labor, that is, keep the employees in periods when there is not enough work. This will increase costs in the short run, but the firm will avoid costs of searching, hiring and training new employees if and when demand rises again (Becker, 1962; Oi, 1962; Rosen, 1966). The more specialized the employees are, the more expensive (and difficult) it will be to rehire workers, the higher the costs of firing/(re)hiring, and the more likely it becomes that the firm will hoard labor. In addition, the amount of uncertainty related to when (and if) demand will readjust to pre-crisis levels will also affect the incentives for labor hoarding. Bloom, Bond, and Van Reenen (2007) find that higher levels of uncertainty lead to preference for the status quo (doing as before), which in this context is keeping employees that might be costly to replace later.

The pit-stop argument also works in favor of labor hoarding since the firm can use the excess capacity of employees on training and solving organizational problems, thus increasing the firm's stock of human capital. Similar to R&D capital, human capital investments have a two component cost structure, where one component is the out of pocket costs associated with training employees (e.g., course fee), and the other is the opportunity costs associated with taking an employee out of her ordinary work. Reductions in demand increase the level of excess capacity, which lowers the opportunity costs of human capital investments, and this gives firms stronger incentives to invest. To put it more bluntly, idle employees that the firm wants to retain might as well work on building human capital through training or efforts to solve organizational problems. Human capital investments thus become "cheaper" when demand falls, and the demand curve for capital (D) will shift outward due to the positive shift in investment opportunities (see Fig. 10). This implies a positive effect on human capital investments. This notion of recessions as reorganizations is supported by several studies advocating the pit-stop

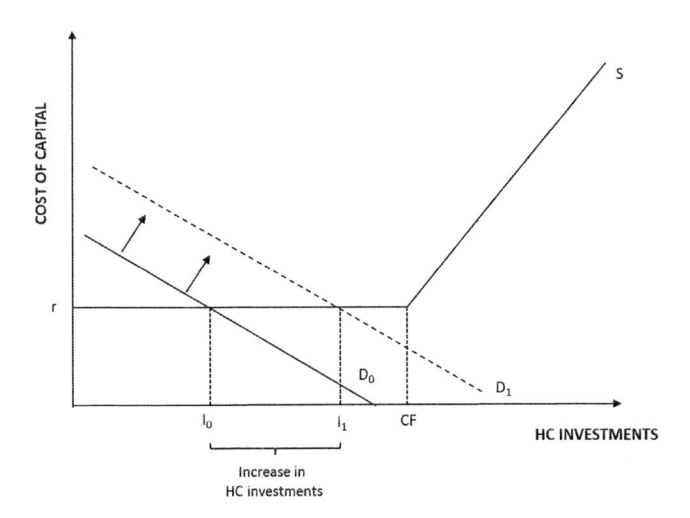

Fig. 10. Increase in Investment Opportunities for Human Capital Investments.

view (Aghion & Saint-Paul, 1998; Caballero & Hammour, 1996; Davis & Haltiwanger, 1990; Hall, 1991).

Proposition 8. Investment opportunities in human capital increase when demand falls.

The opportunity cost component as a share of total costs are larger for human capital than for R&D investments, and the pit-stop effects of recessions will therefore be relatively stronger. This implies that the positive effect of demand reductions on investment opportunities in human capital is greater than for R&D investments, and also that it is greater than the (purely negative) relationship between demand reductions and investment opportunities in physical capital.

Proposition 9. The effect of demand reductions on investment opportunities in human capital will be more positive than for physical capital.

Changes in Access to Internal Funding

Reductions in demand reduce firms' cash flow and thereby also their access to internal funding. If internal finance falls to the point where the firm is unable to finance all the labor hoarding it would ideally undertake, the firm is forced to turn to credit, and/or reduce labor hoarding by turning to layoffs. Reducing labor hoarding will of course mean reducing the opportunity to exploit the reduced opportunity cost of human capital investments. In other words, human capital investments are reduced not because the firms do not have the incentives to maintain them, but because their ability to do so is limited by their ability to finance the labor hoarding.

Empirical studies of job creation and destruction over the business cycle find that the rate of job destruction increases in recessions, while job creation is rather unresponsive to the business cycle (e.g., Davis & Haltiwanger, 1990). However, while there is net job destruction in recessions, much of this activity takes place within a relatively small number of firms that make large cutbacks (Davis & Haltiwanger, 1990). Since a much larger share of firms are affected by demand reductions, than the share of firms that turn to layoffs, the evidence suggests that labor hoarding is a widespread phenomenon. Put differently, a fall in demand has to be of a certain size before a firm starts laying off employees in response to a demand shock it believes will be temporary (see Fig. 11 for details). Accordingly, the relationship between reductions in access to internal finance and human capital investments is a kinked, negative function.

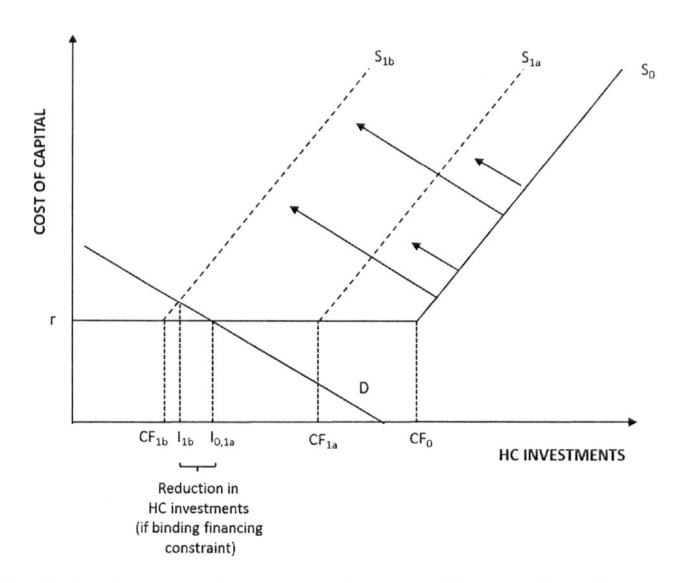

Fig. 11. Reductions in Access to Internal Finance for Human Capital Investments.

Proposition 10. The relationship between internal finance and human capital investment is a kinked function. Up until the point where internal finance suffices to fully fund labor hoarding, the investment levels are insensitive to changes in internal finance. Beyond this point reductions in access to credit will reduce human capital-investment.

Next we compare the relative effects of internal finance on human capital investments with those of physical capital. Here, the argument is similar to the one discussed for R&D in Proposition 4. As for R&D, human capital investments are usually financed internally (Becker, 1962), which implies that the intersection between the demand- and supply curve for human capital investments will be located to the left of the CF-point. When a recession hit and reduces firms' access to internal finance (inward shift in the supply curve), this will not affect human capital investments unless the new intersection between the supply- and demand curve is located to the right of the CF-mark. This is similar to the behavior of R&D investments, although it will take a relatively larger reduction in access to credit to surpass the CF-point for human capital investments. This is because the equilibrium for human capital investments will be located further to the left than for R&D investments. For physical capital a comparable shift in the supply curve would have an immediate detrimental effect on investments because firms already finance a part of such investments externally.

Proposition 11. Compared to physical capital, human capital investments are less sensitive to changes in internal finance when the ability to hoard labor is unconstrained, but more sensitive when the ability to hoard labor *is* constrained.

Changes in Access to Credit

When internal finance is insufficient to finance labor hoarding, the firm has to turn to credit if it wants to avoid laying off valuable employees. However, using credit to finance labor hoarding directly is difficult. Employees cannot be owned, human capital has low salvage value, and they represent very poor collateral (Becker, 1962; Nickell & Bell, 1995). Consequently, much like R&D, using credit to finance labor hoarding is likely to be limited by unused borrowing capacity in existing physical assets (Almeida & Campello, 2007), and the supply curve for external finance will be upward sloping. This is illustrated in Fig. 12.

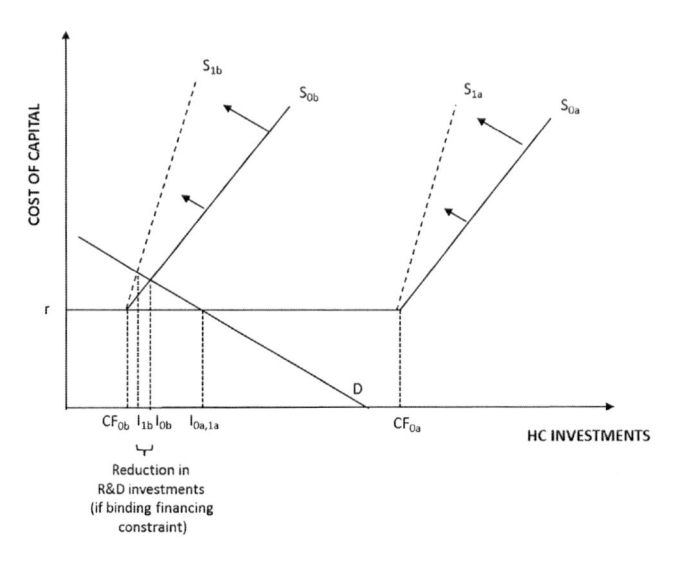

Fig. 12. Reductions in Access to Credit for Human Capital Investments.

As firms exploit more of the unused borrowing capacity in physical capital, credit become increasingly expensive. More expensive credit makes labor hoarding less attractive and the threshold of adjustment costs necessary for hoarding increases. This in turn means that the number of layoffs of employees that would have been hoarded absent financing problems increases, and human capital investments decline.

Proposition 12. The relationship between access to credit and human capital investment is a kinked function, where the kink is located at the point where internal finance just suffices to finance all desired labor hoarding.

If we compare the relative effects of access to credit for human capital- and physical investments, the argument is similar to the argument comparing the effect for R&D and physical investments. That is, the supply of credit curve for human capital is, as for R&D, mainly the supply curve for unused debt capacity in existing physical assets. This means that the supply curve for external finance will be steeper than for physical investments, and that the steepness will increase relatively more in recessions. However, since the fall in internal finance has to be relatively larger for human capital to make credit financing relevant, human capital investments will be relatively less sensitive to credit.

Proposition 13. Compared to physical capital, human capital investments are less sensitive to changes in credit when the ability to hoard labor is unconstrained, but more sensitive when the ability to hoard labor *is* constrained.

Net Effects

Based on the above discussions, changes in demand should have a nonlinear relationship to human capital investments: Reduced opportunity costs associated with training employees when excess capacity rises, increase firms' incentives to invest in human capital. This effect will increase up to a point where the cost of carrying excess capacity becomes too high, that is, when the expected gains from retaining and training employees will be lower than the forgone savings from layoffs, and the firm will increasingly turn to layoffs. This, in turn, reduces human capital investments. Conversely, the opportunity costs of training and investments in organizational capital increases when demand increases, and investments should then fall (Bean, 1990). For sufficiently large increases the firm will have to start hiring, which will tend to drive the need for training upward. The change in investments in training and organizational capital should therefore be a negative cubic function of demand problems. That is, if demand increases, investments should fall. If demand is reduced, investments should initially increase, but eventually decrease (for sufficiently large reductions in demand) as firms turn to layoffs instead of labor hoarding. Similar to R&D investments this pattern is what a negative cubic function traces out (see Fig. 13), but the nonlinearity is stronger for human capital investments because the opportunity cost effect is stronger, and the credit effects are weaker.

The net effect of recessions will be equal to the investment opportunity effect up to the point where the ability to hoard labor depends on access to finance. This is because the investment opportunity effect is present as long as the firm has incentives to hoard labor, while the two financing effects only apply when a binding financing constraint exists. From this point the negative effect of recessions on human capital investments increases rapidly (see Fig. 6). For less severe negative demand shocks, the positive investment opportunity effect implies a countercyclical relationship between recessions and human capital investments. Empirical studies have found this predicted countercyclical pattern of investments in human capital both on firm level (López-García et al., 2013), and on the individual level

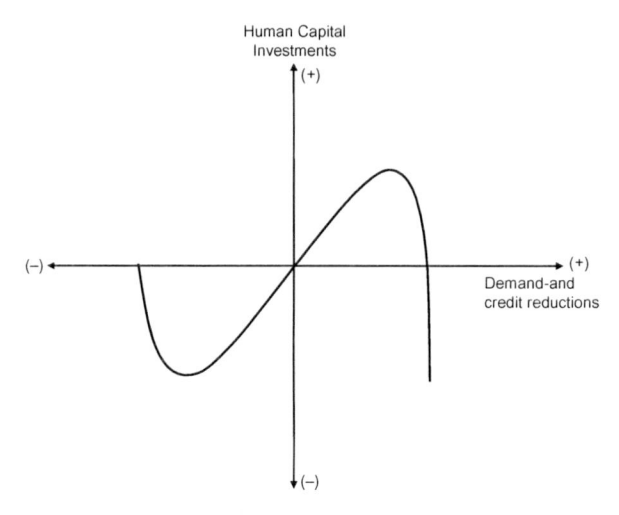

Fig. 13. Net Effects Human Capital Investments.

in the form of increased college enrollments in recessions as individuals use their own excess capacity to accumulate skills in such periods (DeJong & Ingram, 2001; Dellas & Sakellaris, 2003; Heylen & Pozzi, 2007). Also, Geroski and Gregg (1997) found that firms were less likely to cut back on investments related to training of their employees than to cut other investments during the UK recession in the early 1990s. The discussion of human capital investments in recessions are summarized in Fig. 13.

Proposition 14. The relationship between reductions in demand and human capital investments is a negative cubic function, and the nonlinearity of human capital investments is stronger than for R&D investments.

CONCLUSION

The central premise of the present chapter has been that the strategy literature has been virtually silent on the issue of recessions, and that this constitutes a regrettable sin of omission. Furthermore, we have argued that a key route to rectify this omission is to focus on how recessions affect investment behavior, and thereby firms stocks of assets and capabilities, which ultimately will affect competitive outcomes.

The key contribution we have attempted to make here is at the front end of this link, that is, on how recessions affect investment behavior, while we have remained silent on the implications of our propositions for competitive outcomes. We believe a focus on how investment behavior is affected must come before a discussion of the ensuing consequences, which is why we have focused on investment and not performance consequences (see Table 1 for a summary). Nevertheless, it seems pertinent to offer some illustrative thoughts on the implications for competitive outcomes in this concluding section.

For example, we have pointed out that under some circumstances recessions will have a positive effect on investments in human and organizational capital, since excess capacity can imply a de facto subsidy of the (opportunity) costs of making such investments. One might speculate that this will put pressure on competitive advantages that are founded on advantages in human- and organizational capital, for example if followers experience slightly more excess capacity than leaders. We can also speculate that this tendency will be stronger when incentives to hoard labor are strong.

We have also pointed out that firms attempt to shield R&D investments in recessions, but that the ability to do so depends on financing constraints. A firm that cannot fully fund R&D internally will face serious cost increases as it turns to external finance for R&D, and if it cannot borrow to maintain R&D it must cut its investment. Because of the high adjustment costs of R&D, this could create a lasting negative effect on competitiveness. Consider the effects of this from a game theoretic perspective.

Table 1. Summary of the Effects of a Negative Demand- and Credit Shock on Investments.

	Physical Capital	R&D	Human Capital
Investment opportunities	Strongly negative	Zero or weakly positive	Strongly positive
Availability of internal funds	Negative	Zero effect when unconstrained, strongly negative effect when constrained	Zero effect when unconstrained, strongly negative effect when constrained
Reduction in availability of external credit	Negative	Zero effect when unconstrained, strongly negative effect when constrained	Zero effect when unconstrained, strongly negative effect when constrained

It would seem likely that a firm barely able to keep up its R&D would make an inviting target for a better financed competitor. If the stronger firm could lower the weaker firm's margins slightly, it could inflict long lasting damage to its competitor by manipulating it to make irreversible cuts in R&D.

More generally, we believe that the discussion here shows that some of the common background assumptions in strategy are highly problematic during recessions. For example, the strategy literature typically assumes that a number of markets are reasonably well functioning, most notably financial markets, so that positive NPV-investments will be financed. The business cycle literature in economics and finance provide ample evidence that this assumption is violated during a recession, and this can have important implications for competitive behavior – investment behavior in particular.

Another common background assumption in the strategy literature is that the *ability* to finance profitable investments does not vary across different asset types. That is, while capital markets do assess the risk/return profile of different investments, there is no discrimination for or against tangible assets once the risk is taken into account. This means that firms are free to allocate their investments so that the expected marginal returns are equal across different asset types. Again, this is not necessarily the case during recessions. Since intangible assets are typically weaker collateral than physical capital, funding for intangible assets will be particularly difficult for firms that cannot finance these by retained profit or equity reserves (Aghion et al., 2012; Hall, 2002, 2010). So the more dependent you are on credit, the less unused borrowing capacity your physical assets have, the more difficult it will be to finance investments in intangibles and the more you will have to cut in such investments. Moreover, the *incentives* to invest during recessions will also vary across different asset types. As we have seen some investments become less attractive during periods of low demand, while other investments become relatively cheaper and hence more attractive during a recession.

In sum, then, recessions and the financial market frictions associated with (or causing) recessions may create serious distortions in both the level and composition of investment – factors that are important to competitive behavior and ultimately competitive outcomes. This is something strategy researchers cannot sweep under the rug if we want to understand the strategic implications of recessions.

There are many items on the agenda if the strategy field wants to fill this void. One such example is the role of firm heterogeneity. In this chapter, we have not really focused a lot on firm heterogeneity since our primary goal has been to compare and contrast different asset types and the different components of a recessionary shock. More work is needed to understand firm heterogeneity and how it affects both the exposure to demand- and credit shocks, and the way firm responds to them. We think the general framework in this chapter may also be useful for confronting heterogeneity head on, but other approaches will surely also be needed. A nice example of this is the work in finance on how internal capital markets might affect the financing constraints a firm faces during a recession (Dimitrov & Tice, 2006; Kuppuswamy & Villalonga, 2010).

Another potentially fruitful dimension is to gain better understanding of how investment decisions are actually made. It is often difficult to determine econometrically from secondary data if an observed change in firms' investment behavior is caused by changing opportunities, scarce financing, some real option logic, or by perceived adjustment costs. This is problematic since it inhibits our ability to learn about which firms will respond in what way. One interesting approach that may complement conventional techniques is to observe or ask decision makers directly why they respond the way they do. Campello, Graham, et al. (2010) is a source of inspiration in this respect, because they survey CFO's about which changes they made in investments during a recessions and why they acted as they did. Again, more work of this nature would be useful, not only on investment behavior, but on other types of competitive behavior as well.

A third possible direction for future research is related to how strategic interaction is affected by recessions and business cycles. Are firms' possibility for influencing competitors' behavior different in a recession compared to normal times? Which situations and firm properties lead firms to become more or less aggressive in a recession? Which firms make attractive targets in a recession? How do firms in oligopolistic markets capitalize on strength during a recession? So far, all these questions remain unanswered. However, inspiration about these issues can (once again) be drawn from economics, where authors such as Chevalier and Scharfstein (1996) and Rotemberg and Saloner (1986) have laid a foundation. The house on top of this foundation remains to be raised, however.

In closing, almost any question that the strategy field asks can be formulated as a question about whether this phenomenon, mechanism, or whatever, is materially affected by recessions or not, and if yes, how? So, if the strategy field decides to start taking recessions and business cycles seriously, it will open the door to an abundance of research opportunities.

NOTES

1. The logic here implies that internal finance is used before external finance, which is consistent with the pecking order theory of corporate finance (e.g., Myers & Majluf, 1984).
2. The cost of internal capital (r) is here shown as a horizontal line, indicating that a firm can invest its internal capital outside the firm (in the market).
3. We concede that this proposition may not hold if expected future interest rates are very high. If so, firms may cut R&D instead. We do however believe that it will hold for most realistic levels of expected future interest rates.

ACKNOWLEDGMENT

We thank an anonymous AiSM reviewer, Belén Villalonga, Peter G. Klein, and participants at the Academy of Management Meeting, Orlando 2013 for providing helpful comments. We also thank the research project "Crisis, Restructuring and Growth" at NHH Norwegian School of Economics for financial support. The usual caveats apply.

REFERENCES

Acharya, V. V., & Viswanathan, S. (2011). Leverage, moral hazard, and liquidity. *The Journal of Finance*, 66(1), 99–138.

Agarwal, R., Barney, J. B., Foss, N. J., & Klein, P. G. (2009). Heterogeneous resources and the financial crisis: Implications of strategic management theory. *Strategic Organization*, 7, 467–484.

Aghion, P., Angeletos, G.-M., Banerjee, A., & Manova, K. (2010). Volatility and growth: Credit constraints and the composition of investment. *Journal of Monetary Economics*, 57(3), 246–265.

Aghion, P., Askenazy, P., Berman, N., Cette, G., & Eymard, L. (2012). Credit constraints and the cyclicality of R&D Investment: Evidence from France. *Journal of the European Economic Association*, 10(5), 1001–1024.

Aghion, P., & Saint-Paul, G. (1998). Virtues of bad times: Interaction between productivity growth and economic fluctuations. *Macroeconomic Dynamics*, 2(3), 322–344.

Almeida, H., & Campello, M. (2007). Financial constraints, asset tangibility, and corporate investment. *Review of Financial Studies*, 20(5), 1429–1460.

Barlevy, G. (2007). On the cyclicality of research and development. *The American Economic Review*, 97(4), 1131–1164.

Barney, J. B. (1986). Strategic factor markets: Expectations, luck, and business strategy. *Management Science*, 32(10), 1231–1241.

Barney, J. B. (1991). Firm resources and sustained competitive advantage. *Journal of Management*, *17*(1), 99–120.
Bean, C. R. (1990). Endogenous growth and the procyclical behaviour of productivity. *European Economic Review*, *34*(2–3), 355–363.
Becker, G. (1962). Investment in human capital: A theoretical analysis. *Journal of Political Economy*, *70*, 9–49.
Bernanke, B. S. (1983). Irreversibilities, uncertainty, and cyclical investment. *Quarterly Journal of Economics*, *93*, 85–106.
Bernanke, B. S., & Gertler, M. (1989). Agency costs, net worth, and business fluctuations. *American Economic Review*, *79*(1), 14–31.
Bernanke, B. S., & Gertler, M. (1990). Financial fragility and economic performance. *Quarterly Journal of Economics*, *105*, 97–114.
Bernanke, B. S., Gertler, M., & Gilchrist, S. (1996). The financial accelerator and the flight to quality. *Review of Economics and Statistics*, *78*(1), 1–15.
Bertoni, F., Colombo, M. G., & Croce, A. (2010). The effect of venture capital financing on the sensitivity to cash flow of firm's investments. *European Financial Management*, *16*(4), 528–551.
Bhagat, S., & Obreja, I. (2013). Employment, corporate investment and cash flow uncertainty. *SSRN eLibrary*. Retrieved from http://ssrn.com/paper=1923829
Bhagat, S., & Welch, I. (1995). Corporate research & development investments international comparisons. *Journal of Accounting and Economics*, *19*(2–3), 443–470.
Bloom, N. (2007). Uncertainty and the dynamics of R&D. *American Economic Review*, *97*(2), 250–255.
Bloom, N., Bond, S., & Van Reenen, J. (2007). Uncertainty and investment dynamics. *Review of Economic Studies*, *74*(2), 391–415.
Bond, S., Harhoff, D., & Van Reenen, J. (2005, July/December). Annales d'Économie et de Statistique No. 79/80. Contributions in memory of Zvi Griliches (pp. 433–460). L'INSEE/GENES. Retrieved from http://www.jstor.org/stable/20777584
Bougheas, S., Görg, H., & Strobl, E. (2003). Is R&D financially constrained? Theory and evidence from Irish manufacturing. *Review of Industrial Organization*, *22*(2), 159–174.
Bovha Padilla, S., Damijan, J. P., & Konings, J. (2009). *Financial constraints and the cyclicality of R&D investment: Evidence from Slovenia*. LICOS Discussions Paper 239/2009. Katholieke Universiteit Leuven.
Braun, M., & Larrain, B. (2005). Finance and the business cycle: International, inter-industry evidence. *The Journal of Finance*, *60*(3), 1097–1128.
Bromiley, P., Navarro, P., & Sottile, P. (2008). Strategic business cycle management and organizational performance: A great unexplored research stream. *Strategic Organization*, *6*(2), 207–219.
Brown, J. R., Fazzari, S. M., & Petersen, B. C. (2009, February). Financing innovation and growth: Cash flow, external equity and the 1990s R&D boom. *Journal of Finance*, *64*(1), 151–185.
Caballero, R. J., & Hammour, M. L. (1996). On the timing and efficiency of creative destruction. *The Quarterly Journal of Economics*, *111*(3), 805–852.
Campello, M. (2003). Capital structure and product markets interactions: Evidence from business cycles. *Journal of Financial Economics*, *68*(3), 353–378.
Campello, M., Giambona, E., Graham, J. R., & Harvey, C. R. (2010). *Liquidity Management and Corporate Investment During a Financial Crisis*. National Bureau of Economic Research Working Paper Series, No. 16309.

Campello, M., Graham, J. R., & Harvey, C. R. (2010). The real effects of financial constraints: Evidence from a financial crisis. *Journal of Financial Economics*, *97*(3), 470–487.
Canepa, A., & Stoneman, P. (2008). Financial constraints to innovation in the UK: Evidence from CIS2 and CIS3. *Oxford Economic Papers*, *60*(4), 711–730.
Carpenter, R. E., & Petersen, B. C. (2002). Capital market imperfections, high-tech investment, and new equity financing. *The Economic Journal*, *112*(477), F54–F72.
Chava, S., & Purnanandam, A. (2011). The effect of banking crisis on bank-dependent borrowers. *Journal of Financial Economics*, *99*(1), 116–135.
Chevalier, J. A., & Scharfstein, D. S. (1996). Capital-market imperfections and countercyclical markups: Theory and evidence. *The American Economic Review*, *86*(4), 703–725.
Comin, D., & Gertler, M. (2006). Medium-term business cycles. *The American Economic Review*, *96*(3), 523–551.
Czarnitzki, D., & Hottenrott, H. (2011). R&D investment and financing constraints of small and medium-sized firms. *Small Business Economics*, *36*(1), 65–83.
Davis, S. J., & Haltiwanger, J. (1990). Gross job creation and destruction: Microeconomic evidence and macroeconomic implications. *NBER Macroeconomics Annual*, *5*, 123–168.
DeJong, D. N., & Ingram, B. F. (2001). The cyclical behavior of skill acquisition. *Review of Economic Dynamics*, *4*(3), 536–561.
Dellas, H., & Sakellaris, P. (2003). On the cyclicality of schooling: Theory and evidence. *Oxford Economic Papers*, *55*(1), 148–172.
Dierickx, I., & Cool, K. (1989). Asset stock accumulation and sustainability of competitive advantage. *Management Science*, *35*(12), 1504–1511.
Dimitrov, V., & Tice, S. (2006). Corporate diversification and credit constraints: Real effects across the business cycle. *Review of Financial Studies*, *19*(4), 1465–1498.
Duchin, R., Ozbas, O., & Sensoy, B. A. (2010). Costly external finance, corporate investment, and the subprime mortgage credit crisis. *Journal of Financial Economics*, *97*(3), 418–435.
Eisfeldt, A. L. (2004). Endogenous liquidity in asset markets. *The Journal of Finance*, *59*(1), 1–30.
Eisfeldt, A. L., & Rampini, A. A. (2006). Capital reallocation and liquidity. *Journal of Monetary Economics*, *53*(3), 369–399.
Fatas, A. (2000). Do business cycles cast long shadows? Short-run persistence and economic growth. *Journal of Economic Growth*, *5*(2), 147–162.
Fazzari, S., Hubbard, R. G., & Petersen, B. C. (1988). Financing constraints and corporate investment. *Brookings Papers on Economic Activity*, *1*(August), 141–195.
Filippetti, A., & Archibugi, D. (2011). Innovation in times of crisis: National Systems of innovation, structure, and demand. *Research Policy*, *40*(2), 179–192.
Gali, J., & Hammour, J. L. (1993). *Long run effects of business cycles*. Columbia: Graduate School of Business.
Geroski, P. A., & Gregg, P. (1997). *Coping with recession: UK company performance in adversity*. Cambridge: Cambridge University Press.
Geroski, P. A., & Walters, C. F. (1995). Innovative activity over the business cycle. *The Economic Journal*, *105*(July), 916–928.
Gertler, M., & Hubbard, R. G. (1988). Financial factors in business fluctuations. *Financial Market Volatility: Causes, Consequences, and Policy Recommendations*: Federal Reserve Bank of Kansas City, 1988.

Ghemawat, P. (2009). The risk of not investing in a recession. *MIT Sloan Management Review*, 50(3), 30−38.
Gilchrist, S., & Sim, J. W. (2007). *Investment during the Korean financial crisis: A structural econometric analysis*. National Bureau of Economic Research Working Paper Series, No. 13315.
Gorodnichenko, Y., & Schnitzer, M. (2010). *Financial constraints and innovation: Why poor countries don't catch up*. National Bureau of Economic Research Working Paper Series, No. 15792.
Gugler, K. (2001). *Corporate governance and economic performance*. Oxford: Oxford University Press.
Hall, B. H. (1992). *Investment and research and development at the firm level: Does the source of financing matter?* National Bureau of Economic Research Working Paper Series, No. 4096.
Hall, B. H. (2002). *The financing of research and development*. National Bureau of Economic Research Working Paper Series, No. 8773.
Hall, B. H. (2010). The financing of innovative firms. *Review of Economics and Institutions*, 1(1, Spring), 1−30.
Hall, R. E. (1991). Recessions as reorganizations. Paper presented at the NBER Macro Annual Conference.
Hall, R. E., Blanchard, O. J., & Hubbard, R. G. (1986). Market structure and macroeconomic fluctuations. *Brookings Papers on Economic Activity*, 1986(2), 285−338.
Harhoff, D. (1998). Are there financing constraints for R&D and investment in German manufacturing firms? *Annals of Economics and Statistics/Annales d'Économie et de Statistique*, (49/50), 421−456.
Heylen, F., & Pozzi, L. (2007). Crises and human capital accumulation/ crises et accumulation de capital humain. *Canadian Journal of Economics/Revue Canadienne D'économique*, 40(4), 1261−1285.
Himmelberg, C. P., & Petersen, B. C. (1994). R&D and internal finance: A panel study of small firms in high-tech industries. *The Review of Economics and Statistics*, 76(1), 38−51.
Hovakimian, A., & Hovakimian, G. (2009). Cash flow sensitivity of investment. *European Financial Management*, 15(1), 47−65.
Hubbard, R. G. (1997). *Capital-market imperfections and investment*. NBER Working Paper Series, Working Paper 5996. National Bureau of Economic Research.
Ivashina, V., & Scharfstein, D. (2010). Bank lending during the financial crisis of 2008. *Journal of Financial Economics*, 97(3), 319−338.
Kuppuswamy, V., & Villalonga, B. (2010). *Does diversification create value in the presence of external financing constraints? Evidence from the 2007−2009 financial crisis*. Working Paper 10−101. Harvard Business School.
Latham, S., & Braun, M. (2011). Economic recessions, strategy, and performance: A synthesis. *Journal of Strategy and Management*, 4(2), 96−115.
Li, D. (2011). Financial constraints, R&D investment, and stock returns. *Review of Financial Studies*, 24(9), 2974−3007.
López-García, P., Montero, J. M., & Moral-Benito, E. (2013). Business cycles and investment in productivity-enhancing activities: Evidence from Spanish firms. *Industry and Innovation*, 20(7), 611−636.

Mancusi, M. L., & Vezzulli, A. (2010). *R&D, innovation, and liquidity constraints*. KITeS Working Papers 30/2010 Bocconi University.
Mascarenhas, B., & Aaker, D. A. (1989). Strategy over the business cycle. *Strategic Management Journal*, *10*(2), 199–210.
McGahan, A. M., & Porter, M. E. (2002). What do we know about variance in accounting profitability? *Management Science*, *48*(7), 834–851.
Mohnen, P., Palm, F., van der Loeff, S., & Tiwari, A. (2008). Financial constraints and other obstacles: Are they a threat to innovation activity? *De Economist*, *156*(2), 201–214.
Müller, E., & Zimmermann, V. (2009). The importance of equity finance for R&D activity. *Small Business Economics*, *33*(3), 303–318.
Myers, S. C., & Majluf, N. S. (1984). Corporate financing and investment decisions when firms have information that investors do not have. *Journal of Financial Economics*, *13*(2), 187–221.
Nickell, S., & Bell, B. (1995). The collapse in demand for the unskilled and unemployment across the OECD. *Oxford Review of Economic Policy*, *11*(1), 40–62.
Oi, W. (1962). Labor as a quasi-fixed factor. *Journal of Political Economy*, *70*, 538–555.
Ouyang, M. (2011). On the cyclicality of R&D. *Review of Economics and Statistics*, *93*(2), 542–553.
Paunov, C. (2012). The global crisis and firms' investments in innovation. *Research Policy*, *41*(1), 24–35.
Peteraf, M. A. (1993). The cornerstones of competitive advantage: A resource-based view. *Strategic Management Journal*, *14*(3), 179–191.
Petersen, B., & Strongin, S. (1996). Why are some industries more cyclical than others? *Journal of Business & Economic Statistics*, *14*(2), 189–198.
Rafferty, M. (2003). Do business cycles influence long-run growth? The effect of aggregate demand on firm-financed R&D expenditures. *Eastern Economic Journal*, *29*(4), 607–618.
Rosen, S. (1966). *Short-run employment variation on class I railroads in the U.S., 1947–1963*. Chicago, IL: University of Chicago.
Rotemberg, J. J., & Saloner, G. (1986). A supergame-theoretic model of price wars during booms. *The American Economic Review*, *76*(3), 390–407.
Savignac, F. (2008). Impact of financial constraints on innovation: What can be learned from a direct measure. *Economics of Innovation and New Technology*, *17*(6), 553–569.
Schneider, C., & Veugelers, R. (2010). On young highly innovative companies: Why they matter and how (not) to policy support them. *Industrial and Corporate Change*, *19*(4), 969–1007.
Shleifer, A., & Vishny, R. W. (1992). Liquidation values and debt capacity: A market equilibrium approach. *The Journal of Finance*, *47*(4), 1343–1366.
Tong, H., & Wei, S.-J. (2008). *Real effects of the subprime mortgage crisis: Is it a demand or a finance shock?* National Bureau of Economic Research Working Paper Series, No. 14205.
Ughetto, E. (2008). Does internal finance matter for R&D? New evidence from a panel of Italian firms. *Cambridge Journal of Economics*, *32*(6), 907–925.
Wälde, K., & Woitek, U. (2004). R&D expenditure in G7 countries and the implications for endogenous fluctuations and growth. *Economics Letters*, *82*(1), 91–97.
Wernerfelt, B. (1984). A resource-based view of the firm. *Strategic Management Journal*, *5*(2), 171–180.

THE EFFECT OF INSTITUTIONAL FACTORS ON THE VALUE OF CORPORATE DIVERSIFICATION

Venkat Kuppuswamy, George Serafeim and Belén Villalonga

ABSTRACT

Using a large sample of diversified firms from 38 countries we investigate the influence of several national-level institutional factors or "institutional voids" on the value of corporate diversification. Specifically, we explore whether the presence of frictions in a country's capital markets, labor markets, and product markets, affects the excess value of diversified firms. We find that the value of diversified firms relative to their single-segment peers is higher in countries with less-efficient capital and labor markets, but find no evidence that product market efficiency affects the relative value of diversification. These results provide support for the theory of internal capital markets that argues that internal capital allocation would be relatively more beneficial in the presence of frictions in the external capital markets. In addition, the results show that diversification can be beneficial in the presence of frictions in the labor market.

Keywords: Diversification; conglomerate discount; institutions; capital markets; labor markets; international

The effect of corporate diversification on firm value has been a focus of significant scholarly inquiry and debate over the past two decades. Core to this debate has been the so-called diversification discount. The "diversification discount" refers to the empirical observation that diversified firms are on average undervalued relative to their single-segment peers (Berger & Ofek, 1995; Lang & Stulz, 1994). While initially seen as evidence of value destruction from corporate diversification, subsequent work (Campa & Kedia, 2002; Villalonga, 2004a, 2004b) has shown that the finding of an average discount in the United States can be attributed entirely to sample-selection biases, calling into question the interpretation of the discount as evidence of value destruction arising from diversification. Furthermore, the finding that the discount found using Compustat data disappears when corporate operations are classified into business units using more fine-grained data calls into question the mere existence of a discount in the United States (Villalonga, 2003). It is worth noting, however, that the focus of this debate has been on the average effect of diversification on firm value. Scholars on both sides of the debate have found significant variance across diversified firms in the discounts and premiums at which they trade relative to single-segment firms, yet the sources of this variance have received much less attention (Stein, 2003). Moreover, outside of the United States the evidence about the mere existence of a discount is mixed, and has been subject to much less scrutiny (Villalonga, 2003). The present study seeks to fill this gap by examining how the strength of a country's institutional environment affects the value added by corporate diversification.

Prior work examining corporate diversification in an international context has tended to choose sample countries with similar degrees of institutional development. In separate studies, Lins and Servaes (1999, 2002) explore the existence of a diversification discount in well-developed institutional environments as well as emerging markets. While these studies reveal the presence of a diversification discount in both well-developed and weak institutional contexts as well as the role that ownership structures may play, they shed less light on whether (and which) aspects of a country's institutional environment influence the value of diversification. Similarly, while studies have shown that conglomerates or business groups in emerging markets can add significant value to member firms leading to a valuation premium for diversified groups (Khanna & Palepu, 2000; Khanna & Rivkin, 2001), it remains to be seen which factors related to institutional development explain a significant portion of the cross-sectional variance regarding the value of diversification across the world. Doing so requires a representative sample of firms from different institutional environments as well as measures of institutional development on multiple dimensions.

One effort in this regard is the work of Fauver, Houston, and Naranjo (2003), who attempt to link a country's state of capital market development to the value of internal capital allocation, but fail to find an effect. However, this study is limited in several key respects. First, due to poor coverage of emerging markets during the sample period (between 1991 and 1995), their international sample consists primarily of firms from developed institutional contexts. As a result, the lack of a relationship between the efficiency of external capital markets and the value of corporate diversification may be due to insufficient variation in this institutional factor. Second, the study did not examine whether aspects of the institutional environment highlighted in prior theoretical work, such as the quality of the country's labor market and the efficiency of its product markets, do in fact influence the value of diversification (Khanna & Palepu, 2010). Third, as prior scholars have highlighted, endogeneity issues are a significant factor in any analysis of the value added by diversification (Villalonga, 2003). Consequently, the lack of self-selection models cast concern over their prior findings. Finally, since the primary explanatory variables regarding institutional efficiency vary only at the country-level, standard errors must be corrected by clustering at the country-level. Consequently, in light of the limitations of prior work in this domain, Stein (2003) notes that "taken together, the results from this effort thus far seem inconclusive."

In this chapter, we investigate whether and how the value of corporate diversification varies with institutional development. Namely, which institutional factors, if any, drive the observed differences in the value of diversification across firms and countries? To answer this question, we assemble a large data set consisting of diversified firms from 38 countries over the 15-year period from 1995 to 2009. We focus on several institutional variables that might affect the value of diversification, including the efficiency of a country's capital markets, labor markets, and product markets. Specifically, we analyze whether these institutional variables explain the variance in the value of diversified firms across different countries, as well as within the same country over time.

Consistent with Stein's (1997) internal capital markets theory, which suggests that the ability of diversified firms to fund and pursue projects by reallocating funds from other divisions is significantly more valuable in settings with frictions in the external capital market, we find that the value of diversified firms relative to their single-segment peers is indeed higher in countries with less-efficient capital markets. In addition, we find evidence that the efficiency of the country's labor market also has a significant effect on the excess value of diversified firms. In countries where frictions in the labor markets are present, the value of diversified firms relative to their single-segment peers is greater. This finding supports Khanna and Palepu's (2010) argument that other institutional voids besides those that may exist in capital markets can also influence the value of corporate diversification. However, we find that the efficiency of a country's product market does not influence the relative value of diversified firms, after the state of the external capital markets and labor markets are accounted for. This finding suggests that frictions in the input factor markets, for example, capital and labor, dominate frictions in the output factor market, as determinants of the value of diversification.

In addition to our cross-sectional analysis of the value of diversification, we estimate models with country fixed effects to examine whether changes in the institutional environment of a given country over time influence the relative value of its diversified firms. Consistent with Shleifer and Vishny (1991), Hubbard and Palia (1999), and Kuppuswamy and Villalonga (2011), we find evidence that as capital markets become more efficient, the value of corporate diversification decreases. Changes in other institutional factors within a country have no significant impact on the value of diversification. It is important to note, however, that these other factors exhibit little longitudinal variation within a given country, which makes difficult to identify their effect on the value of diversification using just changes within a country over time.

The rest of the chapter proceeds as follows. The section "The Institutional Environment and the Value of Corporate Diversification" describes our predictions about the effect of institutional factors on the value of corporation diversification. The section "Data and Variables" describes the sample and the data. The section "How Do Institutional Factors Affect the Value of Corporate Diversification Across the World?" presents the results of our analysis of whether and which institutional factors explain the variation in the value of diversification around the world.

The next section presents some robustness checks. The section "Do Within-Country Changes in Institutional Factors Affect the Value of Corporate Diversification?" analyzes within-country changes in the value of diversification. The last section is the conclusion.

THE INSTITUTIONAL ENVIRONMENT AND THE VALUE OF CORPORATE DIVERSIFICATION

The value of internal capital allocation and thus, corporate diversification, is likely to depend on a firm's institutional environment (Williamson, 1975). Specifically, the literature on internal capital markets has highlighted several potential benefits and costs to internal capital allocation, the net effect of which should vary with the institutional context. The main benefit of internal capital allocation is the ability of corporate headquarters to engage in "winner picking," whereby funds can be diverted away from one division to pursue more promising projects in another division that might be capital-constrained in more focused firms (Stein, 1997). Focused or stand-alone firms may face capital constraints regarding such projects due to imperfections in the external capital market arising from information asymmetries or a generalized shortage of credit offered by the external markets (Kuppuswamy & Villalonga, 2011; Stein, 1997).

However, internal capital markets also present a "dark side," where the CEO or divisional managers may engage in rent-seeking behavior that leads to a misallocation of corporate resources (Rajan, Servaes, & Zingales, 2000; Scharfstein & Stein, 2000). In institutional contexts where external capital markets are inefficient and fraught with imperfections, the benefits of "winner picking" become more significant and counter the costs of rent-seeking behavior to a greater extent. As a result, diversification is likely to be more valuable in countries with less-efficient external capital markets (Khanna & Palepu, 2000). To this end, recent work has found that firms in capital-intensive industries are more likely to belong to a conglomerate when they operate in a country with inefficient external capital markets (Belenzon, Berkovitz, & Rios, 2013). Furthermore, firms that are affiliated with business groups receive support from other member firms when they suffer cash-flow shocks, avoiding bankruptcy and negative spillovers toward firms in the rest of the group (Gopalan, Nanda, & Seru, 2007). Focusing on the incidence of inta-group loans between group-affiliated firms, scholars have predicted and found evidence that more capital-intensive firms receive loans from less capital-intensive ones in order to fund capital-intensive projects (Almeida & Wolfenzon, 2006; Buchuk, Larrain, Muñoz, & Urzúa Infante, 2014). We extend these empirical findings by investigating whether the financing advantages highlighted in prior work translate into a valuation advantage for diversified firms in countries with less-efficient external capital markets.

Apart from the efficiency of external capital markets, prior work notes that the presence of other "institutional voids" may also increase the value of corporate diversification (Khanna & Palepu, 1999). In particular, frictions in a country's labor market may substantially increase the transaction costs associated with operating a stand-alone business relative to a diversified operation (Williamson, 1975). Inefficiencies in the labor market may arise from a variety of sources including the limited supply of talent from professional or technical schools, the decreased ability of employees to leave their existing employer and move to another one, and undue governmental inference in wage negotiations between labor and business (Khanna & Palepu, 1999, 2010). Such frictions in the labor market can significantly increase the costs associated with searching for and securing the technical and managerial talent needed for a promising project. Internal labor markets operated by diversified firms in such environments can minimize these transaction costs. For example, diversified firms have the ability to source managerial talent from other existing divisions. Indeed, Tate and Yang (2012), who analyze the labor market consequences of corporate diversification within the United States, find that workers in diversified firms have greater cross-industry mobility within and across firms, and that diversified firms benefit from the opportunity to redeploy workers internally from declining to expanding industries. Moreover, the ability to expose internal talent to a diverse set of situations and business activities may enable diversified firms to develop internal talent and overcome limitations in educational infrastructure. As a result, corporate diversification may be more valuable in contexts with voids in their labor market institutions.

Another institutional void concerns the efficiency of a country's product markets. Specifically, this refers to the extent to which a country's regulatory and political context promotes fair and effective competition among firms in the product marketplace. Barriers to entry instituted by direct government intervention or excessive regulatory hurdles can lead to the lack of entry of intermediaries such as retailers, who are needed to facilitate the sale of goods and services to consumers (Khanna & Palepu, 2010). Similarly, import tariffs and processing hurdles set up by customs authorities can limit the timely supply of necessary inputs to firms, restricting their ability to compete downstream. Moreover, regulatory roadblocks can impede the ability of firms to exploit new business opportunities that might emerge through the introduction of new products or services. Finally, direct government involvement, through state control of enterprises or subsidies to certain groups may further distort the ability to compete fairly in certain industries. Unlike stand-alone enterprises, divisions in diversified companies can overcome some of these obstacles by leveraging the experience and resources of other divisions within the company. For example, diversified firms may be able to overcome the lack of suitable intermediaries for the distribution and sale of its products from one business by deploying its distribution and retail assets from another. Furthermore, a diversified firm may be able to leverage its experience and relationships with regulatory authorities from one business to expedite the administrative process required to pursue new opportunities in another line of business. Diversified firms may also be able to exploit economies of scope through the sharing of common inputs between divisions (Penrose, 1959). Consequently, they may be able to reduce the risk of a supply disruption, if the necessary raw materials are available from other divisions. As a result, diversification is likely to be more valuable in institutional environments characterized by inefficient product markets.

DATA AND VARIABLES

Sample

Our sample consists of 10,164 diversified and 21,737 single-segment firms across the world that we draw from the Worldscope international database.[1] Worldscope maintains financial and business segment data on publicly listed companies across the world.[2] The aggregate market capitalization of companies in the Worldscope database stands at approximately 95% of the total value of the world's markets (Thomson Financial, 2003). While the database targets publicly listed firms from 53 countries, its coverage of emerging markets is quite weak before 1995 (Lins & Servaes, 2002). Therefore, our sample period begins in 1995, and ends in 2009. Worldscope records financial data regarding a firm's 10 largest business segments, each of which is assigned a 4-digit Standard Industrial Classification (SIC) code to indicate its industry affiliation.

Following previous literature, we classify diversified firms as those with at least two segments with distinct 4-digit SIC codes (Berger & Ofek, 1995; Villalonga, 2004a, 2004b). Due to a significant degree of missing asset totals for individual segments, we focus on the sales figures of individual segments in constructing both our dependent variable as well as selecting firms into our sample. Following Berger and Ofek (1995), we restrict our sample of diversified firms to those firm-year observations where the segment totals are not subject to significant under or over-reporting. Specifically, we restrict our sample to those diversified firms for which the sum of segment sales was within 5% of the firm's total sales in that year. Furthermore, we ensure that our sample firms had no segments with one-digit SIC codes of 0 (agriculture), 6 (financial), or 9 (government). In total, we have 35,886 firm-year observations from 10,164 diversified firms across 38 countries. Table 1 shows a breakdown of the number of observations per country. Firms from the United States, Japan, and United Kingdom represent 45%, 18%, and 11% of the sample, with a substantial number of observations also coming from Australia, Canada, China, France, Germany, Hong Kong, India, Malaysia, Singapore, Sweden, Taiwan, and Thailand.

Measures

Dependent Variable
The dependent variable of our study is *Excess Value*, a measure developed by Berger and Ofek (1995) that represents the value of a diversified firm relative to its single-segment peers. Excess values are computed as the natural logarithm of the ratio between a firm's market value and its imputed value at the end of the year. A firm's imputed value is the sum of its segments' imputed values, which are obtained by multiplying the segment's sales total by the median market-to-sales ratio of single-segment firms in the same industry, country, and year. The industry matching is carried out using the narrowest SIC grouping that includes at least five single-segment firms. Due to potential over or under-reporting of segment sales totals (within our 5% threshold), we gross up or down the imputed value by the percentage deviation in firm sales and segment sales totals. Furthermore, following prior literature on the diversification discount, we exclude outliers from our analysis. Specifically, we exclude observations with excess values that fall beyond the two standard deviations from the mean. Yet our results are very similar if we define

Table 1. Breakdown of Diversified Firm Observations by Country.

Country	N	% of Sample	Mean Excess Value	Median Excess Value
Australia	511	1.42	−0.418	−0.500
Belgium	5	0.01	0.035	0.446
Brazil	40	0.11	0.093	−0.042
Canada	1,138	3.17	−0.294	−0.313
Chile	4	0.01	−0.062	0.020
China	1,548	4.31	−0.091	−0.112
Czech Republic	16	0.04	0.450	0.473
Denmark	29	0.08	−0.328	−0.323
Finland	48	0.13	−0.358	−0.396
France	965	2.69	−0.085	−0.093
Germany	958	2.67	−0.117	−0.149
Greece	33	0.09	−0.076	−0.177
Hong Kong	655	1.83	−0.375	−0.465
India	573	1.6	−0.073	−0.061
Indonesia	159	0.44	0.063	0.164
Ireland	10	0.03	−0.590	−0.565
Israel	60	0.17	−0.014	−0.072
Italy	10	0.03	−0.513	−0.557
Japan	6,493	18.09	−0.154	−0.146
South Korea	90	0.25	−0.079	−0.104
Malaysia	363	1.01	−0.269	−0.279
Mexico	14	0.04	0.303	0.185
Netherlands	75	0.21	−0.456	−0.638
New Zealand	1	0.00	−0.750	−0.750
Norway	61	0.17	−0.251	−0.331
Philippines	14	0.04	0.320	0.334
Poland	21	0.06	0.300	0.423
Russian Federation	11	0.03	0.617	0.860
Singapore	384	1.07	−0.235	−0.203
South Africa	103	0.29	−0.207	−0.209
Spain	6	0.02	−0.680	−0.583
Sweden	336	0.94	−0.300	−0.295
Switzerland	152	0.42	−0.325	−0.291
Taiwan	519	1.45	0.055	0.075
Thailand	347	0.97	0.113	0.123
Turkey	12	0.03	0.545	0.554
United Kingdom	4,035	11.24	−0.217	−0.220
United States	16,087	44.83	−0.250	−0.242
Overall Sample	35,886	100%	−0.207	−0.198

Notes: The table presents a breakdown of the number of diversified-year observations for each country in our sample. In addition we present the mean and median *Excess Value* for diversified firms in each country. *Excess Value* is the natural logarithm of the ratio of a firm's market value to its imputed value. A firm's imputed value is the sum of its segments' imputed values, which are the product of the segment's sales total with the median market-to-sales ratio of at least five single-segment firms in the same industry.

outliers to be excess values that fall beyond the top 1% and bottom 1% of all excess values.

Table 1 shows mean and median excess values per country. As the table shows, there is considerable variation across countries in the value of diversified firms relative to single-segment firms, ranging from a discount of 75% for New Zealand to a premium of 62% for Russia. However, the countries at the tails of the distributions have very few observations. Leaving aside those countries with less than 20 observations, the range narrows down to an average discount of 46% for the Netherlands and a premium of 30% for Poland – still a very wide range.

While our dependent variable measures the value of a diversified firm relative to its single-segment peers, one potential source of bias in this measure is the fact that certain single-segment firms may actually be members of business groups and thus have access to the capital resources of other firms (Khanna & Palepu, 2000). The lack of widespread data on business group affiliations precludes us from accounting for such single-segment firms. Nevertheless, to the extent that certain single-segment comparables may actually have access to the internal capital markets possessed by diversified firms, this should actually bias us away from finding an effect regarding the relative benefits of diversification in contexts with weaker institutions. As a result, our results would represent a conservative estimate on the relative value of diversification in such contexts.

Independent Variables

The core independent variables in our analysis are measures of several key facets of a country's institutional environment – the efficiency of its capital, labor, and product markets. Annual data on the institutional variables are derived from the International Institute for Management Development (IMD) World Competitiveness Yearbook (WCY). Since 1996, IMD has analyzed and ranked the ability of nations to create and maintain an environment that sustains enterprise competitiveness. The yearbook compares the performance of 58 countries based on more than 300 criteria measuring different facets of competitiveness. Approximately two thirds of the data come from statistical databases (international/national sources) and the remaining third from surveys (Executive Opinion Survey). The statistical indicators provided by WCY are acquired from international, national and regional organizations, private institutions and a network of 54 partner institutes worldwide. The Executive Opinion Survey measures perceptions of competitiveness by business executives who are dealing with international business situations. They cover factors that are not easily measurable using output data, such as management practices, labor relations, corruption, environmental concerns, and quality of life.

The measures of capital market efficiency, labor market efficiency, and product market efficiency are logarithms of reversed ordinal country rankings derived from pertinent WCY survey items which are outlined in Table 3. The *Capital Market Efficiency* variable includes measures of the efficiency of banks, stock markets, and other types of financial intermediaries.[3] The *Product Market Efficiency* variable includes measures that reflect both the openness of the product markets to foreign firms, and policies, laws and regulations that directly affect the level of competition in the product market. *Labor Market Efficiency* includes measures of the rigidity of the labor market and policies and laws that affect the supply of labor. To construct each of these variables, the institute first standardizes each of the WCY data items reported in the Appendix in a given year by subtracting its mean and dividing by its cross-country standard deviation. This effectively forces each item to have equal importance. The institute then calculates the mean of the standardized survey items to generate an aggregate measure of capital, labor, and product market efficiency. For each of our institutional variables, the sample countries are assigned an ordinal ranking reflecting their relative performance. Finally, we reverse and take the logarithm of the ordinal rankings so that higher values of our institutional variables reflect contexts with higher efficiency.

Summary statistics and pairwise correlations for the main variables are presented in Table 2. *Excess Value* exhibits a negative univariate correlation with all institutional variables. As expected, all institutional variables exhibit a strong positive correlation (0.36−0.68). However, as we will highlight later in the results section, variance inflation factors computed at the end of each analysis indicate that multicollinearity is not a concern in the analysis (Kutner, Nachtsheim, & Neter, 2004).

Control Variables

In addition to the institutional variables that are the focus of our analysis, we include several control variables in all of our models. Specifically, we include the following firm characteristics: log of total assets, the ratio of cash and marketable securities to the book value of assets, leverage, dividends paid as a percentage of equity, return on assets, and the ratio of capital expenditures to total assets. We also control for the country's economic performance to make sure that our institutional development measures are not merely capturing the country's economic development.[4] In analogous fashion to the institutional measures of our interest, a country's economic

Table 2. Summary Statistics and Pairwise Correlations.

Variable	(1)	(2)	(3)	(4)	(5)	(6)	(7)	(8)	(9)	(10)	(11)
(1) Excess Value	1.00										
(2) Capital Market Efficiency	−0.09	1.00									
(3) Labor Market Efficiency	−0.06	0.36	1.00								
(4) Product Market Efficiency	−0.07	0.68	0.49	1.00							
(5) Economic Performance	−0.04	0.48	0.42	0.41	1.00						
(6) Log Assets	0.13	0.03	0.03	−0.02	0.04	1.00					
(7) % Cash of Assets	0.12	−0.04	−0.01	0.01	−0.02	−0.23	1.00				
(8) Leverage	−0.05	0.05	−0.05	−0.02	0.04	0.15	−0.42	1.00			
(9) Dividends as % of Equity	0.03	0.05	0.00	−0.01	−0.01	0.17	−0.07	0.10	1.00		
(10) Profitability (ROA)	0.01	−0.11	−0.07	−0.09	−0.08	0.33	−0.11	−0.19	0.14	1.00	
(11) % CAPX of Assets	0.05	0.05	0.05	0.03	0.08	0.04	−0.14	0.01	0.03	0.02	1.00
Mean	−0.207	3.786	3.750	3.602	3.868	12.260	0.153	0.524	0.029	−0.018	0.054
Median	−0.198	3.970	3.892	3.584	3.989	12.143	0.096	0.529	0.006	0.027	0.038
St. Dev.	0.650	0.368	0.372	0.205	0.257	1.997	0.169	0.225	0.076	0.202	0.061
Q1	−0.627	3.689	3.689	3.466	3.784	10.953	0.030	0.361	0.000	−0.015	0.017
Q3	0.223	4.025	3.951	3.784	4.025	13.538	0.212	0.676	0.031	0.065	0.069

Notes: The table presents summary statistics and pairwise correlations of variables used in subsequent tables. *Excess Value* is the natural logarithm of the ratio of a firm's market value to its imputed value. A firm's imputed value is the sum of its segments' imputed values, which are the product of the segment's sales total with the median market-to-sales ratio of at least five single-segment firms in the same industry. *Capital Market Efficiency* is the logarithm of the reversed ordinal ranking of a country's capital market efficiency derived from the IMD World Competitiveness Yearbook, published annually (rank reversed so that higher values of this measure correspond to countries with greater efficiency). Similarly, *Labor Market Efficiency*, *Product Market Efficiency*, and *Economic Performance* are logarithms of reversed ordinal rankings of a country's labor market efficiency, product market efficiency, and overall economic performance, all extracted from the IMD World Competitiveness Yearbook.

performance is measured by the logarithm of its reverse WCY rank on that dimension, which takes into account the size, past and forecasted growth, and wealth of the domestic economy, the state of international trade, and international investments.

HOW DO INSTITUTIONAL FACTORS AFFECT THE VALUE OF CORPORATE DIVERSIFICATION ACROSS THE WORLD?

Multivariate OLS Regressions

To examine the effect of our institutional variables on the relative value of diversified firms, we first run an Ordinary Least Squares (OLS) model with *Excess Value* regressed as a function of *Capital Market Efficiency*, *Labor Market Efficiency*, *Product Market Efficiency*, and our control variables. The results are shown in Table 3. Models (1) through (3) include only one of our institutional variables, while Model (4) includes all of them simultaneously as covariates. We note that, while our institutional variables are correlated with one another to a significant degree (see Table 2), multicollinearity does not appear to be a concern in including them together in Model (4): The variance inflation factors computed for each of our covariates is less than 3.5, which is well below the typical threshold of 10 used to signal multicollinearity concerns (Kutner et al., 2004). All models include year fixed effects, and standard errors that are clustered by country and robust to heteroscedasticity.

The results of Models (1)–(3) indicate that when included on their own, *Capital Market Efficiency*, *Labor Market Efficiency*, and *Product Market Efficiency* each have negative coefficients that are significant at the 1% level.[5] In other words, in contexts where capital, labor, or product markets are more efficient, the value of diversified firms relative to their single-segment peers decreases, as expected. In Model (4), where all our institutional variables are included at the same time, *Capital Market Efficiency* and *Labor Market Efficiency* continue to load negatively and significantly. However, after controlling for these other institutional factors, the coefficient of *Product Market Efficiency* turns statistically insignificant. If a country improves its capital market efficiency rank from 55th in the world to 20th, the value of diversified firms relative to single-segment firms decreases by approximately 13% (based on the coefficient in Model (4)).

Table 3. The Effect of Institutional Factors on the Value of Diversification: OLS Regressions.

	(1) Excess Value	(2) Excess Value	(3) Excess Value	(4) Excess Value
Capital Market Efficiency	−0.195***			−0.154***
	(0.046)			(0.053)
Labor Market Efficiency		−0.124***		−0.0830***
		(0.034)		(0.027)
Product Market Efficiency			−0.319***	−0.0647
			(0.058)	(0.086)
Economic Performance	−0.061	−0.107*	−0.081	−0.0170
	(0.057)	(0.0602)	(0.052)	(0.057)
Log Assets	0.060***	0.060***	0.0596***	0.0605***
	(0.012)	(0.012)	(0.012)	(0.012)
Cash Percentage	0.605***	0.608***	0.615***	0.600***
	(0.062)	(0.055)	(0.056)	(0.059)
Leverage	−0.065***	−0.080***	−0.075***	−0.081***
	(0.021)	(0.026)	(0.025)	(0.027)
Dividends	0.167	0.115	0.115	0.162
	(0.165)	(0.172)	(0.190)	(0.162)
ROA	−0.200***	−0.183***	−0.191***	−0.209***
	(0.044)	(0.051)	(0.0445)	(0.042)
CAPX	0.688***	0.713***	0.703***	0.695***
	(0.104)	(0.092)	(0.093)	(0.101)
Year Fixed Effects	Yes	Yes	Yes	Yes
Constant	0.0363	−0.0716	0.527**	0.260
	(0.162)	(0.194)	(0.198)	(0.270)
N	35,886	35,886	35,886	35,886
Number of clusters (countries)	38	38	38	38
Adjusted R^2	0.064	0.059	0.062	0.066

Notes: The table presents multivariate OLS regressions where excess value is modeled as function of three institutional variables — capital market efficiency, labor market efficiency, and product market efficiency. Models (1)–(3) each include only one of these institutional variables, while all three covariates are included together in Model (4). *Excess Value* is the natural logarithm of the ratio of a firm's market value to its imputed value. A firm's imputed value is the sum of its segments' imputed values, which are the product of the segment's sales total with the median market-to-sales ratio of at least five single-segment firms in the same industry. *Capital Market Efficiency* is the logarithm of the reversed ordinal ranking of a country's capital market efficiency derived from the IMD World Competitiveness Yearbook, published annually (rank reversed so that higher values of this measure correspond to countries with greater efficiency). Similarly, *Labor Market Efficiency*, *Product Market Efficiency*, and *Economic Performance* are logarithms of reversed ordinal rankings of a country's labor market efficiency, product market efficiency, and overall economic performance, all extracted from the IMD World Competitiveness Yearbook. Standard errors are clustered by country and are in parentheses. Significance levels are denoted by * (10% level), ** (5% level), and *** (1% level).

Similarly, if a country improves its labor market efficiency rank from 40th in the world to 20th, the relative value of a diversified firm decreases by 6.5%.

Collectively, the results from Model (4) provide evidence that institutional factors have a significant effect on the value of corporate diversification around the world. First, in support of the theory of internal capital markets, we find that the value of internal allocation and thus, the value of diversified firms relative to their single-segment peers is greater in contexts with less-efficient capital markets (Stein, 1997, 2003). Moreover, we find evidence that the presence of frictions in a country's labor market also influences the value of corporate diversification. Consistent with the theory of institutional "voids" in emerging markets, we find that in institutional environments where labor markets are less efficient, the relative value of diversified firms is higher (Khanna & Palepu, 2010). While we find strong evidence that both capital and labor market efficiency influence the value of diversification across the world, there is little evidence that the efficiency of a country's product market affects the value of corporate diversification. Nevertheless, the results of Table 3 provide strong evidence that different institutional factors do influence the value of corporate diversification. A question that still remains unanswered is whether these results are robust to self-selection models that account for the fact that diversification is not pursued randomly (Villalonga, 2004a, 2004b).

Heckman Selection Models

In order to account for the selection of firms into diversified status, we investigate the relationship between institutional factors and the excess value of diversified firms using the Heckman two-step selection model (Heckman, 1979). In this approach, we model the selection of diversified status in the first stage and model excess values for diversified firms in the second stage. We do so by implementing the Heckman selection model using a maximum likelihood estimator, which estimates the two stages simultaneously. Heckman's approach requires the application of exclusion restrictions to at least one variable – which is included in the first-stage selection model but that can be excluded from the second-stage regression model for the selected firms, since it is uncorrelated with the outcome. To this end, we use a variable used in prior work on the diversification discount: an indicator for whether the firm reports a non-zero amount for the minority interest on its balance sheet (Dimitrov & Tice, 2006; Hund,

Monk, & Tice, 2010). The rationale for using a minority interest indicator as an instrument is that it proxies for (possibly diversifying) acquisitions that happened in the past but need not be correlated with contemporaneous segment-level unobservables.

Table 4 displays the results of the Heckman selection models. Similar to the previous table, we have separate selection models for each institutional variable (Models (1)–(3)), and a model with all three institutional variables included at the same time (Model (4)). However, due to the importance of accounting for other institutional factors in the analysis of any one of them, we will focus our discussion of this table on the results of the Model (4). Moreover, in the interest of conserving space, we display just the selection-corrected results of the second stage of the Heckman model for Models (1)–(3), but display both stages for the results of our complete model, Model (4). The first-stage results are similar across all four models, though.

The first stage of the model is estimated with 129,667 observations, 35,886 of them representing diversified firms and the rest single-segment firms. Examining the first stage of the Heckman selection model, we observe that our instrumental variable, *Minority Interest*, has a positive coefficient and is significant at the 1% level. This is consistent with prior work that has found diversified US firms to be significantly more likely to hold a non-zero amount of minority interest on their balance sheets (Dimitrov & Tice, 2006; Hund et al., 2010). While not the main focus of our empirical analysis, we also note that one of our institutional variables, *Labor Market Efficiency*, appears to predict the likelihood that a firm would be diversified. Specifically, firms in countries with less-efficient labor markets are more likely to be diversified, than in contexts where these markets are more efficient. This would be expected if less-efficient labor markets institutional environments do indeed make diversification more valuable. However, we do not find similar associations between our other institutional variables and the likelihood of diversification. Recent work has found that firms exhibit greater levels of vertical integration in contexts with greater contracting hazards and financial development (Acemoglu, Johnson, & Mitton, 2009). Our finding that certain characteristics of the institutional environment also significantly influence the *likelihood* of corporate diversification (i.e., the horizontal scope of the firm) further extends this literature.

Turning to the second stage of the Heckman model, we observe that *Capital Market Efficiency* and *Labor Market Efficiency* both have negative coefficients that are significant at the 1% level. Therefore, consistent with our OLS results from Table 4, we continue to find that the value of diversified firms relative to their single-segment counterparts is greater in institutional settings with frictions in their capital and labor markets. Furthermore, in line with the prior OLS analysis, we again find that *Product Market Efficiency* has an insignificant effect on the value of diversified firms, after accounting for the other institutional factors. Overall, the results of the Heckman selection models in Table 4 provide strong evidence that our earlier findings are not driven by self-selection biases.

Table 4. The Effect of Institutional Factors on the Value of Diversification: Heckman Selection Models.

	(1)	(2)	(3)	(4)	
	Excess Value (2nd stage)	Excess Value (2nd stage)	Excess Value (2nd stage)	Diversified (1st stage)	Excess Value (2nd stage)
Capital Market Efficiency	−0.221*** (0.042)			−0.315 (0.237)	−0.182*** (0.045)
Labor Market Efficiency		−0.135*** (0.037)		−0.275** (0.118)	−0.103*** (0.029)
Product Market Efficiency			−0.343*** (0.057)	0.129 (0.278)	−0.0547 (0.079)
Economic Performance	−0.0471 (0.053)	−0.103* (0.060)	−0.0753 (0.053)	0.324 (0.227)	0.00588 (0.054)
Log Assets	0.0681*** (0.009)	0.065*** (0.011)	0.0653*** (0.010)	0.114*** (0.014)	0.0694*** (0.009)
Cash Percentage	0.591*** (0.058)	0.600*** (0.050)	0.605*** (0.0518)	−0.221 (0.201)	0.584*** (0.0535)
Leverage	−0.049*** (0.017)	−0.072*** (0.023)	−0.0640*** (0.020)	0.209** (0.106)	−0.065*** (0.020)
Dividends	0.168 (0.161)	0.113 (0.173)	0.112 (0.190)	−0.008 (0.340)	0.164 (0.156)
ROA	−0.186*** (0.049)	−0.175*** (0.056)	−0.180*** (0.050)	0.192*** (0.068)	−0.195*** (0.046)
CAPX	0.573*** (0.097)	0.651*** (0.107)	0.623*** (0.084)	−1.717*** (0.566)	0.572*** (0.093)
Minority Interest				0.282*** (0.049)	
Year Fixed Effects	Yes	Yes	Yes	Yes	Yes
Constant	−0.104 (0.122)	−0.148 (0.181)	0.464*** (0.168)	−1.179 (1.344)	0.120 (0.206)
Rho	0.14**	0.08	0.10*		0.15***

Table 4. (*Continued*)

	(1)	(2)	(3)	(4)	
	Excess Value (2nd stage)	Excess Value (2nd stage)	Excess Value (2nd stage)	Diversified (1st stage)	Excess Value (2nd stage)
N	35,886	35,886	35,886	129,667	35,886
Number of clusters (countries)	38	38	38		38

Notes: The table presents the results of Heckman self-selection models where diversified status is modeled as a probit in the first stage, and where the excess value for diversified firms is modeled in the second stage. The first-stage probit requires a sample of both single-segment (N = 93,781) and diversified firms (N = 35,886), while the diversified firms represent the selected group for the second-stage analysis. Heckman's approach requires the application of exclusion restrictions to at least one variable – which is included in the first-stage selection model but that can be excluded from the second-stage regression model for the selected firms, since it is uncorrelated with the outcome. To this end, we use an indicator, *Minority Interest*, for whether the firm reports a non-zero amount for the minority interest on its balance sheet. The key independent variables in these selection models are three institutional variables – capital market efficiency, labor market efficiency, and product market efficiency. Models (1)–(4) each include only one of these institutional variables, while all three covariates are included together in Model (4). Furthermore, only the second stages of the Heckman models are shown for Models (1)–(3), while both stages are shown for Model (4). *Excess Value* is the natural logarithm of the ratio of a firm's market value to its imputed value. A firm's imputed value is the sum of its segments' imputed values, which are the product of the segment's sales total with the median market-to-sales ratio of at least five single-segment firms in the same industry. *Capital Market Efficiency* is the logarithm of the reversed ordinal ranking of a country's capital market efficiency derived from the IMD World Competitiveness Yearbook, published annually (rank reversed so that higher values of this measure correspond to countries with greater efficiency). Similarly, *Labor Market Efficiency*, *Product Market Efficiency*, and *Economic Performance* are logarithms of reversed ordinal rankings of a country's labor market efficiency, product market efficiency, and overall economic performance, all extracted from the IMD World Competitiveness Yearbook. Standard errors are clustered by country and are in parentheses. Significance levels are denoted by * (10% level), ** (5% level), and *** (1% level).

Propensity Score Matching

Villalonga (2004a, 2004b) argues that the diversification discount can be attributed to the difficulty of finding truly comparable single-segment firms. Using propensity score matching to find comparable firms, she finds that excess values increase on average, to the point of turning the average discount found in US data into a premium. It is important to recognize that systematically underestimating the value of diversification is not necessarily a problem for this study, because we are interested in the cross-country variation of the discount rather than the average discount. However, if the bias on the value of diversification introduced by the difficulty of finding appropriate comparable firms varies systematically with institutional factors, then this could bias the estimated coefficients on the institutional factors. In other words, if we are underestimating the value of diversification more in countries with more developed capital and labor markets then this methodological problem could produce our results.

To examine this alternative explanation, we estimate propensity score matching models and derive an adjusted excess value estimate for each country. These bias-corrected excess values are computed using one-to-one nearest neighbor propensity score matching with a caliper of 0.001, where diversified firms are matched to single-segment firms in the same country on the natural logarithm of total assets, return on assets, cash over assets, capital expenditures over assets, leverage, and dividends paid as a percentage of equity. Due to data limitations, we are only able to derive the estimates for 29 out of 38 countries. Consistent with prior literature, we find that the adjusted excess values are higher for 23 out of the 29 countries. The average mean excess value across countries is −12.3% while the adjusted one is −6.4%. However, the underestimation of excess value did not vary much across countries. Because propensity score matching factors in firm-level variables such as size, profitability, leverage, etc., in the estimation of the discount, we calculated the difference between these propensity score matching estimates and the OLS estimates of the discount (Berger & Ofek, 1995). The correlation between this difference and our institutional variables was insignificant.

The univariate correlation between the excess value and the adjusted excess value across countries is 0.95. In summary, the relations documented here between value of diversification and institutions do not seem to be affected by the selection of comparable firms.

ROBUSTNESS CHECKS

OLS and Heckman Models without Diversified Firms from the United States

While our sample has a significant number of observations from countries other than the United States, observations from the United States still account for approximately 45% of our sample. As a result, it is unclear whether our results are driven by the inclusion of these US firms, or whether our institutional variables still explain variation in the value of diversification across a non-US subsample. In the following analysis, we exclude all US firms and model excess values as a function of our institutional factors using both multivariate OLS and Heckman selection models. The results of this analysis on the non-US subsample are presented in Table 5.

Excluding US firms reduces the sample of diversified firms to 19,799 observations. The results of Table 5 are very similar to the results from the prior analyses that included diversified firms from the United States (Tables 3–4). As before, we see that *Capital Market Efficiency* and *Labor Market Efficiency* have negative coefficients that are significant in both the OLS (at the 5% level) and Heckman models (at the 1% level). As a result, we find that the efficiency of capital and labor markets continue to significantly affect the value of diversification across countries outside the United States. Again, the relative value of diversified firms is greater in countries with less-efficient capital and labor markets. These results increase our confidence that the results are not driven solely by the inclusion of US firms.

OLS and Heckman Models with Diversified Firms from Countries with at Least 100 Observations

Just like there may have been a concern that our results are driven by the large number of observations from the United States, another source of concern may lie in the few observations many countries in our sample have. As an additional robustness test, we exclude all countries from our analysis that have less than 100 diversified-year observations. After enforcing this limit, we are left with only 18 counties, and thus clusters with which to adjust our standard errors. Nevertheless, we present the results of both the OLS analysis and the Heckman selection model run on observations from these 18 countries in Table 6.

The results of Table 4 are consistent with the results of the main analysis with observations from 38 countries (Table 3). Again, we find that *Capital Market Efficiency* and *Labor Market Efficiency* have negative coefficients that are significant in both the OLS (at the 5% level and 1% level, respectively) and Heckman models (at the 1% level). As a result, we find that the

Table 5. The Effect of Institutional Factors on the Value of Diversification: Excluding Diversified Firms from the USA.

	OLS	Heckman Selection Model	
	Excess Value	Diversified (1st stage)	Excess Value (2nd stage)
Capital Market Efficiency	−0.111**	−0.245	−0.142***
	(0.053)	(0.229)	(0.0455)
Labor Market Efficiency	−0.065**	−0.214*	−0.086***
	(0.028)	(0.114)	(0.031)
Product Market Efficiency	−0.146	0.205	−0.118
	(0.092)	(0.294)	(0.081)
Economic Performance	0.001	0.448***	0.048
	(0.050)	(0.168)	(0.048)
Minority Interest		0.283***	
		(0.067)	
Controls	Yes	Yes	Yes
Year Fixed Effects	Yes	Yes	Yes
Constant	0.580**	−2.771***	0.190
	(0.260)	(1.023)	(0.249)
N	19,799	66,078	19,799
Number of clusters (countries)	37		37
Adjusted R^2	0.048		
Rho			0.211***

Notes: The table presents the results of both OLS and Heckman self-selection models of excess value where firms from the United States are excluded from the sample. In the Heckman model, diversified status is modeled as a probit in the first stage, and where the excess value for diversified firms is modeled in the second stage. The first-stage probit requires a sample of both single-segment and diversified firms, while the diversified firms represent the selected group for the second-stage analysis. Heckman's approach requires the application of exclusion restrictions to at least one variable − which is included in the first-stage selection model but that can be excluded from the second-stage regression model for the selected firms, since it is uncorrelated with the outcome. To this end, we use an indicator, *Minority Interest*, for whether the firm reports a non-zero amount for the minority interest on its balance sheet. The key independent variables in both the OLS and selection models are three institutional variables − capital market efficiency, labor market efficiency, and product market efficiency. *Excess Value* is the natural logarithm of the ratio of a firm's market value to its imputed value. A firm's imputed value is the sum of its segments' imputed values, which are the product of the segment's sales total with the median market-to-sales ratio of at least five single-segment firms in the same industry. *Capital Market Efficiency* is the logarithm of the reversed ordinal ranking of a country's capital market efficiency derived from the IMD World Competitiveness Yearbook, published annually (rank reversed so that higher values of this measure correspond to countries with greater efficiency). Similarly, *Labor Market Efficiency*, *Product Market Efficiency*, and *Economic Performance* are logarithms of reversed ordinal rankings of a country's labor market efficiency, product market efficiency, and overall economic performance, all extracted from the IMD World Competitiveness Yearbook. Standard errors are clustered by country and are in parentheses. Significance levels are denoted by * (10% level), ** (5% level), and *** (1% level).

Table 6. The Effect of Institutional Factors on the Value of Diversification: Excluding Diversified Firms from Countries with less than 100 Observations.

	OLS	Heckman Selection Model	
	Excess Value	Diversified (1st stage)	Excess Value (2nd stage)
Capital Market Efficiency	−0.153**	−0.369	−0.182***
	(0.055)	(0.273)	(0.046)
Labor Market Efficiency	−0.093***	−0.289**	−0.112***
	(0.028)	(0.132)	(0.028)
Product Market Efficiency	−0.052	0.212	−0.038
	(0.088)	(0.305)	(0.082)
Economic Performance	−0.006	0.203	0.007
	(0.066)	(0.331)	(0.060)
Minority Interest		0.271***	
		(0.052)	
Controls	Yes	Yes	Yes
Year Fixed Effects	Yes	Yes	Yes
Constant	0.201	−0.780	0.098
	(0.276)	(1.693)	(0.220)
N	35,326	126,109	35,326
Number of clusters (countries)	18		18
Adjusted R^2	0.064		
Rho			0.141**

Notes: The table presents the results of both OLS and Heckman self-selection models of excess value where firms from countries with less than 100 observations are excluded from the sample. In the Heckman model, diversified status is modeled as a probit in the first stage, and where the excess value for diversified firms is modeled in the second stage. The first-stage probit requires a sample of both single-segment and diversified firms, while the diversified firms represent the selected group for the second-stage analysis. Heckman's approach requires the application of exclusion restrictions to at least one variable − which is included in the first-stage selection model but that can be excluded from the second-stage regression model for the selected firms, since it is uncorrelated with the outcome. To this end, we use an indicator, *Minority Interest*, for whether the firm reports a non-zero amount for the minority interest on its balance sheet. The key independent variables in both the OLS and selection models are three institutional variables − capital market efficiency, labor market efficiency, and product market efficiency. *Excess Value* is the natural logarithm of the ratio of a firm's market value to its imputed value. A firm's imputed value is the sum of its segments' imputed values, which are the product of the segment's sales total with the median market-to-sales ratio of at least five single-segment firms in the same industry. *Capital Market Efficiency* is the logarithm of the reversed ordinal ranking of a country's capital market efficiency derived from the IMD World Competitiveness Yearbook, published annually (rank reversed so that higher values of this measure correspond to countries with greater efficiency). Similarly, *Labor Market Efficiency*, *Product Market Efficiency*, and *Economic Performance* are logarithms of reversed ordinal rankings of a country's labor market efficiency, product market efficiency, and overall economic performance, all extracted from the IMD World Competitiveness Yearbook. Standard errors are clustered by country and are in parentheses. Significance levels are denoted by * (10% level), ** (5% level), and *** (1% level).

efficiency of capital and labor markets continue to significantly affect the value of diversification across countries with a larger number of observations in our overall sample. Furthermore, if we were to additionally exclude diversified firms from the United States from the analyses in Table 6, we continue to obtain similar results. The results of this table indicate that our main results are not substantially influenced by the inclusion of countries in our sample with relatively few observations.

Imputing Segment Value with a Minimum of Three Comparable Firms

As is standard practice in the literature on the diversification discount, the imputed value of a firm's segment (used to eventually calculate a firm's excess value) was derived from the median market-to-sales ratio of at least five single-segment firms in that industry (Berger & Ofek, 1995; Villalonga, 2004a, 2004b). However, since the requirement of five single-segments firms in the same industry may be too restrictive for certain countries in our sample, we perform an additional analysis with the requirement of only three comparable single-segment firms needed to impute the value of a firm's segment. The drawback of requiring fewer comparable single-segment firms is that the imputed value of a firm's segment may potentially be less reliable and noisier than when we require at least five comparable firms. After computing the modified excess values for diversified firms, we analyze the relationship between our institutional variables and these excess values using both a multivariate OLS regression and a Heckman selection model. However, unlike the previous analysis, we only show models where all our institutional variables are included at the same time. The results of this analysis are presented in Table 5.

The results of Table 7 further support the effect of our institutional variables on the value of corporate diversification around the world. The sample now has increased to 42,034 observations from 35,886 observations, where the new observations come primarily from Australia, China, India, Hong Kong, Japan, Canada, the United Kingdom, and the United States. In particular, after relaxing the requirement of five single-segment comparables to three in order to impute segment values, we continue to find that *Capital Market Efficiency* and *Labor Market Efficiency* have negative and significant coefficients (at the 1% and 10% levels, respectively) in the OLS model. Turning to the Heckman model, we again find that *Capital Market Efficiency* is highly significant at the 1% level.

Table 7. The Effect of Institutional Factors on the Value of Diversification: Segment Value Imputed using at least Three Single-Segment Comparables.

	OLS	Heckman Selection Model	
	Excess Value	Diversified (1st stage)	Excess Value (2nd stage)
Capital Market Efficiency	−0.151***	−0.342	−0.174***
	(0.052)	(0.227)	(0.047)
Labor Market Efficiency	−0.052*	−0.260**	−0.067**
	(0.026)	(0.114)	(0.029)
Product Market Efficiency	−0.060	0.101	−0.053
	(0.080)	(0.275)	(0.075)
Economic Performance	0.005	0.324**	0.022
	(0.045)	(0.163)	(0.045)
Minority Interest		0.290***	
		(0.0461)	
Controls	Yes	Yes	Yes
Year Fixed Effects	Yes	Yes	Yes
Constant	0.057	−1.002	−0.046
	(0.220)	(1.161)	(0.181)
N	42,034	142,767	42,034
Number of clusters (countries)	40		40
Adjusted R^2	0.056		
Rho			0.115***

Notes: The table presents the results of both OLS and Heckman self-selection models of excess value, where the imputed value of a segment requires only three comparable single-segment firms (rather than five). In the Heckman model, diversified status is modeled as a probit in the first stage, and where the excess value for diversified firms is modeled in the second stage. The first-stage probit requires a sample of both single-segment ($N = 100,733$) and diversified firms ($N = 42,034$), while the diversified firms represent the selected group for the second-stage analysis. Heckman's approach requires the application of exclusion restrictions to at least one variable — which is included in the first-stage selection model but that can be excluded from the second-stage regression model for the selected firms, since it is uncorrelated with the outcome. To this end, we use an indicator, *Minority Interest*, for whether the firm reports a non-zero amount for the minority interest on its balance sheet. The key independent variables in both the OLS and selection models are three institutional variables — capital market efficiency, labor market efficiency, and product market efficiency. *Excess Value* is the natural logarithm of the ratio of a firm's market value to its imputed value. A firm's imputed value is the sum of its segments' imputed values, which are the product of the segment's sales total with the median market-to-sales ratio of at least three single-segment firms in the same industry. *Capital Market Efficiency* is the logarithm of the reversed ordinal ranking of a country's capital market efficiency derived from the IMD World Competitiveness Yearbook, published annually (rank reversed so that higher values of this measure correspond to countries with greater efficiency). Similarly, *Labor Market Efficiency*, *Product Market Efficiency*, and *Economic Performance* are logarithms of reversed ordinal rankings of a country's labor market efficiency, product market efficiency, and overall economic performance, all extracted from the IMD World Competitiveness Yearbook. Standard errors are clustered by country and are in parentheses. Significance levels are denoted by * (10% level), ** (5% level), and *** (1% level).

However, in contrast to the OLS results, we find that *Labor Market Efficiency* is more significant at the 5% level, after accounting for self-selection. In summary, we continue to find that the relative value of diversified firms is greater in contexts with inefficient capital and labor markets. In the case of *Product Market Efficiency*, we continue to find that it remains insignificant in influencing the value of diversification across the world. Overall, the results of Table 7 are broadly consistent with the significant results of prior analyses that required five single-segment comparables to impute segment values.

DO WITHIN-COUNTRY CHANGES IN INSTITUTIONAL FACTORS AFFECT THE VALUE OF CORPORATE DIVERSIFICATION?

While institutional factors have been found to explain cross-sectional variation in the value of diversification across the world, it remains to be seen whether changes in these institutional variables also explain within-country variation in the value of diversification over time. Doing so requires country fixed effects to be included in the multivariate analysis, to isolate the effect of changes in our institutional variables within each country. Prior literature has found that the relative value of diversified firms can change over time. Shleifer and Vishny (1991) and Hubbard and Palia (1999) argue that the reason why conglomerate mergers triggered positive market reactions during the 1960s but not during the 1980s is because of the secular increase in the efficiency of external capital markets, which translates into a relative decrease in the perceived efficiency of the alternative – internal capital markets within conglomerates. Servaes (1996) examines changes in the diversification discount in the United States during the conglomerate merger wave (from 1961 to 1976) and finds that while there was a significant discount in the 1960s, the discount was reduced considerably in the early to late 1970s. Kuppuswamy and Villalonga (2011) show that the value of corporate diversification increased during the global financial crisis of 2008–2009, partly due to changes in the relative efficiency of external and internal capital markets. We extend this line of work with an international sample and examine whether changes in the state of the institutional environment within a country explains changes in the value of diversification. Table 8 displays the results of such an analysis.

Table 8. The Effect of Changes in Institutional Factors over Time on the Value of Diversification: A Within-Country Analysis.

	(1) Excess Value	(2) Excess Value	(3) Excess Value	(4) Excess Value
Capital Market Efficiency	−0.102*** (0.033)			−0.111** (0.049)
Labor Market Efficiency		−0.101 (0.066)		−0.098 (0.069)
Product Market Efficiency			−0.004 (0.042)	0.093* (0.047)
Economic Performance	0.050 (0.040)	0.051 (0.045)	0.0201 (0.043)	0.074* (0.043)
Controls	Yes	Yes	Yes	Yes
Year Fixed Effects	Yes	Yes	Yes	Yes
Country Fixed Effects	Yes	Yes	Yes	Yes
Constant	−0.792*** (0.143)	−0.819*** (0.191)	−1.074 (0.187)	−0.801*** (0.151)
N	35,886	35,886	35,886	35,886
Number of clusters (countries)	38	38	38	38
Adjusted R^2	0.078	0.078	0.077	0.078

Notes: The table presents the results of a within-country analysis of excess values over time. Using multivariate OLS regressions with country fixed effects, excess value is modeled as function of three institutional variables — capital market efficiency, labor market efficiency, and product market efficiency. Models (1)–(3) each include only one of these institutional variables, while all three covariates are included together in Model (4). *Excess Value* is the natural logarithm of the ratio of a firm's market value to its imputed value. A firm's imputed value is the sum of its segments' imputed values, which are the product of the segment's sales total with the median market-to-sales ratio of at least five single-segment firms in the same industry. *Capital Market Efficiency* is the logarithm of the reversed ordinal ranking of a country's capital market efficiency derived from the IMD World Competitiveness Yearbook, published annually (rank reversed so that higher values of this measure correspond to countries with greater efficiency). Similarly, *Labor Market Efficiency*, *Product Market Efficiency*, and *Economic Performance* are logarithms of reversed ordinal rankings of a country's labor market efficiency, product market efficiency, and overall economic performance, all extracted from the IMD World Competitiveness Yearbook. Standard errors are clustered by country and are in parentheses. Significance levels are denoted by * (10% level), ** (5% level), and *** (1% level).

Table 8 presents the results of several OLS regression models with each of our institutional variables included separately (Models (1)–(3)), with the final model including all three (Model (4)). Again, each model includes country fixed effects in order to focus on within-country variation in the value of diversification over time. The results of this table show that

Capital Market Efficiency loads significantly in the multivariate analysis (in Models (1) and (4)). However, *Labor Market Efficiency* does not load significantly both when it is included separately as well as together with the other institutional factors. Moreover, while *Product Market Efficiency* has a positive and marginally significant coefficient in the full model (Model (4)), we view this result with suspicion given its lack of significance when included alone in Model (3). It is more than likely that the marginal significance of *Product Market Efficiency* in the full model is due to multicollinearity — significantly high variance inflation factors computed for this model support this argument. While we find no evidence that product and labor market efficiency explain within-country variation in the value of corporate diversification, these results should be interpreted with caution since these institutional variables do not change significantly within most countries over time. Nevertheless, we find significant evidence that changes in the state of a country's capital markets do significantly affect the relative value of corporate diversification within the country over time. Consistent with Shleifer and Vishny (1991), Hubbard and Palia (1999), and Kuppuswamy and Villalonga (2011), we find that a country's capital markets become more efficient over time, the value of internal capital allocation decreases. As a result, the value of diversified firms relative to their single-segment peers is found to decrease.

CONCLUSION

In this chapter, we examine whether and which facets of a country's institutional environment explain the variation in the value of corporate diversification around the world. Using data on diversified firms from 38 countries over a 15-year period, we explore the effect of three key institutional variables — capital market efficiency, labor market efficiency, and product market efficiency — on the excess value of diversified firms relative to their single-segment peers. Using both OLS and self-selection models, we find that capital and labor market efficiency are important drivers of the value of diversification across the world. In doing so, we directly address recent calls to explore the drivers of cross-sectional variance in the diversification discount, rather than its main effect (Stein, 2003). Moreover, these findings validate theoretical work that highlight the importance of other institutional "voids," such as the state of a country's labor market, in analyzing the relative value of diversification across the world

(Khanna & Palepu, 1999, 2010). Finally, we advance the limited literature examining variation in the value of diversification within countries over time (Kuppuswamy & Villalonga, 2011; Servaes, 1996). To our knowledge, the present study represents to first attempt to use an international sample to investigate within-country variation in the value of diversification. In doing so, we show that amongst all the institutional factors we consider, changes in the efficiency of a country's capital markets drive variation in the excess value of diversified firms over time.

While we have taken steps to be conservative with our measures of excess value and have established the persistence of our results across different subsamples, the representativeness of our sample does remain a potential concern. The factors by which companies chose to go public may vary significantly by country. This may potentially bias our across-country analyses of public firms since such factors may be correlated with our institutional measures of interest. However, results from our within-country analysis of corporate diversification indicate that even when we focus on changes in capital market efficiency over time in a given country, we observe a shift in the relative value of diversified firms.

We conclude by identifying a potential avenue for future research. Given the evidence in this chapter that the value of diversification is contingent on the institutional infrastructure of a country, it would be interesting for future research to explore within the same firm how financing arrangements differ for diversification activities across countries with different institutional characteristics. Gaining a better understanding of this process would help us understand better the role of finance in the growth of corporations across countries.

NOTES

1. Our primary sample is restricted to diversified firms. However, single-segment firms are used in the computation of the excess values of our diversified firms as well as in the first stage of the two-step Heckman selection models.

2. For other studies that have used segment data from Worldscope for international firms, see Lins and Servaes (1999), Ashbaugh and Pincus (2001), and Healy, Serafeim, Srinivasan, and Yu (2011).

3. Apart from a country's capital markets, firms could also access capital from foreign sources through Foreign Direct Investment. In unreported analyses, our results are robust to the inclusion of a control variable measuring FDI inflows as a percentage of GDP in all our models.

4. For more information about this measure, see the IMD competitiveness report: http://www.imd.org/research/publications/wcy/upload/ep_list.pdf

5. In addition, we see in all models that ROA has a negative and highly significant coefficient. This counter-intuitive result is driven by the presence of small firms that have high growth opportunities but poor profitability. If we were to restrict our sample to those firms with annual sales above $15 million, the coefficient on ROA would be positive and highly significant.

ACKNOWLEDGMENT

We are grateful to participants at the FMA Napa Valley conference 2012, and seminar participants at UNC and Georgetown University for many helpful comments. All errors are our own.

REFERENCES

Acemoglu, D., Johnson, S., & Mitton, T. (2009). Determinants of vertical integration: Financial development and contracting costs. *The Journal of Finance*, 64, 1251–1290.

Almeida, H. V., & Wolfenzon, D. (2006). A theory of pyramidal ownership and family business groups. *Journal of Finance*, 61(6), 2637–2680.

Ashbaugh, H., & Pincus, M. (2001). Domestic accounting standards, international accounting standards, and the predictability of earnings. *Journal of Accounting Research*, 39, 417–434.

Belenzon, S., Berkovitz, T., & Rios, L. A. (2013). Capital markets and firm organization: How Financial development shapes European corporate groups. *Management Science*, 59(6), 1326–1343.

Berger, P. G., & Ofek, E. (1995). Diversification's effect on firm value. *Journal of Financial Economics*, 37, 39–65.

Buchuk, D., Larrain, B., Munoz, F., & UrzúaInfante, F. (2014). The internal capital markets of business groups: Evidence from intra-group loans. *Journal of Financial Economics*, 112, 190–212.

Campa, J. M., & Kedia, S. (2002). Explaining the diversification discount. *Journal of Finance*, 57, 1731–1762.

Dimitrov, V., & Tice, S. (2006). Corporate diversification and credit constraints: Real effects across the business cycle. *Review of Financial Studies*, 19, 1465–1498.

Fauver, L., Houston, J., & Naranjo, A. (2003). Capital market development, legal systems and the value of corporate diversification: A cross-country analysis. *Journal of Financial and Quantitative Analysis*, 38, 135–157.

Gopalan, R., Nanda, V., & Seru, A. (2007). Affiliated firms and financial support: Evidence from Indian business groups. *Journal of Financial Economics*, 86, 759–795.

Healy, P. M., Serafeim, G., Srinivasan, S., & Yu, G. (2011). *Market competition, government efficiency, and profitability around the world*. Harvard Business School Working Paper No. 12-010.

Heckman, J. J. (1979). Sample selection bias as a specification error. *Econometrica*, 47, 153–161.

Hubbard, R. G., & Palia, D. (1999). A reexamination of the conglomerate merger wave in the 1960s: An internal capital markets view. *Journal of Finance, 54,* 1131–1152.

Hund, J., Monk, D., & Tice, S. (2010). Rational learning and the diversification discount. *Journal of Financial Economics, 96,* 463–484.

Khanna, T., & Palepu, K. (1999). The right way to restructure conglomerates in emerging markets (cover story). *Harvard Business Review, 77,* 125–134.

Khanna, T., & Palepu, K. (2000). Is group affiliation profitable in emerging markets? An analysis of diversified Indian business groups. *The Journal of Finance, 55,* 867–891.

Khanna, T., & Palepu, K. G. (2010). *Winning in emerging markets: A road map for strategy and execution.* Boston, MA: Harvard Business Press.

Khanna, T., & Rivkin, J. W. (2001). Estimating the performance effects of business groups in emerging markets. *Strategic Management Journal, 22,* 45–74.

Kuppuswamy, V., & Villalonga, B. (2011). *Does diversification create value in the presence of external financing constraints? Evidence from the 2008–2009 financial crisis.* Harvard Business School Finance Working Paper No. 1569546.

Kutner, M. H., Nachtsheim, C., & Neter, J. (2004). *Applied linear regression models.* Boston, MA: McGraw-Hill/Irwin.

Lang, L. H. P., & Stulz, R. M. (1994). Tobin's q, corporate diversification, and firm performance. *Journal of Political Economy, 102,* 1248.

Lins, K., & Servaes, H. (1999). International evidence on the value of corporate diversification. *The Journal of Finance, 54,* 2215–2239.

Lins, K. V., & Servaes, H. (2002). Is corporate diversification beneficial in emerging markets? *Financial Management, 31,* 5–31.

Penrose, E. (1959). *The theory of the growth of the firm.* Oxford: Oxford University Press.

Rajan, R., Servaes, H., & Zingales, L. (2000). The cost of diversity: The diversification discount and inefficient investment. *The Journal of Finance, 55,* 35–80.

Scharfstein, D. S., & Stein, J. C. (2000). The dark side of internal capital markets: Divisional rent-seeking and inefficient investment. *The Journal of Finance, 55,* 2537–2564.

Servaes, H. (1996). The value of diversification during the conglomerate merger wave. *Journal of Finance, 51,* 1201–1225.

Shleifer, A., & Vishny, R. W. (1991). Takeovers in the '60s and '80s: Evidence and implications. *Strategic Management Journal, 12,* 51–59.

Stein, J. C. (1997). Internal capital markets and the competition for corporate resources. *The Journal of Finance, 52,* 111–133.

Stein, J. C. (2003). Agency, information and corporate investment. In G. M. Constantinides, M. Harris, & R. M. Stulz (Eds.), *Handbook of the economics of finance* (Vol. 1A, pp. 111–165) [Corporate Finance]. NH, Amsterdam: Elsevier.

Tate, G., & Yang, L. (2012). *The bright side of corporate diversification: Evidence from internal labor markets.* Working Paper. UCLA.

Thomson Financial. (2003). Worldscope database. *Electronic database,* May 2003.

Villalonga, B. (2003). Research roundtable discussion: The diversification discount. *SSRN eLibrary.*

Villalonga, B. (2004a). Diversification discount or premium? New evidence from the business information tracking series. *Journal of Finance, 59,* 479–506.

Villalonga, B. (2004b). Does diversification cause the diversification discount? *Financial Management, 33,* 5–27.

Williamson, O. (1975). *Markets and hierarchies: Analysis and antitrust implications.* New York, NY: Free Press.

APPENDIX: DATA ITEMS USED TO CONSTRUCT INSTITUTIONAL ENVIRONMENT VARIABLES

Data Item	Measure
Capital Market Efficiency	
Bank Efficiency	
Banking sector assets	Percentage of GDP
Banking and financial services	Banking and financial services do support business activities efficiently
Financial institutions' transparency	Financial institutions' transparency is sufficiently implemented
Finance and banking regulation	Finance and banking regulation is sufficiently effective
Financial risk factor	The risk factor in the financial system is adequately addressed.
Stock Market Efficiency	
Stock markets	Stock markets provide adequate financing to companies
Stock market capitalization	Percentage of GDP
Value traded on stock markets	US$ per capita
Listed domestic companies	Number of listed domestic companies
Shareholders' rights	Shareholders' rights are sufficiently implemented
Finance Management	
Credit	Credit is easily available for businesses
Venture capital	Venture capital is easily available for businesses
Corporate debt	Corporate debt does not restrain the ability of enterprises to compete
Labor Market Efficiency	
Labor regulations	Labor regulations do not hinder business activities
Unemployment legislation	Unemployment legislation provides an incentive to look for work
Immigration laws	Immigration laws do not prevent your company from employing foreign labor
Redundancy costs	Number of weeks of salary
Labor market flexibility	Index on rigidity of employment (index 0–100)
Product Market Efficiency	
Openness	
Tariff barriers	Tariffs on imports: Most favored nation simple average rate
Customs' authorities	Customs' authorities do facilitate the efficient transit of goods
Protectionism	Protectionism does not impair the conduct of your business
Public sector contracts	Public sector contracts are sufficiently open to foreign bidders

Appendix. (*Continued*)

Data Item	Measure
Competition and Regulations	
Government subsidies	To private and public companies as a percentage of GDP
Subsidies	Subsidies do not distort fair competition and economic development
State ownership of enterprises	State ownership of enterprises is not a threat to business activities
Competition legislation	Competition legislation is efficient in preventing unfair competition
Parallel economy	Parallel (black-market) economy does not impair economic development
Ease of doing business	Ease of doing business is supported by regulations
Creation of firms	Creation of firms is supported by legislation
Start-up days	Number of days to start a business
Start-up procedures	Number of procedures to start a business

Source: IMD World Competitiveness Reports.

TERMINATION PAYMENT PROVISIONS IN ACQUISITIONS: AN INFORMATION ECONOMICS PERSPECTIVE

Cheng-Wei Wu and Jeffrey J. Reuer

ABSTRACT

In M&A markets, acquirers face a hold-up problem of losing the value of investments they make in due diligence, negotiations, and post-acquisition planning if targets would pursue the options of waiting for better offers or selling to an alternative bidder. This chapter extends information economics to the literature on M&A contracting by arguing that such contracting problems are more likely to occur for targets with better outside options created by the information available on their resources and prospects. We also argue that acquirers address these contracting problems by using termination payment provisions to safeguard their investments. While previous research in corporate strategy and finance has suggested that certain factors can facilitate an acquisition by reducing a focal acquirer's risk of adverse selection (e.g., signals, certifications), we note that these same factors can make the target attractive to other potential bidders and can exacerbate the risk of hold-up, thereby leading acquirers to use termination payment provisions as contractual safeguards.

Keywords: Mergers and acquisitions; acquisition contracts; hold-up risk; information economics; termination provisions

INTRODUCTION

Acquirers often expend significant time and effort prior to the completion of acquisition deals in carrying out due diligence and negotiations as well as in making plans for integration and other post-acquisition management activities (e.g., Hitt, Harrison, & Ireland, 2001; Jemison & Sitkin, 1986; Puranam, Powell, & Singh, 2006; Zollo & Singh, 2004). These tasks are conducted by acquirers in order to be able to exploit the intrinsic value of target firms as well as to identify synergies from acquisitions (e.g., King, Slotegraaf, & Kesner, 2008; Rock, 1994). Since many of these efforts are geared to a focal transaction and do not transfer readily to other targets, they also represent deal-specific investments whose value is lost if the acquirer cannot complete a transaction (e.g., Dikova, Sahib, & van Witteloostuijn, 2010; Gilson & Schwartz, 2005; Williamson, 1991). The target's potential pursuit of outside opportunities therefore creates a contracting problem since the target firm holds the option of waiting for better offers or selling to another firm after the acquirer has made such investments. A seller's ability to hold up a buyer after the announcement of a deal can also contribute to inefficiencies if it leads a buyer to underinvest in valuable M&A deal-making and planning activities in the first place.

Such contracting problems in acquisitions can be more severe when information is widely available on a target firm's resources and prospects. For instance, previous research has suggested that the affiliations a firm has with prominent organizations can signal the firm has attractive prospects and certifies the unobserved quality of the firm (Gulati & Higgins, 2003; Hsu, 2006; Nicholson, Danzon, & McCullough, 2005; Pollock & Gulati, 2007). While these affiliations reduce a focal bidder's risk of overpayment, or adverse selection, and can therefore facilitate an acquisition deal (e.g., Ragozzino & Reuer, 2007), it is important to note that this information is also available to other potential bidders, so it can make the target more attractive to other bidders and increase its outside options. The greater potential for the target to obtain alternative bids contributes to the risk of hold-up before the transaction is executed, as the target can either credibly threaten to sell to another firm to obtain better terms or actually sell to another company.

Faced with the risk of hold-up in M&A deal-making, an acquirer can use termination payment provisions (TPPs) to safeguard its investments during the M&A process. These provisions impose costs on targets if they terminate deals or if they even pursue alternative offers (e.g., Bates & Lemmon, 2003; Coates & Subramanian, 2000; Officer, 2003). For instance, target termination fees require a target firm to pay the acquirer a fixed amount of money if the target does not consummate the deal. As a second example, lockup options provide the acquiring firm with a call option on the common shares of the target at a discount, and these options can be exercised by the acquirer if the target pursues other offers. Termination fees and lockup options can therefore compensate the acquirer for the loss of deal-specific investments. In addition, because TPPs impose costs on the target firm for either terminating the agreement or pursuing other bidders, they have the effect of enhancing deal completion and mitigating potential competition in the first place (e.g., Bates & Lemmon, 2003; Coates & Subramanian, 2000; Jeon & Ligon, 2011). Since the contracting problem of hold-up in M&A negotiations is more serious when a target presents a lower risk of adverse selection to other bidders due to the information available on the target's resources and prospects, we investigate whether TPPs will be more likely to be employed under these conditions.

We carry out this study in the context of acquisitions of newly public firms, and this research context is interesting and appropriate for several reasons. Research has shown that the M&A market involving newly public targets is active because of the attractive growth opportunities they possess as well as the broad dissemination of information on these firms during the process of initial public offerings (IPOs) (e.g., Field & Karpoff, 2002; Mikkelson, Partch, & Shah, 1997). This information can be consequential for acquisitions of IPO target firms because of the valuation uncertainty that often surrounds them due to their intangible assets and limited track records (e.g., Brau, Sutton, & Hatch, 2010; Capron & Shen, 2007; Cohen & Dean, 2005; Sanders & Boivie, 2004). In addition, research suggests that the IPO context offers many different opportunities for firms to provide signals on their prospects, obtain certifications on their resources and capabilities, and convey information to outside exchange partners and investors (e.g., Gulati & Higgins, 2003; Sanders & Boivie, 2004). As we will discuss, several characteristics of firms during and after the IPO process deliver important information on targets to prospective bidders. We therefore address the following core research question: What particular characteristics of IPO target firms can have an impact on the acquirer's usage of TPPs?

Beyond combining the research streams on IPOs and M&A contracting at a broad level, our study makes two specific contributions to the literature on acquisitions within the corporate strategy and finance fields. First, we offer a new theoretical explanation for firms' usage of termination agreements. Previous research in finance has often emphasized the target's perspective and the role of agency costs, arguing that target firm managers use these agreements to sell the firm to a bidder who would extend their employment or offer a severance package (e.g., Bates & Lemmon, 2003; Boone & Mulherin, 2007; Officer, 2003). Our theoretical arguments instead shift the focus to the acquirer's perspective and suggest that TPPs are important tools to manage the potential hold-up problem in acquisition deal-making that arises when the target has outside options in the M&A market due to the reduced adverse selection risk it presents to potential bidders. Second, our study contributes to information economics research in corporate strategy and finance by emphasizing the dual effects of information in markets such as M&A. Specifically, we identify an unexamined drawback of signals, certifications, and other factors that reduce the risk of adverse selection in M&A markets. While such remedies to the overpayment problem can facilitate M&A transactions and reduce information costs for a focal acquirer, as previous studies have suggested, they also can contribute to a different contracting problem (i.e., hold-up) to which parties must attend during M&A deal-making.

THEORY AND HYPOTHESES

Background Literature

Startup firms often possess attractive growth prospects, but the uncertainty surrounding these firms' operations also make it difficult for them to secure financial and other resources from outsiders in order to successfully develop and commercialize new products and technologies (e.g., Amit, Glosten, & Muller, 1990; Shane & Cable, 2002). Although there often exists significant uncertainty surrounding these firms, their interorganizational relationships in markets can provide signals and certifications of the underlying quality of their resources and prospects, thereby facilitating their corporate development activities and market transactions. For example, strategy and management research has suggested that startup firms affiliated with prominent underwriters, venture capitalists (VCs), or alliance partners are often faster to file initial public offerings, obtain higher valuation from the market, and are better able to engage in cooperative product commercialization (e.g., Gulati & Higgins, 2003; Hsu, 2006; Stuart, Hoang, & Hybels, 1999). The basic arguments underlying this research are twofold: First, prominent organizations have strong incentives to discern the quality of their exchange partners carefully to protect their accumulated capital, so any affiliations that are formed between these organizations and new ventures can be considered certifications of the new venture's quality. Second, new ventures also have an interest in forming these affiliations, but there are substantial costs in doing so, particularly for firms of worse quality. Firms that seek out and successfully obtain affiliations with prominent organizations therefore signal to others that they have attractive resources and market prospects.

As a consequence of this two-sided matching process, firms associated with prominent organizations are perceived to be more credible and visible as attractive exchange partners in markets, and this can lead to various follow-on opportunities for the firms, including acquisitions. For example, consistent with these ideas, research has shown that the information firms convey before or during the IPO process can have an impact on their post-IPO corporate activities (e.g., Pollock & Gulati, 2007; Ragozzino & Reuer, 2007). Acquisitions of newly public firms have become more prevalent because many of these firms provide valuable growth opportunities to acquirers (e.g., Field & Karpoff, 2002; Mikkelson et al., 1997). However, acquirers often face the challenge of selecting targets due to information asymmetries. Targets possess private information regarding their resources or prospects, and acquirers might be unable to efficiently discern the quality of targets during acquisition deal-making before developing first-hand experience with the target's resources and capabilities. Under these conditions, buyers bear the risk of adverse selection, or overpayment (e.g., Akerlof, 1970), and in the absence of appropriate remedies, these difficulties impede worthwhile deals from occurring (e.g., Milgrom & Stokey, 1982). For instance, given the paucity of information on private targets, being publicly traded can help them get into the M&A market (e.g., Capron & Shen, 2007), and if a firm is affiliated with financial intermediaries such as a prominent investment bank or venture capitalist during the IPO process, it can be all the more likely to be acquired and capture more value (Brau et al., 2010; Ragozzino & Reuer, 2007; Reuer, Tong, & Wu, 2012).

However, it is important to note that such information on a target's resources and prospects might not only facilitate an acquisition between the target and a focal acquirer, but this information is also widely available to other potential buyers and can reduce their adverse selection risk as well. The target can therefore have a number of outside options to sell the company, and potential competition can also increase after the details of a deal are publicly disclosed. For example, operating synergies an acquirer envisions from access to proprietary technologies or additional production facilities might be revealed, and the increased sales opportunities in new markets as well as the expected cross-fertilization of innovation ideas also might attract attention. The risk of potential competition also exists because of the time gap between the announcement of the acquisition and the deal's execution. For example, several approvals are required before the closing of a deal, including the consent of the bidder's and the target's shareholders, regulatory agencies, and other third parties. The waiting period between signing the M&A agreement and closing the deal can often take many months (e.g., Coates & Subramanian, 2000; Officer, 2003). In this interim period, the target's shareholders might decide to wait for better deals, or other potential bidders might free ride on the information disclosed by the initial acquirer and offer better acquisition proposals (e.g., Bates & Lemmon, 2003; Berkovitch, Bradley, & Khanna, 1989; Officer, 2003). In such situations, initial acquirers experience hold-up risk and can capture less value for at least two reasons. First, in order to complete the deal, the initial acquirer might need to renegotiate with the target, which leads to higher acquisition costs and prolongs the entire process. Second, if the target instead sells to another firm, the initial acquirer loses any deal-specific investments (e.g., efforts associated with due diligence, negotiations, integration planning) and may even incur reputational cost from being seen as weak in the M&A market (e.g., Subramanian, 2003).

Prior literature on transaction cost economics has studied the implications of hold-up in many contractual contexts (e.g., Joskow, 1988; Williamson, 1985). This research suggests that when transaction-specific investment is low, resources and capital invested in a transaction can be readily deployed to other relationships or businesses without loss of value (e.g., Klein, Crawford, & Alchian, 1978; Williamson, 1991). However, the risks and distorted incentives created by the potential for hold-up will rise when an exchange partner can threaten termination of an exchange after the focal party has made transaction-specific investments. In the M&A market, for instance, after the acquirer makes deal-specific investment in an M&A transaction, the target can threaten to terminate the deal, or even actually sell to another bidder, in order to capture more value. Given the presence of non-redeployable deal-specific investments, the acquirer can be held up by the target after the deal announcement. Because the information provided on the target's resources and prospects increases its outside options due to the reduced risk of adverse selection that prospective bidders face, the contracting problem of hold-up is exacerbated under these conditions surrounding M&A deal-making.

To address these issues, the initial acquirer can negotiate penalties to be paid by the target to cover the consequences of deal termination. These aspects of M&A agreements can be defined as TPPs. Two kinds of such provisions are frequently used in M&A deals. First, a target termination fee requires that the target pay a fixed amount of cash to the bidder if the target does not consummate the proposed deal. Second, a lockup option grants the bidder a call option on the common shares of the target firm at a discount and is exercisable if the target terminates the focal deal or pursues an acquisition by another bidder. These provisions could facilitate the deal's completion as well as reduce potential competition (e.g., Bates & Lemmon, 2003; Coates & Subramanian, 2000; Jeon & Ligon, 2011). By agreeing to include TPPs in M&A agreements, target management could encourage the initial acquirer to reveal its valuable private information and to make deal-specific investments to successfully complete a deal. Also, such provisions can be used to save the initial acquirer substantial costs in bidding and re-negotiation that may occur if a bidding competition appears. These cost savings generated from the use of TPPs can be shared between the initial acquirer and the target, thereby allowing the acquirer to compensate the target's loss of pursuing outside options with a higher acquisition premium. Therefore, the granting of TPPs by the target also serves as a commitment to mitigate the acquirer's concern of being held up in the M&A transaction, and thus the target would be able to capture more value from the deal because of the enhanced interest alignment between both parties.

Existing studies of TPPs based on agency considerations have argued that target management can enhance its job security or ensure a severance package by offering TPPs to a friendly bidder, thereby deterring other bidders who might replace target management, yet empirical work has not found much support for this argument. For example, research has demonstrated that TPPs have neutral or even positive effects on target shareholders' returns (e.g., Bates & Lemmon, 2003; Burch, 2001; Coates & Subramanian, 2000; Officer, 2003). These studies provide insights into deal completion and the performance implications for acquirers, but there is less understanding about the antecedents of contracting problems in the M&A market and whether acquirers respond to them by utilizing contractual safeguards in the form of TPPs. We therefore aim at complementing the stream of research on termination agreements in acquisitions by extending information economics to this research stream. Our core proposition is therefore that information on the target's resources and prospects prompt acquirers to use TPPs, and our arguments complement prior research on M&A contracting by offering a new theoretical perspective to complement explanations of TPP rooted in agency theory and by shifting the focus from the target to the acquirer during M&A contracting.

Research Hypotheses

Although several features of IPO firms might convey information on their resources and prospects, we focus on those that are closely tied to the IPO process and have attracted recent research attention in the corporate strategy and finance literatures on IPOs. Compared to more established firms, IPO firms often receive less attention from the financial press and analysts, so investors uncertain about the value of such firms may turn to the signals and certifications associated with the IPO firm's affiliations as well as information produced on these firms by analysts (e.g., Arikan & Capron, 2010; Hsu, 2006; Pollock & Gulati, 2007; Stuart et al., 1999). Following these precedents, in the hypotheses developed below, we examine IPO firms' relationships with reputable investment banks, venture capitalists, and alliance partners, and their coverage by security analysts. These four variables represent different sources of information about an IPO firm at different stages. For example, the backing of venture capitalists can reflect the firm's growth prospects since it was a startup; a firm's pre-IPO alliances can convey its resource endowments that are in demand by strategic partners; the affiliation with reputable underwriters can demonstrate expectations about a firm's potential after going public; finally, the coverage of analysts can offer timely information about a firm's operations. This set of variables therefore captures some of the most important sources of information on such firms' resources and prospects that can mitigate the risk of adverse selection by bidders.

Investment Bank Reputation
IPO firms' associations with investment banks can provide useful information to investors because of the way in which IPO firms and underwriters

match with each other for firms undertaking IPOs. Investment banks are highly selective in the clients they choose to take public (e.g., Beatty & Ritter, 1986) and seek to take public those firms that present less risk to their accumulated reputational capital (e.g., Carter & Manaster, 1990; Gulati & Higgins, 2003). The most prominent underwriters have the greatest incentive to engage in extensive due diligence and screen out firms that are speculative or expose the firm to legal liabilities (e.g., Beatty & Welch, 1996; Tinic, 1988), which makes forming relationships with them difficult to imitate. In addition, higher quality firms have an incentive to bond themselves to the most prominent underwriters or borrow their reputations to obtain a higher sales price when going public (Draho, 2004).

Given the aforementioned sorting process, acquirers can use the reputation of the IPO firm's underwriter to judge the IPO firm's quality and future prospects. Thus, even if information asymmetries surround the sale of newly public firms, acquirers can select target firms affiliated with a reputable underwriter to reduce their risk of adverse selection. However, as we have emphasized previously, such information can be useful not only to the initial acquirer but also to other bidders that might approach the target or the target could also pursue. Other bidders also experience a reduced risk of adverse selection, so the target is attractive to other firms and has greater outside options in the M&A market as a consequence. It follows that the initial acquirer bears the risk of losing attractive targets and its deal-specific investments, given the attractiveness of the target's outside opportunities. Hence, the initial acquirer has an incentive to protect itself with TPPs to reduce the risk of hold-up and safeguard the value of its investments during M&A deal-making processes. We therefore hypothesize:

H1. The likelihood of an acquirer using termination payment provisions will be positively associated with the reputation of the IPO target's investment bank.

Venture Capitalist Backing
Just as IPO firms' associations with investment banks can offer information on the target's resources and prospects and carry consequences for M&A contracting, the same argument can also hold for IPO firms' relationships with venture capitalists. While all firms rely on underwriters to take them public, only a fraction of firms that go public are backed by VCs. Evidence shows that less than 1% of entrepreneurial firms receive funding from VCs (Megginson & Weiss, 1991), and that VCs' selectivity in choosing portfolio

companies similarly has the effect of certifying a firm's resources and prospects (Higgins & Gulati, 2003; Hurry, Miller, & Bowman, 1992; Stuart et al., 1999). VCs' repeat business also relies upon the accumulation of reputation capital, creating opportunities for risk signaling and bonding (Gompers, 1996), as noted above.

Venture capitalists also conduct extensive due diligence before making each additional round of investment, and they approach such investment choices with selectivity as well (e.g., Li, 2008). Compared to investment banks, VCs will therefore have a longer relationship with the organization and be more aware of the details about its businesses and operations (e.g., Megginson & Weiss, 1991). In addition, as VCs often specialize in certain industries, this expertise lends additional credence to their investment decisions over time (e.g., Jain & Kini, 1995). Backing by a VC reduces not only the risk of adverse selection for the focal acquirer but also the risk of adverse selection for other potential bidders. This enhances the attractiveness of the target in the M&A market, increases its outside options, and elevates the potential for hold-up during M&A deal-making. As before, we posit that acquirers will find it valuable to utilize TPPs as contractual safeguards under these conditions:

H2. The likelihood of an acquirer using termination payment provisions will be higher for an IPO target with venture capitalist backing than for other IPO targets.

Pre-IPO Alliances
While the above two hypotheses emphasize that IPO firms' relationships with financial intermediaries can certify their quality and provide signals to acquirers on their future prospects, the IPO firm's relationships with other firms can affect M&A contracting for similar reasons. For example, Jensen (2004) argues that firms' alliance activities are not only a mechanism for resource exchange but also an important source of information on the firm's resources and prospects. Research has also shown that firms active in alliance activities are often associated with positive market performance (e.g., Koh & Venkatraman, 1991), as well as improved growth, survival, and innovation rates in the future (e.g., Gulati, 1999; Mitchell & Singh, 1996; Singh & Mitchell, 2005). Unlike other potential exchange partners, alliance partners are more likely to have detailed information on the focal firm's particular resources or technologies, so alliances also provide positive information on the extent to which a firm's resources and capabilities are in demand by other organizations. Similar to other exchange partners,

alliance partners also carry out due diligence on firms, so their decisions to collaborate provide information on their judgments about a firm's resources and prospects (e.g., Eisenhardt & Schoonhoven, 1996; Hitt, Dacin, Levitas, Arregle, & Borza, 2000).

Moreover, the fact that new ventures can bear significant costs to enter into alliances suggests that they can offer signals to other organizations. For instance, in biotechnology–pharmaceutical alliances, biotech companies receive substantially discounted payments from pharmaceutical companies when forming their first alliance. The discounted payments accepted by the biotech firms can be seen as a reimbursement to the pharmaceutical company for bearing the information costs associated with due diligence, and other biotech firms lacking growth prospects could find such practice costly to follow. The biotech firm then is able to recoup the first alliance discount by obtaining a higher subsequent valuation from venture capitalists and equity markets (Nicholson et al., 2005). To the extent that alliances convey information on the target's resources and prospects that reduces the risk of adverse selection for other bidders, these alliances similarly can elevate the risk of hold-up during M&A deal-making and prompt acquirers to use TPPs as contractual safeguards:

H3. The likelihood of an acquirer using termination payment provisions will be positively associated with the number of alliances formed by the IPO target.

Analyst Coverage
Whereas the above three hypotheses concern the firms' relationships with other organizations prior to or during the IPO process, analyst coverage after public offerings can also help acquirers mitigate valuation uncertainty because it conveys timely information on the firm's resources and prospects (e.g., Jennings & Mazzeo, 1993; McNichols & O'Brien, 1997). Analysts specialized in particular industries issue regular reports and forecasts on the quality and investment potential of firms, which increases investors' awareness of the firm as well as reduces bidders' costs to obtain information about the firm (Jennings & Mazzeo, 1993). Research indicates that not every firm is covered by analysts, and analysts initiate coverage only when they are optimistic about a firm's future prospects (McNichols & O'Brien, 1997). Due to the close scrutiny exercised by analysts, their coverage therefore certifies the resources and prospects possessed by a firm, enabling outside investors to draw inferences about the underlying quality of a firm. Supporting this contention, evidence shows that newly public firms

followed by more analysts have better long-term prospects than others with less coverage (e.g., Das, Guo, & Zhang, 2006).

In addition, analysts have had an incentive not to cover poorly performing firms, as this would jeopardize future investment banking business and reduce trading commissions from investors (e.g., Bhushan, 1989; McNichols & O'Brien, 1997). More importantly, analysts may also lose their jobs when the accuracy of their earnings forecasts declines (Mikhail, Walther, & Willis, 1999). As a consequence, analysts' initiation of coverage also conveys that the firm has attractive resources and prospects. Because such information is observable not only to the focal acquirer but also to other potential bidders, the availability of the target's outside options increases as does the acquirer's need to protect itself through TPPs. Based upon the foregoing logic, we predict:

H4. The likelihood of an acquirer using termination payment provisions will be positively associated with the number of analysts following the IPO target.

METHODS

Sample and Data

The base sample for this study was obtained from Thomson Financial's Securities Data Corporation (SDC) database, which provides detailed coverage of firms' IPO, M&A, and alliance activities. The SDC database has been widely used in prior studies on acquisitions, including those focusing on TPPs (e.g., Bates & Lemmon, 2003; Boone & Mulherin, 2007; Coates & Subramanian, 2000; Officer, 2003). Our sample of IPO firms was constructed by first drawing all initial public offerings of common shares by US firms from 1991 to 2005. Following prior IPO research (e.g., Ritter, 1991), we excluded IPOs associated with real estate investment trusts, closed-end mutual funds, unit offerings, spin-offs, leveraged buyouts, and offerings by firms operating in the financial services sector.

The initial sample then was merged with acquisition data from SDC to identify acquisitions of IPO firms. We excluded deals involving spin-offs, carveouts, recapitalizations, self-tenders, exchange offers, buybacks, privatizations, as well as M&A transactions without data on TPPs. We also restricted our focus to the first offer to acquire a majority interest in the target after it went public. Additionally, we followed prior work on post-IPO acquisitions and focused on targets that had undergone an initial public offering no longer than five years prior to the M&A transaction (e.g., Field & Karpoff, 2002; Ragozzino & Reuer, 2007). Prior research has suggested that the impact of firms' pre-IPO affiliations can have long-term effects on firms (e.g., Hsu, 2006; Pollock & Gulati, 2007; Stuart et al., 1999), in part because post-IPO information might not be readily available (e.g., Arikan & Capron, 2010). Thus, the five-year timeframe enables us to strike a balance between an attempt to capture the effects of this information and to limit the effects of confounding corporate activities or decisions on M&A outcomes. Finally, we matched the sample with the Compustat database and the Center for Research in Securities Prices (CRSP) data files to obtain accounting and financial information for targets and acquirers. After implementing these sampling screens and dropping observations with missing values for the variables described below, the final sample consisted of 444 deals.

Variables and Measurement

Dependent Variables
The first dependent variable in our analysis is a dichotomous measure indicating whether or not an acquiring firm used a termination fee for the acquisition. *Target Termination Fee* equals one when there was a termination fee used in the deal, and zero when no such provision was included. Since a buyer can better safeguard its deal-specific investments by establishing a larger amount of termination fee in the M&A contract, our second dependent variable is *Amount of Target Termination Fee*, which is defined as termination fees as a percentage of target's total assets. Given that different forms of TPPs are unique and might have distinct antecedents, we also examined separately the usage of lockup options in deals to test the hypotheses previously developed. *Lockup Option* is a dummy variable indicating whether or not a lockup option was included in the deal. Finally, as we describe below, we wish to examine how firms layer TPPs in the form of termination fees and lockup options on top of each other in designing M&A deals, because prior studies as well as our data showed that lockup options are used less frequently but in conjunction with termination fees (e.g., Boone & Mulherin, 2007). We therefore also constructed a count variable (i.e., *Number of TPPs*) to capture the number of target TPPs in the deal. Data on TPPs are reported in the SDC database for each deal, yet prior research has shown that the accuracy of SDC data on termination

provisions improves with deal size (Boone & Mulherin, 2007), so we also reviewed the SEC filings in the EDGAR system to ensure the accuracy of this information.

Independent Variables

Our first theoretical variable is the prominence of the firm's investment bank (e.g., Gulati & Higgins, 2003; Stuart et al., 1999). In order to test H1, we measured *Investment Bank Reputation* by employing the ranking index first developed by Carter and Manaster (1990) and supplemented by Loughran and Ritter (2004). The index was constructed from investment banks' positions in tombstone announcements, which list members of the underwriting syndicate. A value of nine was assigned to the most prestigious underwriters and one for penny stock underwriters. Given that IPOs are often co-managed by underwriting syndicates, we followed previous studies by identifying the lead underwriter for each issuing firm (e.g., Stuart et al., 1999) and matched the rankings to get their corresponding scores. Data for the lead underwriter were drawn from the new issues module of the SDC database.

Our second theoretical variable indicates whether or not the firm was backed by a venture capitalist at the time of its public offering. While all firms are taken public by underwriters, not all IPO firms are backed by VCs. Venture capitalists are adept at discerning young organizations' resources and prospects prior to making investments, and the presence of a venture capitalist at the time of IPO therefore conveys positive information on the firm's resources and prospects (e.g., Megginson & Weiss, 1991). In testing H2, we followed IPO research and specified *Venture Capitalist Backing* as a dummy variable that assumes a value of one if the IPO firm was backed by a venture capitalist, and zero otherwise (e.g., Brau et al., 2010). Data for this variable were also obtained from the new issues module in the SDC database.

Our third theoretical variable is the firm's number of pre-IPO alliances, which reflects the extent to which the firm's resources are in demand by other organizations (e.g., Gulati, 1999; Jensen, 2004; Stuart et al., 1999). Just as investment banks and venture capitalists vet firms prior to making investments, so do alliance partners (e.g., Nicholson et al., 2005), so the firm's ability to form alliance partnerships conveys positive information on the firm's resources and future potential. We used the SDC database to track a firm's activities in alliances and then counted the number of alliances up to three years before an IPO. To address the skewness of this measure and the fact that some firms do not enter alliances, we defined the variable *Pre-IPO Alliances* as the log of one plus the number of alliances formed prior to going public.

Our final theoretical variable captures the IPO firm's analyst coverage, and in order to test H4, we measured analyst coverage by counting the number of analysts who provide earnings forecasts of the firm in the year prior to the acquisition announcement (e.g., Hong, Lim, & Stein, 2000). Due to skewness that was evident for this measure, we used the log of one plus the number of analysts to define the variable *Analyst Coverage*. The data on this variable were obtained from the Institutional Brokers Estimate System (I/B/E/S), and firms not covered by I/B/E/S are assumed to have no analyst coverage (e.g., Jensen, 2004).

Control Variables
We incorporated a series of controls for features of IPO targets, acquirers, and M&A deals to account for other factors that might be related to the theoretical variables as well as the design of the focal M&A agreement. At the target firm level, we first controlled for *IPO Underpricing*, or the IPO firm's first-day stock returns, as firms that underprice more might attract more attention from potential investors or exchange partners in the M&A market (e.g., Chemmanur, 1993; Demers & Lewellen, 2003). IPO underpricing was measured as the percentage difference between the IPO firm's first-day closing price and the offer price. Data for this measure were assembled from the SDC database. Next, we considered the product announcements after an IPO, since such announcements could help a firm garner market attention and are related to the firm's underlying innovation capability (e.g., Heil & Robertson, 1991; Zahra & Nielsen, 2002). Specifically, we compiled news articles within the Lexis-Nexis database and measured *New Product Announcements* by summing up the number of Lexis-Nexis headlines containing each firm name and possible new product activity (e.g., innovation, new product, and new service) in the year prior to the acquisition. We then included a control for *IPO Firm Tobin's Q*, reflecting the market-based performance of a firm as well as the growth opportunities that potential bidders can obtain (e.g., Bates & Lemmon, 2003; Lang & Stulz, 1994; Officer, 2003). This variable was measured by following the approach suggested by Chung and Pruitt (1994), using data from Compustat and CRSP. We also controlled for the size of the firm as information on large targets is more publicly available, though larger targets might also represent more complex deals, which makes the protection of deal-specific investments important (e.g., Bates & Lemmon, 2003; Coff, 2003; Officer, 2003). *IPO Firm Size* was measured as the natural log of

the IPO firm's total assets in millions of dollars, and the data were collected from Compustat.

In order to capture target management's interests in negotiating TPPs to select acquirers who can offer them job security or a severance package, we incorporated a number of variables that are associated with agency problems. Firms with substantial cash flows would create potential conflicts between managers and shareholders, while these excess cash flows also make firms attractive acquisition targets in the M&A market (e.g., Burch, 2001). Drawing upon Burch's (2001) work, we defined *IPO Firm Free Cash Flow* as operating income before depreciation minus total income taxes, changes in deferred taxes, preferred and common stock dividends, and interest expense, all divided by total assets. Data for this measure were collected from Compustat. Prior research on TPPs also suggested that firms' corporate governance characteristics can influence the inclusion of TPPs in M&A deals. We therefore considered the following three corporate governance variables for the IPO target. First, boards composed primarily of insiders are less independent and are more likely to favor managers' interests during acquisitions (e.g., Bange & Mazzeo, 2004; Coff, 2003), so we controlled for the percentage of insiders on the board (i.e., *Inside Directors*). Second, when the chief executive officer (CEO) and board chair positions are held by the same person, the board's monitoring ability might be hindered during the acquisition process (e.g., Bange & Mazzeo, 2004; Bates, Becher, & Lemmon, 2008), and thus target managers are more likely to act in their own interests, so we controlled for CEO duality (i.e., *CEO Duality*). Third, managers of target firms with lower institutional ownership might be subject to less oversight and hence might be more likely to use TPPs to secure their benefits (e.g., Burch, 2001). Thus, we also included the percentage of shares held by IPO targets' institutional investors (i.e., *Institutional Ownership*). Data for these three variables were derived from the Compact Disclosure.

Several variables capturing M&A deal characteristics were also incorporated as controls. First, acquirers potentially need to pay higher premiums to induce targets to agree to TPPs (e.g., Fishman, 1989; Jennings & Mazzeo, 1993) since targets can have bargaining power when their forgone outside options are valuable. We defined *Acquisition Premium* as the percentage difference between the price the seller receives and the seller's stock price four weeks prior to the announcement date reported in the SDC database for each deal. Second, for similar reasons we controlled for termination fee grants by bidders as reciprocal commitments (e.g., Bates & Lemmon, 2003; Officer, 2003). *Acquirer Termination Fee* is a dummy variable, indicating the presence or absence of bidder termination fee clauses in M&A agreements. Additionally, previous studies have shown that the usage of TPPs is associated with the method of payment in acquisition deals (e.g., Bates & Lemmon, 2003; Boone & Mulherin, 2007; Coates & Subramanian, 2000; Officer, 2003), so we added a dummy variable *Cash Offer*, given that cash deals can be executed more quickly to forestall competitors (e.g., Fishman, 1989). We next controlled for whether or not the M&A deal was a *Tender Offer*, or related to hostile acquisitions attempts (e.g., Schwert, 2000) and thus reduce the likelihood of a negotiated deal provision. Prior research indicates that acquisition advisors help reduce the information asymmetry between acquirers and targets (e.g., Servaes & Zenner, 1996), and because an IPO firm might have continuous relationship with its underwriters for information exchange or other financial services (e.g., Arikan & Capron, 2010; Eccles & Crane, 1988; James, 1992), acquirers might choose the IPO target's underwriter as advisor during negotiations to gain additional information on the firm. Specifically, *Acquisition Advisor* is a dichotomous variable indicating whether or not the acquirer used the IPO target's underwriter as advisor in the M&A deal. We also controlled for whether or not the M&A transaction was a cross-border deal (i.e., *Cross Border*). Cross-border transactions can require significant due diligence efforts and are often abandoned during negotiations (Dikova et al., 2010), yet foreign acquirers also seek less control and integration due to the uncertainties they face (e.g., Gatignon & Anderson, 1988; Kang & Kim, 2010). Data for these variables were obtained from the SDC database.

At the acquirer firm level, we first controlled for prior relationships between the acquirer and the target. Firms that have engaged in alliances in the past may be more aware of each other's resources and prospects (e.g., Porrini, 2004) and thus the efforts on due diligence and deal negotiations may be reduced. *Prior Ties* therefore equals one when there was any alliance formed between the acquirer and the IPO target in the five years prior to the acquisition announcement, and zero otherwise. Data for this variable was collected from the SDC alliance module. In addition, we included a control for the acquiring firm's M&A experience. Acquirers that have significant acquisition experience may be able to select better targets or integrate them more efficiently (e.g., Barkema & Schijven, 2008; Pennings, Barkema, & Douma, 1994; Zollo, 2009) and might be more apt to use complex termination provisions in their acquisition agreements. We used the SDC database to track a firm's acquisition activities and counted its number of acquisitions in the three years preceding the focal deal. To address the skewness of this variable, we took the log of the number of acquisitions plus one to construct this measure (i.e., *Acquirer M&A Experience*).

Finally, we also incorporated controls for potential differences in M&A across industries and time. Moeller, Schlingemann, and Stulz (2005) noted that competition for corporate control is more intense during peak merger waves. We therefore controlled for the volume of acquisitions in the IPO target's industry at the three-digit standard industrial classification (SIC) level during the 12 months prior to the announcement of the focal deal (i.e., *Industry Acquisition Activity*). Alternatively, we included IPO target's sector fixed effects to distinguish targets' sectors of operations, and we obtained results similar to those reported below. We also captured economy-wide influences by including a series of dummies indicating the announcement year of the focal deal (i.e., *Year Fixed Effects*).

Statistical Method

Given that target termination fee and lock option variables are dichotomous, models associated with these two dependent variables were estimated using logit models. To exploit the potential heterogeneity in the value of the different sources of information on targets' resources and prospects, we also estimated standardized coefficients to investigate the relative importance of the four theoretical variables in affecting the usage of target termination fees and lockup options. Moreover, since the size of target termination fee is constructed as the percentage of target's total assets, this variable is truncated at 0 and 1, and thus we estimated two-limit Tobit models to test the hypotheses (e.g., Maddala, 1983). Finally, we used negative binomial regressions to estimate the number of TPPs in the deal, as overdispersion was evident in model estimations. We also ran Poisson regressions and obtained qualitatively similar results as those presented later.

RESULTS

Table 1 presents the descriptive statistics and correlations for all the variables in the analyses. Eighty-four percent of the acquisitions had provisions for termination fees whereas 10% of the M&A deals had lockup options. On average, the amount of target termination fee is about 11% of the target's total assets. The average IPO target had entered 0.4 alliances before going public, announced 1.0 new products or services, and was covered by 4.7 analysts before being acquired. Roughly half of the IPO firms received funding from venture capitalists (i.e., 57%), and a quarter of the acquisitions were tender offers (i.e., 25%). Sixteen percent of the deals were cross-border transactions, and only 2% of deals involve prior alliance relationships between the acquirer and the target. The average acquirer had carried out 6.3 acquisitions in the three years prior to the focal deal.

We also noted several interesting correlations among the variables. Firms with greater analyst coverage tended to be those that were taken public by reputable underwriters ($p < 0.001$), were VC backed ($p < 0.01$), and had been active in forming alliances prior to going public ($p < 0.05$). Additionally, firms that were affiliated with reputable underwriters, backed by venture capitalists, and had more pre-IPO alliances as well as analyst coverage are more likely to have new product announcements ($p < 0.01$). Lastly, experienced acquirers tend to acquire targets associated with prominent underwriters ($p < 0.05$). There are not particularly large correlations among the variables, and inspection of variance inflation factors (VIFs) confirmed that multicollinearity is not a concern for model estimation (i.e., the maximum VIF is 2.74).

Table 2 presents the results associated with target termination fees to test the four hypotheses. In Models 1 and 3, we set up baseline specifications that include all of the control variables to estimate the presence or absence of target termination fees, and the amount of target termination fees, respectively. Models 2 and 4 augment the baseline specifications with the four theoretical variables. All of baseline and full models are highly significant ($p < 0.001$) and the four theoretical variables are jointly significant for the two dependent variables tested (i.e., $\chi^2 = 10.89$, $p < 0.05$; and $\chi^2 = 10.95$, $p < 0.05$, respectively).

H1 predicts that acquirers are more likely to employ TPPs for IPO targets taken public by reputable underwriters. The coefficient estimates for the investment bank reputation variable are positive and significant in Models 2 and 4 (both $p < 0.05$), providing support for H1. In a parallel fashion, our second hypothesis posits that TPPs are more likely to be used by acquirers when an IPO target was backed by a venture capitalist than when VC backing was absent. However, the coefficient for venture capitalist backing is not significant in Models 2 and 4, so we do not find support for H2 in models for target termination fees.

H3 posits that a target firm's alliance activities can similarly increase the usage of TPPs. The coefficient for the pre-IPO alliances variable is not significant, so H3 is not supported for termination fees. When we calculated

Table 1. Descriptive Statistics and Correlation Matrix.[a]

	Mean	S.D.	1	2	3	4	5	6	7	8	9	10
1. Target Termination Fee	0.84	0.37	—									
2. Lockup Options	0.10	0.30	0.07	—								
3. Investment Bank Reputation	7.50	1.99	0.18***	0.13**	—							
4. Venture Capitalist Backing	0.57	0.50	0.09†	0.10*	0.28***	—						
5. Pre-IPO Alliances	0.41	0.97	0.05	0.15**	0.15**	0.21***	—					
6. Analyst Coverage	4.73	4.10	0.22***	0.12*	0.44***	0.14**	0.11*	—				
7. IPO Underpricing	0.25	0.54	0.08†	0.04	0.08†	0.14**	0.07	0.03	—			
8. New Product Announcements	0.99	3.33	0.16***	0.22***	0.15**	0.16***	0.18***	0.23***	0.19***	—		
9. IPO Firm Tobin's Q	2.55	3.38	0.12*	0.23***	0.07	0.06	0.02	0.05	0.20***	0.14**	—	
10. IPO Firm Size	4.57	1.37	0.06	0.01	0.49***	−0.13**	−0.01	0.57***	−0.03	0.04	−0.08†	—
11. IPO Firm Free Cash Flow	−0.11	0.34	−0.02	−0.01	−0.04	−0.31***	−0.12**	0.17***	−0.07	−0.06	0.01	0.43***
12. Inside Directors	0.35	0.19	−0.12**	−0.01	−0.16***	−0.17***	−0.10*	−0.12**	−0.03	0.04	−0.01	−0.08†
13. CEO Duality	0.51	0.50	−0.02	−0.06	−0.09†	−0.14**	0.02	0.02	−0.05	0.00	−0.03	0.05
14. Institutional Ownership	0.31	0.23	0.17***	0.11*	0.27***	0.08†	0.02	0.38***	−0.06	0.09†	0.11**	0.39***
15. Acquisition Premium	0.45	0.46	0.14**	0.03	0.06	0.11*	0.06	0.02	0.05	0.05	−0.04	−0.08
16. Acquirer Termination Fee	0.20	0.40	0.22***	0.08	0.06	−0.07	0.01	0.15**	0.05	0.06	0.02	0.18***
17. Cash Offer	0.36	0.48	−0.02	−0.19***	−0.03	0.03	−0.01	0.00	−0.04	−0.03	−0.13**	−0.06
18. Tender Offer	0.25	0.44	0.07	−0.11*	0.08†	−0.03	−0.08†	0.04	−0.09†	−0.03	−0.06	0.08†
19. Acquisition Advisor	0.05	0.23	0.05	0.12*	0.11*	0.01	−0.05	0.07	−0.01	0.04	0.06	0.13**
20. Cross Border	0.16	0.37	−0.06	−0.09†	0.11*	−0.06	0.07	0.11*	−0.07	0.07	−0.06	0.18***
21. Prior Ties	0.02	0.14	−0.11*	0.01	0.05	0.03	0.14**	0.07	0.08†	0.07	−0.03	0.02
22. Acquirer M&A Experience	6.34	9.85	0.15**	0.19***	0.10*	0.01	0.03	0.07	0.00	0.07	0.09†	0.08†
23. Industry Acquisition Activity	381.72	644.18	0.20***	0.17***	0.03	0.24***	0.18***	0.03	0.22***	0.22***	0.22***	−0.23***

	11	12	13	14	15	16	17	18	19	20	21	22
1. Target Termination Fee												
2. Lockup Options												
3. Investment Bank Reputation												
4. Venture Capitalist Backing												
5. Pre-IPO Alliances												
6. Analyst Coverage												
7. IPO Underpricing												
8. New Product Announcements												
9. IPO Firm Tobin's Q												
10. IPO Firm Size												
11. IPO Firm Free Cash Flow	—											
12. Inside Directors	0.07	—										
13. CEO Duality	0.07	−0.05	—									
14. Institutional Ownership	0.22***	−0.17***	0.04	—								
15. Acquisition Premium	−0.09†	0.03	−0.12*	−0.08†	—							
16. Acquirer Termination Fee	0.07	−0.09*	0.04	0.03	−0.09*	—						
17. Cash Offer	−0.04	−0.01	−0.06	−0.03	0.05	−0.17***	—					
18. Tender Offer	0.04	0.04	0.02	0.05	0.16***	−0.13**	0.40***	—				
19. Acquisition Advisor	0.07	−0.13**	0.01	0.12*	−0.04	0.11*	−0.05	0.04	—			
20. Cross Border	0.06	−0.07	0.09†	0.06	0.04	−0.08†	0.16***	0.21***	0.08†	—		
21. Prior Ties	−0.05	−0.01	0.01	−0.03	0.04	−0.03	0.03	0.03	−0.03	0.02	—	
22. Acquirer M&A Experience	0.03	0.02	0.11*	0.06	0.06	−0.02	−0.18***	0.03	0.03	0.02	0.02	—
23. Industry Acquisition Activity	−0.29***	0.08†	0.01	−0.05	0.20***	−0.00	−0.13**	−0.04	−0.09†	−0.14**	0.00	0.19***

[a] $N = 444$. † $p < 0.10$; * $p < 0.05$; ** $p < 0.01$; *** $p < 0.001$.

Table 2. Usage and Amount of Target Termination Fees.[a]

Independent Variables	Usage of Target Termination Fee		Amount of Target Termination Fee	
	Model 1	Model 2	Model 3	Model 4
Intercept	−2.042†	−2.012†	−0.136*	−0.168*
	(1.109)	(1.187)	(0.067)	(0.080)
Year Fixed Effects	Incl.	Incl.	Incl.	Incl.
Industry Acquisition Activity	0.237*	0.221†	0.015*	0.014†
	(0.116)	(0.120)	(0.007)	(0.007)
IPO Underpricing	0.279	0.356	0.032	0.034
	(0.353)	(0.360)	(0.036)	(0.036)
New Product Announcements	0.861**	0.747*	0.016	0.012
	(0.319)	(0.346)	(0.013)	(0.013)
IPO Firm Tobin's Q	0.165	0.142	0.035***	0.035***
	(0.151)	(0.150)	(0.008)	(0.008)
IPO Firm Size	0.096	−0.239	−0.025***	−0.043***
	(0.169)	(0.190)	(0.007)	(0.009)
IPO Firm Free Cash Flow	−0.011	0.106	−0.035	−0.025
	(0.863)	(0.950)	(0.030)	(0.034)
Inside Directors	−1.452†	−1.382†	−0.031	−0.020
	(0.753)	(0.799)	(0.036)	(0.035)
CEO Duality	−0.107	−0.121	−0.003	0.001
	(0.307)	(0.320)	(0.018)	(0.019)
Institutional Ownership	2.260*	1.872*	0.170***	0.144**
	(0.908)	(0.879)	(0.042)	(0.045)
Acquisition Premium	0.864	0.787	0.077***	0.075***
	(0.583)	(0.602)	(0.021)	(0.021)
Acquirer Termination Fee	2.662**	2.645**	0.049	0.048
	(1.015)	(1.024)	(0.033)	(0.034)
Cash Offer	−0.220	−0.277	−0.030†	−0.027†
	(0.401)	(0.417)	(0.016)	(0.016)
Tender Offer	0.674	0.654	−0.000	−0.003
	(0.478)	(0.500)	(0.016)	(0.016)
Acquisition Advisor	0.089	0.040	−0.004	−0.007
	(0.863)	(0.891)	(0.029)	(0.028)
Cross Border	−0.796	−0.856†	−0.012	−0.012
	(0.495)	(0.499)	(0.047)	(0.017)
Prior Ties	−2.073**	−2.284**	−0.121**	−0.125**
	(0.777)	(0.803)	(0.047)	(0.046)
Acquirer M&A Experience	0.280	0.262	0.023**	0.022**
	(0.195)	(0.201)	(0.008)	(0.008)
Investment Bank Reputation		0.154*		0.012*
		(0.065)		(0.006)
Venture Capitalist Backing		−0.291		−0.007
		(0.365)		(0.021)

Table 2. (*Continued*)

Independent Variables	Usage of Target Termination Fee		Amount of Target Termination Fee	
	Model 1	Model 2	Model 3	Model 4
Pre-IPO Alliances		−0.067		−0.020
		(0.438)		(0.021)
Analyst Coverage		0.718**		0.031**
		(0.228)		(0.012)
χ^2	76.29***	81.44***	264.27***	278.14***

$^a N = 444.$ $^\dagger p < 0.10$; $*p < 0.05$; $**p < 0.01$; $***p < 0.001$.

the number of pre-IPO alliances using an alternative five-year time window, we found that this measure was very highly correlated with the three-year count measure ($r = 0.97$), and that the coefficient for this measure had the same sign and a similar level of significance across the models. H4 suggests that a target's analyst coverage will increase the usage of TPPs. The positive and significant coefficient of analyst coverage in Models 2 and 4 (both $p < 0.01$) shows that the likelihood of acquirers utilizing TPPs increases with the number of analysts providing coverage of the IPO firm.

We then test our hypotheses in models for lockup options. The first two columns of Table 3 present logistic regression models analyzing the usage of lockup options in the acquisition deal. Model 5 is a base model of all the M&A deals including only control variables. Model 6 introduces the four theoretical variables to test our hypotheses and they are also jointly significant (i.e., $\chi^2 = 13.38$, $p < 0.01$). The significant and positive coefficient of the investment bank reputation again supports H1 ($p < 0.10$). However, the insignificant coefficient of venture capitalist backing does not provide support for H2 either. It might be that VC backing is associated with other considerations than signaling or certification that work against the usage of TPPs. For example, prior studies show that VC firms often continue to hold the shares of companies they fund and serve on the boards even after public offerings (e.g., Gompers & Lerner, 1998; Lin & Smith, 1998), and thus VCs might represent an active, large block shareholder that could help mitigate the managers' incentives to act in their own interests during acquisitions. Interestingly, the positive and significant coefficient of pre-IPO alliances in Model 6 ($p < 0.01$) provides support for H3, which may suggest that this effect is more relevant for lockup options rather than termination fees. In contrast, we found the effect of analyst coverage on the use of lockup options to be non-significant.

Table 3. Lockup Options as Termination Payment Provisions.[a]

Independent Variables	Usage of Lockup Option		Number of Termination Payment Provisions	
	Model 5	Model 6	Model 7	Model 8
Intercept	−8.185***	−10.284***	−0.704***	−0.801***
	(1.857)	(2.368)	(0.178)	(0.196)
Year Fixed Effects	Incl.	Incl.	Incl.	Incl.
Industry Acquisition Activity	0.379[†]	0.263	0.047**	0.034*
	(0.224)	(0.240)	(0.016)	(0.016)
IPO Underpricing	0.021	0.193	−0.002	0.001
	(0.260)	(0.284)	(0.043)	(0.043)
New Product Announcements	0.930**	0.718*	0.119***	0.083*
	(0.337)	(0.331)	(0.034)	(0.034)
IPO Firm Tobin's Q	0.099*	0.099*	0.018*	0.015*
	(0.046)	(0.046)	(0.007)	(0.007)
IPO Firm Size	0.232	0.108	0.009	−0.055[†]
	(0.209)	(0.256)	(0.025)	(0.029)
IPO Firm Free Cash Flow	−1.093	−0.763	−0.081	−0.018
	(0.997)	(1.039)	(0.073)	(0.077)
Inside Directors	−0.304	0.181	−0.254[†]	−0.193
	(0.940)	(1.051)	(0.132)	(0.132)
CEO Duality	−0.555	−0.419	−0.061	−0.053
	(0.468)	(0.452)	(0.047)	(0.047)
Institutional Ownership	1.222	1.197	0.360***	0.288**
	(1.031)	(1.094)	(0.103)	(0.109)
Acquisition Premium	0.058	−0.100	0.131*	0.111*
	(0.370)	(0.401)	(0.054)	(0.055)
Acquirer Termination Fee	0.533	0.671	0.260***	0.261***
	(0.466)	(0.522)	(0.047)	(0.047)
Cash Offer	−1.086[†]	−1.034	−0.012	−0.012
	(0.616)	(0.654)	(0.062)	(0.062)
Tender Offer	−0.598	−0.490	0.023	0.029
	(0.615)	(0.666)	(0.055)	(0.055)
Acquisition Advisor	1.805*	2.128**	0.149[†]	0.156[†]
	(0.764)	(0.808)	(0.079)	(0.080)
Cross Border	−1.379	−1.662	−0.127[†]	−0.143*
	(1.012)	(1.051)	(0.067)	(0.067)
Prior Ties	−1.121	−2.276	−0.409	−0.492[†]
	(1.243)	(1.385)	(0.271)	(0.265)
Acquirer M&A Experience	0.607*	0.644*	0.076**	0.074**
	(0.254)	(0.285)	(0.024)	(0.024)
Investment Bank Reputation		0.234[†]		0.038*
		(0.131)		(0.017)
Venture Capitalist Backing		0.630		−0.010
		(0.531)		(0.053)

Table 3. (*Continued*)

Independent Variables	Usage of Lockup Option		Number of Termination Payment Provisions	
	Model 5	Model 6	Model 7	Model 8
Pre-IPO Alliances		0.978**		0.095*
		(0.336)		(0.044)
Analyst Coverage		0.020		0.115**
		(0.542)		(0.044)
χ^2	102.75***	114.37***	150.10***	163.15***

[a]$N = 444$. †$p < 0.10$; *$p < 0.05$; **$p < 0.01$; ***$p < 0.001$.

To investigate the relative importance of the four theoretical variables for the use of target termination fees and lockup options, we reestimated Models 2 and 6 by examining standardized coefficients for key variables. Specifically, we found that in models for target termination fees, analyst coverage had the greatest standardized beta ($\beta = 0.21$) and was followed by investment bank reputation ($\beta = 0.11$), venture capitalist backing ($\beta = -0.06$), and pre-IPO alliances ($\beta = -0.02$). On the other hand, models on lockup options show that pre-IPO alliances ranked at the top ($\beta = 0.18$) and was followed by investment bank reputation ($\beta = 0.15$), venture capitalist backing ($\beta = 0.09$), and analyst coverage ($\beta = 0.01$). Therefore, our results suggest that whereas investment bank reputation matters for both provisions, analyst coverage matters the most in the use of target termination fees, and pre-IPO alliances is the most important variable in predicting the usage of lockup options.

The previous disaggregate analyses consider the usage of the two TPPs as independent choices. We explored the dependent variables further and found that when lockup options are used, they are used alone in only four cases (i.e., 8.9%) and in conjunction with termination fees in 41 cases (i.e., 91.1%). In addition, given that termination fees are used much more often, it is evident that lockup options are layered on top of termination fees to offer additional safeguards for a deal. For example, Boone and Mulherin (2007) found that compared to target termination fees, lockup options are more likely to be found in larger deals that may require more efforts for due diligence related activities. We therefore reestimated the models using a negative binomial regression to capture the number of TPPs used in M&A agreements (see Models 7 and 8 in Table 3). Consistent with our hypotheses, acquirers use more extensive deal protection when the IPO target was underwritten by a reputable investment bank ($p < 0.05$), was actively engaged in alliances before going public ($p < 0.05$), and received extensive analyst coverage ($p < 0.01$). We further examined the economic significance of the variables. When the values of all other variables are set at their means, one standard deviation increase in the value of investment bank reputation increases the likelihood of using more termination provisions by 4%. Similarly, a rise in the value of pre-IPO alliances from its mean to one standard deviation over mean raises the likelihood of using more provisions by 9%. Finally, when the analyst coverage is one standard deviation higher than mean, the increase in using more termination provisions is 11%. In sum, H1, H3, and H4 are supported, but there is no significant effect for VC backing (H2).

Turning to the control variables, there are some noteworthy results that we will briefly summarize. As would be expected, acquirers are more likely to secure deals with IPO targets possessing attractive growth opportunities ($p < 0.05$) (e.g., Bates & Lemmon, 2003; Officer, 2003). It is also interesting that TPPs are used more frequently when an agreement contains bidder termination fees ($p < 0.001$), showing that termination fee negotiated by bidders are reciprocal commitments that compensate for targets' concession in termination provisions (e.g., Bates & Lemmon, 2003; Officer, 2003). Similarly, TPPs are negotiated for transactions with higher premiums ($p < 0.05$), which is suggestive of the costs acquirers bear in inducing targets to forgo outside options (e.g., Fishman, 1989; Jennings & Mazzeo, 1993). Among the corporate governance variables, only institutional ownership is a significant determinant of termination provisions, but consistent with the prior studies we found that the higher the level of a target's institutional ownership, the higher the acquirer's likelihood of using TPPs (e.g., Burch, 2001). Combined with the insignificance of targets' free cash flow, this finding does not support the argument that TPPs are generally used by self-serving target managers who would sacrifice acquisition premiums to secure their continued employment (e.g., Officer, 2003). There is also evidence that acquirers from foreign countries are less likely to use termination provisions ($p < 0.05$), perhaps owing to lower levels of operational integration (e.g., Gatignon & Anderson, 1988; Kang & Kim, 2010), which necessitates less deal-specific investments in M&A planning. Finally, experienced acquirers are apt to use complex termination provisions ($p < 0.01$), either because they are better at selecting better targets and integrating them more extensively, or because they are simply more aware of more sophisticated termination provisions for their M&A agreements (e.g., Barkema & Schijven, 2008; Zollo & Singh, 2004).

Supplementary Analyses

In order to assess the robustness of our findings, we also conducted a few additional analyses. First, we examined if there might be substitutive effects between the four theoretical variables in affecting the usage of TPPs. The marginal value of one source of information conveyed by the IPO target may be lower when prospective bidders already face lower adverse selection risk owing to other information available on the target's resources and prospects (e.g., Long, 2002). After mean-centering the four theoretical variables and constructing six interaction terms among them, we found that there is only one negative and significant interaction effect − between investment bank reputation and analyst coverage (i.e., $p < 0.05$). This result indicates that the effect of investment bank reputation on the use of TPPs may be diminished when the IPO target is followed by a large number of analysts. Thus, there is only modest evidence for the substitutability among signals.

We also investigated if the influence of the variables might decay over time after the firm goes public. Specifically, we followed Arikan and Capron (2010) and formed interaction terms between the time from the IPO to acquisition and the three pre-IPO variables (i.e., investment bank reputation, venture capitalist backing, and pre-IPO alliances). However, we found that none of the interaction terms was significant, providing no evidence that the impact of the different sources of information on the target's resources and prospects is greater immediately upon the IPO and diminishes within the five-year time window.

DISCUSSION

Contributions and Implications

Our study makes several contributions to theory and research on acquisitions. To begin with, we extend information economics to the context of M&A contracting in order to offer a new theoretical explanation for the design of M&A deals and the contractual safeguards firms use in such transactions. Studies on TPPs have applied agency theory and considered whether TPPs are used by the target's management in exchange for continued employment or whether the target's management uses TPPs as a bargaining basis to improve the return to the target's shareholders (e.g., Bates & Lemmon, 2003; Boone & Mulherin, 2007; Burch, 2001; Coff,

2003; Officer, 2003). Our study therefore complements prior research on M&A contracts by arguing that information on a target's resources and prospects can contribute to contracting problems in M&A markets. We suggest that through the usage of TPPs, acquirers can address the hold-up risk that grows in importance as a target presents lower risk of adverse selection to prospective bidders and has more outside options in M&A markets. The empirical evidence we present on the determinants of termination fees and lockup options is consistent with this core theoretical proposition we advance. In bringing this new theoretical explanation to M&A contracting, we shift attention from agency theoretic considerations on the target side to the risks acquirers encounter, and we identify a new source of contracting problems for M&A deals.

This study also contributes to information economics research in strategy and management by identifying a specific downside of signals, certifications, and other remedies to adverse selection that are nonexclusionary, or apply to more than one potential bidder. For instance, prior studies often consider the positives of signals such as their impact on the firms' access to resources or ability to attain higher valuations (e.g., Gulati & Higgins, 2003; Stuart et al., 1999). However, when a target has more outside options due to the signals it has conveyed, this creates the contracting problems of hold-up in negotiations and motivates acquirers to negotiate TPPs in acquisition contracts. Signals therefore have particular downsides that have been neglected in previous research on the many follow-on benefits they provide. Given our emphasis on the determinants of TPPs, it would be valuable in future research to consider how M&A contracting practices and information on targets' resources and prospects affect the performance of acquirers, just as it would be valuable to use information economics to investigate contracting problems in other research contexts.

Limitations and Future Research Directions

In addition to investigating these avenues for future research, extensions might also address several limitations of our study. First, our empirical analyses focus on the usage of TPPs in acquisitions involving IPO target firms in the United States. Future research can therefore investigate the generalizability of our findings by studying the use of TPPs in deals involving more established targets or targets in other countries. Information problems and their remedies might be less relevant for target firms that are more established, and such firms might present less attractive growth opportunities or intangible assets to potential bidders. For example, lockup options sometimes also convey voting rights to the focal acquirer, which could provide better safeguards to acquirers (e.g., Boone & Mulherin, 2007). Therefore, lockup options might be less likely employed in acquisitions of established targets. In addition, targets in other host countries such as emerging markets might exacerbate foreign acquirers' information disadvantages compared to local bidders and increase efforts at due diligence given the lack of reliable company information and the underdevelopment of institutions (e.g., Peng, Sun, Pinkham, & Chen, 2009; Raff, Ryan, & Stähler, 2009), reinforcing a need for cross-country comparisons.

Second, we have restricted our arguments and analyses to information conveyed on the targets having undergone an IPO, and future research may empirically examine the informational effects of TPPs themselves in M&A markets. Prior research has already shown that TPPs are associated with a higher probability of deal completion and a lower likelihood of actual competition (e.g., Bates & Lemmon, 2003; Coates & Subramanian, 2000; Jeon & Ligon, 2011). Since targets who accept TPPs may lose the opportunity to receive superior alternative bids, it is less likely for targets to employ TPPs to attract more potential bidders. Leshem (2012) theoretically modeled the effect of TPPs on bidding competition and proposed that the presence of TPPs can indicate an acquirer's high valuation of a target, which could discourage other potential bidders from occurring. It would be helpful for future research to provide more empirical evidence on how the information generated by M&A contracts and other facets of acquisitions shape competition in the market.

Third, future research could also consider other ways that acquirers might address potential contractual hazards in M&A markets, and other theoretical perspectives might be useful for such investigations. As one example, it is possible that an acquirer can establish a "reputation for toughness" by engaging in high-profile bidding contests and paying more than other competing bidders (e.g., Kreps & Wilson, 1982; Milgrom & Roberts, 1982). Acquirers with such a reputation may be less likely to use TPPs to protect their deal-specific investments because their reputation deters other potential bidders. Therefore, it would be interesting to use different perspectives to investigate ways that acquirers might try to soften competition in factor markets and determine whether acquirers can enhance the value they obtain from acquisitions as a consequence (e.g., Barney, 1988).

Finally, our secondary data do not allow us to observe directly the time and efforts invested by the acquirer during the processes of due diligence, negotiations, and integration planning. Hence, future research based on fieldwork or surveys would be valuable to explore the heterogeneity of bidders' deal-specific investments in acquisitions and managers' perceptions of the outside options for the targets they pursue. Such methodologies could also provide important insights into the details of how managers select between different types of termination provisions as well as other remedial mechanisms to contracting problems in M&A. Research that goes beyond the antecedents of TPPs and examines the consequences of these facets of M&A contracts in processes such as negotiations and post-acquisition integration would also be valuable.

REFERENCES

Akerlof, G. A. (1970). The market for "lemons": Quality uncertainty and the market mechanism. *Quarterly Journal of Economics, 84*, 488–500.

Amit, R., Glosten, L., & Muller, E. (1990). Entrepreneurial ability, venture investments, and risk sharing. *Management Science, 36*, 1233–1246.

Arikan, A. M., & Capron, L. (2010). Do newly public acquirers benefit or suffer from their pre-IPO affiliations with underwriters and VCs? *Strategic Management Journal, 31*, 1257–1289.

Bange, M. M., & Mazzeo, M. A. (2004). Board composition, board effectiveness, and the observed form of takeover bids. *Review of Financial Studies, 17*, 1185–1215.

Barkema, H. G., & Schijven, M. (2008). How do firms learn to make acquisitions? A review of past research and an agenda for the future. *Journal of Management, 34*, 594–634.

Barney, J. B. (1988). Returns to bidding firms in mergers and acquisitions: Reconsidering the relatedness hypothesis. *Strategic Management Journal, 9*, 71–78.

Bates, T. W., Becher, D. A., & Lemmon, M. L. (2008). Board classification and managerial entrenchment: Evidence from the market for corporate control. *Journal of Financial Economics, 87*, 656–677.

Bates, T. W., & Lemmon, M. L. (2003). Breaking up is hard to do? An analysis of termination fee provisions and merger outcomes. *Journal of Financial Economics, 69*, 469–504.

Beatty, R. P., & Ritter, J. (1986). Investment banking, reputation and the underpricing of initial public offers. *Journal of Financial Economics, 15*, 213–232.

Beatty, R. P., & Welch, I. (1996). Issuer expenses and legal liability in initial public offerings. *Journal of Law and Economics, 39*, 545–602.

Berkovitch, E., Bradley, M., & Khanna, N. (1989). Tender offer auctions, resistance strategies, and social welfare. *Journal of Law, Economics, and Organization, 5*, 395–412.

Bhushan, R. (1989). Firm characteristics and analyst following. *Journal of Accounting and Economics, 11*, 255–274.

Boone, A. L., & Mulherin, J. H. (2007). Do termination provisions truncate the takeover bidding process? *Review of Financial Studies, 20*, 461.

Brau, J. C., Sutton, N. K., & Hatch, N. W. (2010). Dual-track versus single-track sellouts: An empirical analysis of competing harvest strategies. *Journal of Business Venturing, 25*, 389–402.

Burch, T. R. (2001). Locking out rival bidders: The use of lockup options in corporate mergers. *Journal of Financial Economics, 60,* 103–141.
Capron, L., & Shen, J. C. (2007). Acquisitions of private vs. public firms: Private information, target selection, and acquirer returns. *Strategic Management Journal, 28,* 891–911.
Carter, R., & Manaster, S. (1990). Initial public offerings and underwriter reputation. *Journal of Finance, 45,* 1045–1067.
Chemmanur, T. J. (1993). The pricing of initial public offerings: A dynamic model with information production. *Journal of Finance, 48,* 285–304.
Chung, K. H., & Pruitt, S. W. (1994). A simple approximation of Tobin's Q. *Financial Management, 23,* 70–74.
Coates, J. C., IV, & Subramanian, G. (2000). A buy-side model of M&A lockups: Theory and evidence. *Stanford Law Review, 53,* 307–396.
Coff, R. W. (2003). Bidding wars over R&D-intensive firms: Knowledge, opportunism, and the market for corporate control. *Academy of Management Journal, 46,* 74–85.
Cohen, B. D., & Dean, T. J. (2005). Information asymmetry and investor valuation of IPOs: Top management team legitimacy as a capital market signal. *Strategic Management Journal, 26,* 683–690.
Das, S., Guo, R., & Zhang, H. (2006). Analysts' selective coverage and subsequent performance of newly public firms. *Journal of Finance, 61,* 1159–1185.
Demers, E., & Lewellen, K. (2003). The marketing role of IPOs: Evidence from internet stocks. *Journal of Financial Economics, 68,* 413–437.
Dikova, D., Sahib, P. R., & van Witteloostuijn, A. (2010). Cross-border acquisition abandonment and completion: The effect of institutional differences and organizational learning in the international business service industry, 1981–2001. *Journal of International Business Studies, 41,* 223–245.
Draho, J. (2004). *The IPO decision: Why and how companies go public.* Cheltenham, UK: Edward Elgar.
Eccles, R. G., & Crane, D. B. (1988). *Doing deals: Investment banks at work.* Boston, MA: Harvard Business School Press.
Eisenhardt, K. M., & Schoonhoven, C. B. (1996). Resource-based view of strategic alliance formation: Strategic and social effects in entrepreneurial firms. *Organization Science, 7,* 136–150.
Field, L. C., & Karpoff, J. M. (2002). Takeover defenses of IPO firms. *Journal of Finance, 57,* 1857–1889.
Fishman, M. J. (1989). Preemptive bidding and the role of the medium of exchange in acquisitions. *Journal of Finance, 44,* 41–57.
Gatignon, H., & Anderson, E. (1988). The multinational corporation's degree of control over foreign subsidiaries: An empirical test of a transaction cost explanation. *Journal of Law, Economics, and Organization, 4,* 305–336.
Gilson, R. J., & Schwartz, A. (2005). Understanding MACs: Moral hazard in acquisitions. *Journal of Law, Economics, and Organization, 21,* 330.
Gompers, P., & Lerner, J. (1998). Venture capital distributions: Short-run and long-run reactions. *Journal of Finance, 53,* 2161–2183.
Gompers, P. A. (1996). Grandstanding in the venture capital industry. *Journal of Financial Economics, 42,* 133–156.
Gulati, R. (1999). Social structure and alliance formation patterns: A longitudinal analysis. *Administrative Science Quarterly, 20,* 397–420.

Gulati, R., & Higgins, M. C. (2003). Which ties matter when? The contingent effects of interorganizational partnerships on IPO success. *Strategic Management Journal, 24*, 127–144.

Heil, O., & Robertson, T. S. (1991). Toward a theory of competitive market signaling: A research agenda. *Strategic Management Journal, 12*, 403–418.

Higgins, M. C., & Gulati, R. (2003). Getting off to a good start: The effects of upper echelon affiliations on underwriter prestige. *Organization Science, 14*, 244–263.

Hitt, M. A., Dacin, M. T., Levitas, E., Arregle, J. L., & Borza, A. (2000). Partner selection in emerging and developed market contexts: Resource-based and organizational learning perspectives. *Academy of Management Journal, 43*, 449–467.

Hitt, M. A., Harrison, J. S., & Ireland, R. D. (2001). *Creating value through mergers and acquisitions*: New York, NY: Oxford University Press.

Hong, H., Lim, T., & Stein, J. C. (2000). Bad news travels slowly: Size, analyst coverage and the profitability of momentum strategies. *Journal of Finance, 55*, 265–295.

Hsu, D. H. (2006). Venture capitalists and cooperative start-up commercialization strategy. *Management Science, 52*, 204–219.

Hurry, D., Miller, A. T., & Bowman, E. H. (1992). Calls on high-technology: Japanese exploration of venture capital investments in the United States. *Strategic Management Journal, 13*, 85–101.

Jain, B. A., & Kini, O. (1995). Venture capitalist participation and the post-issue operating performance of IPO firms. *Managerial and Decision Economics, 16*, 593–606.

James, C. (1992). Relationship-specific assets and the pricing of underwriter services. *Journal of Finance, 47*, 1865–1885.

Jemison, D. B., & Sitkin, S. B. (1986). Corporate acquisitions: A process perspective. *Academy of Management Review, 11*, 145–163.

Jennings, R. H., & Mazzeo, M. A. (1993). Competing bids, target management resistance, and the structure of takeover bids. *Review of Financial Studies, 6*, 883–909.

Jensen, M. (2004). Who gets Wall street's attention? How alliance announcements and alliance density affect analyst coverage. *Strategic Organization, 2*, 293.

Jeon, J. Q., & Ligon, J. A. (2011). How much is reasonable? The size of termination fees in mergers and acquisitions. *Journal of Corporate Finance, 17*, 959–981.

Joskow, P. L. (1988). Asset specificity and the structure of vertical relationships: Empirical evidence. *Journal of Law, Economics, and Organization, 4*, 95.

Kang, J. K., & Kim, J. M. (2010). Do foreign investors exhibit a corporate governance disadvantage? An information asymmetry perspective. *Journal of International Business Studies, 41*, 1415–1438.

King, D. R., Slotegraaf, R. J., & Kesner, I. (2008). Performance implications of firm resource interactions in the acquisition of R&D-intensive firms. *Organization Science, 19*, 327–340.

Klein, B., Crawford, R. G., & Alchian, A. A. (1978). Vertical integration, appropriable rents, and the competitive contracting process. *Journal of Law and Economics, 21*, 297–326.

Koh, J., & Venkatraman, N. (1991). Joint venture formations and stock market reactions: An assessment in the information technology sector. *Academy of Management Journal, 34*, 869–892.

Kreps, D. M., & Wilson, R. (1982). Reputation and imperfect information. *Journal of Economic Theory, 27*, 253–279.

Lang, L. H. P., & Stulz, R. M. (1994). Tobin's Q, corporate diversification, and firm performance. *Journal of Political Economy, 102*, 1248–1280.

Leshem, S. (2012). A signaling theory of lockups in mergers. *Wake Forest Law Review, 47*, 101–124.

Li, Y. (2008). Duration analysis of venture capital staged financing. *Journal of Business Venturing, 23*, 497–512.

Lin, T. H., & Smith, R. L. (1998). Insider reputation and selling decisions: The unwinding of venture capital investments during equity IPOs. *Journal of Corporate Finance, 4*, 241–263.

Long, C. (2002). Patent signals. *University of Chicago Law Review, 69*, 625–679.

Loughran, T., & Ritter, J. (2004). Why has IPO underpricing changed over time? *Financial Management, 33*, 5–37.

Maddala, G. S. (1983). *Limited-dependent and qualitative variables in econometrics*. Cambridge, UK: Cambridge University Press.

McNichols, M., & O'Brien, P. C. (1997). Self-selection and analyst coverage. *Journal of Accounting Research, 35*, 167–199.

Megginson, W. L., & Weiss, K. A. (1991). Venture capitalist certification in initial public offerings. *Journal of Finance, 46*, 879–903.

Mikhail, M. B., Walther, B. R., & Willis, R. H. (1999). Does forecast accuracy matter to security analysts? *Accounting Review, 74*, 185–200.

Mikkelson, W. H., Partch, M. M., & Shah, K. (1997). Ownership and operating performance of companies that go public. *Journal of Financial Economics, 44*, 281–307.

Milgrom, P., & Roberts, J. (1982). Predation, reputation, and entry deterrence. *Journal of Economic Theory, 27*, 280–312.

Milgrom, P., & Stokey, N. (1982). Information, trade and common knowledge. *Journal of Economic Theory, 26*, 17–27.

Mitchell, W., & Singh, K. (1996). Survival of businesses using collaborative relationships to commercialize complex goods. *Strategic Management Journal, 17*, 169–195.

Moeller, S. B., Schlingemann, F. P., & Stulz, R. M. (2005). Wealth destruction on a massive scale? A study of acquiring-firm returns in the recent merger wave. *Journal of Finance, 60*, 757–782.

Nicholson, S., Danzon, P. M., & McCullough, J. (2005). Biotech-pharmaceutical alliances as a signal of asset and firm quality. *Journal of Business, 78*, 1433–1464.

Officer, M. S. (2003). Termination fees in mergers and acquisitions. *Journal of Financial Economics, 69*, 431–467.

Peng, M. W., Sun, S. L., Pinkham, B., & Chen, H. (2009). The institution-based view as a third leg for a strategy tripod. *Academy of Management Perspectives, 23*, 63–81.

Pennings, J. M., Barkema, H., & Douma, S. (1994). Organizational learning and diversification. *Academy of Management Journal, 37*, 608–640.

Pollock, T. G., & Gulati, R. (2007). Standing out from the crowd: The visibility-enhancing effects of IPO-related signals on alliance formation by entrepreneurial firms. *Strategic Organization, 5*, 339–372.

Porrini, P. (2004). Can a previous alliance between an acquirer and a target affect acquisition performance? *Journal of Management, 30*, 545–562.

Puranam, P., Powell, B. C., & Singh, H. (2006). Due diligence failure as a signal detection problem. *Strategic Organization, 4*, 319–348.

Raff, H., Ryan, M. J., & Stähler, F. (2009). Whole versus shared ownership of foreign affiliates. *International Journal of International Organization, 27*, 572–581.

Ragozzino, R., & Reuer, J. J. (2007). Initial public offerings and the acquisition of entrepreneurial firms. *Strategic Organization, 5*, 155–176.

Reuer, J. J., Tong, T. W., & Wu, C.-W. (2012). A signaling theory of acquisition premiums: Evidence from IPO targets. *Academy of Management Journal, 55*, 667–683.

Ritter, J. R. (1991). The long-run performance of initial public offerings. *Journal of Finance, 46*, 3–27.

Rock, R. H. (1994). Economic drivers of M&A. In M. L. Rock, R. H. Rock, & M. Sikora (Eds.), *The mergers and acquisitions handbook* (2nd ed.). New York, NY: McGraw-Hill.

Sanders, W. G., & Boivie, S. (2004). Sorting things out: Valuation of new firms in uncertain markets. *Strategic Management Journal, 25*, 167–186.

Schwert, G. W. (2000). Hostility in takeovers: In the eyes of the beholder? *Journal of Finance, 55*, 2599–2640.

Servaes, H., & Zenner, M. (1996). The role of investment banks in acquisitions. *Review of Financial Studies, 9*, 787–815.

Shane, S., & Cable, D. (2002). Network ties, reputation, and the financing of new ventures. *Management Science, 48*, 364–381.

Singh, K., & Mitchell, W. (2005). Growth dynamics: The bidirectional relationship between interfirm collaboration and business sales in entrant and incumbent alliances. *Strategic Management Journal, 26*, 497–521.

Stuart, T. E., Hoang, H., & Hybels, R. C. (1999). Interorganizational endorsements and the performance of entrepreneurial ventures. *Administrative Science Quarterly, 44*, 315–349.

Subramanian, G. (2003). The drivers of market efficiency in Revlon transactions. *Journal of Corporation Law, 28*, 691–714.

Tinic, S. M. (1988). Anatomy of initial public offerings of common stock. *Journal of Finance, 43*, 789–822.

Williamson, O. E. (1985). *The economic institutions of capitalism*. New York, NY: Free Press.

Williamson, O. E. (1991). Comparative economic organization: The analysis of discrete structural alternatives. *Administrative Science Quarterly, 36*, 269–296.

Zahra, S. A., & Nielsen, A. P. (2002). Sources of capabilities, integration and technology commercialization. *Strategic Management Journal, 23*, 377–398.

Zollo, M. (2009). Superstitious learning with rare strategic decisions: Theory and evidence from corporate acquisitions. *Organization Science, 20*, 894–908.

Zollo, M., & Singh, H. (2004). Deliberate learning in corporate acquisitions: Post-acquisition strategies and integration capability in US bank mergers. *Strategic Management Journal, 25*, 1233–1256.

CAN YOU BELIEVE IT? MANAGERIAL DISCRETION AND FINANCIAL ANALYSTS' RESPONSES TO MANAGEMENT EARNINGS FORECASTS

Guoli Chen and Craig Crossland

ABSTRACT

Financial analysts act as crucial conduits of information between firms and stakeholders. However, comparatively little is known about how these information intermediaries evaluate the believability and importance of corporate disclosures. We argue that a firm's level of managerial discretion, or latitude of executive action, acts as a cue for financial analysts, which helps them interpret and respond to voluntary management earnings forecasts. Our study provides strong, robust evidence that financial analysts find management forecasts significantly less believable in low-discretion than in high-discretion environments, and therefore tend to be much less responsive to these forecasts. We also show that managerial discretion is especially impactful on analysts' responses in those circumstances where analysts are typically most uncertain about how to interpret management forecasts.

Keywords: Managerial discretion; earnings forecasts; management guidance; strategic leadership; information intermediaries; analyst forecast revision

How do stakeholders evaluate, and make sense of, a firm's actions? In particular, how do disparate groups of stakeholders — such as citizens, consumers, suppliers, and employees — decide how to assess and act upon difficult-to-interpret, but economically meaningful, firm announcements and disclosures? Increasingly, answers to these questions in the organization science literature invoke the importance of third parties known as information intermediaries, or "infomediaries" (Fombrun, 1996; Fombrun & Shanley, 1990). Infomediaries — such as financial analysts, regulatory bodies, and the media — help stakeholders to interpret the nature and veracity of firm disclosures (e.g., Deephouse & Heugens, 2009; Pollock & Rindova, 2003, Zavyalova, Pfarrer, Reger, & Shapiro, 2012). In turn, infomediaries have a strong impact on a firm's reputation, prestige, social approval, and, therefore, competitive advantage (Deephouse & Carter, 2005; Martins, 2005, Pollock, Rindova, & Maggitti, 2008).

However, although helpful, these answers merely shift the locus of decision-making one link further along the chain. If stakeholders interpret firm disclosures based on infomediaries' insights, how, then, do infomediaries generate these insights in the first place? When faced with uncertain, materially important, forward-looking statements — such as R&D projections or new product-market proposals — how do infomediaries decide what to believe?

In our study, we focus on one particular type of infomediary — financial analysts — and one form of voluntary firm disclosure — corporate earnings forecasts. There are two main sources of quarterly earnings per share (EPS) forecasts for public firms: analysts and company management (Cotter, Tuna, & Wysocki, 2006). Analysts typically issue an earnings forecast for the next quarter immediately following the firm's release of actual earnings for the previous quarter. Sometimes, but not always, company management will subsequently release its own earnings forecast ("management guidance") for that quarter. Analysts are generally incentivized to be as accurate as possible in their forecasts (Hong & Kubik, 2003) and therefore are expected to respond to any new information contained in the management guidance and revise their earlier forecast accordingly. However, although management forecasts often represent a firm's best estimate of future earnings, such forecasts may still be inaccurate, and at times may even be intentionally biased (Kasznik, 1999; Rogers & Stocken, 2005). Thus, when a management forecast is materially different from the original analyst forecast, analysts are faced with the question of how much, if at all, to respond. In our chapter, we argue that financial analysts evaluate the credibility and meaningfulness of firm disclosures based, at least in part, on a firm's level of managerial discretion, or latitude of executive action (Hambrick & Finkelstein, 1987).

Broadly, we argue that financial analysts will find unexpected firm announcements less believable in low-discretion contexts. In these contexts, factors such as firm-level constraints, low industry dynamism, and minimal means-ends ambiguity are more likely to lead to consistent, path-dependent performance over time (Hambrick, Finkelstein, Cho, & Jackson, 2004). Thus, analysts will be more certain of their *original* earnings predictions and will view guidance more skeptically. In contrast, in high-discretion contexts, characterized by few firm-level constraints, rapid and dynamic industry change, and greater means-ends ambiguity, past performance will be a less useful predictor of future performance. Chief Executive Officers (CEO) matter more and will have greater influence on the outcomes of their firms. Thus, analysts will be less certain of their original predictions and less skeptical of management forecasts that depart materially from analysts' original forecasts. We therefore hypothesize that, in high-discretion situations, analysts will make significantly greater revisions to their original forecasts in responding to a management guidance surprise. In subsequent hypotheses, we extend the logic of our main hypothesis by examining the differential impact of discretion as a function of contextual characteristics (forecast direction and timing) that affect analysts' levels of uncertainty. To test our hypotheses, we use an 11-year sample of 1,051 firms that provided a total of 5,373 management earnings forecasts.

Our study offers several important contributions. First, we provide a deeper understanding of the role, function, and influence of financial analysts in interpreting firm behavior. Whereas prior research has demonstrated that infomediaries make sense of firm actions for stakeholders, our study offers a theoretically grounded explanation of how this process actually unfolds. Second, we further develop the construct of managerial discretion. To our knowledge, this is the first study to examine the impact of discretion on external stakeholders' responses to economically meaningful firm announcements. In summary, our study integrates strategy and finance research to generate a deeper understanding of the interactions between firms and external stakeholders.

CORPORATE EARNINGS FORECASTS

Although the general topic of corporate earnings forecasts has been considered at length within finance and accounting research (Ramnath, Rock, & Shane, 2008; Verrecchia, 2001), there is relatively little work on this topic in the management literature. However, the work that does exist (e.g., Benner, 2010; Benner & Ranganathan, 2012; Pfarrer, Pollock, & Rindova, 2010; Westphal & Clement, 2008; Wiersema & Zhang, 2011) suggests that analyst and management forecasts provide great scope to explore questions of fundamental relevance to management scholars (Zhang & Gimeno, 2010; Zhu & Westphal, 2011).

Analyst Earnings Forecasts

Financial analysts provide most corporate earnings forecasts. Based on financial, operational, and strategic analyses, an analyst generates periodic reports on a small number of public firms (usually 10–20 in a particular industry or sector). The primary output of an analyst's report is a "buy, sell, or hold" decision (Schipper, 1991). Arguably the most important contributing input to this decision is the analyst's forecast of the firm's future quarterly earnings per share (EPS, or earnings). Investors perceive earnings to be the accounting variable possessing the most information content, and, therefore, to be the most important variable for determining the value of the firm (Givoly & Lakonishok, 1984). Analysts tend to issue next-quarter earnings forecasts immediately after a firm's previous-quarter earnings announcement (Cotter et al., 2006; see Fig. 1). Analysts are generally incentivized to be as accurate as possible in their forecasts (e.g., Dechow, Hutton, & Sloan, 2000; Hong & Kubik, 2003).

Management Earnings Forecasts

A second, less common, source of company earnings forecasts is the firm itself. Management forecasts are voluntary disclosures that fulfill a similar

```
┌─────────────────┐      ┌─────────────────┐      ┌─────────────────┐
│ Analysts issue  │      │ Analysts issue  │      │ Determine if firm│
│ initial forecast│      │ revised forecast│      │ meets/beats      │
│ for current     │      │      (AF)       │      │ forecasts        │
│ quarter (PAF)   │      │                 │      │                  │
└────────┬────────┘      └────────┬────────┘      └────────┬─────────┘
         │                        │                        │
         ▲                        ▲                        ▲
┌─────────────────┐      ┌─────────────────┐      ┌─────────────────┐
│ Prior actual    │      │ Management issues│      │ Next actual     │
│ earnings        │      │ forecast (MF)    │      │ earnings        │
│ announcement    │      │                  │      │ announcement    │
└─────────────────┘      └─────────────────┘      └─────────────────┘
```

Management Guidance Surprise (MGS) = MF − PAF
Analyst Forecast Revision (AFR) = AF − PAF

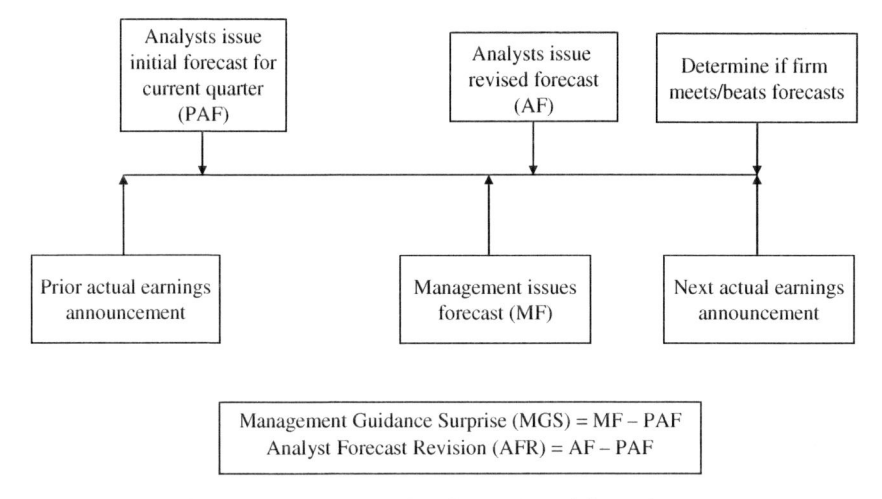

Fig. 1. Earnings Announcement Timeline. Adapted from Cotter et al. (2006).

function as analysts' reports — providing market participants with information about a firm's expected future earnings (Hirst, Koonce, & Venkataraman, 2008) — and therefore act as explicit information asymmetry-reducing signals (cf. Connelly, Certo, Ireland, & Reutzel, 2011; Riley, 2001). These forecasts tend to be released approximately mid-way between the original analyst forecasts and the actual earnings announcement (see Fig. 1).[1] We use the term "management guidance surprise" (or simply "guidance surprise") to describe the difference between an earlier analyst earnings forecast and a subsequent management forecast. If the management forecast is higher than the prior analyst forecast (PAF), this is an upward guidance surprise; if lower, a downward guidance surprise. For example, if the prior consensus (i.e., mean) analyst forecast for a firm were $2.00 per share and the management forecast were $1.50, this would represent a $0.50 downward guidance surprise.

A range of studies have examined the factors that influence the likelihood and frequency of management forecast issuance (Anilowski, Feng, & Skinner, 2007; Tucker, 2007). For instance, firms operating in environments with less volatility (Waymire, 1985) provide more regular forecasts, as do better performing firms (Miller, 2002). More generally, though, most research suggests that managers provide earnings forecasts in order to decrease information asymmetry between firms and investors (Ajinkya & Gift, 1984; Coller & Yohn, 1997). In a survey of several hundred Chief

Financial Officers (CFO), over 80% believed that voluntary guidance reduced the information risk that investors assigned to a stock, and over 90% believed that it promoted a firm's reputation for transparent and accurate reporting (Graham, Harvey, & Rajgopal, 2005). Early disclosure of bad news (i.e., lower expected earnings) is associated with especially strong perceptions of management credibility (Mercer, 2005).

In turn, a stronger reputation for transparency can have substantial economic benefits, as it is associated with a reduction in the firm's cost of capital (Leuz & Verrecchia, 2000), greater liquidity (Diamond & Verrecchia, 1991), and lower risk of litigation (Brown, Hillegeist, & Lo, 2005; Cao & Narayanamoorthy, 2011; Skinner, 1994). Investors are more likely to invest in firms that provide greater disclosure (Ajinkya, Bhoraj, & Sengupta, 2005), and a reputation for providing accurate forecasts is associated with a stronger positive stock market reaction to good news (Hutton & Stocken, 2007). Accordingly, management forecasts "represent one of the key voluntary disclosure mechanisms by which managers establish or alter market earnings expectations, preempt litigation concerns, and influence their reputation for transparent and accurate reporting" (Hirst et al., 2008, p. 315).

Of course, such benefits can only accrue to the extent to which a firm issues accurate management guidance. Forecasting errors, particularly repeated errors, can be quite harmful to a firm (Graham et al., 2005). Thus, the incentives of managers and market participants are often aligned (Hirst et al., 2008). However, at times, managers may be relatively more likely to issue inaccurate or even biased forecasts. Most simply, some forecasts are harder to make than others, resulting in a higher possibility of honest inaccuracy. For instance, less-experienced managers (Chen, 2004), and managers whose firms are facing exogenous shocks (Kasznik, 1999), tend to make less accurate forecasts. Somewhat more nefariously, bad-news forecasts — which tend to temporarily depress a firm's stock price — are significantly more common around the times when managers' stock option awards are issued (Aboody & Kasznik, 2000), and are also more likely to be followed by insider trading (Rogers & Stocken, 2005). And, firms may be inclined to intentionally issue pessimistic guidance in order to encourage analysts to reduce their forecasts and thereby make it easier for the firm to exceed expectations (Baik & Jiang, 2006). Therefore, although many management forecasts do indeed represent a firm's unbiased estimate of future earnings, analysts tend to be wary in their evaluations and are often hesitant to take forecasts at face value (Hassell, Jennings, & Lasser, 1988).

Analysts' Responses to Management Forecasts

Researchers have examined a range of consequences of management forecasts, focusing primarily on stock market reactions (e.g., Baginski, Conrad, & Hassell, 1993). In our study, we examine the reactions of financial analysts. The term "analyst forecast revision" (or "analyst revision") represents the difference between an earlier analyst forecast and a subsequent analyst forecast for the same quarter (see Fig. 1). Continuing the example from the section above, if the subsequent consensus analyst forecast were $1.75, this would represent a $0.25 analyst revision. Analysts often respond to management forecasts by revising their own forecasts, based in part on the management guidance surprise (Hassell et al., 1988). However, the extent to which the revised analyst forecast matches the management forecast varies considerably across firms and situations (Clement, Frankel, & Miller, 2003).

This empirical context is notable for several reasons. First, as argued above, management forecasts are economically meaningful corporate communications, and analysts are incentivized to be as accurate as possible in their own forecasts (e.g., Dechow et al., 2000). Second, although analysts are motivated to respond accurately to management forecasts, evaluating the believability of such forecasts is often highly challenging (Waymire, 1985). Third, the format of management forecasts is highly similar across industries and over time, thus aiding comparability (Hirst et al., 2008). This research context is therefore ideally suited to addressing the broad question of how infomediaries evaluate the credibility of meaningful firm announcements.

MANAGERIAL DISCRETION

Over the last several decades, a growing body of work has examined the construct of managerial discretion, which Hambrick and Finkelstein (1987, p. 378) defined as the extent to which an executive possesses a wide range of alternative actions that fall within the "zone of acceptance of powerful parties." Discretion exists when there is an absence of constraint − an executive is free to select from a range of strategic options − and considerable means-ends ambiguity − the impact of any given action is unclear a priori, and there are multiple, equally plausible alternative approaches (cf. Hambrick, 2007). Research in this domain suggests that firms differ greatly in the capacity of their executives to engage in a wide range of strategic actions (e.g., Finkelstein & Boyd, 1998; Hambrick & Abrahamson, 1995).

In low-discretion contexts − such as stable industries like utilities, where individual executives have much less influence − path-dependence and inertia mean that future firm actions and performance are heavily predictable based solely on past actions and performance (Hambrick et al., 2004). Irrespective of an executive's cognitions, experience, characteristics, or motivation, firm behavior and performance will be highly predictable based on previous firm and industry performance (Hambrick et al., 2004). In high-discretion contexts, though − such as rapidly changing industries like computer software, where there are few constraints and considerable ambiguity between means and ends − executives have great scope to impart their own idiosyncratic stamps on their firms (Hambrick & Abrahamson, 1995). Thus, firm actions and performance can vary greatly from one time period to the next, and accurate long-term predictions will be much more difficult to make.[2]

Most empirical work within this domain has examined the implications of firm-level and industry-level sources of managerial discretion (e.g., Abrahamson & Hambrick, 1997; Keegan & Kabanoff, 2008; Peteraf & Reed, 2007). This work can be divided into two broad streams. First, a number of studies have shown that managerial discretion influences the extent to which organizations are a reflection of their top managers (Hambrick & Mason, 1984). Executives' cognitions and characteristics are reflected in firm-level outcomes to the extent to which executives possess discretion (Hambrick, 2007). For example, the link between CEO hubris and firm risk taking (Li & Tang, 2010) is stronger in a high-discretion context.

A second stream of research examines the implications of boards' recognition of managerial discretion differences. This work is based on the premise that boards implicitly or explicitly recognize variability in the magnitude of discretion and take actions accordingly, especially with regard to executive compensation. When CEOs are seen to have the potential to make a consequential impact on firm outcomes (for good and ill), they tend to be compensated in line with this assumption (Finkelstein & Hambrick, 1988). Thus, in high-discretion contexts, CEOs receive greater total compensation and a greater proportion of incentive-based compensation (e.g., Boyd & Salamin, 2001; Cho & Shen, 2007; Finkelstein & Boyd, 1998).

We therefore see evidence that discretion varies across contexts, and initial evidence that decision-makers within firms recognize these differences. However, to this point, no research has examined whether or not observers and stakeholders outside the firm interpret firm actions differently in line with differences in discretion. We address this shortcoming with our current study by examining how financial analysts use managerial discretion as a type of contextual cue to help them respond to meaningful firm announcements.

Managerial Discretion and Analysts' Responses to Management Forecasts

If a firm issues a management earnings forecast that is the same or very similar to the prior consensus analyst forecast (i.e., a small guidance surprise), there is little pressure on analysts to substantially amend their forecast. However, when the surprise is large, analysts need to make a rapid assessment of the accuracy of the management forecast in order to decide whether and how comprehensively to respond (Williams, 1996). On the one hand, a large guidance surprise might be a legitimate source of credible, material information about earnings. If so, this should influence analysts to substantially revise their initial forecasts, resulting in an updated consensus forecast quite close to the management forecast. On the other hand, though, guidance could be viewed more skeptically, as an attempt by management to influence analysts toward a more desirable earnings prediction (Ajinkya & Gift, 1984). If so, this should influence analysts to *not* revise their original forecast.

In low-discretion situations, firm performance variability from one time period to the next tends to be lower (Crossland & Hambrick, 2007; Hambrick et al., 2004). First, because individual managers experience greater levels of constraint, they have fewer opportunities to make broad changes in the strategic goals and actions of the firm. Second, because there is lower means-ends ambiguity, there will be greater consensus concerning a firm's most appropriate course of action, and thus fewer distinct strategic options from which to select. Overall, therefore, external observers are far better able to predict future performance from past performance. Analysts making their initial earnings forecasts in such situations will be heavily influenced by prior firm-level and industry-level earnings announcements. The magnitude and trajectory of past performance will be more informative, and analysts will be more certain that their initial forecasts are accurate. External observers will therefore be more skeptical of management forecasts that differ substantially from prior consensus analyst forecasts, and thus will discount the information disclosed in the management forecasts to a greater extent.

However, in high-discretion situations, performance variability from one time period to the next can be considerable. First, because mangers operate under fewer constraints, they have more scope to idiosyncratically decide upon different strategic courses of action. Second, because there is greater means-ends ambiguity, powerful firm stakeholders are likely to allow managers to pursue a wider range of competitive approaches. In contexts such as these – often characterized by resource munificence, few governance constraints, rapid changes in customer demand, and discontinuous shifts in technology – past performance provides far less guidance toward future performance. Analysts will be less convinced of the accuracy of their initial forecasts, more attuned to managerial pronouncements, more open to the possibility that expected earnings will differ from their original forecasts and more likely to find large management guidance surprises more believable.

Therefore, we argue that the impact of management guidance surprise on analyst revision will be significantly affected by managerial discretion. In low-discretion contexts, the relationship between guidance surprise and analyst revision may still be positive, but will be much weaker. In high-discretion contexts, the guidance surprise-analyst revision relationship will be significantly stronger (more positive). Thus, we hypothesize:

Hypothesis 1. Managerial discretion will positively moderate the relationship between management guidance surprise and analyst forecast revision.

Our main hypothesis predicted that analysts' responses to management forecasts will be influenced by managerial discretion, with our core logic being that discretion acts as a cue to help analysts resolve their uncertainty in interpreting management forecasts. If our logic is correct, and if managerial discretion does indeed help to reduce analysts' uncertainty, we would expect to see that the impact of managerial discretion will be strongest in those circumstances where analysts are typically most uncertain.[3] To examine this idea, we draw upon insights from work in the accounting literature that explores the characteristics of corporate earnings forecasts. We focus on two important forecast dimensions – direction and timing. We argue that the positive moderating effect of discretion will be stronger: (1) when there is an upward (rather than downward) guidance surprise, and (2) when a management forecast is issued in the fourth quarter (rather than earlier quarters).

Upward Guidance Surprises versus Downward Guidance Surprises

A management forecast may be categorized as an upward surprise (when the management forecast is higher than the prior consensus analyst forecast), a downward surprise (when the management forecast is lower than the prior consensus analyst forecast), or neutral (when the management forecast confirms the analyst forecast). Accounting research suggests that analysts tend to be more convinced of the accuracy of downward guidance surprises (Skinner, 1994). First, managers that are aware of, but do not disclose, material negative information prior to the actual earnings announcement are at greater risk of legal action from shareholders alleging the firm should have disclosed such information more quickly (Alexander, 1991). Second, beyond formal legal obligations, firms' informal reputations in the eyes of market participants may suffer in light of one or more negative earnings surprises (Graham et al., 2005). Analysts therefore tend to perceive downward surprises as being more credible. In contrast, analysts will experience greater uncertainty when faced with an upward guidance surprise.

Therefore, following an upward surprise, when analysts are relatively less sure of the correct interpretation, contextual cues such as managerial discretion will become especially salient. Analysts will rely even more heavily on discretion in evaluating managerial guidance surprises and thus the moderating influence of discretion will be larger; there will be a substantial difference in the guidance surprise-analyst revision relationship across low- and high-discretion contexts. In contrast, following a (more believable) downward guidance surprise, when analysts will be more confident in the accuracy of the management forecast, cues such as managerial discretion will be relatively less important and less useful to an analyst. The moderating impact of discretion will be smaller; for a downward guidance surprise of a particular magnitude, we should see a relatively similar extent of analyst revision in both low- and high-discretion contexts. We therefore hypothesize a second-order moderating relationship:

Hypothesis 2. The moderating impact of managerial discretion on the guidance surprise-analyst revision relationship will vary as a function of the direction of the guidance surprise; specifically, managerial discretion will be a significantly stronger positive moderator when an upward surprise occurs versus when a downward surprise occurs.

Fourth-Quarter Forecasts versus Earlier-Quarter Forecasts

We propose a related argument for our next hypothesis. Just as prior research has shown that analysts' levels of certainty tend to vary as a function of the direction of the guidance surprise, other work indicates that the timing of the management forecast is also important (Baginski & Hassell, 1990). Firms may issue management forecasts in interim quarters (first, second, or third quarter) or the fourth quarter. Analysts tend to be significantly more uncertain when evaluating fourth-quarter disclosures than earlier-quarter disclosures because of the nature of the information being conveyed (e.g., Baginski & Hassell, 1990; Jeter & Shivakumar, 1999). Earlier-quarter management forecasts provide more information about underlying firm quality, which is more fundamental and less subject to unexpected changes. In contrast, managers often incorporate more transient, short-term information in fourth quarter forecasts, as managers are more likely to release such information closer to the financial year-end (Stickel, 1989). Transient information is more difficult to evaluate, but is crucial for making accurate forecasts, resulting in greater analyst uncertainty when evaluating fourth-quarter forecasts.

Accordingly, in the fourth quarter, when analysts are less certain of how to respond to management forecasts, they will tend to rely more heavily on cues such as managerial discretion. The moderating impact of discretion will therefore be larger in the fourth quarter; there will be a substantial difference in the guidance surprise-analyst revision relationship across low-discretion and high-discretion contexts. However, in earlier quarters, when analysts are more certain and relatively more confident in the believability of management guidance surprises, discretion will be a less important cue with which to evaluate firm announcements. The moderating impact of discretion will be smaller; an earlier-quarter guidance surprise of a particular magnitude will be associated with a relatively similar extent of analyst revision in both low- and high-discretion contexts. Therefore, we hypothesize a further second-order moderating relationship:

Hypothesis 3. The moderating impact of managerial discretion on the guidance surprise-analyst revision relationship will vary as a function of the timing of the guidance surprise; specifically, managerial discretion will be a significantly stronger positive moderator when a management forecast is issued in the fourth quarter versus when it is issued in earlier quarters.

METHODS

Sample

We used the First Call database to create an initial sample of all quarterly management forecasts issued by U.S. public firms from 1997 to 2007 inclusive. We retained all management forecasts where the firm was rated by at least three analysts (both before and after the management forecast). If a firm issued more than one management forecast in a specific quarter, we used the forecast which was closest to the actual earnings announcement date. A management forecast can be in several forms: point (e.g., $1 per share), range (e.g., $0.90−1.10 per share), open-ended (e.g., greater than $0.90 per share), or qualitative (no numerical estimates). Following prior research (e.g., Anilowski et al., 2007), we used the exact value of point (i.e., $1 per share in the example above) and open-ended forecasts (i.e., $0.90 per share), the midpoint for range forecasts (i.e., $(0.90+1.10)/2 = $1 per share), and omitted qualitative management forecasts. In addition, we omitted "earnings pre-announcements" (management forecasts issued after the end of the fiscal quarter), because they are actually preliminary earnings announcements rather than forecasts (Rogers & Stocken, 2005), and also omitted firms for which accounting data (from Compustat) or market data (from Center for Research in Security Prices (CRSP)) was incomplete. This procedure yielded a final sample of 5,373 management forecasts from 1,051 firms.

Variables

Analyst Forecast Revision

To capture the responsiveness of analysts to management guidance surprises, we examined the extent to which analysts updated their prior forecasts. Consistent with other work in this area, we focused on the consensus analyst forecast (instead of individual analyst forecasts), which is equivalent to the mean of all earnings forecasts from analysts covering the same company for the same quarter (e.g., Cotter et al., 2006; Williams, 1996). As Fig. 1 indicates, we labeled the analyst forecast consensus prior to the management forecast as PAF_{it} for firm i in quarter t (PAF_{it} is the most recent consensus forecast available 30 days before the management forecast (Feng, Li, & McVay, 2009)). We labeled the corresponding analyst forecast consensus following the management forecast as AF_{it}. To maximize the likelihood that analysts were reacting to the management guidance surprise instead of other exogenous events, we only included consensus updates that were issued within five days of the management forecast (Cotter et al., 2006).[4] Our dependent variable — *analyst forecast revision* (AFR_{it}) — was calculated as AF_{it} minus PAF_{it}, scaled by the share price at the end of the prior quarter (Baginski & Hassell, 1990).

Management Guidance Surprise
We operationalized *management guidance surprise* (MGS_{it}) as the difference between the management forecast (MF_{it} in Fig. 1), and the prior analyst forecast consensus (PAF_{it}), scaled by the share price at the end of the prior quarter.

Upward and Downward Guidance Surprises
Depending on the valence of the difference, we further categorized guidance surprises into three groups. A positive value of MGS_{it} indicates that management has guided the forecast upward (Baginski & Hassell, 1990). Thus, we operationalized the variable *upward surprise* as the value of MGS_{it} if MGS_{it} was positive, and zero otherwise. In contrast, a negative value of MGS_{it} indicates that management has guided the forecast downward. We operationalized the variable *downward surprise* as the value of MGS_{it} if MGS_{it} was negative, and zero otherwise. The third group includes those (relatively few) cases where MGS_{it} was zero, with the management forecast confirming the PAF.[5] In our empirical analyses of Hypothesis 2, this third group is the omitted one.

Fourth-Quarter Forecast
We operationalized *fourth-quarter forecast* as a binary variable, equal to one if a management forecast concerned earnings in the fourth quarter of the firm's financial year, and zero otherwise.

Managerial Discretion
Following prior literature, we used a suite of different measures to operationalize *managerial discretion* (e.g., Hambrick & Abrahamson, 1995; Li & Tang, 2010). We used three industry-level measures (capital intensity, market volatility, and market munificence), based on quarterly data at the three-digit SIC industry level, and three firm-level measures (firm size, firm age, and R&D intensity).

Capital intensity was operationalized as the industry average of net value of property, plant, and equipment divided by the number of employees (Hambrick & Abrahamson, 1995; Hay & Morris, 1979). A higher level of capital intensity induces strategic rigidity and commits firms to long-term courses of action (Ghemawat, 1991). Thus, greater capital intensity is a reflection of lower managerial discretion. To ease the interpretation of our results, we reverse-coded this variable in our analyses (e.g., Hypothesis 1 will receive support if the management guidance-capital intensity interaction is a positive and significant predictor of analyst forecast revision).

Market volatility was operationalized as the volatility of industry sales (Bergh & Lawless, 1998; Keats & Hitt, 1988), which we calculated as the standard error of the regression slope for industry sales over the previous five years, divided by the mean of industry sales over the same period. Market volatility suggests demand instability, which creates mean-ends ambiguity and enhances managerial discretion. In contrast, a highly stable market leaves little room for executives to make critical changes in important domains, such as production capability and staffing, thus reduces managerial discretion (Hambrick & Finkelstein, 1987). Therefore, greater market volatility is a reflection of greater managerial discretion.

Market munificence was operationalized as the average growth in industry sales over the previous five years (Keats & Hitt, 1988; Li & Tang, 2010). Industries with high growth rates are accompanied by unprogrammed decision-making, competitive variation, and ambiguous means-ends linkages. Thus, greater market munificence is a reflection of greater discretion.

Firm size, measured by log-transformed total assets, is an important indicator of organizational inertia (Hambrick & Finkelstein, 1987). The larger the firm, the greater its inertia, and the smaller the amount of managerial discretion (Finkelstein & Hambrick, 1990). Large firms have established routines and experience greater difficulty in enacting dramatic change (Aldrich, 1979; Audia & Greve, 2006); thus, their behavior is more path-dependent. We reverse-coded this variable in our analyses to ease the interpretation of our results.

Firm age is another determinant of organizational inertia, which will act as a constraint upon managerial discretion (Hambrick & Finkelstein, 1987). The greater a firm's age, the more likely that the firm has established routines and tends to engage in fewer exploratory activities (Nelson & Winter, 1982). By contrast, managers in younger firms tend to have greater opportunities to shape the organization and its scope. Firm age was measured by the number of years the firm had been listed on the relevant stock exchange (Feng et al., 2009). Data were collected from CRSP. Similar to firm size, we reverse-coded this variable.

R&D intensity is a measure of product differentiability (Hay & Morris, 1979). Managers in firms characterized by high R&D intensity have greater discretion in allocating firm resources. Relatedly, such firms are less likely to have stable and smooth earnings over times. We operationalized R&D intensity as R&D expenses divided by total sales. We replaced missing data with zero (Villalonga, 2004).

Control Variables
We drew from the finance and accounting literatures to generate a comprehensive list of control variables in our analyses, including firm characteristics, management forecast characteristics, and earnings characteristics. Firm characteristics included *firm profitability* (return on assets) and *acquisition activities* (a dummy variable indicating whether the focal firm had engaged in a merger or acquisition in the prior, current, or next quarters). We also controlled for the effect of corporate governance conditions by including *CEO duality* (a dummy variable coded as one if the CEO was also board chair) and *outsider ratio* (the percentage of independent directors on the board).

In terms of management forecast characteristics, we controlled for *stock market reaction* to the management forecast, which was operationalized as the three-day cumulative abnormal return surrounding the forecast date (Pfarrer et al., 2010). Prior research suggests that the market reaction increases the believability of the management forecast and thus has a positive effect on the analyst forecast revision (Williams, 1996). Another factor influencing analysts' interpretations is *prior accuracy* of management forecasts, which we operationalized as the absolute difference between the most recent prior management forecast and actual earnings, scaled by the share price at the end of prior quarter (Williams, 1996). We also controlled for management *forecast horizon*, measured by the number of days between the date of the management forecast and the date of the actual earnings announcement.

Our earnings quality variables included *auditor opinion* (a dummy variable indicating that an auditor issued an unqualified, or "clean," opinion of the firm's financial statements, which indicates the auditor believed that the audited company's statements were presented fairly according to Generally Accepted Accounting Principles (GAAP)), and *earnings volatility* (the standard deviation of EPS over the last 12 quarters). We also controlled for prior analyst *forecast dispersion* (the standard deviation of the individual analyst forecasts prior to the management forecast). These factors reflect the general information environment, which might potentially influence analysts' abilities to make accurate predictions concerning firm earnings.

Correction for Potential Endogeneity

Providing a management forecast is voluntary and managers that do issue a forecast are likely to have distinct reasons for doing so. Therefore, in our analyses, we needed to address the reasons why some firms issue forecasts in a particular quarter and others do not. To address this potential estimation bias, we used a two-stage Heckman selection model. In the first stage, we regressed a firm's decision to issue a forecast (a dummy variable equal to one if a firm issued a management forecast in a quarter) on a number of factors that have been documented in prior literature to influence the likelihood of issuing a management forecast (Feng et al., 2009). These variables included management incentives (industries with higher litigation risks, the existence of corporate restructuring), firm characteristics (firm size, profitability, firm beta, market-to-book ratio), and analyst forecasting environment (individual analysts' forecast dispersion, earnings volatility, number of analysts following the firm). To successfully control for endogeneity, at least one independent variable needs to be identified that is associated with the dependent variable in the first-stage model, but is not related to the dependent variable in the second-stage model (Larcker & Rusticus, 2010). This variable is the number of analysts following the firm. Previous studies have documented that this variable is positively related to management forecast issuance (Feng et al., 2009). However, the number of analysts following the firm is not significantly associated with management forecast accuracy and analyst forecast revision. The detailed results of this first-stage model are reported in Appendix. All variables were found to be significant predictors of guidance likelihood. Based on the first-stage regression, we calculated the Inverse Mills ratio and included it into our second-stage models, which we used to test our hypotheses.

Model Specifications

We created a panel dataset for our empirical analyses in which the level of analysis is the firm-quarter. In all our empirical tests we used fixed-effect regression models, in which we also included year dummies. The model we used to test Hypothesis 1 is:

$$\text{AFR}_{it} = \beta_0 + \beta_1 \text{MGS}_{it} + \beta_2 \text{MD}_{it} + \beta_3 \text{MGS}_{it} * \text{MD}_{it} + \text{controls} + e_{it} \quad (1)$$

where AFR_{it} is the analyst forecast revision for firm i in quarter t; MGS_{it} is the management guidance surprise for firm i in quarter t; and MD_{it} is managerial discretion measured by three industry-level indicators (MD-capital intensity, MD-market volatility, and MD-market munificence) and three firm-level indicators (MD-firm size, MD-firm age, and MD-R&D intensity). We also created interaction terms between MGS_{it} and each indicator of MD_{it}, for a total of six distinct interactions (and six β_3 coefficients). Hypothesis 1 will receive support if the coefficients for the β_3 variables are positive and significant.

The model we used to test Hypothesis 2 is:

$$\begin{aligned}\text{AFR}_{it} = &\beta_0 + \beta_1 \text{upward surprise}_{it} + \beta_2 \text{ downward surprise}_{it} \\ &+ \beta_3 \text{MD}_{it} + \beta_4 \text{MD}_{it} * \text{upward surprise}_{it} \\ &+ \beta_5 \text{MD}_{it} * \text{downward surprise}_{it} + \text{controls} + e_{it}\end{aligned} \quad (2)$$

where upward surprise$_{it}$ is the value of management guidance surprise when the management forecast is higher than the prior analyst consensus; and downward surprise$_{it}$ is the value of management guidance surprise when the management forecast is lower than the prior analyst consensus. We also created interactions between upward surprise$_{it}$ and MD_{it}, and interactions between downward surprise$_{it}$ and MD_{it}. Hypothesis 2 is a second-order interaction; we argue that the moderating impact of discretion on the guidance surprise-analyst revision relationship will be significantly stronger when the guidance surprise is upward than when the guidance surprise is downward. Thus Hypothesis 2 will receive support if β_4 is greater than β_5 and the difference is statistically significant.

Similar to Hypothesis 2, Hypothesis 3 is a second-order interaction; we argued that the moderating impact of discretion on the guidance surprise-analyst revision relationship would be significantly stronger when a forecast was issued in the fourth quarter than when it was issued in earlier quarters. The full model is as follows:

$$\begin{aligned}\text{AFR}_{it} = &\beta_0 + \beta_1 \text{MGS}_{it} + \beta_2 \text{MD}_{it} + \beta_3 \text{Qtr4} + \beta_4 \text{MGS}_{it} * \text{Qtr4} + \beta_5 \text{MD}_{it} * \text{MGS}_{it} \\ &+ \beta_6 \text{MD}_{it} * \text{Qtr4} + \beta_7 \text{MD}_{it} * \text{MGS}_{it} * \text{Qtr4} + \text{controls} + e_{it}\end{aligned} \quad (3)$$

where Qtr4 is a dummy variable indicating the management forecast was issued for fourth quarter earnings, and all other variables are as described above. However, to avoid the difficulties of interpreting a three-way interaction (β_7), we followed prior research (e.g., Ho, Wu, & Xu, 2011) and instead used the same model as for Hypothesis 1 (see Eq. (1)), but ran this model separately for two groups: (1) management forecasts issued for earlier quarters, and (2) management forecasts issued for the fourth quarter. For Hypothesis 3 to be supported, we would expect to see that β_3 (MGS$_{it}$ * MD$_{it}$) in our fourth-quarter model is significantly greater than β_3 in our earlier-quarter model.[6]

RESULTS

Table 1 reports descriptive statistics and correlations for all variables used in our analyses. Table 2 reports our tests of Hypothesis 1. Model 1 includes all control variables. Consistent with prior research (e.g., Baginski & Hassell, 1990), the effect of guidance surprise is positive and significant. Note that the coefficient ($\beta = 0.5067$) is less than 1.00, suggesting that analysts tend to respond to, but partially discount, management forecasts when updating their prior forecasts. For instance, if the management guidance surprise were \$1.00, the expected analyst forecast revision would be only \$0.51. In other words, in our sample, analysts discounted management guidance surprises by 49.33% (i.e., $1 - 0.5067 = 0.4933$).

Models 2–7 include six proxies of managerial discretion, and the interactions of these six proxies and guidance surprise. We found, as predicted, that managerial discretion was a positive and significant moderator of the guidance surprise-analyst revision relationship (except for Model 4 in which managerial discretion was measured by market munificence). Specifically, the interactions between guidance surprise and, respectively, MD-capital intensity ($\beta = 1.1812$, $p < 0.01$), MD-market volatility ($\beta = 0.6772$, $p < 0.01$), MD-firm size ($\beta = 0.0934$, $p < 0.01$), MD-firm age ($\beta = 0.0033$, $p < 0.05$) and MD-R&D intensity ($\beta = 2.1275$, $p < 0.01$) were all positive and significant. Thus, we found strong support for Hypothesis 1.

To provide an overall indication of the practical significance of our results for Hypothesis 1, we created a managerial discretion index (MD-index), which was the sum of the standardized scores of our six managerial discretion proxies. We then ran a regression including (a) the control

Table 1. Descriptive Statistics and Correlations.

		Mean	S.D.	1	2	3	4	5	6	7	8	9	10	11	12	13	14	15	16	17	18	19	20	21
1	Analyst forecast revision	−0.001	0.008																					
2	Guidance surprise	−0.001	0.014	0.66																				
3	Upward surprise	0.001	0.012	0.47	0.91																			
4	Downward surprise	−0.002	0.006	0.59	0.46	0.05																		
5	ROA	0.013	0.049	0.04	−0.05	−0.14	0.17																	
6	Acquisition activities	0.429	0.495	0.03	0.02	0.00	0.04	−0.01																
7	CEO duality	0.598	0.490	−0.01	−0.02	−0.04	0.02	0.02	0.02															
8	Outsider ratio	0.758	0.128	0.06	0.04	0.00	0.11	0.04	0.05	0.11														
9	Stock market reaction	0.002	0.110	0.20	0.14	0.05	0.23	0.04	0.00	−0.01	0.09													
10	Prior accuracy	0.003	0.008	0.07	0.01	−0.02	0.07	0.17	0.03	−0.07	−0.01	0.05												
11	Forecast horizon[a]	3.187	0.511	0.08	0.07	0.02	0.13	0.02	0.05	−0.03	0.02	0.11	0.02											
12	Auditor opinion	0.891	0.496	0.02	0.03	0.03	−0.01	0.02	−0.02	−0.02	−0.17	−0.03	−0.01	−0.05										
13	Earnings volatility	0.355	6.155	0.03	0.00	−0.01	0.02	0.07	0.00	−0.01	0.01	0.01	0.03	−0.03	0.03									
14	Forecast dispersion	0.535	0.525	−0.03	−0.03	−0.02	−0.02	−0.01	0.03	0.01	0.02	−0.05	0.00	−0.03	0.00	−0.01								
15	Endogeneity control	0.171	0.125	0.03	0.04	0.07	−0.05	−0.01	0.01	0.02	−0.18	0.02	0.06	−0.38	0.10	0.02	−0.10							
16	Fourth quarter forecast	0.234	0.423	0.02	0.03	0.05	−0.04	0.00	0.10	−0.03	−0.02	0.01	0.03	0.04	0.06	0.00	−0.01	−0.01						
17	MD-capital intensity[b]	−0.244	0.160	−0.01	−0.01	−0.04	0.06	−0.02	0.04	−0.15	−0.04	0.03	0.10	0.09	0.05	−0.01	−0.02	−0.06	0.00					
18	MD-market munificence	0.095	0.150	−0.02	0.01	0.03	−0.04	0.00	−0.01	−0.04	−0.15	−0.04	−0.05	−0.06	0.04	0.01	−0.01	0.09	0.02	−0.16				
19	MD-market volatility	0.067	0.051	−0.02	−0.03	−0.03	−0.01	−0.07	0.03	0.05	−0.09	−0.04	−0.07	0.01	0.08	0.01	0.01	0.09	−0.06	0.18	−0.07			
20	MD-firm size[a,b]	−6.801	1.541	−0.01	−0.03	−0.02	−0.03	−0.06	−0.13	−0.12	−0.24	−0.03	0.01	0.01	0.18	−0.06	0.01	0.34	0.01	0.21	−0.03	0.23		
21	MD-firm age[b]	−10.78	10.502	0.00	0.02	0.04	−0.03	−0.06	0.02	−0.07	−0.18	−0.02	−0.01	0.01	0.09	−0.03	0.02	−0.01	−0.01	0.08	0.05	0.17	0.47	
22	MD-R&D intensity	0.084	0.158	−0.03	−0.02	−0.01	−0.05	−0.16	−0.01	−0.08	0.00	−0.01	−0.07	0.04	0.00	−0.06	0.02	−0.10	0.01	0.27	−0.06	0.07	0.11	0.05

$N = 5,373$; Correlations of 0.03 or higher are significant at the 0.05 level.
[a]Log-transformed.
[b]Reverse-coded.

Table 2. Models Predicting Analyst Forecast Revision.

	(1)	(2)	(3)	(4)	(5)	(6)	(7)
ROA	0.0052†	0.0034†	0.0080**	0.0051†	0.0085**	0.0051†	0.0032
	(0.0027)	(0.0018)	(0.0023)	(0.0027)	(0.0025)	(0.0027)	(0.0020)
Acquisition activities	0.0004	0.0000	0.0002	0.0004	0.0003	0.0004	0.0002
	(0.0003)	(0.0002)	(0.0003)	(0.0003)	(0.0003)	(0.0003)	(0.0002)
CEO duality	−0.0003	−0.0006†	−0.0003	−0.0003	−0.0002	−0.0002	−0.0003
	(0.0004)	(0.0003)	(0.0004)	(0.0004)	(0.0004)	(0.0004)	(0.0003)
Outsider ratio	0.0010	0.0010	0.0009	0.0010	0.0012	0.0010	0.0015
	(0.0016)	(0.0011)	(0.0014)	(0.0016)	(0.0015)	(0.0016)	(0.0012)
Stock market reaction	0.0048**	0.0015*	0.0018*	0.0049**	0.0032**	0.0049**	0.0049**
	(0.0011)	(0.0007)	(0.0009)	(0.0011)	(0.0010)	(0.0011)	(0.0008)
Prior accuracy	0.0072**	0.0027*	0.0051**	0.0072**	0.0067**	0.0071**	0.0052**
	(0.0018)	(0.0012)	(0.0015)	(0.0018)	(0.0017)	(0.0018)	(0.0013)
Forecast horizon	0.0000	−0.0000	−0.0000	0.0000	−0.0000	0.0000	0.0000
	(0.0000)	(0.0000)	(0.0000)	(0.0000)	(0.0000)	(0.0000)	(0.0000)
Auditor opinion	0.0001	−0.0000	0.0001	0.0001	0.0002	0.0001	0.0003
	(0.0003)	(0.0002)	(0.0003)	(0.0003)	(0.0003)	(0.0003)	(0.0002)
Earnings volatility	0.0000	−0.0000	0.0000	0.0000	0.0000	0.0000	0.0000
	(0.0000)	(0.0000)	(0.0000)	(0.0000)	(0.0000)	(0.0000)	(0.0000)
Forecast dispersion	−0.0002	−0.0002	−0.0002	−0.0002	−0.0003	−0.0002	−0.0003
	(0.0002)	(0.0002)	(0.0002)	(0.0002)	(0.0002)	(0.0002)	(0.0002)
Endogeneity control	0.0007	0.0021†	0.0017	0.0006	−0.0000	0.0006	0.0013
	(0.0018)	(0.0012)	(0.0016)	(0.0018)	(0.0017)	(0.0018)	(0.0014)
Fourth quarter forecast	−0.0003	−0.0002	−0.0006†	−0.0003	−0.0004	−0.0003	−0.0002
	(0.0004)	(0.0003)	(0.0003)	(0.0004)	(0.0004)	(0.0004)	(0.0003)
MD-capital intensity	0.0180	0.0114	0.0198†	0.0158	0.0183	0.0186	0.0141
	(0.0118)	(0.0079)	(0.0103)	(0.0117)	(0.0112)	(0.0118)	(0.0090)
MD-market munificence	0.0021	0.0012	0.0018	−0.0001	0.0021	0.0021	0.0025
	(0.0022)	(0.0015)	(0.0019)	(0.0001)	(0.0021)	(0.0022)	(0.0017)
MD-market volatility	0.0063	−0.0213	−0.0596	0.0069	0.0206	0.0054	−0.0488
	(0.0718)	(0.0480)	(0.0627)	(0.0719)	(0.0678)	(0.0718)	(0.0546)

Table 2. (Continued)

	(1)	(2)	(3)	(4)	(5)	(6)	(7)
MD-firm size	0.0008†	0.0006†	0.0008*	0.0008†	0.0003	0.0008†	0.0006†
	(0.0004)	(0.0003)	(0.0004)	(0.0004)	(0.0004)	(0.0004)	(0.0003)
MD-firm age	0.0001	0.0000	−0.0007	0.0001	−0.0001	0.0001	0.0004
	(0.0006)	(0.0004)	(0.0005)	(0.0006)	(0.0006)	(0.0006)	(0.0005)
MD-R&D intensity	−0.0016	−0.0012†	−0.0013	−0.0016	−0.0015	−0.0016	−0.0002
	(0.0011)	(0.0007)	(0.0010)	(0.0011)	(0.0011)	(0.0011)	(0.0009)
Guidance surprise	0.5067**	0.6909**	0.6762**	0.5055**	0.5954**	0.4950**	0.4646**
	(0.0095)	(0.0071)	(0.0102)	(0.0098)	(0.0102)	(0.0110)	(0.0073)
MD-Capital intensity* Guidance surprise		1.1812**					
		(0.0384)					
MD-Market volatility* Guidance surprise			0.6772**				
			(0.0236)				
MD-Market munificence* Guidance surprise				0.0123			
				(0.0202)			
MD-Firm size* Guidance surprise					0.0934**		
					(0.0052)		
MD-Firm age* Guidance surprise						0.0033*	
						(0.0016)	
MD-R&D intensity* Guidance surprise							2.1275**
							(0.0487)
Constant	0.0092	0.0053	−0.0001	0.0086	0.0041	0.0092	0.0112
	(0.0100)	(0.0067)	(0.0088)	(0.0100)	(0.0095)	(0.0100)	(0.0076)
R-squared	0.67	0.85	0.75	0.67	0.71	0.67	0.81

$N = 5,373$. † $p < 0.10$, * $p < 0.05$, ** $p < 0.01$.
Year dummy variables were also included in all models but are not reported to conserve space.

variables shown in Model 1 (from Return on Assets (ROA) to fourth quarter forecast), (b) guidance surprise, (c) MD-index, and (d) the interaction between guidance surprise and MD-index. The main effect of guidance surprise was significant ($\beta = 0.5281$, $p < 0.01$), and the interaction coefficient was also significant ($\beta = 0.1154$, $p < 0.01$). This suggests that, if managerial discretion increases by one standard deviation, the main effect of management guidance on analyst revision increases by 11.54%. Analysts discount management guidance surprises by 35.65% (i.e., $1 - 0.5281 - 0.1154$) in high-discretion contexts, but 47.19% in low-discretion contexts.

Table 3 reports our tests of Hypothesis 2. Model 1 includes all control variables. In these analyses, we separately reports the effects of upward surprises and downward surprises (with zero guidance (i.e., $MGS_{it} = 0$) being the omitted variable). In Model 1, note that the coefficient for upward surprise is 0.4185 and the coefficient for downward surprise is 0.7878. The difference in these coefficients is statistically significant (Chow test: $F = 226.14$, $p < 0.001$). The interpretation of these coefficients is as follows. If, for example, the PAF was $2.00 and the management forecast was $3.00 (a $1.00 upward surprise), the expected updated analyst forecast would be $2.42 ($2.00 + $0.4185). However, if the management forecast was $1.00 (a $1.00 downward surprise), the expected updated analyst forecast would be $1.21 ($2.00 − $0.7878). Consistent with prior research (e.g., Williams, 1996), we therefore see evidence that analysts discount upward guidance surprises (58.15%) considerably more than downward guidance surprises (21.22%).

Models 2–7 in Table 3 include the main effects of our measures of managerial discretion and the interactions between discretion and: (1) upward surprise and (2) downward surprise. All discretion-upward surprise interactions, except for Model 4 in which managerial discretion was measured by market munificence, were positive and significant (MD-capital intensity: $\beta = 0.8200$, $p < 0.01$; MD-market volatility: $\beta = 0.8153$, $p < 0.01$; MD-firm size: $\beta = 0.1676$, $p < 0.01$; MD-firm age: $\beta = 0.0118$, $p < 0.01$; MD-R&D intensity: $\beta = 2.8832$, $p < 0.01$). The discretion-downward surprise interactions were also significant (again except for Model 4), although the coefficients were smaller than those of discretion-upward surprise interactions (MD-capital intensity: $\beta = 0.3471$, $p < 0.01$; MD-market volatility: $\beta = 0.1217$, $p < 0.01$; MD-firm size: $\beta = -0.0869$, $p < 0.01$; MD-firm age: $\beta = 0.0061$, $p < 0.01$; MD-R&D intensity: $\beta = 0.4911$, $p < 0.01$).

Hypothesis 2 predicted that the discretion-upward surprise interactions would be stronger than the discretion-downward surprise interactions (i.e., β_4 in Eq. (2) would be larger than β_5). Consistent with Hypothesis 2, we see that the coefficients for five of the upward surprise interactions were

Table 3. Models Predicting Analyst Forecast Revision (Upward Surprise vs. Downward Surprise).

	(1)	(2)	(3)	(4)	(5)	(6)	(7)
ROA	0.0006	0.0054**	0.0047**	0.0006	0.0050*	0.0005	0.0050**
	(0.0026)	(0.0017)	(0.0018)	(0.0026)	(0.0022)	(0.0026)	(0.0019)
Acquisition activities	0.0003	−0.0000	−0.0000	0.0003	−0.0001	0.0004	0.0002
	(0.0003)	(0.0002)	(0.0002)	(0.0003)	(0.0002)	(0.0003)	(0.0002)
CEO duality	−0.0003	−0.0004	−0.0003	−0.0003	−0.0004	−0.0002	−0.0003
	(0.0004)	(0.0003)	(0.0003)	(0.0004)	(0.0004)	(0.0004)	(0.0003)
Outsider ratio	0.0006	0.0013	0.0009	0.0006	0.0013	0.0004	0.0009
	(0.0015)	(0.0010)	(0.0011)	(0.0015)	(0.0013)	(0.0015)	(0.0011)
Stock market reaction	0.0028**	0.0027**	0.0023**	0.0028**	0.0028**	0.0028**	0.0031**
	(0.0010)	(0.0007)	(0.0007)	(0.0010)	(0.0009)	(0.0010)	(0.0007)
Prior accuracy	0.0055**	0.0026*	0.0034**	0.0055**	0.0048**	0.0052**	0.0041**
	(0.0017)	(0.0011)	(0.0012)	(0.0017)	(0.0014)	(0.0017)	(0.0012)
Forecast horizon	0.0000	0.0000	−0.0000	0.0000	−0.0000	0.0000	0.0000
	(0.0000)	(0.0000)	(0.0000)	(0.0000)	(0.0000)	(0.0000)	(0.0000)
Auditor opinion	0.0001	0.0000	0.0001	0.0001	0.0002	0.0001	0.0002
	(0.0003)	(0.0002)	(0.0002)	(0.0003)	(0.0002)	(0.0003)	(0.0002)
Earnings volatility	0.0000	−0.0000	0.0000	0.0000	0.0000	0.0000	0.0000
	(0.0000)	(0.0000)	(0.0000)	(0.0000)	(0.0000)	(0.0000)	(0.0000)
Forecast dispersion	−0.0002	−0.0001	−0.0001	−0.0002	−0.0001	−0.0002	−0.0002
	(0.0002)	(0.0002)	(0.0002)	(0.0002)	(0.0002)	(0.0002)	(0.0002)
Endogeneity control	0.0008	0.0011	0.0013	0.0007	0.0010	0.0006	0.0004
	(0.0017)	(0.0011)	(0.0012)	(0.0017)	(0.0015)	(0.0017)	(0.0012)
Fourth quarter forecast	−0.0001	−0.0002	−0.0004	−0.0001	−0.0003	−0.0001	−0.0002
	(0.0004)	(0.0002)	(0.0003)	(0.0004)	(0.0003)	(0.0004)	(0.0003)
MD-capital intensity	0.0177	0.0122	0.0141†	0.0151	0.0213*	0.0189†	0.0143†
	(0.0113)	(0.0076)	(0.0079)	(0.0112)	(0.0096)	(0.0113)	(0.0082)
MD-market munificence	0.0021	0.0015	0.0011	−0.0001	0.0021	0.0021	0.0019
	(0.0021)	(0.0014)	(0.0015)	(0.0001)	(0.0018)	(0.0021)	(0.0015)

Table 3. (Continued)

	(1)	(2)	(3)	(4)	(5)	(6)	(7)
MD-market volatility	-0.0338	-0.0202	-0.0056	-0.0337	-0.0074	-0.0383	-0.0494
	(0.0690)	(0.0459)	(0.0480)	(0.0690)	(0.0586)	(0.0687)	(0.0497)
MD-firm size	0.0009*	0.0004	0.0004	0.0009*	0.0005	0.0010*	0.0005†
	(0.0004)	(0.0003)	(0.0003)	(0.0004)	(0.0004)	(0.0004)	(0.0003)
MD-firm age	0.0000	0.0000	-0.0005	-0.0000	-0.0001	-0.0000	0.0002
	(0.0006)	(0.0004)	(0.0004)	(0.0006)	(0.0005)	(0.0006)	(0.0004)
MD-R&D intensity	-0.0009	-0.0015*	-0.0015*	-0.0009	-0.0013	-0.0009	0.0019*
	(0.0011)	(0.0007)	(0.0007)	(0.0011)	(0.0009)	(0.0011)	(0.0008)
Upward surprise	0.4185**	0.1676**	0.1541**	0.4147**	0.5848**	0.3689**	0.4122**
	(0.0108)	(0.0088)	(0.0092)	(0.0559)	(0.0106)	(0.0186)	(0.0078)
Downward surprise	0.7878**	0.5816**	0.7462**	0.7960**	0.6689**	0.7799**	0.7534**
	(0.0208)	(0.0234)	(0.0218)	(0.0429)	(0.0202)	(0.0210)	(0.0172)
MD-capital intensity*		0.8200**					
Upward surprise		(0.0153)					
MD-capital intensity*		0.3471**					
Downward surprise		(0.0284)					
MD-market volatility*			0.8153**				
Upward surprise			(0.0158)				
MD-market volatility*			0.1217**				
Downward surprise			(0.0212)				
MD-market munificence*				0.0041			
Upward surprise				(0.0569)			
MD-market munificence*				-0.0092			
Downward surprise				(0.0474)			
MD-firm size*					0.1676**		
Upward surprise					(0.0055)		
MD-firm size*					-0.0869**		
Downward surprise					(0.0088)		

Table 3. (Continued)

MD-firm age*					0.0118**
Upward surprise					(0.0037)
MD-firm age*					0.0061**
Downward surprise					(0.0017)
MD-R&D intensity*					2.8832**
Upward surprise					(0.0611)
MD-R&D intensity*					0.4911**
Downward surprise					(0.0854)
Constant	0.0106	0.0045	−0.0018	0.0098	0.0049	0.0107	0.0086
	(0.0096)	(0.0064)	(0.0067)	(0.0096)	(0.0082)	(0.0096)	(0.0069)
R-squared	0.70	0.87	0.85	0.70	0.78	0.72	0.84
Chow test of β(MD*upward surprise) = β(MD*downward surprise)		F = 193.17 (p < 0.001)	F = 423.98 (p < 0.001)	F = 1.03 (n.s.)	F = 576.83 (p < 0.001)	F = 19.12 (p < 0.01)	F = 450.56 (p < 0.001)

$N = 5,373$; $^†p < 0.10$; $*p < 0.05$; $**p < 0.01$.
Year dummy variables were also included in all models but are not reported to conserve space.

indeed significantly larger than the corresponding downward surprise interactions. Using a series of Chow tests, we found that β_4 was significantly greater than β_5 for five of the six discretion measures: MD-capital intensity ($F = 193.17$, $p < 0.001$), MD-market volatility ($F = 423.98$, $p < 0.001$), MD-firm size ($F = 576.83$, $p < 0.001$), MD-firm age ($F = 19.12$, $p < 0.01$), and MD-R&D intensity ($F = 450.56$; $p < 0.001$). Therefore, we found strong support for Hypothesis 2.

Table 4 reports our analyses for Hypothesis 3. As noted above, to test Hypothesis 3 we first divided our full sample into two sub-samples: (1) management forecasts issued in quarters 1–3 ($N = 4,112$), and (2) management forecasts issued in quarter 4 ($N = 1,261$). Table 4 contains 12 distinct Models. Models 1, 3, 5, 7, 9, and 11 (odd models) represent the six discretion-guidance surprise interactions for the earlier-quarter forecast sub-sample. Models 2, 4, 6, 8, 10, and 12 (even models) represent the six discretion-guidance surprise interactions for the fourth-quarter forecast sub-sample. Hypothesis 3 will receive support if the managerial discretion-guidance surprise interactions are stronger in the fourth-quarter sub-sample (even models) than the earlier-quarter sub-sample (odd models).

Results indicate that all interactions were positive and significant in the fourth-quarter sub-sample (MD-capital intensity: $\beta = 2.1940$, $p < 0.01$; MD-market volatility: $\beta = 1.1164$, $p < 0.01$; MD-market munificence: $\beta = 0.1985$, $p < 0.05$; MD-firm size: $\beta = 0.1711$, $p < 0.01$; MD-firm age: $\beta = 0.0442$, $p < 0.01$; MD-R&D intensity: $\beta = 2.4500$, $p < 0.01$). Three of the six interactions were positive and significant in the earlier-quarter sub-sample (MD-capital intensity: $\beta = 0.6947$, $p < 0.01$; MD-firm age: $\beta = 0.0071$; $p < 0.01$; MD-R&D intensity, $\beta = 0.6726$, $p < 0.01$), one interaction was negatively significant (MD-firm age: $\beta = -0.0374$, $p < 0.01$), and the remaining two interactions were non-significant (MD-market volatility: $\beta = -2.0234$, n.s.; MD-market munificence: $\beta = 0.0239$, n.s.).

Again using Chow tests, we see that the coefficients for each of the discretion-guidance surprise interactions were significantly larger in the fourth-quarter sub-sample than in the earlier-quarter sub-sample (MD-capital intensity: $F = 281.17$, $p < 0.001$; MD-market volatility: $F = 1300.97$, $p < 0.001$; MD-market munificence: $F = 6.07$, $p < 0.05$; MD-firm size: $F = 1137.31$, $p < 0.001$; MD-firm age: $F = 19.17$, $p < 0.01$; MD-R&D intensity: $F = 642.43$, $p < 0.001$). We therefore found strong support for Hypothesis 3.

We used the combined MD-index described above to illustrate the overall effect of managerial discretion in terms of our two second-order moderators. We ran similar regression models as those presented in Table 3,

Table 4. Models Predicting Analyst Forecast Revision (Earlier Quarters vs. Fourth Quarter).

	(1) Earlier Quarters	(2) Fourth Quarter	(3) Earlier Quarters	(4) Fourth Quarter	(5) Earlier Quarters	(6) Fourth Quarter	(7) Earlier Quarters	(8) Fourth Quarter	(9) Earlier Quarters	(10) Fourth Quarter	(11) Earlier Quarters	(12) Fourth Quarter
ROA	0.0007 (0.0018)	0.0058 (0.0074)	−0.0004 (0.0018)	0.0554** (0.0099)	−0.0002 (0.0018)	0.0086 (0.0175)	−0.0007 (0.0018)	0.0409** (0.0100)	0.0001 (0.0018)	0.0022 (0.0173)	0.0002 (0.0018)	0.0101 (0.0109)
Acquisition activities	0.0001 (0.0002)	−0.0004 (0.0002)	0.0001 (0.0002)	−0.0002 (0.0005)	0.0001 (0.0002)	0.0007 (0.0009)	0.0001 (0.0002)	−0.0008 (0.0005)	0.0001 (0.0002)	0.0001 (0.0009)	0.0001 (0.0002)	0.0004 (0.0006)
CEO duality	−0.0007* (0.0003)	−0.0001 (0.0005)	−0.0006† (0.0003)	0.0010 (0.0007)	−0.0006* (0.0003)	0.0005 (0.0013)	−0.0007† (0.0003)	0.0006 (0.0007)	−0.0006† (0.0003)	−0.0008 (0.0013)	−0.0006* (0.0003)	0.0006 (0.0008)
Outsider ratio	0.0020† (0.0012)	−0.0014 (0.0022)	0.0021† (0.0012)	−0.0031 (0.0029)	0.0020† (0.0012)	−0.0058 (0.0051)	0.0020† (0.0012)	−0.0031 (0.0029)	0.0019 (0.0012)	−0.0049 (0.0050)	0.0022† (0.0012)	−0.0029 (0.0032)
Stock market reaction	0.0044** (0.0008)	0.0007 (0.0014)	0.0055** (0.0008)	0.0020 (0.0018)	0.0055** (0.0008)	0.0027 (0.0032)	0.0059** (0.0008)	−0.0019 (0.0018)	0.0057** (0.0008)	0.0002 (0.0031)	0.0051** (0.0008)	0.0054** (0.0020)
Prior accuracy	0.0043** (0.0013)	0.0009 (0.0023)	0.0054** (0.0013)	−0.0021 (0.0031)	0.0054** (0.0013)	0.0075 (0.0055)	0.0054** (0.0013)	−0.0111 (0.0031)	0.0052** (0.0013)	0.0081 (0.0054)	0.0049** (0.0013)	0.0045 (0.0034)
Forecast horizon	−0.0000 (0.0000)	0.0000* (0.0000)	−0.0000 (0.0000)	0.0000† (0.0000)	−0.0000 (0.0000)	0.0000** (0.0000)	−0.0000 (0.0000)	0.0000** (0.0000)	−0.0000 (0.0000)	0.0000** (0.0000)	−0.0000 (0.0000)	0.0000† (0.0000)
Auditor opinion	0.0000 (0.0002)	0.0003 (0.0004)	0.0001 (0.0002)	0.0005 (0.0005)	0.0001 (0.0002)	0.0007 (0.0009)	0.0001 (0.0002)	0.0002 (0.0005)	0.0001 (0.0002)	0.0004 (0.0009)	0.0001 (0.0002)	0.0005 (0.0006)
Earnings volatility	−0.0000 (0.0000)	0.0000 (0.0000)	−0.0000 (0.0000)	0.0001† (0.0000)	−0.0000 (0.0000)	0.0001* (0.0001)	−0.0000 (0.0000)	0.0001† (0.0000)	−0.0000 (0.0000)	0.0001 (0.0001)	−0.0000 (0.0000)	0.0000 (0.0000)
Forecast dispersion	−0.0001 (0.0002)	0.0001 (0.0003)	−0.0001 (0.0002)	0.0003 (0.0004)	−0.0001 (0.0002)	0.0003 (0.0007)	−0.0001 (0.0002)	−0.0001 (0.0004)	−0.0001 (0.0002)	0.0002 (0.0007)	−0.0002 (0.0002)	0.0002 (0.0004)
Endogeneity control	0.0016 (0.0013)	0.0067** (0.0026)	0.0012 (0.0013)	0.0117** (0.0034)	0.0011 (0.0013)	0.0256** (0.0060)	0.0010 (0.0013)	0.0127** (0.0034)	0.0005 (0.0013)	0.0196** (0.0059)	0.0014 (0.0013)	0.0082* (0.0038)
MD-capital intensity	0.0053 (0.0090)	0.0065 (0.0133)	0.0040 (0.0091)	0.0195 (0.0176)	0.0021 (0.0090)	0.0233 (0.0307)	0.0047 (0.0091)	0.0287 (0.0178)	0.0066 (0.0090)	0.0423 (0.0310)	0.0050 (0.0089)	0.0135 (0.0195)
MD-market munificence	0.0010 (0.0015)	0.0028 (0.0036)	0.0012 (0.0015)	0.0003 (0.0047)	0.0002 (0.0002)	0.0007† (0.0004)	0.0012 (0.0015)	0.0006 (0.0048)	0.0014 (0.0015)	0.0111 (0.0083)	0.0015 (0.0015)	0.0004 (0.0052)
MD-market volatility	−0.0348 (0.0589)	−0.0520 (0.0986)	−0.0386 (0.0600)	−0.1375 (0.1301)	−0.0416 (0.0600)	−0.0057 (0.2323)	−0.0430 (0.0597)	−0.0558 (0.1318)	−0.0378 (0.0594)	0.0775 (0.2286)	−0.0514 (0.0588)	−0.0145 (0.1446)
MD-firm size	0.0006† (0.0003)	0.0013* (0.0005)	0.0006† (0.0003)	−0.0003 (0.0007)	0.0006† (0.0003)	0.0024† (0.0013)	0.0006† (0.0003)	−0.0000 (0.0007)	0.0006† (0.0003)	0.0032* (0.0013)	0.0006† (0.0003)	0.0029** (0.0008)

	Model (1)	Model (2)	Model (3)	Model (4)	Model (5)	Model (6)	Model (7)	Model (8)	Model (9)	Model (10)	Model (11)	Model (12)
MD-firm age	-0.0003 (0.0004)	-0.0002 (0.0002)	-0.0003 (0.0004)	-0.0002 (0.0003)	-0.0004 (0.0004)	-0.0004 (0.0006)	-0.0003 (0.0004)	-0.0002 (0.0003)	-0.0004 (0.0004)	-0.0008 (0.0005)	-0.0002 (0.0004)	-0.0007* (0.0003)
MD-R&D intensity	-0.0012 (0.0008)	-0.0072* (0.0029)	-0.0013† (0.0008)	0.0029 (0.0038)	-0.0013† (0.0008)	-0.0008 (0.0067)	-0.0014† (0.0008)	-0.0043 (0.0038)	-0.0013† (0.0008)	-0.0017 (0.0066)	-0.0008 (0.0008)	-0.0081† (0.0042)
Guidance surprise	0.6092** (0.0146)	0.7504** (0.0095)	0.5577** (0.0145)	0.9348** (0.0163)	0.5647** (0.0140)	0.4825** (0.0224)	0.5517** (0.0138)	0.7644** (0.0131)	0.5495** (0.0137)	0.7994** (0.0352)	0.5591** (0.0134)	0.5198** (0.0124)
MD-capital intensity*Guidance surprise	0.6947** (0.0815)	2.1940** (0.0494)										
MD-market volatility*Guidance surprise			-2.0234 (2.8535)	1.1164** (0.0357)								
MD-market munificence*Guidance surprise					0.0239 (0.0267)	0.1985* (0.0893)						
MD-firm size*Guidance surprise							-0.0374** (0.0088)	0.1711** (0.0056)				
MD-firm age*Guidance surprise									0.0071** (0.0011)	0.0442** (0.0054)		
MD-R&D intensity*Guidance surprise											0.6726** (0.0752)	2.4500** (0.0914)
Constant	0.0041 (0.0044)	0.0066 (0.0061)	0.0039 (0.0045)	-0.0038 (0.0080)	0.0037 (0.0045)	0.0085 (0.0142)	0.0044 (0.0045)	0.0010 (0.0081)	0.0048 (0.0045)	0.0168 (0.0141)	0.0038 (0.0044)	0.0118 (0.0089)
Observations	4,112	1,261	4,112	1,261	4,112	1,261	4,112	1,261	4,112	1,261	4,112	1,261
R-squared	0.73	0.88	0.72	0.87	0.73	0.80	0.73	0.87	0.73	0.80	0.74	0.86
Chow test of β(guidance surprise*managerial discretion) in odd models = β(guidance surprise*managerial discretion) in even models	Model (1) vs. (2) F=281.17 (p<0.001)		Model (3) vs. (4) F=1300.97 (p<0.001)		Model (5) vs. (6) F=6.07 (p<0.05)		Model (7) vs. (8) F=1137.31 (p<0.001)		Model (9) vs. (10) F=19.17 (p<0.01)		Model (11) vs. (12) F=462.43 (p<0.001)	

†p<0.10; *p<0.05; **p<0.01.
Year dummy variables were also included in all models but are not reported to conserve space.

and found that the coefficient for the interaction of MD-index and upward surprise was positive and significant ($\beta = 0.1216$, $p < 0.001$), while the coefficient for the interaction of MD-Index and downward surprise was marginally significant ($\beta = 0.0057$, $p = 0.07$). The difference in the coefficients was statistically significant ($F = 687.91$, $p < 0.001$). In practical terms, when the management forecast was upward, a one standard deviation increase in discretion was associated with a 12.16% increase in the main effect of guidance surprise on analyst revision. However, when the management guidance was downward, a one standard deviation increase in discretion was only associated with a 0.57% increase in the main effect of guidance surprise on analyst revision.

Next, when we ran similar models as those presented in Table 4, we found that the coefficient for the interaction of MD-index and guidance surprise was positive and significant in both the Quarter 4 sub-sample ($\beta = 0.1042$, $p < 0.01$) and the earlier-quarter sub-sample ($\beta = 0.0195$, $p < 0.01$). The difference in these coefficients was statistically significant ($F = 1128.85$, $p < 0.001$). In practical terms, when a forecast was issued in the fourth quarter, a one standard deviation increase in managerial discretion was associated with a 10.42% increase in the main effect of guidance surprise on analyst revision. When a forecast was issued in earlier quarters, though, the corresponding effect of guidance surprise on analyst revision was only 1.95%.

Supplementary Analyses

We conducted several supplementary analyses. First, we examined how management earnings guidance related to firms' (subsequent) actual earnings announcements. See Table 5 for an illustration of the mean PAF, MF, revised AF, and actual earnings for the sample of 5,373 firm-quarters used in our study. As discussed above, analysts were more responsive following downward guidance than upward guidance. However, as shown in Table 5, management forecasts were on average quite accurate in predicting subsequent actual earnings, supporting the idea that firms tend to be incentivized to provide accurate guidance generally (Hirst et al., 2008).

In addition, we further explored the relationship between managerial discretion and management forecast characteristics. We generated a *management forecast error* variable, which was operationalized as the management forecast minus actual earnings, scaled by the share price. A negative value of this variable indicates a pessimistic forecast (actual earnings beat the forecast), while a positive value indicates an optimistic forecast (actual

Table 5. Mean Quarterly Analyst Forecasts, Management Guidance, and Subsequent Earnings Announcements (Scaled by the Share Price at Quarter $t-1$).

	Prior Analyst Forecast	Management Forecast	Revised Analyst Forecast	Actual Earnings
All management forecasts	0.0084	0.0068	0.0075	0.0069
Upward management guidance	0.0071	0.0095	0.0081	0.0094
Downward management guidance	0.0091	0.0053	0.0072	0.0054

$N = 5,373$ Firm-quarters.

earnings fell short of the forecast). We found that management forecast error was positively and significantly correlated with all six measures of managerial discretion ($0.04 < r < 0.08$, $p < 0.01$), which suggests that management forecasts issued in high-discretion contexts tend to be systematically more optimistic than is justified by actual results.

Next, we examined whether managerial discretion is actually a "helpful" cue to analysts, that is, whether discretion helps analysts to be more accurate in predicting actual reported earnings. We calculated the eventual accuracy of all 5,373 consensus forecast revisions (accuracy was operationalized as the reverse of the absolute difference between the final consensus analyst forecast and actual reported earnings, scaled by the share price at the end of last quarter). We then regressed accuracy on MD-index, the absolute value of analyst forecast revision, the interaction of these two predictors, and all control variables reported in Model 1 of Table 2. Results showed that the interaction term was a positive and significant predictor of accuracy ($\beta = 0.3327$, $p < 0.01$). This finding suggests that analysts who update their forecasts more in high-discretion environments (and less in low-discretion environments) do in fact tend to be more accurate in predicting actual earnings.

Finally, we conducted a supplementary analysis to examine the issue of forecast revision heterogeneity at the level of individual analysts (recall that our main analyses are based on consensus (i.e., mean) analyst forecasts). We were particularly interested to see if experienced analysts responded differently than inexperienced analysts. We began by creating a sample comprised of all firm-quarters where an analyst had issued an initial earnings forecast and then an updated forecast following the release of a management earnings forecast ($N = 10,571$ analyst-quarters). We then regressed analyst forecast revision on a vector of available controls, along with MD-Index, analyst firm-specific experience (the number of years that the focal analyst had covered the focal firm), and the interaction of these two variables (see Table 6). Results from this model showed that more

Table 6. Impact of Analyst Experience on Analyst Forecast Revision.

	(1)
ROA	−0.2702*
	(0.1365)
Acquisition activities	0.0029
	(0.0163)
Stock market reaction	−0.3192**
	(0.0512)
Prior accuracy	26.5631**
	(1.1940)
Forecast horizon	0.0012**
	(0.0004)
Auditor opinion	0.0150**
	(0.0054)
Earnings volatility	−0.0034**
	(0.0011)
Forecast dispersion	0.0252*
	(0.0121)
Endogeneity control	−0.6586**
	(0.0914)
Fourth quarter forecast	−0.0505**
	(0.0147)
Management guidance	61.523**
	(1.1301)
Number of firms covered by analyst	−0.0008
	(0.0008)
Years that analyst appears in IBES database	−0.0005
	(0.0013)
Analyst firm-specific experience	0.0093**
	(0.0028)
MD-index	0.504**
	(0.093)
MD-index * analyst firm-specific experience	0.026**
	(0.008)
Constant	0.9166**
	(0.1281)
Observations	10,571
R-squared	0.84

†$p < 0.10$; *$p < 0.05$; **$p < 0.01$. Year dummies not reported.
All coefficients and standard errors multiplied by 100 to aid interpretability.

experienced analysts were significantly more likely to update their original forecasts following management guidance ($\beta = 0.0093$, $p < 0.01$), perhaps suggesting that analysts become more trusting of individual firms over time. Of more relevance, we also found that the interaction of MD-Index and analyst firm-specific experience was positive and significant ($\beta = 0.026$, $p < 0.01$). This finding offers suggestive evidence that analysts increasingly rely on cues such as managerial discretion as they become more experienced.

DISCUSSION

A growing body of research has begun to explore how information intermediaries — such as financial analysts — assist stakeholders in interpreting economically meaningful firm disclosures (Pfarrer et al., 2010). In this study, we examined how analysts use managerial discretion to help them evaluate the believability of one particular type of forward-looking firm disclosure, voluntary management earnings forecasts. Using an 11-year sample of analysts' consensus responses to over 5,000 management forecasts, we found strong evidence that the impact of management guidance surprise on the extent of subsequent analyst forecast revision is significantly influenced by managerial discretion. In low-discretion contexts, analysts find large management guidance surprises less believable and react more conservatively. In contrast, in high-discretion contexts, analysts find guidance surprises more believable and update their prior forecasts far more comprehensively. We also found robust evidence that analysts were influenced by managerial discretion most strongly in those situations where they could be expected to be most uncertain. Specifically, the moderating impact of managerial discretion was especially strong when guidance surprises were upward (vs. downward) and management forecasts were issued in the fourth quarter (vs. earlier quarters).

Implications and Future Research

Our results have implications for research in a number of distinct domains within strategic management. First, we see potential for extending our work in the domain of symbolic management. This research builds on Pfeffer's (1981, p. 4) argument that a fundamental role of management is to "provide explanations, rationalizations, and legitimation for the activities undertaken in the organization." Relatedly, management forecasts can be viewed as not just instrumental decisions arising from a desire to mitigate information asymmetry, but also as an important symbolic act (Fiss & Zajac, 2006). Future work could examine the extent to which discretion relates to the use of management disclosures as symbolic actions. We expect that, in low-discretion firms where substantive actions are more constrained, management will be more likely to engage in symbolic actions. However, our results suggest that observers may also be conscious of this possibility and may therefore be more likely to discount such symbolic actions.

Second, and more generally, we believe that our study helps to inform research into stakeholder and market reactions to corporate announcements, especially those related to major planned changes to a firm's strategic direction or posture (e.g., Woolridge & Snow, 1990). Reports of such announcements are often accompanied by a change in firm valuation, especially when the announcement was unexpected or unplanned. Although market reactions are often viewed as being an endorsement (or vilification) of a particular strategic decision, they may also be illustrative of the extent to which stakeholders believe that such an approach is likely or even possible. Our results suggest that market participants might be using contextual factors such as managerial discretion to frame their interpretations of, and responses to, such transitions.

Third, our study also has cross-disciplinary implications, in particular for the large body of research in finance and accounting that considers the topic of voluntary firm disclosures. Although there is no comprehensive theory of disclosure (Verrecchia, 2001), underpinning most of this work is the assumption that managers disclose information when it is economically rational to do so, that is, when the potential benefits of the disclosure outweigh the potential costs (e.g., Heitzman, Wasley, & Zimmerman, 2010). For example, there is evidence that management forecasts reduce costs associated with information asymmetry, and thus reduce a firm's cost of capital (Leuz & Verrecchia, 2000). However, most work focuses on factors internal to the firm. Our approach illustrates the usefulness of also considering the characteristics of a firm's context when trying to understand responses to firm actions.

Finally, our results suggest that managers of low-discretion firms have a harder time convincing external observers of the believability of their announcements and predictions than their counterparts in high-discretion environments. If our logic holds, we would expect to see evidence that managers from low-discretion firms take greater efforts to be persuasive when providing voluntary disclosures, perhaps by pointing to past evidence of accurate predictions, or by providing greater quantitative evidence to support their claims and predictions. Future research might be able to fruitfully explore such a possibility.

NOTES

1. Occasionally, managers will release earnings guidance after the accounting period has ended, but before actual earnings are released. These "earnings preannouncements" are theoretically and empirically distinct from earnings forecasts (Hirst et al., 2008); therefore, we do not include earnings preannouncements in our sample.
2. A related but distinct construct, also termed managerial discretion, appears in the financial economics literature (e.g., Williamson, 1963). Authors within this stream of research tend to assume that firm rents are a combined function of heterogeneous resource allocation across firms (rent-enhancing) and discretionary decisions by top managers (rent-inhibiting) (Amit & Schoemaker, 1993; Levinthal & Myatt, 1994). Thus, discretion refers to the extent to which managers have the capacity to engage in opportunism and self-dealing, and is therefore associated with shareholder wealth expropriation (e.g., Gedajlovic & Shapiro, 2002; Stulz, 1990). For example, Fox and Marcus (1992) argued that bank debt covenants are associated with a restriction in cash flow and, thus, a reduction in agency problems arising from discretion. In a recent synthesis, Shen and Cho (2005) distinguished between these two versions of discretion as representing "latitude of actions" (Hambrick & Finkelstein, 1987) versus "latitude of objectives" (Williamson, 1963). Although these two different conceptions have some theoretical overlap, in our chapter we follow Hambrick and Finkelstein (1987) in using the term managerial discretion to refer to latitude of actions. We make no assumptions concerning the normative implications of discretion, nor the relationship between discretion and firm performance valence.
3. Note that we are referring here to *analysts'* uncertainty. This is distinct from the means-ends ambiguity (or environmental uncertainty) that characterizes a high-discretion context. In other words, we argue that analysts use the characteristics of a firm's context, and specifically the level of managerial discretion available to the firm, as a cue to reduce their own uncertainty in interpreting management earnings forecasts.
4. In a robustness test we used 15 days as the response window (Feng et al., 2009). Results were unchanged.
5. In our sample, 24% of management forecasts were upward surprises, 68% were downward surprises, and 8% confirmed the prior consensus analyst forecast.
6. We also ran a three-way regression based on Eq. (3), and found significant results for the coefficient of MD_{it} * MGS_{it} * Qtr4. Results are available upon request.

ACKNOWLEDGMENTS

Authors are in alphabetical order and contributed equally. We thank Ethan Burris, Don Hambrick, Mike Pfarrer, Margarethe Wiersema, and participants in the INSEAD research seminar for their helpful comments on earlier drafts of this manuscript. We are also very grateful to Editor Belen Villalonga and two anonymous reviewers for their detailed advice and suggestions. This research was funded in part by the INSEAD Alumni Fund and a 3M Nontenured Faculty Grant at the University of Texas at Austin.

REFERENCES

Aboody, D., & Kasznik, R. (2000). CEO stock option awards and the timing of voluntary corporate disclosures. *Journal of Accounting and Economics, 29*, 73–1000.

Abrahamson, E., & Hambrick, D. C. (1997). Attentional homogeneity in industries: The effect of discretion. *Journal of Organizational Behavior, 18*, 513–532.

Ajinkya, B. P., Bhoraj, S., & Sengupta, P. (2005). The association between outside directors, institutional investors and the properties of management earnings forecasts. *Journal of Accounting Research., 43*, 343–376.

Ajinkya, B. P., & Gift, M. J. (1984). Corporate managers' earnings forecasts and symmetrical adjustments of market expectations. *Journal of Accounting Research, 22*, 425–444.

Aldrich, H. E. (1979). *Organizations and environments*. Englewood Cliffs, NJ: Prentice-Hall.

Alexander, J. C. (1991). Do the merits matter? A study of settlements in securities class actions. *Stanford Law Review, 43*, 497–598.

Amit, R., & Schoemaker, P. J. H. (1993). Strategic assets and organizational rent. *Strategic Management Journal, 14*, 33–46.

Anilowski, C., Feng, M., & Skinner, D. J. (2007). Does earnings guidance affect market returns? The nature and information content of aggregate earnings guidance. *Journal of Accounting and Economics, 44*, 36–63.

Audia, P. G., & Greve, H. R. (2006). Less likely to fail: Low performance, firm size, and factory expansion in the shipbuilding industry. *Management Science, 52*, 83–94.

Baginski, S. P., Conrad, E. J., & Hassell, J. M. (1993). The effects of management forecast precision on equity pricing and on the assessment of earnings uncertainty. *Accounting Review, 68*, 913–927.

Baginski, S. P., & Hassell, J. M. (1990). The market interpretation of management earnings forecasts as a predictor of subsequent financial analyst forecast revision. *Accounting Review, 65*, 175–190.

Baik, B., & Jiang, G. (2006). The use of management forecasts to dampen analysts' expectations. *Journal of Accounting and Public Policy, 25*, 531–553.

Benner, M. J. (2010). Securities analysts and incumbent response to radical technological change: Evidence from digital photography and internet telephony. *Organization Science, 21*, 42–62.

Benner, M. J., & Ranganathan, R. (2012). Offsetting illegitimacy? How pressures from securities analysts influence incumbents in the face of new technologies. *Academy of Management Journal, 55*, 213–233.

Bergh, D. D., & Lawless, M. W. (1998). Portfolio restructuring and limits to hierarchical governance: The effects of environmental uncertainty and diversification strategy. *Organization Science, 9*, 87–102.

Boyd, B. K., & Salamin, A. (2001). Strategic reward systems: A contingency model of pay system design. *Strategic Management Journal, 22*, 777–792.

Brown, S., Hillegeist, S. A., & Lo, K. (2005). *Management forecasts and litigation risk*. Working Paper. SSRN No. 709161. University of British Columbia.

Cao, Z., & Narayanamoorthy, G. S. (2011). The effect of litigation risk on management earnings forecasts. *Contemporary Accounting Research, 28*, 125–173.

Chen, S. (2004). *Why do managers fail to meet their own forecasts?* Working Paper. SSRN No. 490562. University of Washington.

Cho, T. S., & Shen, W. (2007). Changes in executive compensation following an environmental shift: The role of top management team turnover. *Strategic Management Journal, 28*, 745–754.

Clement, M., Frankel, R., & Miller, J. (2003). Confirming management earnings forecasts, earnings uncertainty, and stock returns. *Journal of Accounting Research, 41*, 653–679.

Coller, M., & Yohn, T. L. (1997). Management forecasts and information asymmetry: An examination of bid-ask spreads. *Journal of Accounting Research, 35*, 181–191.

Connelly, B. L., Certo, S. T., Ireland, R. D., & Reutzel, C. R. (2011). Signaling theory: A review and assessment. *Journal of Management, 37*, 39–67.

Cotter, J., Tuna, I., & Wysocki, P. D. (2006). Expectations management and beatable targets: How do analysts react to explicit earnings guidance? *Contemporary Accounting Research, 23*, 593–624.

Crossland, C., & Hambrick, D. C. (2007). How national systems differ in their constraints on corporate executives: A study of CEO effects in three countries. *Strategic Management Journal, 28*, 767–789.

Dechow, P. M., Hutton, A. P., & Sloan, R. G. (2000). The relation between analysts' forecasts of long-term earnings growth and stock price performance following equity offerings. *Contemporary Accounting Research, 17*, 1–32.

Deephouse, D. L., & Carter, S. M. (2005). An examination of differences between organizational legitimacy and organizational reputation. *Journal of Management Studies, 42*, 329–360.

Deephouse, D. L., & Heugens, P. P. M. A. R. (2009). Linking social issues to organizational impact: The role of infomediaries and the infomediary process. *Journal of Business Ethics, 86*, 541–553.

Diamond, D., & Verrecchia, R. (1991). Disclosure, liquidity, and the cost of capital. *Journal of Finance, 46*, 1325–1359.

Feng, M., Li, C., & McVay, S. (2009). Internal control and management guidance. *Journal of Accounting and Economics, 48*, 190–209.

Finkelstein, S., & Boyd, B. K. (1998). How much does the CEO matter? The role of managerial discretion in the setting of CEO compensation. *Academy of Management Journal, 41*, 179–199.

Finkelstein, S., & Hambrick, D. C. (1988). Chief executive compensation: A synthesis and reconciliation. *Strategic Management Journal, 9*, 543–558.

Finkelstein, S., & Hambrick, D. C. (1990). Top-management-team tenure and organizational outcomes: The moderating role of managerial discretion. *Administrative Science Quarterly*, 35, 484–503.

Fiss, P. C., & Zajac, E. J. (2006). The symbolic management of strategic change: Sensegiving via framing and decoupling. *Academy of Management Journal*, 49, 1173–1193.

Fombrun, C. J. (1996). *Reputation: Realizing value from the corporate image*. Boston, MA: Harvard Business School Press.

Fombrun, C. J., & Shanley, M. (1990). What's in a name? Reputation building and corporate strategy. *Academy of Management Journal*, 33, 233–258.

Fox, I., & Marcus, A. (1992). The causes and consequences of leveraged management buyouts. *Academy of Management Review*, 17, 62–85.

Gedajlovic, E., & Shapiro, D. M. (2002). Ownership structure and firm profitability in Japan. *Academy of Management Journal*, 45, 565–575.

Ghemawat, P. (1991). *Commitment: The dynamic of strategy*. New York, NY: Free Press.

Givoly, D., & Lakonishok, J. (1984). The quality of analysts' forecasts of earnings. *Financial Analysts Journal*, 40(September–October), 40–47.

Graham, J., Harvey, C. R., & Rajgopal, S. (2005). The economic implications of corporate financial reporting. *Journal of Accounting and Economics*, 40, 3–73.

Hambrick, D. C. (2007). Upper echelons theory: An update. *Academy of Management Review*, 32, 334–343.

Hambrick, D. C., & Abrahamson, E. (1995). Assessing managerial discretion across industries: A multimethod approach. *Academy of Management Journal*, 38, 1427–1441.

Hambrick, D. C., & Finkelstein, S. (1987). Managerial discretion: A bridge between polar views of organizational outcomes. In B. Staw & L. L. Cummings (Eds.), *Research in organizational behavior* (Vol. 9, pp. 369–406). Greenwich, CT: JAI Press.

Hambrick, D. C., Finkelstein, S., Cho, T. S., & Jackson, E. M. (2004). Isomorphism in reverse: Institutional theory as an explanation for recent increases in intraindustry heterogeneity and managerial discretion. In R. M. Kramer & B. Staw (Eds.), *Research in organizational behavior* (Vol. 26, pp. 307–350). Greenwich, CT: JAI Press.

Hambrick, D. C., & Mason, P. (1984). Upper echelons: The firm as a reflection of its top managers. *Academy of Management Review*, 9, 193–206.

Hassell, J. M., Jennings, R. H., & Lasser, D. J. (1988). Management earnings forecasts: Their usefulness as a source of firm-specific information to security analysts. *Journal of Financial Research*, 11, 303–320.

Hay, D. A., & Morris, D. J. (1979). *Industrial economics: Theory and evidence*. Oxford, UK: Oxford University Press.

Heitzman, S., Wasley, C., & Zimmerman, J. (2010). The joint effects of materiality thresholds and voluntary disclosure incentives on firms' disclosure decisions. *Journal of Accounting and Economics*, 49, 109–132.

Hirst, D. E., Koonce, L., & Venkataraman, S. (2008). Management earnings forecasts: A review and framework. *Accounting Horizons*, 22, 315–338.

Ho, J. L. Y., Wu, A., & Xu, S. X. (2011). Corporate governance and returns on information technology investment: Evidence from an emerging market. *Strategic Management Journal*, 32, 595–623.

Hong, H., & Kubik, J. D. (2003). Analyzing the analysts: Career concerns and biased earnings forecasts. *Journal of Finance*, 58, 313–352.

Hutton, A., & Stocken, P. C. (2007). *Effect of reputation on the credibility of management forecasts*. Working Paper. Boston College.

Jeter, D. C., & Shivakumar, L. (1999). Cross-sectional estimation of abnormal accruals using quarterly and annual data: Effectiveness in detecting event-specific earnings management. *Accounting and Business Research, 29*, 299–319.

Kasznik, R. (1999). On the association between voluntary disclosure and earnings management. *Journal of Accounting Research, 37*, 57–81.

Keats, B. W., & Hitt, M. A. (1988). A causal model of linkages among environmental dimensions, macro organizational characteristics, and performance. *Academy of Management Journal, 31*, 570–598.

Keegan, J., & Kabanoff, B. (2008). Indirect industry-and subindustry-level managerial discretion measurement. *Organizational Research Methods, 11*, 682–694.

Larcker, D. F., & Rusticus, T. O. (2010). On the use of instrumental variables in accounting research. *Journal of Accounting and Economics, 49*, 186–205.

Leuz, C., & Verrecchia, R. (2000). The economic consequences of increased disclosure. *Journal of Accounting Research, 38*, 91–124.

Levinthal, D., & Myatt, J. (1994). Co-evolution of capabilities and industry: The evolution of mutual fund processing. *Strategic Management Journal, 15*(Winter special issue), 45–62.

Li, J., & Tang, Y. (2010). CEO hubris and firm risk taking in China: The moderating role of managerial discretion. *Academy of Management Journal, 53*, 45–68.

Martins, L. L. (2005). A model of the effects of reputational rankings on organizational change. *Organization Science, 16*, 701–720.

Mercer, M. (2005). The fleeting effects of disclosure forthcomingness on management's reporting credibility. *The Accounting Review, 80*, 723–744.

Miller, G. (2002). Earnings performance and discretionary disclosure. *Journal of Accounting Research, 40*, 173–204.

Nelson, R. R., & Winter, S. G. (1982). *An evolutionary theory of economic change*. Boston, MA: Harvard University Press.

Peteraf, M., & Reed, R. (2007). Managerial discretion and internal alignment under regulatory constraints and change. *Strategic Management Journal, 28*, 1089–1112.

Pfarrer, M. D., Pollock, T. G., & Rindova, V. P. (2010). A tale of two assets: The effects of firm reputation and celebrity on earnings surprises and investors' reactions. *Academy of Management Journal, 53*, 1131–1152.

Pfeffer, J. (1981). Management as symbolic action: The creation and maintenance of organizational paradigms. In L. L. Cummings & B. M. Staw (Eds.), *Research in organizational behavior* (Vol. 3, pp. 1–52). Greenwich, CT: JAI Press.

Pollock, T. G., & Rindova, V. P. (2003). Media legitimation effects in the market for initial public offerings. *Academy of Management Journal, 46*, 631–642.

Pollock, T. G., Rindova, V. P., & Maggitti, P. G. (2008). Market watch: Information and availability cascades among the media and investors in the U.S. IPO market. *Academy of Management Journal, 51*, 335–358.

Ramnath, S., Rock, S., & Shane, P. (2008). The financial analyst forecasting literature: A taxonomy with suggestions for further research. *International Journal of Forecasting, 24*, 34–75.

Riley, J. G. (2001). Silver signals: Twenty-five years of screening and signaling. *Journal of Economic Literature, 39*, 432–478.

Rogers, J. L., & Stocken, P. C. (2005). Credibility of management forecasts. *Accounting Review, 80*, 1233–1260.

Schipper, K. (1991). Analysts' forecasts. *Accounting Horizons, 5*(December), 105–121.

Shen, W., & Cho, T. S. (2005). Exploring involuntary executive turnover through a managerial discretion framework. *Academy of Management Review, 30*, 843–854.

Skinner, D. J. (1994). Why firms voluntarily disclose bad news. *Journal of Accounting Research, 32*, 38–60.

Stickel, S. E. (1989). The timing and incentives for annual earnings forecasts near interim earnings announcements. *Journal of Accounting and Economics, 11*, 275–292.

Stulz, R. M. (1990). Managerial discretion and optimal financing policies. *Journal of Financial Economics, 26*, 3–27.

Tucker, J. W. (2007). Is openness penalized? Stock returns around earnings warnings. *Accounting Review, 82*, 1055–1087.

Verrecchia, R. E. (2001). Essays on disclosure. *Journal of Accounting and Economics, 32*, 97–180.

Villalonga, B. (2004). Intangible resources, Tobin's q, and sustainability of performance differences. *Journal of Economic Behavior and Organization, 54*, 205–230.

Waymire, G. (1985). Earnings volatility and voluntary management forecast disclosure. *Journal of Accounting Research, 23*, 268–295.

Westphal, J., & Clement, M. B. (2008). Sociopolitical dynamics in relations between top managers and security analysts: Favor rendering, reciprocity, and analyst stock recommendations. *Academy of Management Journal, 51*, 873–897.

Wiersema, M. F., & Zhang, Y. (2011). CEO dismissal: The role of investment analysts. *Strategic Management Journal, 32*, 1161–1182.

Williams, P. A. (1996). The relation between a prior earnings forecast by management and analyst response to a current management forecast. *Accounting Review, 71*, 103–113.

Williamson, O. E. (1963). Managerial discretion and business behavior. *American Economic Review, 53*, 1032–1057.

Woolridge, J. R., & Snow, C. C. (1990). Stock market reaction to strategic investment decisions. *Strategic Management Journal, 11*, 353–363.

Zavyalova, A., Pfarrer, M. D., Reger, R. K., & Shapiro, D. L. (2012). Managing the message: The effects of firm actions and industry spillovers on media coverage following wrongdoing. *Academy of Management Journal, 55*, 1079–1101.

Zhang, Y., & Gimeno, J. (2010). Earnings pressure and competitive behavior: Evidence from the U.S. electric industry. *Academy of Management Journal, 53*, 743–768.

Zhu, D. H., & Westphal, J. D. (2011). Misperceiving the beliefs of others: How pluralistic ignorance contributes to the persistence of positive security analyst reactions to the adoption of stock repurchase plans. *Organization Science, 22*, 869–886.

APPENDIX: FIRST-STAGE REGRESSION MODEL PREDICTING THE LIKELIHOOD OF MANAGEMENT FORECAST ISSUANCE

	DV: Management Guidance Issuance (Dummy)
Industries with higher litigation risk	0.3381**
	(0.0469)
Corporate restructuring (M&A, acquisition etc.)	0.1127**
	(0.0302)
Firm size	0.0829**
	(0.0092)
Firm profitability (ROA)	2.8832**
	(0.3673)
Firm beta	0.0607**
	(0.0142)
Market-to-book ratio	−0.0980*
	(0.0416)
Forecast dispersion	0.0911*
	(0.0420)
Earnings volatility	1.1595**
	(0.2436)
Number of analysts following the firm	0.0035*
	(0.0017)
Constant	−1.3453**
	(0.0719)
Log Likelihood	−10060.819**

$N = 21{,}415$; *$p < 0.05$; **$p < 0.01$.
Year dummy variables were also included in all models but are not reported to conserve space.

PART II
HOW CAPITAL AND OWNERSHIP STRUCTURES SHAPE STRATEGY

FINANCIAL HEALTH AND PARTNER ATTRACTIVENESS IN THE MARKET FOR INTER-FIRM COLLABORATION

Fabio Zambuto, M. V. Shyam Kumar and Jonathan P. O'Brien

ABSTRACT

We propose that in addition to its resources and capabilities, a firm's capital structure and financial health will act as an important determinant of its attractiveness as an alliance partner. Alliances with leveraged firms are prone to unplanned termination due to financial distress, which puts at risk the value embedded in the collaboration. As a result, ceteris paribus, *highly leveraged firms will be viewed as less desirable partners in the market for interfirm collaboration when compared to low leverage firms. In support of this proposition, we find that when forming an alliance firms tend to partner with other firms with similar levels of leverage: low-leverage firms partner with other low-leverage firms while high-leverage firms partner with other high-leverage firms, as well as with lower quality ones. Furthermore, we show that alliances with highly leveraged firms are more likely to involve equity participation as a form* of ex post protection, especially when they involve partners with relatively lower leverage. Finally, we show that leverage is negatively related to the intensity of alliance activity, suggesting that firms also maintain lower leverage in their capital structure in order to attract potential partners. Overall our results imply that financial policies regarding capital structure have an important role to play in alliancing activity.

INTRODUCTION

What role does a firm's financial health play in its alliancing activity? In the strategy literature, theoretical explanations of alliances (e.g., Teece, 1986) have typically highlighted their efficacy in enabling firms to acquire and access resources residing in other firms. Following these perspectives, key alliance decisions such as firm partnering choices (i.e., whom to partner with) and alliance governance (e.g., equity versus non-equity) have usually been explained from the perspective of the resources and capabilities being combined by parent firms in the alliance, with the objective assumed to be to preserve and maximize the value of these resources over the course of the cooperation. In this chapter, we develop a complementary perspective and argue that apart from these resources and capabilities, a firm's financial policies (i.e., its capital structure) also have an important bearing on various aspects of its alliancing activity. Empirically, we demonstrate that a firm's leverage has a systematic impact on the types of alliance partners it attracts as well as the choice of alliance governance. Moreover, we also show that the imperative to be perceived as an attractive alliance partner in the market for inter-firm collaboration can induce some firms to maintain lower leverage in their capital structures.

Our hypotheses are based on two central arguments. First, we propose that the role of financial policies in alliancing activity is important because of a critical ex post hazard in alliances: the risk of unplanned termination. Unplanned termination occurs when one partner unilaterally withdraws from the relationship before its objectives have been achieved (Reuer & Arino, 2002; Reuer & Zollo, 2005; Sadowski & Duysters, 2008). The costs associated with such unanticipated termination can be substantial because the efforts devoted to the alliance and the resources developed within it (such as joint technologies or marketing know-how) are often sunk and cannot be fully recovered if the relationship is prematurely terminated. Moreover, such events can also be particularly frustrating because neither firm may wish to terminate the alliance, but one firm may simply be unable to continue to contribute effort to the alliance, thereby preventing strategic goals from being achieved.

Prior evidence points to a strong link between firm financial health and unplanned termination in alliances. Reports from the popular press indicate that firms often withdraw from an alliance and sell their stakes to their partners or to external firms to raise cash and pay down debt.[1] In a recent paper documenting the effects of bankruptcy of an alliance partner, Boone and Ivanov (2012) find that firms experience a significant negative stock price reaction when an alliance partner files for bankruptcy.[2] In addition they also find that the non-bankrupt alliance partners experienced a significant drop in profitability and investment levels in the subsequent two years. Taken together, the evidence suggests that financial constraints are an important cause of alliance termination and have potentially detrimental performance consequences.

Building on this perspective, our second argument is that leverage is an important determinant of partner attractiveness in numerous transactions, including alliances. The relationship between partner attractiveness and leverage has been previously highlighted by stakeholder theories of debt and capital structure. These theories were developed in response to Modigliani and Miller's (1958) work, which suggests that in the presence of corporate tax savings, firms should maximize debt in their capital structure while minimizing equity. To explain the limits on debt, stakeholder perspectives argue that as leverage increases, employees, customers, and suppliers impose various costs on the firm (e.g., demanding higher compensation or paying lower prices) due to the increased probability of bankruptcy and financial distress (Cornell & Shapiro, 1987). These costs ultimately induce firms to limit the amount of debt in their capital structure. Thus, higher leverage makes a firm a less-attractive transaction partner (Titman, 1984) and creates disincentives for stakeholders to make relationship-specific investments. Our study extends this reasoning to the context of alliances and argues that leverage similarly makes a firm an unattractive alliance partner since it increases the risk of unplanned termination.

Based on our central arguments that financial health and the implied risk of unplanned termination influence a firm's attractiveness as an alliance partner, we develop and test several hypotheses. First, we demonstrate that firms tend to form alliances with partners characterized by relatively similar levels of leverage. This double-sided matching of leverage occurs in the market for collaboration because low-leverage firms prefer other low-leverage firms as partners, whereas high-leverage firms are constrained to partner with other high-leverage firms due to the risks of unanticipated termination. Our analyses confirm that firm leverage and partner leverage are positively associated. Moreover, we also hypothesize and find that a firm's leverage is negatively associated with its partners Tobin's Q, suggesting that levered firms are also constrained to partner with lower quality firms.

The second important result we obtain is that we also demonstrate that the propensity to use equity-based agreements in alliances increases both as a firm's leverage increases and as the *difference* in leverage across the alliance partners increases. Prior literature extensively argues that equity is effective in aligning incentives and in containing appropriability hazards in an alliance relationship. We complement these studies and show that equity is also important because it provides an enforceable mechanism and a safeguard through which specific investments can be salvaged by a lower levered partner in the event of premature termination by a more leveraged firm (Pisano, 1989). Finally, we posit that a value maximizing firm interested in forming alliances would anticipate the costs of leverage and ex ante limit debt in its capital structure. Accordingly, we demonstrate that after controlling for potential endogeneity, a firm's leverage is negatively related to the number of alliances it forms. This result suggests alliance-intensive firms maintain lower leverage in their capital structure, presumably to induce other firms to enter into partnerships with them and make relationship-specific investments.

Our research makes three important contributions to the literature. First, we highlight that financial constraints and capital structure have significant implications for alliancing activity. While it stands to reason that when entering into an alliance, partners will gauge each other's attractiveness not just in terms of the resources they possess but also in terms of their ability to sustain the venture in financial terms, this intuition has neither been formalized nor its implications fully explored. We seek to fill this gap. Second, and relatedly, we show that financial constraints and leverage provide us with an enhanced understanding of how firms select their alliance partners and the form of governance they choose. Third, in the spirit of this special volume, our study also highlights a unique link between corporate strategy and corporate finance. While there has been a vast literature on the determinants of capital structure, this literature has so far not recognized the role of alliances in determining leverage. Our study adds to this stream and suggests that the desire to be perceived as an attractive strategic alliance partner is another potentially important factor that can cause firms to maintain a lower leverage in their capital structure.

THEORY AND HYPOTHESES

As noted at the outset, the literature on partner selection is vast and multi-dimensional and has highlighted numerous factors. Central to these various streams is the theme that firms enter into alliances based on the resources and capabilities of the partner. While access to a partner's complementary resources may be a critical driver of alliance formation, the value of the collaboration might never be realized if financial distress by one partner disrupts the continuity of the alliance and undermines a partner's ability to devote consistent efforts. Thus, resource considerations should be traded off against the risk implied by partner financial health. Alliance research has acknowledged the importance of firm financial health, in the sense that it has assumed capital constraints and cost-sharing as common motivations for firms to form alliances. However, to the best of our knowledge, little if any of the prior works look at the role of leverage in making a firm a more or less attractive transacting partner. For instance, several scholars suggest that financially constrained firms tend to form alliances more because they lack the necessary financial resources to prosper independently (Lerner, Shane, & Tsai, 2003; Patzelt, Shepherd, Deeds, & Bradley, 2008; Stuart, 2000). Nonetheless, while these studies have paid attention to firm financial health to the extent that it determines the need for external financial resources, they mostly overlook its implications for the risks involved in alliances. Below, we try to fill this gap by integrating the alliance literature with insights from stakeholder theories of capital structure.

Stakeholder theories of capital structure have argued and shown that firm leverage can potentially impose costs on stakeholders such as employees, customers buying long-lived assets, dependent suppliers, or any other stakeholders exchanging unique products and services with the firm (Banerjee, Dasgupta, & Kim, 2008; Kale & Shahrur, 2007; Titman, 1984). In particular, unique products and services often involve investments that are relation-specific, whose value is maximized only as long as the two parties transact with each other (Williamson, 1985). If the relationship is terminated due to financial distress or bankruptcy, these investments lose value. Thus, as higher leverage implies a greater risk of bankruptcy and financial distress, external stakeholders are often reluctant to invest in relation-specific assets with highly levered firms unless they are compensated, ex ante, by better terms.

Investments involved in alliances with highly levered firms expose partners to similar costs and risks. Firms turn to alliances when they want to create assets which are specialized in conjunction with those of other firms. Indeed, by combining their resources and capabilities in unique ways, firms are able to obtain productivity gains not imitable by other competitors and create a relational competitive advantage (Dyer & Singh, 1998). For instance, many manufacturing firms form collaborations with their suppliers in order to buy inputs tailored to their particular needs and this allows them to reduce costs, time to market, or improve product quality. However, the existence of highly complementary assets is not sufficient to create an advantage, as partners must also develop ad hoc structures and inter-organizational processes to allow the creation, sharing or exchange of resources and capabilities across firms' boundaries. In this respect, Teece (1986) notes that during an alliance, interactions with a particular transacting partner are repeated and intense. Such interactions call for close formal and informal coordination mechanisms that enable the flow of information, and are greatly facilitated by an alliance structure as opposed to by arm's length transactions (Agarwal, Croson, & Mahoney, 2010). For example, in R&D alliances, firms develop inter-firm knowledge sharing routines that are purposefully designed to facilitate knowledge exchanges between partners. Moreover, as the alliance progresses over time, partners inevitably generate and accumulate knowledge about each other's products, expertise and organizational processes. While such interactions and coordination mechanisms facilitate innovation, they also inevitably build relationship-specific assets. If one partner prematurely terminates the venture due to reasons such as financial distress, the value of the resources or shared knowledge is significantly diminished (Boone & Ivanov, 2012). Thus, despite its best intentions, a highly levered partner inevitably puts at risk the continuity of an alliance and the value of the investments undertaken by both sides because its weak financial position may result in unplanned termination.

In addition to loss of relationship-specific assets, high leverage can also give rise to additional costs even when there is little immediate risk of bankruptcy because leverage influences a firm's incentives to meet implicit commitments to stakeholders. Implicit commitments are too state-contingent to be reduced to a written form, and thus during periods of cash shortfalls a levered firm may have incentives to default on those claims in order to shore up its financial health (Cornell & Shapiro, 1987). Consequently, scholars have demonstrated that highly levered firms are more likely to provide their customers lower quality inputs and skimp on follow-up services for existing products (Cornell & Shapiro, 1987; Maksimovic & Titman, 1991).[3] In the context of alliances, one important implicit claim is the commitment to provide high-quality effort over the duration of the alliance. During financially tough times levered firms may reduce critical resource contributions to the alliance, such as cash flows and managerial resources and personnel (Inkpen, 2000; Khanna, Gulati, & Nohria, 1998). Under these circumstances, the alliance partner is either faced with the prospect of terminating the alliance and losing its relationship-specific assets or continuing the alliance despite the half-hearted efforts of the levered partner. This problem could be partially mitigated if effort levels could be contractually specified ex ante, but such terms are difficult to write given the contingencies involved. Consequently, a leveraged firm's commitment to provide high-quality effort over the duration of the alliance remains an unenforceable implicit claim, which is a critical factor from the perspective of the partner in the alliance (although, as we note below, equity alliances may mitigate these concerns).

In addition to reduced effort, a lower levered firm is exposed to another form of ex post opportunism when partnering with a levered counterpart. A firm experiencing financial distress could try to extract concessions from a more financially healthy partner by threatening termination of the alliance and requesting either financial support or renegotiation for more favorable terms. Thus, a lower levered firm may once again be faced with the choice between terminating the alliance and losing the value of its relation-specific investments or perpetuating the alliance despite ex post opportunistic behavior (Arino, Ragozzino, & Reuer, 2008; Reuer & Arino, 2002) by subsidizing the levered partner in some manner.[4]

It is important to note that while our first argument is that high leverage may cause unplanned termination despite partner best intentions, our last two arguments make the point that highly levered firms could also extract gains by being opportunistic. Alternatively, it could be argued that since highly levered firms are likely to face financial constraints, they may need to form more alliances in order to extricate themselves from their financial troubles. These pressures could make the desperate firm more (and not less) amenable to making the alliance work and thus be less opportunistic. However, as soon as concerns about financial distress arise and firm survival is put at threat, any such inter-firm commitments are rapidly undermined by the potential of extracting wealth from financially strong alliance partners. Hence, the overall effect of higher leverage is to increase risks related to partner's commitment towards the alliance.

In summary, while alliances help firms access complementary partner resources, they also inevitably involve the presence of relationship-specific assets, which raise the costs of premature termination. Partnering with highly leveraged firms not only increases the risk of premature termination, but also exposes the unlevered firm to various forms of ex post opportunism such as a lack of effort or bargaining for financial support and more favorable terms. Thus, even though a levered firm might be a source of valuable synergies, the potential value that can be obtained by combining complementary assets must be weighed against the risks posed by partner financial condition. Rational firms should anticipate these risks and take ex ante action by carefully selecting potential partners based on their leverage. This implies that, *ceteris paribus*, low leverage firms are generally more attractive partners and should have greater opportunities to find collaborators. At the same time, they are also likely to face additional opportunism when dealing with highly levered counterparts, and hence they would tend to avoid partnering with such firms. Conversely, highly levered firms will generally be constrained to partner with other highly levered firms because they are perceived as being less attractive. Accordingly, a relatively stable pattern of alliance formation should emerge, wherein firms tend to partner with others characterized by similar levels of leverage.

The argument that alliances will involve partners with similar leverage is consistent with the broader literature on alliance homophily, which suggests that firms end up partnering with others that are similar along some dimension in order to reduce collaboration hazards (Ahuja, Polidoro, & Mitchell, 2009; Chung, Singh, & Lee, 2000; Gulati, 1995; Gulati & Gargiulo, 1999; Kumar & Park, 2012; Podolny, 1994; Stuart, 1998). For instance, Podolny (1994) suggests that although alliances are formed to reduce market uncertainty, they also expose the firm to greater uncertainty about the quality and behavior of prospective partners. When these factors are hard to observe, firms rely on status to infer partner attractiveness, under the assumption that higher status signals reliability and an established reputation of being an effective alliance partner. Firms will generally look for higher status partners not only because they are more attractive, but also because they act as an endorsement to external constituencies (Stuart, Hoang, & Hybels, 1999). Hence, the benefits associated with a high status partner should be especially salient for low status firms. Conversely, higher status firms will generally avoid partnering with such firms, since low status partners have little to offer and could even damage their reputation. Therefore, the most likely alliances are those between firms of similar status. Similarly, other scholars propose that other dimensions of homophily, such as similarity of partner technological profiles or social institutions, can also facilitate interfirm collaboration (e.g., Lane, Salk, & Lyles, 2001; Mowery, Oxley, & Silverman, 1996; Pfeffer & Nowak, 1976; Stuart, 1998).

Building on this logic, we argue that another important dimension along which alliance partners tend to be similar is their capital structure. Financially weak firms pose serious hazards during an alliance and they have more incentives to behave opportunistically. For these reasons, firms will generally want to partner with low-leverage firms because they are more reliable and financially sound. At the same time, these benefits should be especially attractive for high-leverage firms as they are more constrained and in need for additional resources. Conversely, low-leverage firms will have greater incentives to avoid partnering with high-leverage firms not only because they have more to lose, but also because they have greater opportunities to partner with more attractive low-leverage firms. Therefore, we predict the following:

Hypothesis 1. Firms will tend to form alliances with partners characterized by similar levels of leverage.

The influence of a firm's leverage on the risk of unplanned termination will also likely impact the quality of the alliance partners that a firm can attract. One of the primary reasons for engaging in alliances is to combine complementary assets and stimulate innovation. Firms possessing high-quality resources are the most valuable partners because they should be able to generate the most valuable synergies. Consequently, high-quality firms have more bargaining power in the market for collaboration, which they can use in order to partner with the most desirable associates (Rhode-Kropf & Robinson, 2008). We contend that, due to their superior resources endowments, high-quality firms will have the bargaining power to avoid the risks entailed by partnering with highly levered firms. Indeed, during cash flow fluctuations, the lack of incentives to devote consistent efforts by a highly leveraged firm could undermine the realization of synergies. Furthermore, despite best intentions to devote effort, synergies would also not be realized if the alliance terminates prematurely because of a partner's financial difficulties. Thus, higher quality firms face a greater opportunity cost by partnering with highly leveraged counterparts. As a result, high-quality firms will thus tend to select lower levered counterparts.

Hypothesis 2. There is a negative relationship between a firm's leverage and the quality of its partners.

Thus far we have argued that highly leveraged firms are unattractive partners due to greater risks of financial distress and unplanned termination, which dissuades low levered and high-quality firms from forming alliances with them. However, highly leveraged firms can ex ante offer various forms of protection and safeguards in order to attract desirable partners. One particular form of protection that is likely to be effective in this regard is structuring the alliance as an equity joint venture (JV). As Pisano (1989) observes, allocating equity in an alliance requires putting a value on the expected contributions of each firm prior to the commencement of the partnership. Typically it entails negotiations and explicitly drawing out agreements regarding such relative contributions. Once drawn out, these agreements can be legally enforced by the partner (Ryall & Sampson, 2009), which may prevent any subsequent reneging or scaling back of effort on the part of a levered firm. Moreover, any shirking by the leveraged firm reduces the value of the JV and the value of its equity position, which would lower the proceeds it could obtain should it attempt to raise funds by selling its stake in the JV to the partner or to a third party, which are common methods of JV termination (Cuypers & Martin, 2007; Villalonga & McGahan, 2005).

Equity participation and a JV structure also provide other advantages besides ensuring continuity of effort. Typically a JV has a board with members drawn from the constituent partners. Through such a structure, a partner can safeguard its investments by exercising better control and monitoring of the efforts of a highly leveraged firm on a more continuous basis. Moreover, such ongoing control also allows the partner to understand the JV's operations more intimately. In the event of an unplanned termination, the partner may be able to salvage its investments by taking over the venture entirely. The protection provided by equity and a JV structure is, however, also costly for both parties since it involves a greater commitment of resources from the outset (e.g., managerial resources in the form of human capital and employees specifically devoted to the alliance) as compared to alliances which are more similar to arm's length relationships. For a highly leveraged firm, its willingness to devote such resources and human capital acts as a form of credible commitment to sustain the collaboration and devote consistent effort. Conversely, a JV structure should be desirable also from the counterpart's point of view, regardless of its leverage, because to the extent that there is value in collaborating with a leveraged partner, it may be willing to incur such costs upfront. Hence, we predict:

Hypothesis 3. Alliances involving highly levered firms are more likely to be equity-based.

As an extension of hypothesis 3, we also posit that an alliance is more likely to take the form of a JV as the *difference in leverage* between the two partners grows. Although any alliance partner could potentially seek concessions or skimp on future resource commitments, the problem should be particularly acute when one firm is lowly levered and financially healthy while the other is highly levered. Under these conditions, the unlevered firm is particularly vulnerable to the threat that the levered firm may use its financially weak position as justification for renegotiation and extracting concessions. Consequently, lower levered firms have greater incentives to require their highly levered counterparts to commit to the additional protections afforded by an equity JV. Conversely, the additional costs of a JV structure (described above) are less likely to be regarded as warranted when both firms are low leveraged due to the lower threat of opportunistic renegotiation and extracting concessions, given that both partners are financially healthy. Similarly, a JV is also less likely to occur when both firms are highly levered as the weak financial positions of both partners reduce the risk of opportunism (i.e., because there is little wealth to be extracted from a financially weak partner) while making the additional costs of a JV difficult to afford. Hence, we argue the following:

Hypothesis 4. The greater the difference between partners' leverage, the greater the probability that an alliance will take the form of a JV.

Thus far, our theory and level of analysis has focused on the alliance and predicted patterns in partner selection and alliance governance. For our final hypothesis, we take a firm-level perspective and argue that firms that make alliances a strategic priority will adopt lower leverage in order to improve their own attractiveness as an alliance partner. Stakeholder theories provide evidence that in conditions where customers and suppliers incur firm-specific investments, firms maintain a lower level of leverage. In line with this reasoning, Titman and Wessels (1988) show that firms tend to have lower leverage when they operate in durable goods industries, where customers switching costs and relationship-specific assets tend to be high. Banerjee et al. (2008) similarly show that firms with dedicated suppliers (i.e., suppliers for whom more than 10% of sales come from the firm) and dedicated customers (i.e., customers for whom the firm constitutes greater than 10% of sales) maintain lower leverage so that that they can induce these dedicated suppliers or customers to transact primarily with them and develop valuable firm-specific assets. Similarly, Kale and Shahrur (2007) show that the R&D intensity of suppliers and customers is negatively associated with firm leverage, indicating that lower leverage stimulates these stakeholders to invest in technological resources that are likely to be relationship-specific.

If financial health matters to alliance partners like it does to customers and suppliers, we would expect to observe that firms actively seeking alliance partners would similarly adopt lower leverage in order to induce other firms to form partnerships and make specific investments. Furthermore, existing influential alliance partners may also encourage the firm to keep leverage low ex post or even to reduce it further, if necessary in order to protect their relationship-specific investments. Accordingly, we predict:[5]

Hypothesis 5. A firm's leverage will be negatively related to its alliance intensity.

METHODS

Data and Sample

We drew data on all alliances announced between the years 1988 and 2006 from the Securities Data Corporation (SDC) database on mergers, acquisitions, and alliances. We restricted our attention to two partner alliances to ease the comparison among partners' characteristics. In addition, we also excluded from our sample alliances involving financial firms, since leverage has a different interpretation in those industries. For alliances meeting these criteria, information was retrieved on the partners' names, SIC codes, state of incorporation, descriptions of activities involved in the alliance, geographical locations, and other governance-related data such as the presence of equity-exchanges.

Accounting and financial data on the partnering firms were gathered from Compustat. After combining all data, we were left with 4,220 alliances involving 2,074 distinct firms. On average, each of these 2,074 focal firms is associated with 4.1 alliances in our final sample. Our final sample includes alliances in a wide variety of sectors. Adopting Fama and French's twelve industry classification, the distributions of the alliance activity across industrial codes are as follows: computer, software and electronic equipment (48.1%); healthcare, medical equipment and drugs (8.45%); chemical and allied products (1.37%); manufacturing (2.84%); consumer durables (1.59%); telephone and television transmission (2.06%); wholesale, retail and related services (11%); and finance (8.65%). All remaining industries account for minor percentages.

Dependent Variables

In order to test hypothesis 1, which posits that firms with similar levels of leverage will partner with each other, we adopt two approaches. First, as we discuss in greater detail in the results section, we compared differences in leverage among allied firms with the difference in leverage of random matched pairs of firms picked from the entire Compustat database. Second, and more formally, we tested the hypothesis by constructing a hierarchical linear regression model to regress partner leverage on alliance level variables and focal firm leverage. Since firms formed multiple alliances in our sample, we constructed our data set so that each alliance with its corresponding partner and alliance characteristics was nested within the firm. Thus, for the 2,074 firms in our sample, a focal firm's alliance appears as a nested observation within the partners' observations, and correspondingly the same alliance appears as a nested observation within the focal firms' observations. Accordingly, to test this relationship, we measured the partners' market leverage (*PLEV*), where market leverage is computed as total debt divided by total market value of the firm, and the total market value of the firm is the sum of the book value of debt plus total market value of outstanding shares.[6] We similarly constructed a measure of the partners' Tobin's *Q*, *PQ*, to proxy for firm quality and test hypothesis 2, which posits that leveraged firms will attract lower quality partners. The variable *PQ* is computed as: (market value of equity + total assets − common equity)/ (total assets).

Our third and fourth hypotheses relate partners leverage to the choice of the governance form of the alliance. We used a hierarchical model for this analysis as well, and we constructed a dummy variable (*JV*) which takes the value of one when the alliance is a JV and zero otherwise.[7] Finally, our last hypothesis relates a firm's alliance intensity with its own level of leverage. In order to test this hypothesis, we took the entire population of firms in Compustat and structured our sample as a panel data. We then regressed firm leverage (*LEV*) in a given year on the number of alliances formed during that year and other firm-level controls, where leverage is defined as the firm's market leverage.

Key Independent Variables

The variables leverage (*LEV*) and partner leverage (*PLEV*) in the year of alliance formation were also used as independent variables to test hypotheses 1, 2, and 3. To test hypothesis 4, which pertains to the impact of differences in partner leverage on the choice of governance, we also constructed the variable *DELTA*, which is the absolute difference in market leverage between the two partners. Finally, for hypothesis 5, which relates to the effects of alliance intensity on the focal firm's leverage, we constructed the variable *ALLIANCES* as a count of all alliances formed by the focal firm in a given year.

Models

Hypothesis 1 suggests a double-sided matching in the market for collaboration, whereby a highly levered firm is more likely to form alliances with other highly levered firms, while a lower levered firm is more likely to ally with other conservatively financed partners. To test this prediction, the following equation is estimated:

$$PLEV_{ij} = a_{00} + a_{0i} + \tau_t + \gamma_1 PROA_{ij} + \gamma_2 PQ_{ij} + \gamma_3 PRD_{ij} + \gamma_4 PLASSET_{ij} \\ + \gamma_5 LEV_{ij} + \gamma_6 ROA_{ij} + \gamma_7 Q_{ij} + \gamma_8 RD_{ij} + \gamma_9 LASSET_{ij} \\ + \gamma_{10} DOWNTURN_{ij} + \mu_{ij} \quad (1)$$

As groups of alliances formed by the same focal firm are likely to possess common characteristics, and observations related to the same focal firm are likely to be correlated, we employed hierarchical models wherein alliances are nested within firms. Accordingly in Eq. (1), the variables denoted by *P* are partner characteristics and are at the alliance level, which are modeled as nested within the firm. Hence, for alliance *j* formed by focal firm *i* a random intercept term is included in order to capture these dependencies. Similarly, hypothesis 2 examines the impact of leverage on the quality of alliance partners a focal firm is able to attract. To test this hypothesis, we estimated the following hierarchical model where we take the logarithm of Tobin's *q* as the dependent variable (Hirsch & Seaks, 1993), and, as before, alliances are nested within firms:

$$Log(PQ_{ij}) = a_{00} + a_{0i} + \tau_t + \gamma_1 PRD_{ij} + \gamma_2 PLASSET_{ij} + \gamma_3 PROA_{ij} \\ + \gamma_4 PLEV_{ij} + \gamma_5 RD_{ij} + \gamma_6 LASSET_{ij} + \gamma_7 ROA_{ij} + \gamma_8 Q_{ij} \quad (2) \\ + \gamma_9 LEV_{ij} + \gamma_{10} DOWNTURN + \mu_{ij}$$

For both models above, we included several control variables that could impact either a firm's leverage or the quality of the alliance partners it attracts. Partner selection choices can be largely explained by looking at partnering firms' resources, which in turn also determine their level of leverage. Therefore, it is important to control for firms' resources in order to make sure these factors are not driving leverage patterns in our sample of alliances. Firms often seek alliance partners to access their technological skills and know-how (Hitt et al., 2000). These intangible and idiosyncratic resources are less re-deployable and limit a firm's ability to borrow, thus implying that partners possessing higher technological skills and know-how also tend to adopt lower leverage (Vicente-Lorente, 2001). Accordingly, we controlled for the R&D intensity of both the partner firm (*PRD*) and the focal firm (*RD*), defined as the ratio of R&D expenses to total assets. Another common motivation for forming alliances is to gain access to other partners' financial resources (Lerner et al., 2003). More profitable firms are better able to internally generate the financial resources needed to fund their investments and they should be viewed as being more attractive by financially constrained partners. In addition, since they have more internal resources, these firms do not need to take on debt, and thus also tend to be less levered. Conversely, financially constrained firms are more likely to be dependent on external financing to prosper and should be relatively more levered (Myers & Majluf, 1984). To account for these differences we controlled for both the focal firm's and its partner's return on assets (*ROA* and *PROA*, respectively), defined as operating income divided by total assets. Prior research further indicates that larger firms represent the most valuable partners in alliances because they arguably possess greater resources to invest in R&D and tend to be more innovative (Stuart, 2000). On the other hand, large firms usually have greater market power, which they can use to obtain a bargaining advantage over alliance partners (Hitt et al., 2000). Thus, large firms and small firms are likely to seek different kinds of alliance partners. At the same time, bigger firms usually possess established and more diversified businesses and thus they are expected to have easier access to equity markets and may carry lower levels of debt. To control for the effects of size we included the variables *PLASSETS* and *LASSETS*, defined as the natural logarithm of the partner and focal firm's total assets, respectively.

We also controlled for both partners' Tobin's q (*Q* and *PQ*), as this is an accepted proxy for the firm's level of intangible resources (Villalonga, 2004), and for both its current and expected profitability (Huselid, Jackson, & Schuler, 1997). Finally, research has shown that the importance of a firm's financial condition is also influenced by the business cycle, arguably because higher leverage is more likely to lead to financial distress during recessions than during booms (Opler & Titman, 1994). In order to address the impact of economic conditions at the time of alliance establishment we employed a binary variable (*DOWNTURN*) to capture whether the focal firm's industry was experiencing a recession when the alliance was formed. This variable takes the value of one when the firm's 4-digits SIC industry is characterized by negative median sales and median stock return less than −30%, and zero otherwise (Chevalier & Scharfstein, 1995; Opler & Titman, 1994). Also, we added yearly dummies (τ_t) to capture any trend in the selection of partners at the time of alliance formation.

Hypotheses 3 and 4 focus on the impact of leverage on the governance form of an alliance. In order to test these hypotheses, we employ logit models where, as before, alliances are nested within focal firms. The following equations were estimated:

$$Prob(Y_{ij}=1) = \alpha_i + \tau_t + \beta_1 RESEARCH_{ij} + \beta_2 MANUFACT_{ij} + \beta_3 MARKET_{ij}$$
$$+ \beta_4 SUPPLY_{ij} + \beta_5 LICENS_{ij} + \beta_6 SUPRANATION_{ij}$$
$$+ \beta_7 SAMESTATE_{ij} + \beta_8 SAMEIND_{ij} + \beta_9 PRIORALL_{ij}$$
$$+ \beta_{10} AVGASSET_{ij} + \beta_{11} RASSET_{ij} + \beta_{12} RDGAP_{ij} + \beta_{13} AVGROA_{ij}$$
$$+ \beta_{14} DOWNTURN_{ij} + \beta_{15} \mathbf{LEV}_{ij} + \beta_{16} \mathbf{PLEV}_{ij} \qquad (3)$$

$$Prob(Y_{ij}=1) = \alpha_i + \tau_t + \beta_1 RESEARCH_{ij} + \beta_2 MANUFACT_{ij} + \beta_3 MARKET_{ij}$$
$$+ \beta_4 SUPPLY_{ij} + \beta_5 LICENS_{ij} + \beta_6 SUPRANATION_{ij}$$
$$+ \beta_7 SAMESTATE_{ij} + \beta_8 SAMEIND_{ij} + \beta_9 PRIORALL_{ij}$$
$$+ \beta_{10} AVGASSET_{ij} + \beta_{11} RASSET_{ij} + \beta_{12} RDGAP_{ij} + \beta_{13} AVGROA_{ij}$$
$$+ \beta_{14} DOWNTURN + \beta_{15} \mathbf{DELTA}_{ij} \qquad (4)$$

In these models, α_i is the random intercept term, which takes into account dependencies among alliances pertaining to the same focal firm. To test hypothesis 3, we estimate a nested specification (Eq. (3)) where we include both the focal firm's and its partners' level of leverage as our main independent variables (*LEV* and *PLEV*, respectively). Hypothesis 3 implies that both coefficients on these variables will be positive, so that whenever one of the two firms is highly levered chances of a JV increase. Hypothesis 4 extends the previous argument by suggesting that equity governance will also be preferred when the difference in leverage between partners is high, since under these conditions the lower levered firm would once again seek the protection that equity provides in terms of sustained commitment and protection of the value of alliance assets. To test this hypothesis we include the absolute difference among partners leverage (*DELTA*) as our main independent variable.

In these specifications, we also include other controls typically employed in studies of alliance governance form. Previous research indicates that the typology of activities involved in an alliance is a critical consideration as it determines appropriation concerns anticipated at the time of alliance formation (Gulati & Singh, 1998). Moreover, the level of uncertainty associated with alliance activities induces coordination and adaptation requirements that are important determinants of governance choice (Casciaro, 2003). Accordingly, five dummy variables were constructed in order to indicate whether an alliance included research, marketing, manufacturing, supply, or licensing activities (*RESEARCH, MANUFACT, MARKET, SUPPLY, LICENS*, respectively). There is also evidence that the level of trust developed between partners through repeated ties reduces the hazards involved in future alliances, and thus the likelihood that hierarchical control will be adopted (Gulati & Singh, 1998). To capture inter-firm trust we introduced the variable *PRIORALL*, calculated as the number of prior alliances between the two partners during the previous five years. Researchers have also pointed out that cross-border alliances pose more obstacles for participating firms to develop trust as well as greater appropriation concerns than domestic ties because of their inherent difficulty in monitoring partner's efforts and contributions (Gulati & Singh, 1998; Parkhe, 1993). Conversely, other studies focus on competitive effects in alliances bringing together partners in the same industry or geographical areas, and propose that such ties pose greater hazards because firms may systematically try to capture the counter part's knowledge and resources (Oxley & Sampson, 2004). To control for these factors three dummy variables were employed, which capture if partners operated in the same industry,[8] same geographical areas, or if the geographical scope of the alliance was supranational (*SAMEIND, SAMESTATE, SUPRANATION*).

Previous studies of JVs formation usually control for the effect of absolute firm size and/or the asymmetry in partners' size, under the assumption that small firms may lack the necessary resources to afford the costs of more hierarchical governance forms (Harrigan, 1988; Hennart, 1991; Oxley, 1997). In a similar vein, they have also looked at partnering firms' levels of profitability to control for firms' availability of internal financial resources (Casciaro, 2003). To control for these differences we included the variables *AVGASSET* and *AVGROA*, computed as the average of partners' total book assets and return on assets, respectively. We also employed the variable *RASSET*, computed as the ratio of the smaller firms' total assets over the larger firms' total assets as a measure for partners' asymmetry in size. An important finding of previous research is that large capabilities' gaps between firms participating in an alliance increase the cost of knowledge and technology transfer across firms' boundaries, which in turn may require firms to adopt particular governance structures (Oxley, 1997; Teece, 1986). For this reason, we included the variable *RDGAP*, computed as the absolute difference between firms' R&D intensity. A series of dummy variables were also included to account for the SIC code of the alliance, with industrial codes being reclassified according to Fama and French's 12 industries classification. Finally, as before we included the variable *DOWNTURN* along with year dummies (τ_t) to control for any effects related to time or time-varying industry conditions.

Hypothesis 5 examines the relation between a firm's alliance activity and its own level of leverage. In order to test this prediction, we used the entire Compustat population of firms during the period 1988–2006 as our sample and built a panel data set where the unit of analysis is the *firm-year*. Firms operating in financial sectors (SIC codes 6000–6999) were excluded as in other studies of capital structure. We employ fixed-effects instrumental variables regression in order to estimate the following equation:

$$LEV_{it} = a_0 + \tau_t + \gamma_1 RD_{it} + \gamma_2 Q_{it} + \gamma_3 TANGIBLES_{it} + \gamma_4 ROA_{it} + \gamma_5 LASSET_{it} \\ + \gamma_6 CAPINTENS_{it} + \gamma_7 DIV_{it} + \gamma_8 ALLIANCES_{it} + \mu_{it} \qquad (5)$$

In this specification, the variable *ALLIANCES* is treated as endogenous because a firm's capital structure decision and its alliance decisions could be jointly determined. The endogenous variable is instrumented in the first stage by the average number of alliances formed by firms in that industry during that year (*AVGINDALL*). Institutional theorists have explained alliance formation by suggesting that firms succumb to isomorphic pressures and mimic the behavior of other firms in the industry who have successfully entered into alliances (Gulati, 1995). Accordingly, empirical evidence has shown that industry alliance activity is an established antecedent of alliance formation at the firm level (Gulati, 1995; Hagedoorn & Frankort, 2008). On the opposite, industry alliance activity does not impact firm leverage directly, but only through a firm's direct alliances. Also, while a firm's leverage could well impact its alliance activity, there is no reason to think it could impact industry level alliance activity (i.e., reverse causality is less of a concern with an industry level instrument). For these reasons, the instrument should be exogenous with respect to firm leverage and should reflect the broader tendencies within the industry with respect to using alliances as a means for staying competitive. Finally, we also considered the past trend in industry alliance activity, under the assumption that although a firm may have established the need to collaborate, suitable alliance partners could not always be available. Accordingly, we also added the first and second lag of the variable *AVGINDALL* as instruments for the endogenous variable in the first stage.

We also employ standard controls considered as determinants of capital structure in the literature. In addition to the variables used in the model for hypothesis 1, we include *TANGIBLES* to control for the level of assets that can be used as collateral. This variable is computed as the ratio of property, plant, and equipment to the total book value of assets. Similarly, we also controlled for the firm capital intensity (*CAPINTENS*), computed as the ratio of the firms' total book assets over total sales. In order to account for the effect of dividend policies we included the binary variable *DIV*, which takes the value of 1 when a firm distributes dividends. Finally, to minimize the effect of outliers, all variables that were not binary or logged were winsorized at the 1% level.

RESULTS

In the interest of space, we do not report correlation matrices because our data is structured into several distinct datasets and hence doing so would require multiple tables. While multicollinearity was not a concern with our data, some interesting correlations did exist amongst our variables. Focal firm leverage (*LEV*) was positively correlated ($r = 0.199$) with partner leverage (*PLEV*), while it shows a negative correlation ($r = -0.113$) with partner quality (*PQ*). Moreover, both partners' leverage is positively associated with the presence of a JV ($r = 0.195$ and 0.180 for *LEV* and *PLEV*, respectively).

Before discussing the results of our formal hypothesis tests, we present some preliminary analyses in Table 1 which highlight noteworthy patterns in the data that are consistent with our hypotheses. Our primary thesis is that high leverage makes a firm a less attractive alliance partner. An ideal test of this argument would involve analyzing not only the leverage levels of partners among alliances that were actually formed, but also among pairs of firms which *did not enter* into alliances, potentially because leverage

Table 1. Preliminary Analysis.

Panel A: Comparison of differences in leverage

Variable	Mean Value		t (diff.)	p-value
	Alliances	Non-alliances		
|Δ Leverage|	0.1505	0.1971	−10.8413	<0.001
|Δ Book Leverage|	0.1849	0.2428	−8.3029	<0.001
n = 3,492				

Panel B: Focal firm's leverage and characteristics of partners

Percentiles of Leverage	Mean		Median	
	Partner leverage	Partner Q	Partner leverage	Partner Q
0–33	0.110	4.36	0.041	2.44
33–66	0.131	3.85	0.058	2.31
66–99	0.195	2.80	0.125	1.73
n = 11,112				

Panel C: Joint ventures activity across levels of focal firms' leverage

Focal Firm Leverage	Total Alliances	JVs	Percent of JVs
Below the median	4,167	385	9.24
Above the median	1,389	342	24.62
All observations	5,556	727	13.08

Panel D: Joint venture activity across levels of |Δ Leverage|

Percentiles of |Δ Leverage|	Percent of JVs
0–33	8.53
33–66	12.76
66–99	18.10
n = 5,556	

levels or high differences in levels of leverage made the alliance unattractive. If our hypotheses are correct, then firms with high levels of leverage as well as potential alliance pairings with high differences in leverage will systematically fall out of our sample of allied firms. This introduces a form of truncation in our sample, since the distribution of both observed partners' leverage and differences in leverage is truncated from above and is predominantly observed below a certain threshold. As such, for some of our dependent variables (e.g., partner leverage in Eq. (1)), our estimates are likely to be understated, and thus the results of the hypotheses tests from our models are likely to be conservatively biased due to the truncation.[9] That is, if alliances among firms characterized by high levels of leverage were more common, then the inclusion of those observations in our sample would strengthen our estimates of the impact of firm leverage on partner leverage.

To address the possibility that observed alliances are biased toward firms with lower leverage, we compared the absolute differences in partners' leverage among observed alliance pairs with absolute differences from a matched control sample of random pairs. Control firms are those that formed at least one alliance during the time frame considered in the study (1988–2006). For each partner in the alliance we matched a random control firm operating in the same 4-digits SIC code in the same year. For example, if an observed alliance involved a pharmaceutical and a semiconductor firm, we constructed a control dyad between a random control pharmaceutical firm and a random control semiconductor firm. This matched sample controls for industry and year effects and is representative of a population of alliances that might have potentially occurred if counterpart leverage did not matter. If leverage did not affect alliance formation, then there should be no significant difference in leverage between observed alliances and random matched pairings. Panel A of Table 1 reports the difference in leverage between allied pairs of firms and random pairings. Consistent with our arguments, in the sample of observed alliances the average difference in partners' leverage is 15.1%, while the difference in the sample of random pairings is 19.7%, and a t-test confirms that the difference between the sample means is highly significant ($p < 0.001$). Unreported Wilcoxon and binomial sign tests confirm that results are not driven by outliers. Table 1 further shows that the difference among leverage patterns between observed alliances and matched pairings is even more marked when book levels of leverage are considered. Aside from addressing self-selection bias, this preliminary evidence also tentatively corroborates the argument that when a firm looks for alliance partners, it tends to match with counterparts possessing similar levels of leverage. Thus, it appears lower levered firms systematically partner with each other, while high leverage firms are possibly constrained to partner with other high levered firms.

In Panel B of Table 1 we show a similar pattern *within* the observed sample of alliances. We divided all 11,112 firms in our sample into three groups according to observed percentiles of leverage, and then for each group we computed the mean and median value of the partners' Tobin's q and leverage. For firms with the lower observed leverage (0–33 percentiles) the median level of partners' Tobin's q and leverage are 2.44 and 4.1%, respectively. Conversely, for firms with the highest observed leverage (66–99 percentiles) the median partners' Tobin's q drops to 1.73, while average level of partner leverage rises to 12.5%. These statistics are again consistent with our first argument that highly levered firms are less attractive partners and that they tend to form alliances with partners characterized by higher leverage as well as lower quality, thus supporting hypotheses 1–2.

Finally, Panels C and D provide insight into the extent to which a firm's leverage determines the choice of governance form in an alliance. For Panel C, we first computed the median leverage for all firms in the Compustat population, and then compared the number of alliances formed by firms above and below the median. We divided the sample according to the level of leverage of the first partner listed in the alliance, as it appears on SDC.[10] Results show that more highly leveraged firms are substantially less likely to form alliances, even though some research has suggested they may have a greater need to form alliances under some circumstances (Patzel et al., 2008). Furthermore, 24.6% of alliances involving a highly leveraged firm were structured as a JV, whereas only 9.2% of alliances involving a low leveraged firm were structured as JVs. This difference of 15.4% is also highly statistically significant ($p<0.001$).

Panel D examines how the *difference* in leverage across the two alliance partners relates to the likelihood that an alliance will be structured as a JV. We divided alliances into three groups according to observed percentiles of the absolute differences in leverage. JVs appear to be more likely for alliances characterized by relatively higher differences in leverage, increasing from 8.5% when the difference is relatively small to 18.1% when the difference is relatively large. The results of Panels C and D are consistent with our argument that when a firm has high leverage, an alliance is more likely to involve equity as a form of protection and safeguard for lower levered firms. The overall patterns of Table 1 are also consistent with our general argument that firms pay attention to the financial health of alliance partners, and that they structure their transactions in the market for collaboration accordingly.

Before presenting our regression results, we discuss some alternative explanations that may motivate patterns of leverage among allying firms. Perhaps, the underlying issue could be not whether leverage matters, but what factors influence leverage which in turn also impact partner attractiveness and alliance deals. For instance, prior research suggests leverage is negatively related to innovation as the latter produces mostly intangible assets with low collateral value (Simerly & Li, 2000; Vicente-Lorente, 2001). Hence, one potential alternative explanation could simply be that our results are reflecting highly innovative firms partnering with other highly innovative firms, rather than matching due to leverage. However, high-innovation/high-leverage firms are not unusual. To examine these issues, we divided our sample of firms into four cells according to two dimensions: firms with high/low R&D and firms with high/low leverage. High (low) R&D firms were defined as firms that have R&D intensity greater (lower) than the overall Compustat population median. Similarly, we defined categories for high/low leverage based on Compustat median values. After defining the four categories, next we randomly chose one partner (the first listed partner in SDC) and examined the leverage/R&D distribution of these firms. When considering the first listed partner in the alliance, it appears that 81% of our sample of alliances involves high R&D firms. It is noteworthy that amongst these firms, almost 19% had above median leverage. Moreover, if innovation explained our results, leverage should make no difference to the alliances of R&D intensive firms, and the chances of an equity JV should be roughly the same irrespective of whether a high R&D firm has low leverage or high leverage. However, while high R&D-low leverage firms form JVs in only 5.3% of the cases, this fraction increases to 12.1% for high R&D-high leverage firms. This pattern cannot be explained by R&D intensity and it is consistent with the idea that high leverage also introduces further hazards in the alliance.[11]

Alternatively, it could also be argued that highly levered firms tend partner with lowly levered ones quite often as a result of resource considerations, thus violating our proposed matching among partners characterized by similar leverage. For instance, in biotech-pharma alliances, while the biotech firm's intangible assets may prevent it from adopting higher leverage, the pharma partner can usually take on significant amounts of debt due to its greater tangible assets and cash flows (Gopalakrishnan, Scillitoe, & Santoro, 2008). Accordingly, most alliances should occur between firms possessing very different levels of leverage (due to their different underlying assets), while alliances between firms with similar leverage (high-high or low-low) should be less common. Again, our results in Panel A of Table 1 are inconsistent with this explanation, as observed differences in partners leverage are systematically smaller (and not greater) than differences computed for random pairs.

Table 2 presents the results for our hierarchical regression models that are used to test hypotheses 1 and 2. Note that while Table 1 was based on all 5,556 observed alliances for which both partners' leverage and Tobin's q figures are available, the results in Tables 2 and 3 are based on a reduced sample of 4,220 alliances due to a loss in observations because of missing data for other controls and independent variables. In column 1 of Table 2

Table 2. Hierarchical Models for Partners' Leverage and Partners' Quality.

Dependent Variable	(1) PLEV	(2) LOG(PQ)
Partner variables		
PLEV		−1.814***
		(0.0444)
PQ	−0.00821***	
	(0.000409)	
PLASSETS	0.0252***	−0.0264***
	(0.000692)	(0.00311)
PROA	−0.256***	0.446***
	(0.00794)	(0.0354)
PRD	−0.396***	1.187***
	(0.0174)	(0.0747)
Focal firm variables		
LEV	0.106***	−0.118*
	(0.0130)	(0.0485)
LASSETS	0.000281	0.00695+
	(0.00108)	(0.00355)
Q	−0.000175	0.0121***
	(0.000472)	(0.00183)
ROA	0.00894	−0.118**
	(0.00938)	(0.0365)
RD	−0.0120	−0.263***
	(0.0196)	(0.0763)
DOWNTURN	−0.0178	−0.0929*
	(0.0114)	(0.0470)
Intercept	−0.0376**	1.129***
	(0.0135)	(0.0530)
N	8,440	8,440
Groups	2,074	2,074
Avg. obs. per group	4.1	4.1

Standard errors in parentheses: +$p < 0.10$; *$p < 0.05$; **$p < 0.01$; ***$p < 0.001$.

the dependent variable is partner leverage (*PLEV*), and in column 2 the dependent variable is partner quality (*PQ*). The likelihood ratio tests confirm that in both models the inclusion of a random intercept for each focal firm offers significant improvement over a linear regression model with only fixed effects ($p < 0.001$). Hypothesis 1 predicts that firms will tend to form alliances with partners possessing similar levels of leverage. Consistent with hypothesis 1, column 1 reveals that firm leverage (*LEV*) is positively related to partner leverage ($p < 0.001$). Thus, the higher (lower) a focal firm's leverage, the higher (lower) the levels of leverage of its counterparts.

The second column of Table 2 tests hypothesis 2, which argued that alliances with highly levered firms entail significant risks for good quality firms looking to derive valuable synergies. Thus, good quality firms tend to avoid high leverage partners and, all else being equal, the latter are constrained to partner with firms of relatively lower quality. Consistent with this argument, the coefficient on the variable *LEV* is negative and significant at the $p < 0.05$ level, implying that higher leverage for a firm generally translates into lower quality alliance partners. In terms of the controls, model (2) indicates that at the focal firm level, higher Q firms tend to partner with other high quality partners. Also, bigger firms tend to partner with high Q firms, possibly in order to access the latter's growth opportunities. In addition, R&D intensive firm (which may possess higher growth opportunities) appear to look for partners characterized by lower levels of Q in order to access their tangible assets in place. Similarly, after controlling for the effect of Q, more profitable firms also tend partner with lower quality firms, potentially for access to assets in place. Finally, the negative and significant coefficient on the variable *DOWNTURN* suggests that firms whose industry is experiencing a downturn tend to attract lower Q firms arguably because they offer reduced growth prospects and are thus perceived as being less attractive.

Table 3 reports results from the hierarchical logit models used to test the impact of leverage on the choice of governance form. Hypothesis 3 argues that alliance partners are more likely to opt for the added protections afforded by a JV structure when the partners are highly levered. The positive and significant ($p < 0.001$) coefficients on the variables *LEV* and *PLEV* in model 1 of Table 3 support this hypothesis. Hypothesis 4 further argues that the costs of allying with a high-leverage firm can be especially high for low-leverage counterparts, and thus alliances characterized by greater *difference* among partners' leverage are more likely to take the form of a JV. In model 2 we test this prediction by including the absolute difference between the partners' leverage (*DELTA*). As expected, the coefficient on this variable is positive and significant ($p < 0.001$), supporting hypothesis 4. As a robustness check, we also estimated this model with a standard (i.e., non-hierarchical) logit model computed for the sample of 4,220 alliances and results are qualitatively unchanged.

In terms of the controls, most of the coefficients on our dummies accounting for the activities involved in the collaboration (*RESEARCH, MANUFACT, SUPPLY, LICENS*) and the coefficients on the variables

Table 3. Hierarchical Logit Models for Governance Choice (JV).

	(1)	(2)
LEV	1.996***	
	(0.310)	
PLEV	1.727***	
	(0.275)	
DELTA		1.014***
		(0.296)
DOWNTURN	−0.0205	−0.0851
	(0.343)	(0.339)
SAME_IND	−0.231+	−0.193
	(0.132)	(0.131)
RESEARCH	−0.153	−0.221+
	(0.119)	(0.119)
MANUFACT	1.470***	1.519***
	(0.115)	(0.114)
MARKET	−0.280*	−0.340**
	(0.118)	(0.118)
SUPPLY	−1.942***	−1.824***
	(0.393)	(0.391)
LICENS	−2.258***	−2.326***
	(0.204)	(0.203)
SUPRANATION	−1.353***	−1.379***
	(0.227)	(0.228)
SAME_STATE	0.140	0.144
	(0.127)	(0.126)
PRIORALL	0.106	0.114+
	(0.0693)	(0.0691)
RDGAP	−0.914+	−1.422**
	(0.482)	(0.501)
RASSETS	0.780***	0.832***
	(0.185)	(0.184)
AVGASSETS	0.000000763	0.00000690***
	(0.00000208)	(0.00000195)
AVGROA	0.468	0.0398
	(0.491)	(0.470)
_cons	−4.116***	−3.893***
	(0.425)	(0.430)
N	8,440	8,440
Groups	2,074	2,074
Avg. obs. per group	4.1	4.1

Standard errors in parentheses: $^+p < 0.10$; $^*p < 0.05$; $^{**}p < 0.01$; $^{***}p < 0.001$.

SUPRANATION and *SAME_IND* mirror previous studies on alliance governance (Casciaro, 2003; Oxley, 1997; Oxley & Sampson, 2004; Pisano, Russo, & Teece, 1988). However, the variable *MARKET* was found to have a negative impact in our study, while extant literature finds no significant effect. Similarly, the variable *SAMESTATE* had no significant effect in our analysis, while extant literature documents a significant negative relationship (Oxley & Sampson, 2004). The coefficient on the variable *PRIORALL* is positive and marginally significant only in model 2, consistently with studies showing that partners with repeated ties tend to adopt more complex contractual forms of governance (Casciaro, 2003; Oxley & Sampson, 2004; Van de Vrande, Vanhaverbeke, & Duysters, 2009). The negative impact of *RDGAP* mirrors Kogut and Chang (1991) and suggests firms with similar levels of sophisticated technological capabilities adopt equity JVs, potentially to share surplus related to the knowledge generated. Both *AVGASSET* and *RASSET* appear to have a significant positive influence, while previous studies report conflicting findings (Oxley, 1997).

Table 4 reports results for our leverage model related to hypothesis 5. In this model, the variable *ALLIANCES* is treated as endogenous and it was instrumented in the first stage by the average number of alliances formed in an industry in a given year, along with the first and second lag of this measure. A not reported identification test rejects the null hypothesis that excluded instruments are not relevant ($p<0.001$), while the over-identification test fails to reject the null that the instruments are uncorrelated with the error and thus valid (p-value $= 0.51$). Finally, the endogeneity tests rejects the null that the variable *ALLIANCE* can be treated as strictly exogenous, and thus confirms that instrumental variables are needed (p-value $= 0.066$). Results from the second stage fixed-effects IV regression show that after accounting for endogeneity, *ALLIANCES* has a significant ($p<0.05$) negative coefficient, thus corroborating hypothesis 5. Hence, it appears that firms intensively engaging in alliances tend to adopt lower levels of leverage, presumably to be considered more attractive partners and to encourage relation-specific investments. The control variables produced results consistent with typical models of capital structure (Banerjee et al., 2008).

Finally, in Table 5 we replicate our main analyses for the subsample of alliances in the computer, software and electronic sector. Indeed, our sample draws on the broader population of alliances established during the period 1988–2006 and included in SDC. This represents a very heterogeneous sample in terms of both the industry composition and the economic conditions at the time of alliance formation, raising concerns that our results may be driven by unobserved cross industry heterogeneity. Accordingly, as

Table 4. Fixed-Effects Instrumental Variable Regression on Firm's Leverage.

	(1)
ALLIANCES	−0.0151*
	(0.00654)
RD	−0.118***
	(0.00963)
Q	−0.0150***
	(0.000421)
TANGIBLES	0.135***
	(0.00397)
ROA	−0.135***
	(0.00409)
LASSETS	0.0299***
	(0.00143)
CAPINTENS	−0.000708***
	(0.000118)
DIV	−0.0488***
	(0.00317)
Year fixed effects	Yes
N	55,388
R^2	0.132
Adj. R^2	0.011
F	314.5
Prob > F	0.000

Standard errors in parentheses: $^+p < 0.10$; $^*p < 0.05$; $^{**}p < 0.01$; $^{***}p < 0.001$.

nearly half of our sample encompasses alliances in the computer, software and electronic sector, we restrict our attention only to this subsample under the assumption that it should be less vulnerable to the effects of unobserved variation across sectors. To further control for inter-industry heterogeneity we added in this analysis also three sub-industry dummies (IND_DUMMY1, IND_DUMMY2, IND_DUMMY3), which further capture whether a focal firm operated in the computer, software, or electronic equipment sector, respectively. Prior research also points to the competitive effects of leverage and suggests that rivals (i.e., firms operating in the same industry) tend to behave more aggressively when a firm is highly levered − such as, for example, by drastically reducing prices and engaging in predation (Chevalier, 1995a, 1995b). As similar competitive effects could also be active in alliances between rival firms, we included the variable SAME_SUB_IND, which takes on the value of one when partners in the alliance belong to the same sub-industry.[12] As expected, results from

Table 5. Analyses for the Subsample of Alliances in the Computer, Software, and Electronic Sectors.

Dependent Variables	(1) PLEV	(2) LOG(PQ)	(3) JV	(4) JV
Independent variables				
PLEV		−1.964***	1.649***	
		(0.0781)	(0.468)	
LEV	0.0334*	−0.0915	1.494**	
	(0.0170)	(0.0846)	(0.557)	
DELTA				1.464**
				(0.479)
Partner controls				
PQ	−0.00447***			
	(0.000408)			
PLASSETS	0.0248***	−0.0291***		
	(0.000904)	(0.00494)		
PROA	−0.259***	0.582***		
	(0.0102)	(0.0556)		
PRD	−0.447***	1.055***		
	(0.0263)	(0.137)		
Firm controls				
Q	−0.000105	0.00771***		
	(0.000430)	(0.00215)		
LASSETS	0.000342	0.00797		
	(0.00115)	(0.00565)		
ROA	−0.00715	−0.135*		
	(0.0114)	(0.0571)		
RD	0.0680*	−0.531***		
	(0.0282)	(0.141)		
DOWNTURN	−0.0308*	−0.156*	−0.204	−0.411
	(0.0155)	(0.0781)	(0.589)	(0.583)
IND_DUMMY1	−0.00287	0.0133	−1.001**	−1.112***
	(0.00755)	(0.0370)	(0.318)	(0.317)
IND_DUMMY2	0.00918	−0.0503	−0.349	−0.431+
	(0.00738)	(0.0366)	(0.262)	(0.256)
IND_DUMMY3	−0.0205**	0.0575	−0.905**	−1.070***
	(0.00731)	(0.0362)	(0.286)	(0.275)
Alliance controls				
SAME_SUB_IND	−0.00580	0.0312	−0.191	−0.170
	(0.00422)	(0.0213)	(0.169)	(0.170)
RESEARCH			−0.292	−0.296
			(0.191)	(0.191)
MANUFACTUR			1.986***	2.060***
			(0.180)	(0.179)
MARKET			−0.101	−0.144
			(0.191)	(0.191)

Table 5. (*Continued*)

Dependent Variables	(1) PLEV	(2) LOG(PQ)	(3) JV	(4) JV
SUPPLY			−1.278**	−1.308**
			(0.459)	(0.459)
LICENS			−2.070***	−2.088***
			(0.286)	(0.285)
SUPRANATION			−1.415***	−1.384***
			(0.407)	(0.409)
SAME_STATE			−0.0613	−0.00786
			(0.203)	(0.203)
PRIORALL			0.0614	0.0680
			(0.0907)	(0.0901)
RDGAP			−0.301	−0.634
			(0.798)	(0.811)
RASSETS			−0.131	−0.0486
			(0.310)	(0.309)
AVGASSETS			0.00000406	0.00000783*
			(0.00000355)	(0.00000334)
AVGROA			−1.130	−1.381+
			(0.758)	(0.746)
Intercept	−0.0550**	1.135***	−22.24	−24.87
	(0.0184)	(0.0920)	(5324.6)	(20890.8)
N	4,058	4,058	4,058	4,058

Standard errors in parentheses: $^+ p < 0.10$; $*p < 0.05$; $**p < 0.01$; $***p < 0.001$.

models shown in Table 5 largely support all our hypotheses except for hypothesis 2, which appears not to be supported at least in our restricted subsample of alliances arguably because of the smaller sample size.

DISCUSSION AND CONCLUSIONS

In this research, we show that financial health and leverage are important considerations in selecting alliance partners. We argue that highly levered partners are less attractive in the context of an alliance for multiple reasons. First, highly leveraged partners are more prone to liquidation and bankruptcy risks, and thus they expose the alliance (and all investments involved) to the threat of unplanned termination, potentially even despite the firms' best intentions. Second, we also argued that even when liquidation is not imminent, highly levered firms have incentives to default on their implicit claims and reduce their efforts toward the alliance. Finally, a high-leverage firm facing financial distress may threaten to prematurely terminate an alliance in order to obtain more favorable terms. Rational firms will anticipate these ex post risks and hence will evaluate each other's level of leverage when structuring transactions in the market for collaboration.

Using a large sample of strategic alliances, we show several empirical patterns consistent with this theoretical framework. The first part of our analysis clearly suggests that counter-part leverage is critical during the process of partner selection. A double-sided matching of leverage levels emerges, whereby low-leverage firms partner with other low-leverage firms and high-leverage firms seem to be constrained to partner with other high-leverage firms. Similarly, we also find that after controlling for partner quality, highly levered firms tend to ally with relatively lower quality counterparts. These findings provide additional insight to the broader literature on homophily in alliances (Gulati, 1995; Podolny, 1994; Stuart, 1998) and to recent works applying the theory of marriage to the context of the market for collaboration (Becker, 1974; Rhode-Kropf & Robinson, 2008). This literature shows that firms tend to partner with others that are similar along some dimension − such as Tobin's q (Kumar, 2010; Kumar & Park, 2012), technology profile, status, and so forth − and that this matching occurs in order to minimize the costs of ex post integration while maximizing value. Our study proposes another dimension along which alliance partners tend to be similar: their capital structure. This matching occurs because in the context of alliances, partner attractiveness is not determined exclusively by its resource endowments but also by its financial health, as firms appear to take into account both aspects when scanning for potential partners.

Our second set of results reveals an important link between firm leverage and the choice of governance form in alliances. Our findings show that leverage increases the probability of an alliance being structured as a JV. Equally interestingly, JVs appear to be more likely in the presence of greater difference among partners' leverage. Stakeholder theories of capital structure point out that high leverage makes firms less attractive transacting partners without suggesting any ex post mechanisms to mitigate concerns related to capital structure decisions. In this respect, our study has important implications because it provides additional insight by theorizing the importance of governance structures as an ex post contractual solution to such a situation. Leveraged firms can adopt equity in order to support their exchanges in the face of termination risks. Thus, equity-based governance induces relation-specific investments not only by aligning incentives through shared surplus, but also by providing an enforceable mechanism to mitigate the hazards posed by high-leverage partners.

This evidence also has interesting implications for research analyzing alliance governance from a transaction cost perspective and from a real option perspective. From a transaction cost view, our analysis shows that leverage is a critical source of relational uncertainty at the transaction level. Thus, in contrast to work that has explained governance choices by looking only at appropriability hazards (e.g., Pisano, 1989), our analysis calls for a broader view by showing that some exchange hazards may also arise from firm-level characteristics such as leverage which may lead to the adoption of equity governance. Furthermore, firms have to protect themselves not just from overt opportunism, but also from a partner firm's unintentional inability to live up to its contractual and implicit obligations.

From a real options perspective, our results also provide additional insight into the dueling options often inherent in the tradeoff between flexibility and commitment (Folta & O'Brien, 2004). According to a real options logic, firms value flexibility when faced with high uncertainty (Cuypers & Martin, 2007; Santoro & McGill, 2005; Steensma & Corley, 2001; Tong, Reuer, & Peng, 2008). Thus, they prefer less hierarchical governance modes in order to avoid the opportunity costs of irreversible investments in a shared venture. However, our study suggests that firms may be willing to commit to a more hierarchical form when faced with uncertainty arising from a partner's bankruptcy risks. By increasing barriers to exit with a JV structure, a firm mitigates the uncertainty associated with a leveraged partner as any potential scaling back of commitment from the relationship becomes more expensive. Although this sacrifices the deferment option, it also provides the low-leverage firm with the option to take on the venture in the event of unplanned termination by the partner. As a result, although it comes with an ex ante cost, this lack of flexibility reduces ex post sunk costs much more effectively as compared to a non-equity agreement in the presence of a high leverage firm.

Our analysis also documents the impact of alliances on firm's leverage decisions. Our findings corroborate the idea that high leverage introduces additional risks in an alliance, and thus leverage limits a firm's ability to transact in the market for collaboration. Accordingly, we found that alliance-intensive firms tend to adopt lower levels of leverage, potentially to attract better partners and induce specific investments. This is an important result because we believe that in a world where alliances have become an increasingly critical element of corporate strategic choices, more debate should be encouraged to understand their implications for firm characteristics, including such important decisions as capital structure. In this respect, our study is important not only because it provides preliminary evidence that alliance activity matters for leverage decisions, but it also demonstrates implications of leverage in terms of partner selection and contractual governance.

Future research could extend the present work in several ways. First, it would be worth exploring the importance of alliance heterogeneity with respect to its impact on leverage decisions in greater depth. Alliances substantially differ in terms of specificity of investments involved, partner and strategic uncertainty, and organizational structure. As a result, it would be useful to examine the capital structure implications of alliances from a portfolio perspective, rather than just an individual alliance perspective as we have done. Another interesting avenue for future research is to analyze whether bankruptcy risks influence other contractual characteristics of alliances as well. For example, firms allying with highly levered counterparts may prefer agreements with a predetermined duration or with a limited scope in order to limit the dependence on the counterpart. While lack of detailed data on our sample of alliances prevented us from studying these issues, future research on these topics could prove highly insightful.

Finally, we note an important limitation of our study in that we only analyzed the negative aspects of partner leverage. To a certain extent, we overcome this limitation when we show that high-leverage firms offer equity participation as a form of commitment toward the alliance in order to attract better partners. However, there may also be other benefits associated with highly levered partners. Extant literature suggests that financially constrained (i.e., highly levered) firms are more prone to form alliances in order to develop projects that they would not be able to pursue independently (Lerner et al., 2003; Patzel et al., 2008). Thus, while bringing instability, leverage could also force firms to externalize valuable projects that would be otherwise lost, and non-levered firms may be able to capitalize upon these opportunities. Future work could study the circumstances under which this may happen, such as how the liquidity of the market impacts alliancing behavior. Overall, our study takes an important first step at demonstrating a link between capital structure, financial health and alliance activity.

NOTES

1. For example, in 1997, Eli Lilly sold its 40% stake in its JV with Dow Chemical, named Dow Elanco, and used the proceeds of 900 million USD to pay

down debt from a recent acquisition. Similarly, General Mills sold its stake in its European JV with Pepsico for 750 million USD as part of its debt reduction efforts.

2. As an example, in 2005, the shares of brake manufacturer Pacifica fell by nearly 10% when its customer and joint venture partner, Delphi, filed for bankruptcy. A key part of Pacifica's operations was a plant that it operated jointly with Delphi to supply brakes to GM.

3. The short-term gains from such tactics would immediately benefit a firm's shareholders. On the other hand, if customers later detect opportunistic behavior and react by punishing the firm, the debt holders would bear most of the costs as they bear most of the downside risks of the firm.

4. For example, in 2009, the financially constrained De Beers asked its joint venture partner, Mountain Province Diamond, for a renegotiation of their existing agreement. The new terms were less financially onerous for De Beers and required Mountain Province to reimburse De Beers a significant portion of historic sunk costs in exchange for increased control rights in the venture. Similarly, in October 2001, Telstra rescued its debt-laden joint venture partner Austar by providing additional funding for the venture, causing shares in Austar to soar 69%.

5. This implies that a firm's leverage and its alliance activity are jointly determined. Hence, it is important to test the above argument by controlling for potential endogeneity, a point that we address in the "Methods" section.

6. Results are qualitatively unchanged if we use the book value of total assets in the denominator.

7. Following previous works on alliance governance, we exclude minority equity positions and define equity alliances as joint ventures only. However, our results are virtually unchanged when we also considered these arrangements as equity alliances.

8. To determine if a pair of firms operated in the same industry we referred to their reported four-digits SIC codes. Results are not significantly affected when three-digits SIC codes are considered.

9. Hausman and Wise (1977) emphasize that OLS applied to a sample truncated from above generally produces estimators biased toward zero.

10. Results are qualitatively unchanged when the second partner is considered.

11. Chances of a JV also increase after taking into account alliance partner level of innovativeness. For example, when considering only alliances involving two high R&D firms, chances of a JV increase from 4.5% for low leverage firms to 10.5% for high leverage firms.

12. Results are qualitatively unchanged when this variable is defined by considering partners' four-digits SIC codes.

ACKNOWLEDGMENTS

The authors wish to thank the volume editor Belén Villalonga and two anonymous reviewers for their valuable and insightful comments, which helped improve the chapter. The authors would also like to thank Giovanna Lo Nigro for her useful suggestions on the ideas developed in this chapter.

REFERENCES

Agarwal, R., Croson, R., & Mahoney, J. T. (2010). The role of incentives and communication in strategic alliances: An experimental investigation. *Strategic Management Journal*, *31*(4), 413–437.

Ahuja, G., Polidoro, F., & Mitchell, W. (2009). Structural homophily or social asymmetry? The formation of alliances by poorly embedded firms. *Strategic Management Journal*, *30*(9), 941–958.

Arino, A., Ragozzino, R., & Reuer, J. J. (2008). Alliance dynamics for entrepreneurial firms. *Journal of Management Studies*, *45*(1), 147–168.

Banerjee, S., Dasgupta, S., & Kim, Y. (2008). Buyer-supplier relationships and the stakeholder theory of capital structure. *The Journal of Finance*, *63*(5), 2507–2552.

Becker, G. S. (1974). *A Theory of Marriage*. In T. W. Schultz (Ed.), *Economics of the family: Marriage, children, and human capital*. UMI.

Boone, A. L., & Ivanov, V. I. (2012). Bankruptcy spillover effects on strategic alliance partners. *Journal of Financial Economics*, *103*(3), 551–569.

Casciaro, T. (2003). Determinants of governance structure in alliances: The role of strategic, task and partner uncertainties. *Industrial and Corporate Change*, *12*(6), 1223–1251.

Chevalier, J. A. (1995a). Capital structure and product-market competition: Empirical evidence from the supermarket industry. *The American Economic Review*, *85*(3), 415–435.

Chevalier, J. A. (1995b). Do LBO supermarkets charge more? An empirical analysis of the effects of LBOs on supermarket pricing. *The Journal of Finance*, *50*(4), 1095–1112.

Chevalier, J. A., & Scharfstein, D. S. (1995). Liquidity constraints and the cyclical behavior of markups. *The American Economic Review*, *85*(2), 390–396.

Chung, S. A., Singh, H., & Lee, K. (2000). Complementarity, status similarity and social capital as drivers of alliance formation. *Strategic Management Journal*, *21*(1), 1–22.

Cornell, B., & Shapiro, A. C. (1987). Corporate stakeholders and corporate finance. *Financial Management*, *16*(1), 5–14.

Cuypers, I. R. P., & Martin, X. (2007). Joint ventures and real options: An integrated perspective. In J. J. Reuer & W. T. Tony (Eds.), *Real option theory* (Vol. 24, pp. 103–144). Advances in Strategic Management. Bingley, UK: Emerald Group Publishing Limited.

Dyer, J., & Singh, H. (1998). The relational view: Cooperative strategies and sources of interorganizational competitive advantage. *Academy of Management Review*, *23*(4), 660–679.

Folta, T. B., & O'Brien, J. P. (2004). Entry in the presence of dueling options. *Strategic Management Journal*, *25*(2), 121–138.

Gopalakrishnan, S., Scillitoe, J. L., & Santoro, M. (2008). Tapping deep pockets: The role of resources and social capital on financial capital acquisition by biotechnology firms in biotech-pharma alliances. *Journal of Management Studies*, *45*(8), 1354–1376.

Gulati, R. (1995). Social structure and alliance formation patterns: A longitudinal analysis. *Administrative Science Quarterly*, *40*(4), 619–652.

Gulati, R., & Gargiulo, M. (1999). Where do interorganizational networks come from? *American Journal of Sociology*, *104*(5), 1439–1493.

Gulati, R., & Singh, H. (1998). The architecture of cooperation: Managing coordination costs and appropriation concerns in strategic alliances. *Administrative Science Quarterly*, *40*(4), 781–814.

Hagedoorn, J., & Frankort, H. T. (2008). The gloomy side of embeddedness: The effects of overembeddedness on inter-firm partnership formation. *Advances in Strategic Management*, 25, 503–530.

Harrigan, K. R. (1988). Strategic alliances and partner asymmetries. In F. J. Contractor & P. Lorange (Eds.). *Cooperative strategies in international business*. Lexington, MA: Lexington Books.

Hausman, J. A., & Wise, D. A. (1977). Social experimentation, truncated distributions, and efficient estimation. *Econometrica*, 45(4), 319–339.

Hennart, J. F. (1991). The transaction costs theory of joint ventures: An empirical study of Japanese subsidiaries in the United States. *Management Science*, 37(4), 483–497.

Hirsch, B. T., & Seaks, T. G. (1993). Functional form in regression models of Tobin's q. *The Review of Economics and Statistics*, 75(2), 381–385.

Hitt, M. A., Dacin, M. T., Levitas, E., Arregle, J. L., & Borza, A. (2000). Partner selection in emerging and developed market contexts: Resource-based and organizational learning perspectives. *Academy of Management Journal*, 43(3), 449–467.

Huselid, M. A., Jackson, S. E., & Schuler, R. S. (1997). Technical and strategic human resources management effectiveness as determinants of firm performance. *Academy of Management Journal*, 40(1), 171–188.

Inkpen, A. C. (2000). Research notes and communications: A note on the dynamics of learning alliances: Competition, cooperation, and relative scope. *Strategic Management Journal*, 21, 775–779.

Kale, J. R., & Shahrur, H. (2007). Corporate capital structure and the characteristics of suppliers and customers. *Journal of Financial Economics*, 83(2), 321–365.

Khanna, T., Gulati, R., & Nohria, N. (1998). The dynamics of learning alliances: Competition, cooperation, and relative scope. *Strategic Management Journal*, 19(3), 193–210.

Kogut, B., & Chang, S. J. (1991). Technological capabilities and Japanese foreign direct investment in the United States. *The Review of Economics and Statistics*, 73(3), 401–413.

Kumar, M. S. (2010). Differential gains between partners in joint ventures: Role of resource appropriation and private benefits. *Organization Science*, 21(1), 232–248.

Kumar, S., & Park, J. C. (2012). Partner characteristics, information asymmetry, and the signaling effects of joint ventures. *Managerial and Decision Economics*, 33(2), 127–145.

Lane, P. J., Salk, J. E., & Lyles, M. A. (2001). Absorptive capacity, learning, and performance in international joint ventures. *Strategic Management Journal*, 22(12), 1139–1161.

Lerner, J., Shane, H., & Tsai, A. (2003). Do equity financing cycles matter? Evidence from biotechnology alliances. *Journal of Financial Economics*, 67(2), 411–446.

Maksimovic, V., & Titman, S. (1991). Financial policy and reputation for product quality. *The Review of Financial Studies*, 4(1), 175–200.

Modigliani, F., & Miller, M. H. (1958). The cost of capital, corporation finance and the theory of investment. *The American Economic Review*, 48(3), 261–297.

Mowery, D. C., Oxley, J. E., & Silverman, B. S. (1996). Strategic alliances and interfirm knowledge transfer. *Strategic Management Journal*, 17, 77–91.

Myers, S. C., & Majluf, N. S. (1984). Corporate financing and investment decisions when firms have information that investors do not have. *Journal of Financial Economics*, 13(2), 187–221.

Opler, T. C., & Titman, S. (1994). Financial distress and corporate performance. *The Journal of Finance*, 49(3), 1015–1040.

Oxley, J. E. (1997). Appropriability hazards and governance in strategic alliances: A transaction cost approach. *Journal of Law Economics and Organization, 13*(2), 387–409.
Oxley, J. E., & Sampson, R. C. (2004). The scope and governance of international R&D alliances. *Strategic Management Journal, 25*(8–9), 723–749.
Parkhe, A. (1993). Strategic alliance structuring: A game theoretic and transaction cost examination of interfirm cooperation. *Academy of Management Journal, 36*(4), 794–829.
Patzelt, H., Shepherd, D. A., Deeds, D., & Bradley, S. W. (2008). Financial slack and the venture managers decisions to seek a new alliance. *Journal of Business Venturing, 23*(4), 465–481.
Pfeffer, J., & Nowak, P. (1976). Joint ventures and interorganizational interdependence. *Administrative Science Quarterly, 21*(3), 398–418.
Pisano, G. P. (1989). Using equity participation to support exchange: Evidence from the biotechnology industry. *Journal of Law, Economics & Organization, 5*(1), 109–126.
Pisano, G. P., Russo, M. V., & Teece, D. (1988). Joint ventures and collaborative arrangements in the telecommunications equipment industry. In D. Mowery (Ed.), *International collaborative ventures in US manufacturing* (pp. 23–70). Cambridge, MA: Ballinger.
Podolny, J. M. (1994). Market uncertainty and the social character of economic exchange. *Administrative Science Quarterly, 39*(3), 458–483.
Reuer, J. J., & Arino, A. (2002). Contractual renegotiations in strategic alliances. *Journal of Management, 28*(1), 47–68.
Reuer, J. J., & Zollo, M. (2005). Termination outcomes of research alliances. *Research Policy, 34*(1), 101–115.
Rhode-Kropf, M., & Robinson, D. T. (2008). The market for mergers and the boundaries of the firm. *The Journal of Finance, 63*(3), 1169–1211.
Ryall, M. D., & Sampson, R. C. (2009). Formal contracts in the presence of relational enforcement mechanisms: Evidence from technology development projects. *Management Science, 55*(6), 906–925.
Sadowski, B., & Duysters, G. (2008). Strategic technology alliance termination: An empirical investigation. *Journal of Engineering and Technology Management, 25*(4), 305–320.
Santoro, M. D., & McGill, J. P. (2005). The effect of uncertainty and asset co-specialization on governance in biotechnology alliances. *Strategic Management Journal, 26*(13), 1261–1269.
Simerly, L., & Li, M. (2000). Environmental dynamism, capital structure and performance: A theoretical integration and an empirical test. *Strategic Management Journal, 21*(1), 31–49.
Steensma, K. H., & Corley, K. G. (2001). Organizational context as a moderator of theories on firm boundaries for technology sourcing. *Academy of Management Journal, 44*(2), 271–291.
Stuart, T. E. (1998). Network positions and propensities to collaborate: An investigation of strategic alliance formation in a high-technology industry. *Administrative Science Quarterly, 43*(3), 668–698.
Stuart, T. E. (2000). Interorganizational alliances and the performance of firms: A study of growth and innovation rates in a high-technology industry. *Strategic Management Journal, 21*(8), 791–811.
Stuart, T. E., Hoang, H., & Hybels, R. C. (1999). Interorganizational endorsements and the performance of entrepreneurial ventures. *Administrative Science Quarterly, 44*(2), 315–349.

Teece, D. J. (1986). Profiting from technological innovation: Implications for integration, collaboration, licensing and public policy. *Research Policy, 15*(6), 285–305.

Titman, S. (1984). The effect of capital structure on a firms liquidation decision. *Journal of Financial Economics, 13*(1), 137–151.

Titman, S., & Wessel, R. (1988). The determinants of capital structure choice. *Journal of Finance, 43*(1), 1–19.

Tong, T. W., Reuer, J. J., & Peng, M. W. (2008). International joint ventures and the value of growth options. *Academy of Management Journal, 51*(5), 1014–1029.

Van de Vrande, V., Vanhaverbeke, W., & Duysters, G. (2009). External technology sourcing: The effect of uncertainty on the governance mode choice. *Journal of Business Venturing, 24*(2), 62–80.

Vicente-Lorente, J. (2001). Specificity and opacity as resource-based determinants of capital structure: Evidence for Spanish manufacturing firms. *Strategic Management Journal, 22*(2), 157–177.

Villalonga, B. (2004). Intangible resources, Tobin's q, and sustainability of performance differences. *Journal of Economic Behavior & Organization, 54*(2), 205–230.

Villalonga, B., & McGahan, A. M. (2005). The choice among acquisitions, alliances, and divestitures. *Strategic Management Journal, 26*(13), 1183–1208.

Williamson, O. E. (1985). *The economic institutions of capitalism.* New York, NY: The Free Press.

ACTIVE INVOLVEMENT OF PRIVATE EQUITY FIRMS IN PORTFOLIO COMPANIES AND ITS PERFORMANCE EFFECTS

Christian Landau

ABSTRACT

We investigate whether active involvement of private equity firms in their portfolio companies during the holding period of a later-stage private equity investment is related to increased levels in operating performance of these companies. Our analysis of unique survey data on 267 European buyouts and secondary performance data on 29 portfolio companies using partial least squares structural equation modeling indicates that private equity firms, that is, their board representatives, can increase operating performance not only by monitoring the behavior of top managers of portfolio companies, but also by becoming involved in strategic decisions and supporting top managers through the provision of strategic resources. Strategic resources, in particular expertise and networks, provided by private equity firm representatives in the form of financial and strategic involvement are associated with increases in the financial performance and competitive prospects of portfolio companies. Operational *involvement, however, is not related to changes in operating performance. In addition to empirical insights into the different types of involvement and their effects, this chapter contributes to the buyout literature by providing support for the suggested broadening of the theoretical discussion beyond the dominant perspective of agency theory through developing and testing a complementary resource-based view of involvement. This allows taking into account not only the monitoring, but also the more entrepreneurial supporting element of involvement by private equity firms.*

Keywords: Leveraged buyout (LBO); management buyout (MBO); private equity; active financial investors; active board members; resource-based view

INTRODUCTION

Private equity firms are active financial investors who become involved in portfolio companies after a buyout with the intention of increasing the value of their investment objects through improvements in operating performance (Jensen, 1989a). This involvement takes place during the holding period of a private equity investment through the monitoring and influencing of top management decisions by members of the private equity firm who serve on the boards of portfolio companies (Wright, 2013). In this chapter we are interested in the question whether the intensity of different types of involvement is associated with improvements in the operating performance of portfolio companies. Our analysis is focused on later-stage investments, that is, we examine the involvement by private equity firms in established companies that have been taken over from former owners via a buyout; we do not address venture capital firms' involvement in young ventures.

Increasing operating performance of portfolio companies through active involvement represents one of three value generation levers available to private equity firms (Berg & Gottschalg, 2005). Improvements in operating performance during the holding period are of growing importance to private equity firms (Wright, 2013), since the effectiveness of the other two value generation mechanisms, that is, financial engineering during the initial structuring of the buyout and capitalization on arbitrage when selling a portfolio company, has declined over recent years, respectively (Hoskisson, Wei, Xiwei, & Jing, 2013; Kaplan, 2009).

Private equity firms generally do not assume day-to-day operations in portfolio companies (Klein, Chapman, & Mondelli, 2013). Hence, they have only limited direct influence on operating performance. The responsibility as well as the knowledge and skills to improve a portfolio company's operating performance rest primarily with its top management team. Hence, private equity firms can only indirectly influence operating performance via the company's top management team. To do so, private equity firm members serve as representatives on the board of portfolio companies (Hoskisson et al., 2013). In this function they become involved with the top management team of a portfolio company on a continuous basis during the holding period.

Private equity firm board representatives carry out two value creating functions. The first is monitoring top managers to ensure they act in the interest of the company's owners and improve operating performance. The second is influencing decisions and supporting top managers in their attempt to improve performance (Wright, 2013). While monitoring and its effects are considered to be well researched, the support function of private equity firms is less understood. However, the latter is considered to be of higher relevance for the recent European buyout wave than for the previous U.S. buyout wave, which emphasized monitoring by private equity firms and efficiency improvements (Hoskisson et al., 2013). In this chapter we are interested in both functions, but pay special attention to the support function of board representatives.

To capture both functions we use a dual theoretical approach. We supplement the agency-theoretic logic that actions of a private equity firm's board representatives create value through monitoring top managers with the recently proposed resource-based argument that other forms of involvement also add value, if they provide portfolio companies with access to strategic resources which support top managers in their attempt to improve operating performance (Wood & Wright, 2009; Zahra & Filatotchev, 2004). Based on this general view, we develop a set of hypotheses which take a fine-grained look at how active involvement by private equity firm board representatives takes place and contributes to portfolio company performance. We pay special attention to forms of involvement that reflect resource-providing support and to effects on the competitiveness of portfolio companies as well as on changes in top managers' decision-making. Furthermore, because it represents the time frame during which private equity firms are able to actively influence top managers via board representation, we limit our analysis of involvement to the holding period and compare performance to the time before the buyout.

We test our hypotheses using survey data on 267 portfolio companies and secondary performance data on 29 portfolio companies. Our analysis applying partial least squares structural equation modeling shows that actions of private equity firms' representatives aimed at monitoring and supporting top managers are both positively associated with increases in financial performance and a portfolio company's competitive prospects. While involvement in financial and strategic matters is shown to be related to performance improvements, we are unable to detect any performance effects of operational involvement.

Our study contributes to the advancement of research on buyouts by supporting the proposed broadening of the theoretical discussion beyond the perspective of agency theory and by providing empirical insights into different types of involvement and their effects during the recent European buyout wave (Wright, 2013). Furthermore, our findings are of interest beyond the specific context of buyout research. Our results relate to the literature on support by venture capital firms in early-stage investments. Moreover, our findings are of interest to researchers who draw on the analogy of headquarters and private equity firms for conducting studies on value creation by the corporate headquarters of multi-business firms.

THEORY AND STATE OF RESEARCH

Agency-Theoretic View of Buyouts and the Role of Private Equity Firms

Following the seminal work of Jensen (1989a, 1989b), finance and management researchers have traditionally discussed buyouts from the perspective of agency theory (Jensen & Meckling, 1976) and argued that private equity firms reduce agency costs (Cumming, Siegel, & Wright, 2007; Renneboog, Simons, & Wright, 2007). Private equity firms are assumed to be better than former owners of portfolio companies at reducing managerial discretion and opportunistic behavior, and at intensifying pressure to improve organizational efficiency.

Previous research has identified three governance mechanisms that private equity firms use to reduce the opportunistic behavior of top managers and increase organizational efficiency (Hoskisson et al., 2013). The first is the use of strong financial incentives for top managers, that is, stock ownership and variable compensation to reduce their motivation for opportunistic behavior and to maximize their interest in increasing the company's efficiency and operating performance (e.g., Fox & Marcus, 1992; Jensen, 1986; Wiersema & Liebeskind, 1995). In addition to these positive incentives, private equity firms apply two governance mechanisms that reduce the decision scope of top managers and the potential for actual and undetected opportunistic behavior. The first of these two is indirect control of top managers through the high levels of debt that private equity firms use to finance a buyout (e.g., Cotter & Peck, 2001; Lichtenberg & Siegel, 1990; Shleifer & Vishny). The third governance mechanism is direct control in the form of continuous monitoring of top management behavior (e.g., Nikoskelainen & Wright, 2007; Palepu, 1990; Walsh & Kosnik, 1993). While the first two of the three governance mechanisms are mostly applied during the initial structuring of the buyout, monitoring of top managers is a continuous process performed by board representatives and of stronger relevance during the holding period. Therefore, we focus on the monitoring aspect of governance in the context of this chapter.

The central notion of agency theory that buyouts reduce agency costs through means of governance has been the theoretical basis for a large body of empirical literature, in particular on the first buyout wave in the U.S. during the 1980s and early 1990s. Overall, past empirical research provides wide support for the agency-theoretic view on buyouts, making it the dominant theoretical perspective in private equity research (Meuleman, Wright, Manigart, & Lockett, 2009a; Wood & Wright, 2009). A large number of studies have found theoretically postulated post-buyout improvements in operating performance, using factor-level productivity, accounting data, and stock-market performance as performance measures. They generally ascribe improvements in financial performance to one or several of the previously mentioned governance mechanisms. For comprehensive recent reviews of this literature, the interested reader is referred to Cumming et al. (2007), Kaplan and Strömberg (2009), and Wright (2007).

Agency-theoretic research on buyouts has a strong focus on the short-term financial performance effects of buyouts. Empirical studies generally measure performance at the time of or a few years after the exit of the private equity firm. However, several authors have pointed out that private equity firms might negatively affect portfolio companies by inducing short-term thinking, which in turn negatively impacts the company's innovativeness, strategic flexibility, and competitive ability in the long run (Bacon, Wright, Ball, & Meuleman, 2013; Folta & Janney, 2004; Palepu, 1990; Rappaport, 1990; Zahra, 1995; Zahra & Fescina, 1991). Driven by high levels of debt and pressure from private equity firms, buyouts are suspected of forcing top managers to increase short-term financial performance at the expense of the portfolio company's ability to compete with rivals and generate long-term financial performance (Klein et al., 2013). Contrasting this view, a few existing studies using longer term frames of post-exit performance and studies applying stock-market-based performance measures provide some support for the notion that buyouts are beneficial for portfolio companies also in the long term (e.g., Wright et al., 1995; Wright, Wilson, & Robbie, 1996). A recent study by Wilson, Wright, Siegel, and Scholes (2012) even finds portfolio companies to perform better in times of recession than their peers. However, compared to the body of knowledge on short-term performance improvements, little is known so far about long-term financial performance effects and strategic issues, such as the development of a portfolio company's competitiveness after a buyout.

Entrepreneurial and Resource-Based View of Buyouts and the Role of Private Equity Firms

Researchers are increasingly challenging the strong focus of early research on agency theory, stating that its theoretical representation of value creation processes initiated through buyouts is incomplete. Critics of agency-centered research, for example, Meuleman et al. (2009a) and Wright, Hoskisson, and Busenitz (2001), argue that the focus of agency theory on potentially opportunistic top managers and efficiency improvements takes a rather pessimistic view of top managers and neglects the upward potential inherent to many buyouts. For example, Wright, Robbie, and Albrighton (2000) make the conceptual argument of viewing buyouts as enablers and enhancers of strategic renewal and entrepreneurial growth. Meuleman et al. (2009a) find empirical evidence for this view in their comparison of divisional and non-divisional buyouts. The results of several empirical studies on employment development (see Bacon et al., 2013 for a review) as well as on patent filings and innovation in portfolio companies further support this perspective (Lerner, Sorensen, & Strömberg, 2011; Ughetto, 2010). Overall, recent publications seem to come to the conclusion that buyouts facilitate higher levels of entrepreneurship and innovation in portfolio companies (Klein et al., 2013).

Since the entrepreneurial potential of buyouts is not captured by agency theory (Arthurs & Busenitz, 2006), contemporary studies are supplementing agency-theoretic arguments with complementary theories to develop a more comprehensive theoretical understanding of buyouts. The introduction of resource-based theory to buyout research has been proposed previously by several authors (e.g., Barney, Wright, & Ketchen, 2001; Peteraf & Barney, 2003). However, with the exception of Meuleman et al. (2009a), the literature still lacks empirical studies that diligently pursue and test a resource-based logic on value creation through buyouts in conjunction with agency-theoretic arguments.

According to the resource-based view, a portfolio company's ability to generate competitive advantage and operating performance is dependent on its resources and capabilities (Amit & Schoemaker, 1993; Barney, 1991; Mahoney, 2001; Peteraf, 1993). Thus, even if perfectly efficient governance mechanisms, for example, monitoring by private equity firm representatives were put in place, a portfolio company's operating performance might simply be hampered due to the fact that it lacks the strategic resources required to respond entrepreneurially to market developments (Bruining, Bonnet, & Wright, 2004; Ireland, Hitt, & Sirmon, 2003; Meuleman, Wright, Manigart, & Lockett, 2009b; Wan, Hoskisson, Short, & Yiu, 2011), and develop its full market potential (Zahra & Filatotchev, 2004; Zahra, Filatotchev, & Wright, 2009). In fact, frequently being small, former family-owned businesses or non-core divisions of conglomerates rather than entire, publicly-held corporations prior to their buyouts, many European portfolio companies lack the resources required for growth and performance improvements (Bae & Hoje, 2002; Bruining et al., 2004; Chrisman, Chua, & Litz, 2004; Dawson, 2011; Meuleman et al., 2009a).

With strategic resources essential to a portfolio company's performance, the identification of resource gaps, their subsequent elimination, and the reconfiguration of existing resources to better fit environmental conditions become crucial tasks (Arthurs & Busenitz, 2006; Eisenhardt & Martin, 2000; Grant, 1991; Teece, Pisano, & Shuen, 1997). The top management team bears primary responsibility for the development and management of a portfolio company's strategic resources (Mahoney, 1995; Sirmon, Hitt, & Ireland, 2007). In their attempts to make a portfolio company more competitive, top managers will try to develop missing resources and capabilities internally or acquire resources externally (Lee, Lee, & Pennings, 2001; Maritan & Peteraf, 2011; Meuleman et al., 2009a). A private equity firm can support top managers in their quest for improving the resource base and closing resource gaps during the holding period (Barney, Ketchen, & Wright, 2011). In particular, a private equity firm will add value if it provides unique complementary resources to which a portfolio company would otherwise not have had access (Arthurs & Busenitz, 2006; Zahra et al., 2009).

By providing supporting resources, private equity firms differ from alternative sources for later-stage finance, such as bank debts and equity via public ownership (Gorman & Sahlman, 1989; Hellmann, Lindsey, & Puri, 2008), and show strong similarities to venture capital firms. Venture capital firms are known for being actively involved investors and for providing a number of valuable intangible resources to portfolio companies, for example, financial and strategic knowledge, reputation, and networks (e.g., Arthurs & Busenitz, 2006; Hellman, Hellmann, Puri, & Puri, 2000; Hochberg, Ljungqvist, & Lu, 2007; Hsu, 2004; Sapienza & Manigart, 1996). Similarly to venture capital firms, private equity firms possess no physical resources but intangible resources in addition to financial resources (Berg, 2005). Based on these resources, board members are not only able to carry out the previously mentioned monitoring function, but also serve as advisors to top managers (Barney, 2001; Hillman & Dalziel, 2003; Smart & Waldfogel, 1994). In this regard private equity firm board members are perceived to be better entrepreneurial board members than former owners (Klein et al., 2013).

HYPOTHESES DEVELOPMENT

Board Member Involvement from the Perspective of Agency Theory

Private equity firms have comprehensive information and control rights (Nikoskelainen & Wright, 2007; Singh, 1990). Therefore, private equity firm representatives are likely to detect opportunistic activities among top managers and prevent them from engaging in such actions (Weir, Laing, & Wright, 2005). Following the lines of agency theory, intensified monitoring after a buyout should therefore lead to an increase in the operating performance of portfolio companies. However, governance improvements per se, such as intensified monitoring, have no direct impact on portfolio company performance (Phan & Hill, 1995). Agency theory implies that the primary toehold of monitoring is the behavior of top managers (Wood & Wright, 2009). Therefore, intensified monitoring should be associated with a change in the behavior of top managers, which in turn leads to improved operational performance of portfolio companies. Hence, the performance enhancing effects of monitoring occur indirectly.

Top manager behavior represents a complex, multi-facet construct. In the course of this chapter we focus on top mangers' decision-making behavior. Previous research has found significant changes in the way top managers make and implement decisions after a buyout (Baker & Wruck,

1989; Green, 1992; Wright et al., 2000). With fewer possibilities for undetected opportunistic behavior, top managers will show higher levels of stockholder orientation when making decisions (Bull, 1989; Wright et al., 2001; Zahra, 1995). As a consequence, decisions will become less political and more goal-oriented (Green, 1992). Furthermore, once decisions have been taken, they will be carried out efficiently and effectively (Bruining et al., 2004). Finally, private equity firms have been found to induce more entrepreneurial thinking and acting amongst top managers during the decision-making and implementation process (Klein et al., 2013; Wright et al., 2000).

All changes in decision-making and implementation eventually reflect a higher level of shareholder orientation in decision-making and in attempts to increase the efficiency of managerial processes (Klein et al., 2013). In this chapter, we refer to any or several aspects of the previously mentioned behavior as decision-making with increased ownership orientation. Due to increased levels of monitoring, we expect top managers to show higher levels of such behavior during the holding period and at the time of exit compared to the time before the buyout. Hence, we hypothesize:

Hypothesis 1. The intensity of monitoring by a private equity firm's board representatives during the holding period is positively associated with an increase of owner-orientation in the decision-making of a portfolio company's top managers between the buyout and the time of exit.

Following the lines of agency theory, top managers' decision-making behavior itself will become more efficient and will emphasize actions that aim to improve organizational efficiency after a buyout (Lichtenberg & Siegel, 1990; Liebeskind, Wiersema, & Hansen, 1992). Top managers better utilize slack resources, eliminate wasteful spending, and abandon projects (Fox & Marcus, 1992; Phan & Hill, 1995; Singh, 1990). For example, previous research has shown that top managers sell unused assets and reduce working capital (Easterwood, Seth, & Singer, 1989; Holthausen & Larcker, 1996; Wright, Thompson, & Robbie, 1992), cut back on diversification (Seth & Easterwood, 1993; Wiersema & Liebeskind, 1995), initiate cost-cutting and cash management initiatives (Baker, 1992; Muscarella & Vetsuypens, 1990; Singh, 1990; Smith, 1990), and eliminate hierarchies (Bruining, Boselie, Wright, & Bacon, 2005; Easterwood et al., 1989; Fox & Marcus, 1992). These efficiency-increasing attempts will be reflected in the operating performance of a portfolio company, in particular in its financial performance. Hence, we hypothesize that increased levels of owner-orientation in the decision-making of top managers will be related to improvements in financial performance during the holding period.

Hypothesis 2a. An increase in the level of owner-orientation in top management decision-making processes during the holding period is positively associated with an increase in the financial performance of a portfolio company between the buyout and the time of exit.

While short-term increases in financial performance during the holding period are widely recognized in existing empirical studies, a unanimous answer to the question about the long-term and post-buyout impact of changes in the behavior of top managers is yet to be found. It is of interest to private equity firms that top managers take decisions which immediately increase organizational efficiency. However, a portfolio company's value at the time of exit is determined by its potential to compete successfully in the future and generate cash flows. Hence, private equity firms' monitoring top managers will not only emphasize short-term-oriented behavior, but also ownership-oriented behavior in the sense that top managers prepare the portfolio company for future challenges beyond the holding period. Being monitored to do so and having incentives through their own equity stake in portfolio companies, top managers will show a change in mindset and will emphasize long-range strategic acting over a short-term focus on financial performance (Wright et al., 2000).

It is difficult to evaluate future financial performance at the time of exit. However, it is possible to assess expectations about a portfolio company's ability to compete successfully in the future, which is an antecedent of future long-term financial performance. For example, studies by Palepu (1990) and Phan and Hill (1995) find increased levels of competitiveness in portfolio companies. In this chapter, we refer to an evaluation of a portfolio company's capacity to participate successfully in the marketplace and to compete with rivals in the future as a subjective assessment of it competitive prospects. Given that top managers are monitored to engage in ownership-oriented decision-making behavior that ensures the long-term survival and success of a portfolio company, we expect to find not only an increase in financial performance after a buyout, but also improved competitive prospects. Hence, we hypothesize:

Hypothesis 2b. An increase in the level of owner-orientation in top management decision-making processes during the holding period is positively associated with an increase in the competitive prospects of a portfolio company between the buyout and the time of exit.

Board Member Involvement from the Perspective of the Resource-Based View

Board members might not only carry out the previously addressed monitoring function, but also serve as advisors to top managers and support them by giving them access to the private equity firm's resources (Barney, 2001; Hillman & Dalziel, 2003; Smart & Waldfogel, 1994). In fact, board members themselves represent valuable resources (Castanias & Helfat, 2001). They can provide top managers of portfolio companies with board capital (Zahra et al., 2009). This comprises their knowledge, skills, experience, and personal networks (Hite & Vetsuypens, 1989; Rogers, Holland, & Haas, 2002; Zahra & Filatotchev, 2004). Board members representing private equity firms on portfolio company boards have usually worked for several years in financial institutions or as executives of large corporations prior to joining the private equity firm (Bacon, Wright, Demina, Bruining, & Boselie, 2008; Barber & Goold, 2007; Bruining & Wright, 2002; Kaufman & Englander, 1992). During this time, they developed expertise, skills, and networks in their respective fields and industries (Bacon et al., 2008; Collis & Montgomery, 1995; Hoskisson et al., 2013). Therefore, board members possess high levels of human and social capital (Lazarova & Taylor, 2009; Nahapiet & Ghoshal, 1998). In addition, they can draw on the private equity firm's organizational resources, that is, its financial resources, reputation, and organizational networks to support portfolio companies (Meuleman et al., 2009a).

Board representatives and their human and social capital are of unique value for portfolio companies for two reasons. First, portfolio companies are rather small firms. Such firms generally have greater difficulties than larger corporations in attracting highly qualified board members or hiring excellent human resources. However, the specific setting of private equity provides their representatives with incentives to serve on the boards of rather small companies. Second, private equity board members are better in providing social capital than other external parties, for example, strategy and financial consultants. Compared with consultants, private equity firm representatives have stronger incentives to support portfolio companies. This is due to the fact that they have a personal equity stake in the portfolio company via their participation in the private equity fund that was used to buyout the company. Furthermore, private equity representatives generally provide advice and support to portfolio companies without extra compensation. Additionally, certain resources provided by board members are subject to market failure and hard to trade on factor markets. For example, access to the personal network of board members can neither be bought nor provided by consultants. Serving on the board of portfolio companies provides private equity firm representatives with an opportunity to leverage such underutilized and often non-depleting resources.

Board members can support top managers of portfolio companies in financial, strategic, and operational matters (Meuleman et al., 2009a). Private equity firm representatives with a financial background, for example, in investment banking, can contribute their expertise to support top managers in conducting financial and asset management. This includes, for example, introducing new financial instruments and restructuring both a company's working capital and its non-current assets (Anders, 1992; Baker & Wruck, 1989; Seth & Easterwood, 1993). Furthermore, board members can use their experience as well as a private equity firm's network and reputation to support top managers in negotiating favorable conditions for debt financing (Demiroglu & James, 2010; Folta & Janney, 2004; Hillman & Dalziel, 2003; Zahra et al., 2009). Finally, even though private equity firms are reluctant to provide further equity during the holding period, a private equity firm can provide additional funds to finance attractive growth projects. This is in particular the case when a portfolio company can neither provide sufficient financial resources nor acquire debt to finance innovative projects (Dawson, 2011).

In the following, we refer to one or several actions by private equity firm board representatives related to influencing the financial management or asset structure of a portfolio company as financial involvement. Because these actions represent a provision of one or several strategic resources, financial involvement will be associated with an increase in performance. Since financial involvement aims at reducing interest pay, improving cash management, releasing unnecessarily tied-up resources, etc., we expect it to be related to increases in financial performance during the holding period. However, advice on better financial management and restructuring of the company will not only improve financial performance in the short term, but also help to prepare the portfolio company for future challenges. Therefore, we expect financial involvement to be related to a portfolio company's competitive prospects as well. Hence, we hypothesize:

Hypothesis 3a. The intensity of financial involvement by private equity firm representatives with top managers during the holding period is positively associated with an increase in the financial performance of a portfolio company between the buyout and the time of exit.

Hypothesis 3b. The intensity of financial involvement by private equity firm representatives with top managers during the holding period is positively associated with an increase in the competitive prospects of a portfolio company between the buyout and the time of exit.

Board members with top executive experience in non-financial companies are referred to as operating partners (Barber & Goold, 2007; Kester & Luehrman, 1995). They can use their experience to support top managers in strategic matters (Carpenter & Westphal, 2001; Hillman & Dalziel, 2003). Compared to representatives with investment banking experience, operating partners have more specific industry and management knowledge. Hence, they can become more involved in the actual operations of portfolio companies and cooperate with top managers. In particular, they can introduce new business and operational knowledge (Bacon et al., 2013; Hoskisson et al., 2013). For instance, they can become involved in developing the competitive strategy of a portfolio company (Bruining et al., 2004) and in the strategic restructuring activities often initiated in conjunction with buyouts (Singh, 1990; Wiersema & Liebeskind, 1995). In particular, a private equity firm's network and knowledge of mergers and acquisitions are useful for corporate development activities, that is, in gaining access to partners for acquisitions, divestments or alliances, and in executing such transactions (Hoskisson et al., 2013; Meuleman et al., 2009b; Zahra et al., 2009).

In the following, we refer to one or several actions by private equity firm board representatives related to influencing the strategy or corporate development activities of a portfolio company as strategic involvement. The strategic resources provided through the involvement will support top managers to improve the company's strategy. Hence, we expect strategic involvement to be associated with increases in financial performance during the holding period. Furthermore, strategic involvement should, in particular, support portfolio company top managers in preparing the company for the future and lay the foundation for long-term success. Thus, we expect strategic involvement to be related not only to improvements in financial performance, but also to competitive prospects. Hence, we hypothesize:

Hypothesis 4a. The intensity of strategic involvement by private equity firm representatives with top managers during the holding period is positively associated with an increase in the financial performance of a portfolio company between the buyout and the time of exit.

Hypothesis 4b. The intensity of strategic involvement by private equity firm representatives with top managers during the holding period is positively associated with an increase in the competitive prospects of a portfolio company between the buyout and the time of exit.

Board members with operational industry knowledge or a professional background as management consultants might also use their experience to support top managers of portfolio companies in improving specific operational processes (Bacon et al., 2013; Kaplan & Strömberg, 2009). In this case they would spend a lot of time with portfolio companies and strongly cooperate with top managers. In the following, we refer to any action aiming to support top managers in developing or implementing new operational business processes as operational involvement. The provision of operational knowledge and expertise through operational involvement should, in particular, be related to improvements in financial performance, but can also have an impact on future competitiveness. Hence, we hypothesize:

Hypothesis 5a. The intensity of operational involvement by private equity firm representatives with top managers during the holding period is positively associated with an increase in the financial performance of a portfolio company between the buyout and the time of exit.

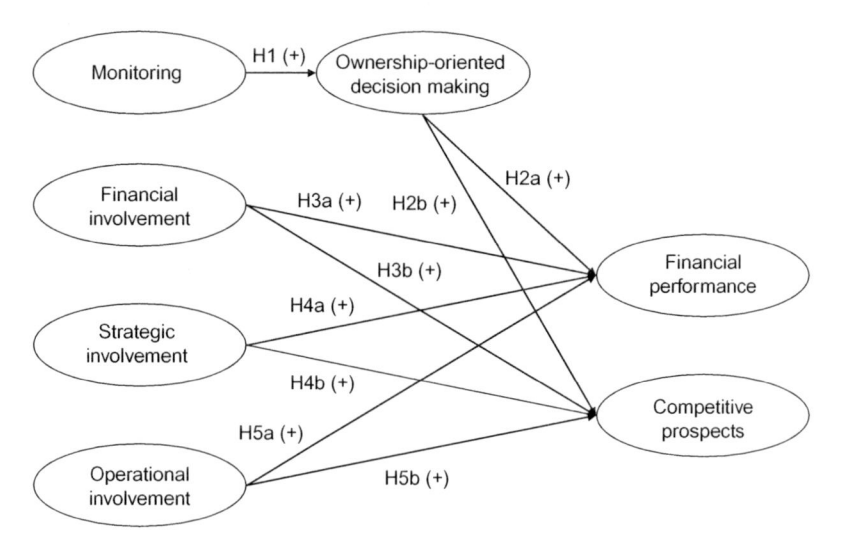

Fig. 1. Research Model.

Hypothesis 5b. The intensity of operational involvement by private equity firm representatives with top managers during the holding period is positively associated with an increase in the competitive prospects of a portfolio company between the buyout and the time of exit.

All nine hypotheses can be combined in our research model that is shown in Fig. 1.

METHODOLOGY

Data and Sample

Because we address the involvement of private equity firm representatives with top managers, detailed data are required on the actions of representatives as well as on the performance development of portfolio companies during the holding period. Since these data are not publicly available and the minimal disclosure requirements are a significant obstacle to academic buyout research based on secondary data (Dess & Robinson, 1984; Singh, 1990), we largely rely on data that was collected through a survey (Phan & Hill, 1995). We surveyed European portfolio companies subject to a buyout during the period January 1997 to March 2007. The firms were identified using the databases Venture Xpert and Private Equity Insight, leading to a survey population of 4,475 firms. CEOs and CFOs of the identified portfolio companies (Phan & Hill, 1995) were sent a paper-based questionnaire in November 2007. We chose these respondents because private equity firm representatives almost exclusively interact with them for implementing governance mechanisms and for providing resources. In addition, top managers of portfolio companies have the best insight into changes made by private equity investors and can provide information on performance.

In total, 315 questionnaires were returned by January 2008, representing a return rate of 7%. Twelve questionnaires had missing values and were excluded. Ten additional answers were omitted from the sample, because respondents were not members of the top management team or had joined the portfolio company after the exit of the private equity firms and, hence, did not represent qualified informants. We also excluded all portfolio companies in which the buyout had taken place less than six months prior to the survey to ensure that the private equity firms' actions had time to show an effect. A total of 26 cases were eliminated, resulting in a final sample size of 267 portfolio companies.

While a survey gives us unique insights into portfolio companies, it also subjects our data to a number of biases that need to be discussed and controlled. To test for non-response bias we compared the answers of early and late respondents and found non-response bias of irrelevant size (Armstrong & Overton, 1977).

In order to reduce sources of common method bias ex-ante, we made use of the procedural remedies recommended by Podsakoff et al. (2003) in designing our survey instrument. However, we rely largely on data from a single respondent for each portfolio company. Despite the potential problems associated with obtaining data from a single source, this approach was one of the few ways to collect data required for this study. Thereby, we potentially faced a problem with common method variance due to common rater effects. Our ex-post test for the existence of common method variance, using Harman's single-factor test, indicated that common method bias does not appear to be a problem; 24 factors account for 32.6–0.4% of the variance, thus no general factor emerged in the un-rotated factor structure (Podsakoff & Organ, 1986). Following Ucbasaran, Westhead, and Wright (2009), we also compared the distribution of respondents' ratings on the different indicators: ratings show high variance and are quite dispersed, which leads to the conclusion that common method bias does not seem to be a major issue.

It is common practice to complement the respondent's answers to survey questions with secondary data sources, in particular to mitigate common method bias. However, there was only limited potential for this approach in our research setting. First, being privately held, portfolio companies have low disclosure requirements for performance data that can be recorded in secondary sources. Hence, secondary databases include no or incomplete information on portfolio companies. Second, this approach would require the identification of portfolio companies to match data sources. However, we had to guarantee top managers anonymity to encourage participation; in our case this hampered combining data sources. Despite these difficulties, we were able to complement our survey data with secondary data for a limited number of portfolio companies. In our survey we gave top managers the opportunity to voluntarily disclose their company's name. Thereby, we were able to identify 153 portfolio companies. We then searched the MindGlobal database for relevant performance information on these companies. We were able to identify performance data for 29 portfolio companies. The limited results of our search highlight the difficulties in gathering secondary performance data for buyout studies (Singh, 1990). Because it was not possible to perform a meaningful test of our hypotheses with this limited set, we had to rely mainly on our survey data to test our research model. However, we were able to use the secondary performance data on the 29 portfolio companies to validate the survey measure of one of our two dependent variables.

Finally, we adopted methodological requirements to keep key informant bias to a minimum and evaluated the potential for the existence of a key informant bias (Kumar, Stern, & Anderson, 1993). We identified the appropriate informants for assessing changes made by private equity firms by relying solely on the assessments made by CEOs and CFOs of portfolio companies (Huber & Power, 1985). Questionnaires indicating other informants were excluded from the sample. Relying on one single informant is common in research areas if the main informant is surveyed (Sharfman, 1998). An assessment made by members of the portfolio company's top management was considered sufficient for our research purpose as these managers have the necessary information with which to evaluate private equity firms' measures, are key decision makers in the company and preside over the necessary degree of insight (Kumar et al., 1993).

Measures

Choice of Measurement Approach

With the exception of financial performance we chose a latent variable design for measuring their variables. Because monitoring and all three forms of involvement represent multi-facet constructs, a latent variable design using several measures allows a better measurement than a single measure. As no prior study on buyouts has tried to directly measure involvement, new measures were developed. A fundamental aspect in the development of measurement models for latent constructs is the decision whether to use reflective or formative constructs (Diamantopoulos & Winklhofer, 2001; Jarvis, MacKenzie, & Podsakoff, 2003). We chose a formative construct specification for monitoring, financial involvement, strategic involvement, and operational involvement, since the indicators of a construct represent a bundle of activities that board members might perform (Podsakoff, Shen, & Podsakoff, 2006; Williams, Vandenberg, & Edwards, 2009). Similarly to the different types of involvement, ownership-orientation of decision-making and competitive prospects cannot be measured easily by one specific indicator either. They are abstract traits and facets of success in a wider sense. Such variables are typically assumed to be of a latent nature and are measured with reflective indicators

(Hulland, 1999). Hence, we chose a reflective measurement for these variables.

As classic procedures for scale development are specified for the design of reflective measurement models only, they are not applicable for the development of indicators for formative constructs. Thus, we followed the C-OAR-SE-procedure as it can be used to develop formative measurement models as well (Rossiter, 2002). The C-OAR-SE-procedure pays special attention to ex-ante content validity of measurement models, which is ensured by systematic construct definition and classification as well as by incorporating experts into the scale development process. Accordingly, we first classified object, attribute, and rater identity of our constructs and then developed specific items for the six latent constructs in an iterative process based on 52 expert interviews. We started the indicator development process by identifying an initial set of potential value creating actions on theoretical grounds. Expert interviews were then conducted to confirm the empirical relevance of the indicators, develop the specific wording of items, and identify additional actions by private equity firms to ensure content validity. Our measurement models are listed in Tables A.1 and A.2.

Dependent Variables
By comparing pre-buyout performance and performance at the time of exit, both dependent variables measure a change in performance of a portfolio company during the holding period. To measure financial performance we opted for a single-item measure (Bergkvist & Rossiter, 2007). Since it has been used in previous studies, we chose a portfolio company's return of capital as a measure of financial performance (Meuleman et al., 2009b; Phan & Hill, 1995). As pointed out earlier, gathering specific performance data on portfolio companies poses great challenges (Singh, 1990). Portfolio companies are not required to publish financial data and they are also very reluctant to voluntarily release sensitive information. Hence, instead of asking top managers for absolute values on pre-buyout and post-exit performance, they were requested to report the percentage change in the company's return on capital employed (ROCE) over the time period between the buyout and time of exit (Meuleman et al., 2009b). In the event the portfolio company was still owned by a private equity firm, top managers were requested to report the percentage change from the buyout until the time of the survey. Seven answer categories, from a decrease to an increase of more than six percentage points, were provided. This approach allowed reducing potential biases associated with the chosen survey design (Mezias & Starbuck, 2003).

In order to validate our performance measurement, we performed a correlation analysis of the top managers' answers on the change in ROCE and retrieved the additional performance information we retrieved from MindGlobal. To do this, we calculated the change in ROCE between the buyout and the time of exit/time of the survey, based on the data from the MindGlobal database. The required information was available for 35 portfolio companies. From these we had to exclude six cases where the buyout had taken place in 2007, as it was not possible to determine a change in ROCE since the fiscal year 2007 had not elapsed at the time of the survey. The identified change in ROCE for the remaining 29 cases was then classified using the same seven categories as in our survey. The correlation analysis revealed a strong and significant correlation between the top managers' answers and the secondary data ($r = 0.741$, $p < 0.01$), giving us confidence in using our survey data for hypotheses testing.

As mentioned in the hypothesis development, we use the construct of competitive prospects for assessing the change in competitiveness of a portfolio company after the buyout and as a proxy for future financial performance, which cannot yet be determined at the time of exit. We define competitive prospects as the long-term capacity of a portfolio company to participate successfully in the marketplace and compete with rivals in the future. In order to measure these prospects, top managers were required to evaluate the extent to which the portfolio company can react more flexibly to market trends, better deal with future competitive threats and opportunities, compete more successfully in the long run, and navigate future challenges compared to the time before the buyout.

Independent Variables
We define monitoring as the sum of all actions taken by representatives of a private equity firm on a portfolio company's board, which aim to detect and deter efficiency-destroying, opportunistic behavior of top managers. In the survey top managers were asked to rate on a five point Likert scale the extent to which representatives of the private equity firm changed objectives/key performance indicators of top management, signaled more rigorous countermeasures to top management, and increased the frequency of board meetings and other forms of interaction with top management.

Financial involvement is defined as the sum of all actions taken by a private equity firm to influence the financial and asset management of a portfolio company. These actions are based on the experience, skills, and networks of private equity representatives in the financial community. Five theoretically based and empirically relevant actions by private equity firms were used to measure financial involvement. Top managers were asked to rate on a five point Likert scale to which extent representatives of private equity firms provided access to additional equity, introduced new types of financial instruments, provided access to external sources of funds, became involved in the optimization of the portfolio company's working capital, and supported top managers to optimize the portfolio company's capital structure.

We define strategic involvement as the sum of all actions by a private equity firm, which aim to support the strategy and corporate development activities of a portfolio company's top managers. Three activities by private equity firms were used to measure strategic involvement on five point Likert scales. Top managers were asked to what extent board representatives from the private equity firm became involved in the company's strategy, established contact to potential transaction partners for acquisitions, divestures or alliances, and supported the implementation of such transactions. These actions represent the experience, skills, and networks of private equity firm representatives in the area of strategic management.

Operational involvement is defined as the sum of all actions by a private equity firm, which aims to support the activities of a portfolio company's top managers targeted at improving operational business processes. Compared with strategic involvement, this type of involvement is more specific and requires private equity firms to have experience and skills in operational management. We asked top managers about the extent, measured on a five point Likert scale, to which the private equity firm highlighted areas for the improvement of operational business processes, became involved in the redesign of business processes, and supported top managers in the implementation of redesigned business processes.

Finally, as outlined earlier, we define owner-oriented decision-making in the context of this chapter as the extent to which the top management team's decision-making and implementation takes place in the interest of the company's owners. It is measured using five reflective indicators that reflect changes in the top management team's decision-making and implementation processes. Top managers were asked to rate on a five point scale the extent to which they agree with the statements that since the buyout management makes decisions more quickly, carries out decisions more rigorously, decides more rationally and with more goal orientation, thinks and acts less politically, and thinks and acts more like entrepreneurs.

We accomplished a pre-test for all measurement models consisting of latent variables with 10 experts. The indicator-allocation-test was used for the pre-test. Proportion-of-substantive-agreement-indices and substantive-validity-coefficient indices were calculated for each indicator or construct. Results were uncritical as both indices were above the critical thresholds of 0.8 and 0.6. As a consequence, we can concede sufficient levels of expert validity to all constructs (Anderson & Gerbing, 1991).

Control Variables
We controlled for a number of factors that might provide alternative explanations for performance differences of portfolio companies. Due to the variation in size and industry of portfolio companies, we controlled for their size measuring the sales volume, and for industry environment using a dummy variable to account for companies operating in a manufacturing versus a service industry. Furthermore, we controlled for the time when the buyout took place, whether buyouts were a primary or secondary buyout, took place in the UK or continental Europe, and whether they were performed by an Anglo-Saxon or Continental European private equity firm. We also controlled for the duration of the holding period measured in years and whether a company was still part of the portfolio of the private equity firm or had been resold at the time of the survey. We included a dummy variable to take potential syndication of private equity firms into account. Furthermore, we controlled whether our respondents had worked with the portfolio company prior to the buyout or joined it as part of the buyout. To capture resource support by external parties other than the private equity firm's representatives, we controlled for use of strategic and financial consultants. Finally, we introduced a last control variable to take into consideration the effect of cooperation with other portfolio companies that might have been initiated by private equity firms.

RESULTS

Assessment of Measurement Models

We first evaluated the reliability and validity of our measurement models before assessing the quality of our structural model and testing our hypotheses (Chin, 1998; Hulland, 1999). Since the traditional assessments of reliability and validity is not applicable to formative constructs, we assessed formative measurement models separately from reflective constructs (Bagozzi, 1994; Diamantopoulos, Riefler, & Roth, 2008). All calculations were performed using smartPLS and SPSS 21 (Ringle, Wende, & Will, 2005) (Table A.3).

We evaluated the reliability and validity of our reflectively specified variables based on the criteria suggested by Hair et al. (2001) and Henseler, Ringle, and Sinkovics (2009). As shown in Table A.4, all reflective indicators are significantly associated with their respective constructs and all loadings are above the threshold of 0.7, indicating high levels of indicator reliability (Bagozzi, Yi, & Phillips, 1991; Götz, Liehr-Gobbers, & Krafft, 2010). Since all indicator loadings fall into a narrow range, we can also assert convergent reliability for all reflective constructs (Chin, 2010). Further, all reflective measurement models show sufficient levels of internal consistency. Table A.4 reveals that values for Cronbach's Alpha (a) and composite reliability (ρ_c) exceed the threshold of 0.7 (Bagozzi & Yi, 1988; Nunnally & Bernstein, 1994). As all constructs show levels for average variance extracted (AVE) above the critical value of 0.5, sufficient convergent validity is also given (Fornell & Larcker, 1981; Götz et al., 2010). Finally, we assessed discriminant validity (Bagozzi & Phillips, 1982; Henseler et al., 2009). We examined uni-dimensionality based on the cross loadings of indicators, which showed that no reflective indicator loads higher on the other endogenous constructs in our model (Hair, Sarstedt, Ringle, & Mena, 2012). Additionally, we checked the Fornell–Larcker criterion (Fornell & Larcker, 1981). Based on the data in Tables A.5 and A.6, both tests assert sufficient levels of discriminant validity.

Since their different measurement logic renders the use of criteria designed for reflective constructs (Diamantopoulos & Siguaw, 2006), we used the guidelines of Hair et al. (2001) and Henseler et al. (2009) to evaluate formative constructs. We tested for multicollinearity using variance inflation factors (VIF) (Cassel, Hackl, & Westlund, 1999; Diamantopoulos & Winklhofer, 2001). As shown in Table A.7, all VIF are below commonly cited value of 10 and also below the more conservative threshold of 5 (Hair, Ringle, & Sarstedt, 2011), indicating no concerning levels of multicollinearity (Belsley, Kuh, & Welsch, 1980; Götz et al., 2010). Further, we assessed indicator weights and their significance using non-parametric bootstrapping (Chin, 1998; Tenenhaus, Vinzi, Chatelin, & Lauro, 2005). The results show that most indicators significantly influence their corresponding constructs and that there are differences in their relative importance (Götz et al., 2010). However, since there is no boundary value that has to be met (Chin, 1998) and because each indicator represents an integral part of our construct definition, we did not eliminate indicators with small weights (Jarvis et al., 2003).

Assessment of the Structural Model

We evaluated our structural model using Stone-Geisser criterion (Q^2) (Geisser, 1975; Stone, 1974), VIF at the structural level (Götz et al., 2010), and coefficient of determination (R^2) (Chin, 1998). Values for Q^2 were obtained by means of the blindfolding procedure, using an omission distance of 7 (Tenenhaus et al., 2005; Wold, 1982). The results are shown in Table A.8. As the values for Q^2 are above the critical threshold of 0 and because VIF are well below critical values, we can ascribe predictive relevance and no problematic levels of multicollinearity (Götz et al., 2010). Acceptable R^2 values depend on the research context (Hair et al., 2011). For financial performance the value of R^2 is moderate; for ownership-oriented decision-making and competitive prospects R^2 can be characterized as moderate to substantial (Chin, 1998). As we are analyzing a special component of performance improvements, that is, the contribution through involvement, these levels of R^2 are realistic.

We evaluated the sign and magnitude of path coefficients as well as the t-values, which were obtained by applying non-parametric bootstrapping (Chin, 1998; Efron & Tibshirani, 1993; Tenenhaus et al., 2005). Further, we calculated total effects (Cohen, 1988). The effects of our control variables are summarized in Table A.9. With regard to the proposed relationships of our research model, the data summarized in Table A.10 give us reason to support six hypotheses because coefficients show the expected signs are above the value of 0.1 and are significant at a level of $p < 0.05$ or higher, while we have to reject three hypotheses (Table A.11).

Our results show a strong association between monitoring intensity and increases in ownership-orientated decision-making of top managers. Increased levels of this behavior are in turn significantly associated with improvements in the financial performance of portfolio companies and their competitive prospects. Hence, we find supporting evidence for hypotheses 1, 2a, and 2b. Likewise, our results give reason to support hypotheses 3a and 3b, since we find significant relationships between the financial involvement by private equity firm representatives and financial performance as well as the competitive prospects of portfolio companies. Strategic involvement is shown to be significantly related to increases in competitive prospects, but not to the financial performance of portfolio companies. Hence, while we find support for hypothesis 4b, we have to reject 4a. Finally, since we find no significant associations of operational involvement either with financial performance or competitive prospects, we reject hypotheses 5a and 5b.

A closer look at total effects reveals that actions associated with monitoring have about the same total effect on financial performance and competitive prospects as the combined total effects of significant forms of involvement. The total effect of monitoring on financial performance is only slightly lower than the effect of financial involvement; the effect of monitoring on competitive prospects is marginally higher than the combined effects of financial and strategic involvement. For both, monitoring and supporting forms of involvement, the total effects on competitive prospects are twice as high as on financial performance.

DISCUSSION AND CONCLUSION

Contribution

Our results are primarily of importance to the literature on buyouts; they are however also of relevance to researchers interested in value creation by venture capital firms and corporate headquarters. We contribute to the buyout literature in three major ways. First, our findings support the proposed usefulness of the joint use of agency theory and the resourced-based view (Meuleman et al., 2009a). Our empirical findings are well in line with empirical studies that attribute improvements in the financial performance of portfolio companies to changes in governance mechanisms and a reduction of agency costs. However, our results also show that private equity firms can go beyond this by providing resources to portfolio companies through involvement. We thereby contribute to the development of the resource-based view of supporting involvement. Through the investment of financial resources in portfolio companies private equity firms take on a capitalist entrepreneurial role (Klein et al., 2013), and leverage intangible resources, for example, experience, reputation, and networks, which are hard to trade on factor markets. The fact that the total effect of monitoring is about the same size as the sum of the total effects of resource-provision involvement implies that agency theory should not be replaced by the resource-based view or other theories, but rather be supplemented by complementary approaches. Thus, our findings support the revitalization currently taking place in the theoretical discussion on buyouts, which is largely stuck in the 1990s (Wood & Wright, 2009). For private equity firms, the ability to add value by a supporting portfolio companies represents a way to differentiate themselves in the increased competition for funds from investors and attractive portfolio companies (Lerner, 2011; Nielsen, 2008).

Second, our findings provide novel empirical insights into buyouts. Authors have called for more research on buyouts in Continental Europe (Weir et al., 2005; Wright, 2013) and studies based on survey data (Wood & Wright, 2009). By using survey data on companies from the UK as well as Continental Europe, we help to advance research beyond archival data and the focus on North America (Amess, 2002).

A third contribution this chapter makes is that it helps to open the black box of how involvement by private equity firm representatives supports performance improvements. To our best knowledge, the explicit analysis of a change in top manager behavior, as implied by agency theory, represents a novelty in private equity research. Together with our analysis of the different types of potential resource-providing forms of involvement our study helps to develop a finer-grained picture of involvement and its effects during the holding period of private equity investments. Our findings on competitive prospects are of particular interest in this context. They are of relevance to the debate on whether private equity firms are short-term-oriented investors and harm portfolio companies' long-term survival.

Their findings on buyouts are also of interest to the related literature on the involvement of venture capital firms in early-stage investments. Studies have found venture capital firms to have value adding monitoring and support functions (e.g., Hellmann & Puri, 2002; Hochberg, 2012; Kaplan & Strömberg, 2004). In contrast to the buyout literature, there is a consensus among researchers that venture capital firms can improve the competitiveness and performance of portfolio companies by providing support and becoming involved in key decisions (e.g., MacMillan, Kulow, & Khoylian, 1989; Sapienza, 1992; Sapienza & Manigart, 1996; Schefczyk & Gerpott, 2001). Our results help to build similar knowledge on this function in the context of later-stage investment. However, resource-based support in the case of buyouts is different to the venture capital context. Unlike early-stage ventures, portfolio companies represent mature firms. Hence, they do not require support for the setting up or professionalization of operations. Similarly, even though private equity firms often exchange top managers, portfolio companies typically have professional management teams and require less support in setting up general management processes (Hellmann & Puri, 2002). However, involvement reflecting the provision of specific knowledge or network access adds value not only in early-stage, but also in later-stage investments.

Finally, our findings are of relevance to researchers who are interested in diversified conglomerates and value creation by corporate headquarters. Private equity firms and their portfolio companies are sometimes cited as a special type of (unrelated) multi-business firm (Collis, 1996; Goold & Luchs, 1993; Klein et al., 2013). While there are a number of differences between the corporate center of a multi-business firm and a private equity firm as the owner of several portfolio companies, there are also several similarities between both organizational forms (Baker & Montgomery, 2009). In particular, both entities have to justify their existence as a capital market intermediary and the existence of the portfolio as a whole (Campbell, Goold, & Alexander, 1995a; Collis & Montgomery, 1998). They have to create value by performing certain functions more efficiently than through market transactions or within portfolio companies (Foss, 1997; Teece, 1982). Such "parenting effects" generally unfold through the influencing effect of managers and the improved operating performance of business units (Foss, 1997; Goold & Campbell, 2002; Porter, 1987).

Previous multi-business firm research has identified an administrative and an entrepreneurial value creation function of corporate headquarters (Chandler, 1991). These relate strongly to the monitoring and support function of a private equity firm. Interestingly, we find private equity firms that generally seek no integration across portfolio companies and hence forfeit any potential synergy (Jensen, 1989a) can contribute to operating performance beyond their "loss preventive" monitoring function. In contrast to the often followed perspective in multi-business firm research, the value they create through their entrepreneurial function does not stem from horizontal synergy via the integration of portfolio companies and their resources, but from the interaction of the headquarters with business units. It results from leveraging resources that are embedded within the private equity firms and its members and shared with portfolio companies. Thereby, private equity firms go beyond the minimum parenting role and take on an active value adding parenting role (Goold & Campbell, 2002). In order to do so, they use a mixture of informal strategic and financial control to add value to their portfolio companies (Campbell & Goold, 1990; Goold, 1991).

Private equity firms pursue a specific parenting style. They represent a small temporal "headquarter," combining elements of financial control and informal strategic control. Their portfolio companies provide a specific parenting opportunity for this style (Campbell et al., 1995a; Campbell, Goold, & Alexander, 1995b). However, parenting opportunities are of limited duration (Collis, 1996). Once all the resources of the private equity firm have been leveraged, a portfolio company needs a new parent company that can provide additional value creating resources and is therefore resold. This logic of temporally adding value to businesses can be generalized to a certain extent to headquarters of similar characteristics managing similar portfolio companies as private equity firms. For a detailed discussion of value creation through interaction between business units and corporate centers using private equity firms as an example, the interested reader is referred to a recent study by Landau and Bock (2013).

Limitations

As any empirical work, our study is subject to a number of limitations. First, buyouts are a heterogeneous phenomenon, which we do not take into account in our analysis. However, it could be argued that the relevance of monitoring and support by board members depend on the buyout type.

Second, we measure changes in financial performance and competitive prospects between the buyout and exit. However, the length of the holding period of a private equity investment varies between one and seven years in our sample. Thus, we neglect the temporal component in assessing performance improvements, which is particularly important in the private equity industry where the internal-rate-of-return serves as the key performance indicator for an investment. Also, the costs private equity firms incur to monitor top managers and provide resources are not taken into consideration. Furthermore, we look at differences between private equity firms and changes in portfolio companies over time. This approach only allows us to say that active private equity firms are more successful in increasing operating performance during the holding period than less active firms. Determining whether they are also the "better parent company" in relation to other owners of portfolio companies is not possible. This would require a comparison of portfolio companies with similar firms under different ownership regimes.

A third potential limitation of our results lies in our decision to use a survey to generate our data. It has to be kept in mind that, even though our analysis reveals no problematic levels of common method variance, all variables with the exception of financial performance are measured with perceptual self-reported data from top managers. In particular, in the case of ownership-orientation of decision-making, evaluated by top managers themselves, this approach might reduce construct validity. Also, subjective reports about buyouts that took place in the past might be biased due to the fact that respondents might not remember all aspects of involvement.

Fourth, even though we place strong emphasis on the development process of our newly conceptualized measurement models and have applied the comprehensive C-OAR-SE procedure, which aims to ensure high content validity of constructs, we run the risk of validity problems as all of our measurement models are newly conceptualized. This issue is particularly the case for ownership-oriented decision-making and competitive prospects, but also for formative constructs, since each indicator represents an essential component of the construct and mistakenly omitting an indicator would reduce the validity of our measurement.

Fifth, our data show a slight overrepresentation of portfolio companies from Scandinavian and German-speaking countries and an underrepresentation of British, French, and South European countries. Furthermore, even though we controlled for the time of the buyout, it should be kept in mind that our sample includes private equity investments that took place throughout almost one decade.

Future Research

Based on the findings and the limitations of this study we can make a number of suggestions for future research projects. First, while our study examines monitoring and resource-providing involvement as independent aspects of involvement, future work should test whether these factors mutually reinforce each other. Second, private equity research should increasingly take on a contingency perspective. In particular, future studies have to take the heterogeneity of buyout types as moderators into account (Bacon et al., 2013; Nikoskelainen & Wright, 2007; Wood & Wright, 2009). Further interesting contingencies that might have an impact on operating performance are external factors such as the industry context of portfolio companies within Europe (Wright et al., 1994), and internal factors such as size, financial standing, growth perspectives, and initiators of buyouts. Different portfolio companies might need different parenting styles by private equity firms. Further, the institutional context (Meuleman & Wright, 2011; Pe'er & Gottschalg, 2011) might influence monitoring and involvement by private equity firms.

The fact that we find that it possible for private equity firm representatives to increase operating performance by providing resources to portfolio companies opens up a number of interesting future research questions. From the perspective of portfolio companies, we consider analyzing in detail how top managers can use the resources provided by private equity firms to build up resources and capabilities in portfolio companies and how organizational learning can actually take place to be promising next steps in the advancement of resource-based research on private equity firms. In this context, future research might take a more elaborate perspective than the simple resource-provision perspective of this chapter. Monitoring and support could be seen as measures to induce dynamic capabilities in portfolio companies (Arthurs & Busenitz, 2006). From the perspective of private equity firms, a relevant question for future research would be how private equity firms learn and build up resources and capabilities over time. Further, the question arises as to whether private equity firms are more successful if they focus on portfolio companies that have a particular need for the resources private equity firms can provide. Thus, specialization and experience of private equity firms become important aspects of value addition (Cressy, Munari, & Malipiero, 2007) as well as looking at portfolio structures from a resource-needs perspective.

Third, future research should address further mediating factors. Our study focuses on owner-orientation of decision-making as one dimension of management behavior. The analysis of factors such as entrepreneurial orientation or innovative capabilities of portfolio companies represent promising concepts to advance our understanding of the upside potential of buyouts.

REFERENCES

Amess, K. (2002). Management buyouts and firm-level productivity − evidence from a panel of UK manufacturing firms. *Scottish Journal of Political Economy, 49*, 304−317.

Amit, R., & Schoemaker, P. (1993). Strategic assets and organizational rent. *Strategic Management Journal, 14*, 33−46.

Anders, G. (1992). The barbarians in the boardroom. *Harvard Business Review, 70*, 79−87.

Anderson, J., & Gerbing, D. (1991). Predicting the performance of measures in a confirmatory factor analysis with a pretest assessment of their substantive validities. *Journal of Marketing Research, 76*, 732−740.

Armstrong, S., & Overton, T. (1977). Estimating nonresponse bias in mail surveys. *Journal of Marketing Research, 14*, 396−402.

Arthurs, J., & Busenitz, L. (2006). Dynamic capabilities and venture performance − The effects of venture capitalists. *Journal of Business Venturing, 21*, 195−215.

Bacon, N., Wright, M., Ball, R. O. D., & Meuleman, M. (2013). Private equity, HRM, and employment. *Academy of Management Perspectives, 27*, 7−21.

Bacon, N., Wright, M., Demina, N., Bruining, H., & Boselie, P. (2008). The effects of private equity and buy-outs on HRM in the UK and the Netherlands. *Human Relations, 61*, 1399−1433.

Baker, G. P., & Montgomery, C. A. (2009). *Conglomerates and LBO associations: A comparison of organizational forms*. Harvard Business School Working Paper No. 10-024. September 2009.

Bae, S., & Hoje, J. (2002). Consolidating corporate control – Divisional versus whole company leveraged buyouts. *Journal of Financial Research, 25*, 247–263.

Bagozzi, R. (1994). Structural equation models in marketing research – Basic principles. In R. Bagozzi (Ed.), *Principles of marketing research* (pp. 317–386). Cambridge: Blackwell.

Bagozzi, R., & Phillips, L. (1982). Representing and testing organizational theories – A holistic construal. *Administrative Science Quarterly, 27*, 459–489.

Bagozzi, R., & Yi, Y. (1988). On the evaluation of structural equation models. *Journal of the Academy of Marketing Science, 16*, 74–97.

Bagozzi, R., Yi, Y., & Phillips, L. (1991). Assessing construct validity in organizational research. *Administrative Science Quarterly, 36*, 421–458.

Baker, G. P. (1992). Beatrice: A study in the creation and destruction of value. *The Journal of Finance, 47*, 1081–1119.

Baker, G., & Wruck, K. (1989). Organizational changes and value creation in leveraged buyouts – The case of O.M. Scott & Sons. *Journal of Financial Economics, 25*, 163–190.

Barber, F., & Goold, M. (2007). The strategic secret of private equity. *Harvard Business Review, 85*, 53–61.

Barney, J. (1991). Firm resources and sustained competitive advantage. *Journal of Management, 17*, 99–120.

Barney, J. (2001). Resource-based theories of competitive advantage – A ten-year retrospective on the resource-based view. *Journal of Management, 27*, 643–650.

Barney, J., Ketchen, D., & Wright, M. (2011). The future of resource-based theory – Revitalization or decline. *Journal of Management, 37*(5), 1299–1315.

Barney, J., Wright, M., & Ketchen, D. (2001). The resource-based view of the firm – Ten years after 1991. *Journal of Management, 27*, 625–641.

Belsley, A. D., Kuh, E., & Welsch, R. E. (1980). *Regression diagnostics*. New York, NY: Wiley.

Berg, A. (2005). *What is strategy for buyout associations*. Berlin: EVCA.

Berg, A., & Gottschalg, O. (2005). Understanding value generation in buyouts. *Journal of Restructuring Finance, 2*, 9–37.

Bergkvist, L., & Rossiter, J. R. (2007). The predictive validity of multiple-item versus single-item measures of the same constructs. *Journal of Marketing Research, 44*, 175–184.

Bruining, H., Bonnet, M., & Wright, M. (2004). Management control systems and strategy change in buyouts. *Management Accounting Research, 15*, 155–177.

Bruining, H., Boselie, P., Wright, M., & Bacon, N. (2005). The impact of business ownership change on employee relations: Buy-outs in the UK and the Netherlands. *International Journal of Human Resource Management, 16*, 345–365.

Bruining, H., & Wright, M. (2002). Entrepreneurial orientation in management buy-outs and the contribution of venture capital. *Venture Capital, 4*, 147–168.

Bull, I. (1989). Financial performance of leveraged buyouts – An empirical analysis. *Journal of Business Venturing, 4*, 263–279.

Campbell, A., & Goold, M. (1990). Adding value from corporate headquarters. In D. Hussey (Ed.), *International review of strategic management* (pp. 219–240). Hoboken, NJ: Wiley

Campbell, A., Goold, M., & Alexander, M. (1995a). Corporate strategy – The quest for parenting advantage. *Harvard Business Review*, 73, 120–132.
Campbell, A., Goold, M., & Alexander, M. (1995b). The value of the parent company. *California Management Review*, 38, 79–97.
Carpenter, M. A., & Westphal, J. D. (2001). The strategic context of external network ties – Examining the impact of director appointments on board involvement in strategic decision making. *Academy of Management Journal*, 44, 639–660.
Cassel, C., Hackl, P., & Westlund, A. (1999). Robustness of partial least-squares method for estimating latent variable quality structures. *Journal of Applied Statistics*, 26, 435–446.
Castanias, R., & Helfat, C. (2001). The managerial rents model – Theory and empirical analysis. *Journal of Management*, 27, 661–678.
Chandler, A. (1991). The functions of the HQ unit in the multibusiness firm. *Strategic Management Journal*, 12, 31–50.
Chin, W. (1998). The partial least squares approach to structural equation modeling. In G. Marcoulides (Ed.), *Modern methods for business research* (pp. 295–336). Mahwah, NJ: Lawrence Erlbaum Associates.
Chin, W. (2010). How to write up and report PLS analyses. In V. Vinzi, W. Chin, J. Henseler, & H. Wang (Eds.), *Handbook of partial least squares: Concepts, methods and applications* (pp. 655–690). Heidelberg: Springer.
Chrisman, J. J., Chua, J. H., & Litz, R. A. (2004). Comparing the agency costs of family and non-family firms: Conceptual issues and exploratory evidence. *Entrepreneurship Theory & Practice*, 28, 335–354.
Cohen, J. (1988). *Statistical power analysis for behavioral sciences*. Hillsdale, NJ: Lawrence Erlbaum Associates.
Collis, D. J. (1996). Corporate strategy in multibusiness firms. *Long Range Planning*, 29, 416–418.
Collis, D., & Montgomery, C. (1995). Competing on resources. *Harvard Business Review*, 73, 118–128.
Collis, D., & Montgomery, C. (1998). Creating corporate advantage. *Harvard Business Review*, 76, 70–83.
Cotter, J., & Peck, S. (2001). The structure of debt and active equity investors – The case of the buyout specialist. *Journal of Financial Economics*, 59, 101–147.
Cressy, R., Munari, F., & Malipiero, A. (2007). Playing to their strengths? Evidence that specialization in the private equity industry confers competitive advantage. *Journal of Corporate Finance*, 13, 647–669.
Cumming, D., Siegel, D., & Wright, M. (2007). Private equity, leveraged buyouts and governance. *Journal of Corporate Finance*, 13, 439–460.
Dawson, A. (2011). Private equity investment decisions in family firms: The role of human resources and agency costs. *Journal of Business Venturing*, 25, 189–199.
Demiroglu, C., & James, C. M. (2010). The role of private equity group reputation in LBO financing. *Journal of Financial Economics*, 96, 306–330.
Dess, G., & Robinson, R. (1984). Measuring organizational performance in the absence of objective measures – the case of the privately-held firm and conglomerate business unit. *Strategic Management Journal*, 5, 265–273.
Diamantopoulos, A., Riefler, P., & Roth, K. P. (2008). Advancing formative measurement models. *Journal of Business Research*, 61, 1203–1218.

Diamantopoulos, A., & Siguaw, J. A. (2006). Formative versus reflective indicators in organizational measure development: A comparison and empirical illustration. *British Journal of Management, 17*, 263–282.
Diamantopoulos, A., & Winklhofer, H. (2001). Index construction with formative indicators – An alternative to scale development. *Journal of Marketing Research, 38*, 269–277.
Easterwood, J., Seth, A., & Singer, R. (1989). The impact of leveraged buyouts on strategic direction. *California Management Review, 32*, 30–43.
Efron, B., & Tibshirani, R. (1993). *An introduction to the bootstrap*. New York, NY: Chapman & Hall/CRC.
Eisenhardt, K., & Martin, J. (2000). Dynamic capabilities: What are they? *Strategic Management Journal, 21*, 1105–1121.
Folta, T., & Janney, J. (2004). Strategic benefits to firms issuing private equity placements. *Strategic Management Journal, 25*, 223–242.
Fornell, C., & Larcker, D. (1981). Evaluating structural equation models with unobservable variables and measurement errors. *Journal of Marketing Research, 18*, 39–50.
Foss, N. (1997). On the rationals of corporate headquarters. *Industrial & Corporate Change, 6*, 313–338.
Fox, I., & Marcus, A. (1992). The causes and consequences of leveraged management buyouts. *Academy of Management Review, 17*, 62–85.
Geisser, S. (1975). A predictive approach to the random effect model. *Biometrika, 61*, 101–107.
Goold, M. (1991). Strategic control in the decentralized firm. *Sloan Management Review, 32*, 69–81.
Goold, M., & Campbell, A. (2002). Parenting in complex structures. *Long Range Planning, 35*, 219–243.
Goold, M., & Luchs, K. (1993). Why diversify? Four decades of management thinking. *Academy of Management Executive, 7*, 7–25.
Gorman, M., & Sahlman, W. A. (1989). What do venture capitalists do? *Journal of Business Venturing, 4*, 231.
Grant, R. (1991). The resource-based theory of competitive advantage – Implications for strategy formulation. *California Management Review, 33*, 114–135.
Green, S. (1992). The impact of ownership and capital structure on managerial motivation and strategy in management buy-outs: A cultural analysis. *Journal of Management Studies, 29*, 513–535.
Götz, O., Liehr-Gobbers, K., & Krafft, M. (2010). Evaluation of structural equation models using the Partial Least Squares (PLS) approach. In V. Vinzi, W. Chin, J. Henseler, & S. H. Wang (Eds.), *Handbook of partial least squares* (pp. 691–711). Heidelberg: Springer.
Hair, J. F., Ringle, C. M., & Sarstedt, M. (2011). PLS-SEM: Indeed a silver bullet. *Journal of Marketing Theory & Practice, 19*, 139–152.
Hair, J., Sarstedt, M., Ringle, C., & Mena, J. (2012). An assessment of the use of partial least squares structural equation modeling in marketing research. *Journal of the Academy of Marketing Science, 40*, 414–433.
Hellman, T., Hellmann, T., Puri, M., & Puri, T. (2000). The interaction between product market and financing strategy: The role of venture capital. *Review of Financial Studies, 13*, 959–984.

Hellmann, T., Lindsey, L., & Puri, M. (2008). Building relationships early: Banks in venture capital. *Review of Financial Studies*, *21*, 513–541.
Hellmann, T., & Puri, M. (2002). Venture capital and the professionalization of start-up firms: Empirical evidence. *Journal of Finance*, *57*, 169–197.
Henseler, J., Ringle, C., & Sinkovics, R. (2009). The use of partial least squares path modeling in international marketing. *Advances in International Marketing*, *20*, 277–319.
Hillman, A. J., & Dalziel, T. (2003). Boards of directors and firm performance – Integrating agency and resource dependence perspectives. *Academy of Management Review*, *28*, 383–396.
Hite, G., & Vetsuypens, M. (1989). Management buyouts of divisions and shareholder wealth. *Journal of Finance*, *44*, 953–970.
Hochberg, Y. V. (2012). Venture capital and corporate governance in the newly public firm. *Review of Finance*, *16*, 429–480.
Hochberg, Y. V., Ljungqvist, A., & Lu, Y. (2007). Whom you know matters: Venture capital networks and investment performance. *Journal of Finance*, *62*, 251–301.
Holthausen, R., & Larcker, D. (1996). The financial performance of reverse leveraged buyouts. *Journal of Financial Economics*, *42*, 293–332.
Hoskisson, R. E., Wei, S. H. I., Xiwei, Y. I., & Jing, J. I. N. (2013). The evolution and strategic positioning of private equity firms. *Academy of Management Perspectives*, *27*, 22–38.
Hsu, D. H. (2004). What do entrepreneurs pay for venture capital affiliation? *Journal of Finance*, *59*, 1805–1844.
Huber, G. P., & Power, D. J. (1985). Retrospective reports of strategic-level managers: Guidelines for increasing their accuracy. *Strategic Management Journal*, *6*, 171–180.
Hulland, J. (1999). Use of Partial Least Squares (PLS) in strategic management research – A review of four recent studies. *Strategic Management Journal*, *20*, 195–204.
Ireland, R., Hitt, M., & Sirmon, D. (2003). Strategic entrepreneurship – The construct and its dimensions. *Journal of Management*, *29*, 963–989.
Jarvis, C., MacKenzie, S., & Podsakoff, P. (2003). A critical review of construct indicators and measurement model misspecification in marketing and consumer research. *Journal of Consumer Research*, *30*, 199–218.
Jensen, M. (1986). Agency costs of free cash flow, corporate finance, and takeovers. *American Economic Review*, *76*, 323–330.
Jensen, M. (1989a). Active investors, LBOs, and the privatization of bankruptcy. *Journal of Applied Corporate Finance*, *2*, 35–44.
Jensen, M. (1989b). Eclipse of the public corporation. *Harvard Business Review*, *67*, 61–74.
Jensen, M., & Meckling, W. (1976). Theory of the firm – Managerial behavior, agency costs, and ownership structure. *Journal of Financial Economics*, *3*, 305–360.
Kaplan, S. (2009). The future of private equity. *Journal of Applied Corporate Finance*, *21*, 8–20.
Kaplan, S. N., & Strömberg, P. (2009). Leveraged buyouts and private equity. *Journal of Economic Perspectives*, *23*, 121–146.
Kaplan, S. N., & Strömberg, P. E. R. (2004). Characteristics, contracts, and actions: Evidence from venture capitalist analyses. *Journal of Finance*, *59*, 2177–2210.
Kaufman, A., & Englander, E. (1992). Kohlberg KRAVIS Roberts & Co. and the challenge to managerial capitalism. *Business and Economic History*, *21*, 97–108.

Kester, W. C., & Luehrman, T. (1995). Rehabilitating the leveraged buyout. *Harvard Business Review*, *73*, 119–130.

Klein, P. G., Chapman, J. L., & Mondelli, M. P. (2013). Private equity and entrepreneurial governance: Time for a balanced view. *Academy of Management Perspectives*, *27*, 39–51.

Kumar, N., Stern, L., & Anderson, J. (1993). Conducting interorganizational research using key informants. *Academy of Management Journal*, *36*, 1633–1651.

Landau, C., & Bock, C. (2013). Value creation through vertical intervention of corporate centres in single business units of unrelated diversified portfolios – The case of private equity firms. *Long Range Planning*, *46*, 97–124.

Lazarova, M., & Taylor, S. (2009). Boundaryless careers, social capital, and knowledge management: Implications for organizational performance. *Journal of Organizational Behavior*, *30*, 119–139.

Lee, C., Lee, K., & Pennings, J. (2001). Internal capabilities, external networks, and performance – A study on technology-based ventures. *Strategic Management Journal*, *22*, 615–640.

Lerner, J. (2011). The future of private equity. *European Financial Management*, *17*, 423–435.

Lerner, J., Sorensen, M., & Strömberg, P. (2011). Private equity and long-run investment: The case of innovation. *The Journal of Finance*, *66*, 445–477.

Lichtenberg, F., & Siegel, D. (1990). The effects of leveraged buyouts on productivity and related aspects of firm behavior. *Journal of Financial Economics*, *27*, 165–194.

Liebeskind, J., Wiersema, M., & Hansen, G. (1992). LBOs, corporate restructuring, and the incentive-intensity hypothesis. *The Journal of the Financial Management Association*, *21*, 73–88.

MacMillan, I., Kulow, D., & Khoylian, R. (1989). Venture capitalists' involvement in their investments – Extent and performance. *Journal of Business Venturing*, *4*, 27–47.

Mahoney, J. (1995). The management of resources and the resource of management. *Journal of Business Research*, *33*, 91–101.

Mahoney, J. (2001). A resource-based theory of sustainable rents. *Journal of Management*, *27*, 651–660.

Maritan, C., & Peteraf, M. (2011). Building a bridge between resource acquisition and resource accumulation. *Journal of Management*, *5*, 1374–1389.

Meuleman, M., Wright, M., Manigart, S., & Lockett, A. (2009a). Agency, strategic entrepreneurship, and the performance of private equity-backed buyouts. *Entrepreneurship Theory and Practice*, *33*, 213–239.

Meuleman, M., Wright, M., Manigart, S., & Lockett, A. (2009b). Private equity syndication: Agency costs, reputation and collaboration. *Journal of Business Finance & Accounting*, *36*, 616–644.

Meuleman, M., & Wright, M. (2011). Cross-border private equity syndication: Institutional context and learning. *Journal of Business Venturing*, *26*, 35–48.

Mezias, J., & Starbuck, W. (2003). Studying the accuracy of managers' perceptions – A research odyssey. *British Journal of Management*, *14*, 3–17.

Muscarella, C., & Vetsuypens, M. (1990). Efficiency and organizational structure – A study of reverse LBOs. *Journal of Finance*, *45*, 1389–1413.

Nahapiet, J., & Ghoshal, S. (1998). Social capital, intellectual capital, and the organizational advantage. *Academy of Management Review*, *23*, 242–266.

Nielsen, K. M. (2008). Institutional investors and private equity. *Review of Finance*, *12*, 185–219.

Nikoskelainen, E., & Wright, M. (2007). The impact of corporate governance mechanisms on value increase in leveraged buyouts. *Journal of Corporate Finance, 13*, 511–537.

Nunnally, J., & Bernstein, I. (1994). *Psychometric theory*. New York, NY: McGraw-Hill.

Palepu, K. (1990). Consequences of leveraged buyouts. *Journal of Financial Economics, 27*, 247–262.

Pe'er, A., & Gottschalg, O. (2011). Red and blue: The relationship between the institutional context and the performance of leveraged buyout investments. *Strategic Management Journal, 32*, 1356–1367.

Peteraf, M. (1993). The cornerstones of competitive advantage – A resource-based view. *Strategic Management Journal, 14*, 179–191.

Peteraf, M., & Barney, J. (2003). Unraveling the resource-based theory. *Managerial and Decision Economics, 24*, 309–323.

Phan, P., & Hill, C. (1995). Organizational restructuring and economic performance in leveraged buyouts – An ex post study. *Academy of Management Journal, 38*, 704–739.

Podsakoff, P., MacKenzie, S., Jeong-Yeon, L., & Podsakoff, N. (2003). Common method biases in behavioral research – A critical review of the literature and recommended remedies. *Journal of Applied Psychology, 88*, 879–903.

Podsakoff, N., Shen, W., & Podsakoff, P. (2006). The role of formative measurement models in strategic management research – Review, critique, and implications for future research. *Research Methodology in Strategy and Management, 3*, 197–252.

Podsakoff, P., & Organ, D. (1986). Self-reports in organizational research – Problems and prospects. *Journal of Management, 12*, 531–544.

Porter, M. (1987). From competitive advantage to corporate strategy. *Harvard Business Review, 65*, 43–59.

Rappaport, A. (1990). The staying power of the public corporation. *Harvard Business Review, 68*, 96–104.

Renneboog, L., Simons, T., & Wright, M. (2007). Why do public firms go private in the UK? The impact of private equity investors, incentive realignment and undervaluation. *Journal of Corporate Finance, 13*, 591–628.

Ringle, M., Wende, S., & Will, A. (2005). SmartPLS 2.0 (beta).

Rogers, P., Holland, T., & Haas, D. (2002). Value acceleration – Lessons from private-equity masters. *Harvard Business Review, 80*, 94–101.

Rossiter, J. (2002). The C-OAR-SE procedure for scale development in marketing. *International Journal of Research in Marketing, 19*, 305–335.

Sapienza, H. (1992). When do venture capitalists add value. *Journal of Business Venturing, 7*, 9–27.

Sapienza, H. J., & Manigart, S. (1996). Venture capitalist governance and value added in four countries. *Journal of Business Venturing, 11*, 439.

Schefczyk, M., & Gerpott, T. J. (2001). Management support for portfolio companies of venture capital firms: An empirical study of German venture capital investments. *British Journal of Management, 12*, 201.

Seth, A., & Easterwood, J. (1993). Strategic redirection in large management buyouts – The evidence from post-buyout restructuring activity. *Strategic Management Journal, 14*, 251–273.

Sharfman, M. (1998). On the advisability of using CEOs as the sole informant in strategy research. *Journal of Managerial Issues, 10*, 373.

Singh, H. (1990). Management buyouts – Distinguishing characteristics and operating changes prior to public offering. *Strategic Management Journal, 11*, 111–129.

Sirmon, D., Hitt, M., & Ireland, R. (2007). Managing firm resources in dynamic environments to create value — Looking inside the black box. *Academy of Management Review, 32,* 273–292.

Smart, S., & Waldfogel, J. (1994). Measuring the effect of restructuring on corporate performance — The case of management buyouts. *Review of Economics & Statistics, 76,* 503–511.

Smith, A. (1990). Corporate ownership structure and performance: The case of management buyouts. *Journal of Financial Economics, 27,* 143–164.

Stone, M. (1974). Cross-validatory choice and assessment of statistical predictions. *Journal of the Royal Statistical Society, 36,* 111–147.

Teece, D. (1982). Towards an economic theory of the multiproduct firm. *Journal of Economic Behavior & Organization, 3,* 39–63.

Teece, D. J., Pisano, G., & Shuen, A. (1997). Dynamic capabilities and strategic management. *Strategic Management Journal, 18,* 509–533.

Tenenhaus, M., Vinzi, V. E., Chatelin, Y. M., & Lauro, C. (2005). PLS path modelling. *Computational Statistics & Data Analysis, 48,* 159–205.

Ucbasaran, D., Westhead, P., & Wright, M. (2009). The extent and nature of opportunity identification by experienced entrepreneurs. *Journal of Business Venturing, 24,* 99–115.

Ughetto, E. (2010). Assessing the contribution to innovation of private equity investors: A study on European buyouts. *Research Policy, 39,* 126–140.

Walsh, J., & Kosnik, R. (1993). Corporate raiders and their disciplinary role in the market for corporate control. *Academy of Management Journal, 36,* 671–700.

Wan, P., Hoskisson, R., Short, J., & Yiu, D. (2011). Resource-based theory and corporate diversification — Accomplishments and opportunities. *Journal of Management, 37,* 1299–1315.

Weir, C., Laing, D., & Wright, M. (2005). Incentive effects, monitoring mechanisms and the market for corporate control — An analysis of the factors affecting public to private transactions in the UK. *Journal of Business Finance & Accounting, 32,* 909–943.

Wiersema, M., & Liebeskind, J. (1995). The effects of leveraged buyouts on corporate growth and diversification in large firms. *Strategic Management Journal, 16,* 447–460.

Williams, L., Vandenberg, R., & Edwards, J. (2009). Structural equation modeling in management research — A guide for improved analysis. *The Academy of Management Annals, 3,* 543–604.

Wilson, N., Wright, M., Siegel, D. S., & Scholes, L. (2012). Private equity portfolio company performance during the global recession. *Journal of Corporate Finance, 18,* 193–205.

Wold, H. (1982). Soft modeling — The basic design and some extensions. In K. Jöreskog & H. Wold (Eds.), *Systems under indirect observations — Causality, structure, prediction* (pp. 1–54). Amsterdam: Elsevier.

Wood, G., & Wright, M. (2009). Private equity — A review and synthesis. *International Journal of Management Reviews, 11,* 361–380.

Wright, M., Robbie, K., Thompson, S., & Starkey, K. (1994). Longevity and the life-cycle of management buy-outs. *Strategic Management Journal, 15,* 215–227.

Wright, M. (2007). Private equity and management buyouts. In H. Landstrom (Ed.), *Handbook of research on venture capital.* Cheltenham: Edward Elgar.

Wright, M. (2013). Private equity: Managerial and policy implications. *Academy of Management Perspectives, 27,* 1–6.

Wright, M., Robbie, K., Romanet, Y., Thompson, R., Joachismson, R., Bruining, H., & Herst, A. (1995). Management buy-outs in the short and long term. *Journal of Business Finance & Accounting, 22,* 461–482.

Wright, M., Robbie, K., & Albrighton, M. (2000). Entrepreneurial growth through privatization — The upside of management buy-outs. *Academy of Management Review, 25*, 591–601.

Wright, M., Hoskisson, R., & Busenitz, L. (2001). Firm rebirth — Buyouts as facilitators of strategic growth and entrepreneurship. *Academy of Management Executive, 15*, 111–125.

Wright, M., Thompson, R., & Robbie, K. (1992). Venture capital and management-led, leveraged buy-outs: A European perspective. *Journal of Business Venturing, 7*, 47–71.

Wright, M., Wilson, N., & Robbie, K. (1996). The longer-term effects of management-led buyouts. *Journal of Entrepreneurial & Small Business Finance, 5*, 555–569.

Zahra, S. (1995). Corporate entrepreneurship and financial performance — The case of leveraged management buyouts. *Journal of Business Venturing, 10*, 225–247.

Zahra, S. A., & Filatotchev, I. (2004). Governance of the entrepreneurial threshold firm: A knowledge-based perspective. *Journal of Management Studies, 41*, 885–897.

Zahra, S., & Fescina, M. (1991). Will leveraged buyouts kill US corporate research & development. *Academy of Management Executive, 5*, 7–20.

Zahra, S., Filatotchev, I., & Wright, M. (2009). How do threshold firms sustain corporate entrepreneurship? The role of boards and absorptive capacity. *Journal of Business Venturing, 24*, 248–260.

APPENDIX

Table A.1. Construct Definitions and Items.

Construct	Definition	Item	Indicator	Scale
Monitoring (MONI)	The collective sum of all actions taken by representatives of a private equity firm that aim to detect and deter efficiency-destroying opportunistic behavior of top managers		*Please rate the extent to which representatives of your investor have done the following:*	
		MONI01	Changed objectives/key performance indicators for top management	1 (not at all) to 5 (extensively)
		MONI02	Signaled rigorous countermeasures to top management in response to missed objectives	
		MONI03	Increased frequency of board meetings and other forms of interaction with top management	
Financial involvement (FINA)	The collective sum of all actions taken by the representatives of a private equity firm which aim at influencing the financial and asset management of a portfolio company		*Please rate the extent to which representatives of your investor have done the following:*	
		FINA01	Introduced new types of financial instruments	1 (not at all) to 5 (extensively)
		FINA02	Provided you with access to new/more favorable sources of funds	
		FINA03	Helped to find the optimal capital structure	
		FINA04	Provided you with additional equity	
		FINA05	Got involved in the optimization of working capital	
Strategic involvement (STRA)	The collective sum of all actions taken by the representatives of a private equity firm which aim at influencing the strategy and business development activities of a portfolio company		*Please rate the extent to which representatives of your investor have done the following:*	
		STRA01	Got involved in the development of your company's strategy	1 (not at all) to 5 (extensively)
		STRA02	Established contact with potential targets/transaction and alliance partners	
		STRA03	Supported you in the implementation of acquisitions/divestments/strategic alliances	

Construct	Definition	Item	Indicator	Scale
Operational involvement (OPER)	The collective sum of all actions taken by the representatives of a private equity firm which aim at influencing the operational business processes of a portfolio company		*Please rate the extent to which representatives of your investor have done the following:*	
		OPER01	Highlighted potential areas for the improvement of operational business processes	1 (not at all) to 5 (extensively)
		OPER02	Got involved in the redesign of operational business processes	
		OPER03	Supported you in the implementation of redesigned business processes	
Ownership-oriented decision-making (OODM)	The extent to which decision-making processes of top managers reflect higher levels of owner and efficiency orientation		*To which extent do you agree with the following statements? Compared to the time before the buyout, today:*	
		OODM01	Management makes quicker decisions	1 (strongly disagree) to 5 (strongly disagree)
		OODM02	Management carries out decisions more rigorously	
		OODM03	Management makes decisions more rationally and goal orientated	
		OODM04	Management decisions involve less politics	
		OODM05	Management thinks and acts more like entrepreneurs	
Competitive prospects (COPR)	The long-term capacity of a portfolio company to participate successfully in the market place and to compete with rivals		*To which extent do you agree with the following statements? Compared to the time before the buyout, today:*	
		COPR01	Your company can better deal with the challenges of the future	1 (strongly disagree) to 5 (strongly disagree)
		COPR02	Your company can react more flexibly to future market trends	
		COPR03	Your company can better deal with future competitive threats /opportunities	
		COPR04	Your company can compete more successfully in the long term	

Table A.2. Construct Classification.

Construct	Object	Object Classification	Attribute	Attribute Classification	Rater Identity	Rater Classification
Monitoring (MONI)	Private equity firm	Concrete singular	Actions representing monitoring	Abstract formed	Member of top management team	Expert
Financial involvement (FINA)	Private equity firm	Concrete singular	Actions representing a provision of resources for financial and asset management	Abstract formed	Member of top management team	Expert
Strategic involvement (STRA)	Private equity firm	Concrete singular	Actions representing a provision of resources for strategy and business development	Abstract formed	Member of top management team	Expert
Operational involvement (OPER)	Private equity firm	Concrete singular	Actions representing a provision of resources for operational business processes	Abstract formed	Member of top management team	Expert
Ownership-oriented decision-making (OODM)	Top management team	Concrete singular	Facets of decision-making and decision implementation	Abstract eliciting	Member of top management team	Expert
Competitive prospects (COPR)	Portfolio company	Concrete singular	Facets of the capacity to compete in the market and compete with rivals	Abstract eliciting	Member of top management team	Expert

Table A.3. Descriptive Statistics.

Variable	Mean	Values							
Year of buyout	Mean 2004	Cumulated %	2000 6.2	2001 10.9	2002 20.2	2003 31.0	2004 48.1	2005 70.9	2006 100.0
Holding period	Mean 2.59	Cumulated %	<1 year 2.3	1–2 years 32.0	2–3 years 55.5	3–4 years 73.4	4–5 years 84.4	5–6 years 94.1	6–7 years 98.8	>7 years 100.0
Size (Sales)		Size (mill. €) cumulated %	<25 29.3	25–99.9 62.0	100–499.9 89.4	500–1999.9 98.5	>2,000 100.0		

Table A.4. Loadings, *t*-Values, and Quality Criteria of Reflective Constructs.

Construct	Item	Loading	*t*-Value	Constructs	Criterion	Value	Threshold
OODM	OODM01	0.882	59.45	OODM	α	0.886	0.7
	OODM02	0.810	30.25		ρc	0.917	0.7
	OODM03	0.873	51.96		AVE	0.688	0.5
	OODM04	0.786	26.24				
	OODM05	0.790	26.10				
COPR	COPR01	0.926	90.23	COMP	α	0.952	0.7
	COPR02	0.932	65.98		ρc	0.965	0.7
	COPR03	0.952	130.07		AVE	0.873	0.5
	COPR04	0.928	81.03				

Table A.5. Cross Loadings of Reflective Constructs.

	COMP	OODM	FPER
OODM01	0.266	0.836	0.210
OODM02	0.300	0.779	−0.143
OODM03	0.469	0.742	−0.079
OODM04	0.210	0.765	0.254
OODM05	0.277	0.730	0.236
COPR01	0.886	0.266	0.100
COPR02	0.806	0.420	0.144
COPR03	0.867	0.348	0.137
COPR04	0.897	0.246	0.103
FPER	0.168	0.139	0.924

Table A.6. Latent Variable Correlations.

	COPR	FINA	MONI	OODM	OPER	FPER	STRA
COPR	1.000						
FINA	0.390	1.000					
MONI	0.391	0.302	1.000				
OODM	0.674	0.268	0.435	1.000			
OPER	0.231	0.194	0.312	0.258	1.000		
FPER	0.278	0.196	0.073	0.269	0.134	1.000	
STRA	0.266	0.386	0.312	0.161	0.370	0.063	1.000

Table A.7. Loadings, *t*-Values, and Variance Inflation Factors of Formative Constructs.

Construct	Item	Weight	*t*-Value	VIF
MONI	MONI01	0.863	8.645	1.534
	MONI02	0.245	1.803	1.621
	MONI03	−0.056	0.411	1.292
FINA	FINA01	−0.013	0.069	1.497
	FINA02	0.034	1.822	1.653
	FINA03	0.811	5.320	1.637
	FINA04	−0.061	0.388	1.233
	FINA05	−0.010	0.069	1.209
STRA	STRA01	0.445	1.720	1.174
	STRA02	0.360	1.153	1.563
	STRA03	0.455	1.503	1.572
OPER	OPER01	0.673	1.949	2.278
	OPER02	−0.807	2.384	2.392
	OPER03	0.976	3.223	1.182

Table A.8. Variance Inflation Factors of Constructs and Construct Quality Criteria.

Endogenous Construct	Exogenous Construct	VIF	R^2	Q^2
COPR	OODM	0.774	0.557	0.096
	FINA	0.794		
	STRA	0.741		
	OPER	0.804		
	MONI	0.722		
FPER	OODM	0.774	0.164	0.036
	FINA	0.794		
	STRA	0.741		
	OPER	0.804		
	MONI	0.722		
OODM	GOVE	1.233	0.189	0.126

Table A.9. Control Variables.

Variable	Description	For Relation to FINA β	For Relation to FINA t-Value	For Relation to COMP β	For Relation to COMP t-Value
SIZE	Size measured in revenues using five categories from 0 to > €2 bn	0.08	1.348	−0.108	2.38
INDU	Industry measured as dummy variable; 1 = manufacturing industry, 0 = service industry	0.015	0.243	0.054	1.287
YEAR	Buyout age measured in year of buyout	−0.02	0.090	−0.005	1.371
HOLD	Duration of holding period measured in years	0.012	0.059	−0.159	1.522
STIL	Ownership status measured as dummy variable; 1 = already sold; 0 = still owned	−0.055	0.692	−0.098	1.862
TYPE	Buyout type measured as dummy variable; 1 = primary buyout, 0 = secondary buyout	−0.005	0.091	−0.003	0.079
UKPC	Portfolio company home country measured as dummy variable; 1 = UK; 0 = Continental Europe	0.058	0.799	−0.007	0.130
UKUS	Private equity firm home country measured as dummy variable; 1 = US or UK; 0 = Continental Europe	−0.114	1.578	0.034	0.654
ALLO	Intensity of initiation of joint projects by the private equity firm with other portfolio companies measured on a five point Likert scale	0.002	0.034	0.035	0.845
CONS	Intensity of hiring of strategy consultants measured on a five point Liker scale	−0.142	1.958	0.01	0.192
CONF	Intensity of hiring of financial consultants measured on a five point Likert scale	0.035	0.845	0.01	1.181
SYND	Existence of syndicate private equity firms measured as dummy variable; 1 = yes, 0 = no	0.015	0.264	−0.092	0.799
JOIN	Respondent joining measured as dummy variable; 1 = with BO; 0 = before BO	−0.164	2.804	0.106	2.34

Table A.10. Path Coefficients and *t*-Values.

No.	Relationship	Expected Sign	Actual Sign	β	t-Value	Interpretation
H1	MONI =>OODM	+	+	0.435***	7.409	Hypothesis not rejected
H2a	OODM =>FPER	+	+	0.269***	4.103	Hypothesis not rejected
H2b	OODM =>COPR	+	+	0.597***	12.377	Hypothesis not rejected
H3a	FINA =>FPER	+	+	0.152*	2.165	Hypothesis not rejected
H3b	FINA =>COPR	+	+	0.186***	3.465	Hypothesis not rejected
H4a	STRA =>FPER	+	+	0.006	0.083	Hypothesis rejected
H4b	STRA =>COPR	+	+	0.112*	2.195	Hypothesis not rejected
H5a	OPER = FPER	+	+	0.097	1.464	Hypothesis rejected
H5b	OPER = COPR	+	+	0.025	0.534	Hypothesis rejected

*$p < 0.05$; **$p < 0.01$; ***$p < 0.001$.

Table A.11. Total Effects.

Exogenous Construct	β (Total) PERF	β (Total) COPR
FAMA	0.152	0.186
MONI	0.117	0.260
OODM	0.269	0.597
OPER	0.097	0.025
STRA	0.006	0.112

WHEN DO VENTURE CAPITALISTS BECOME BOARD MEMBERS IN NEW VENTURES?

Haemin Dennis Park and H. Kevin Steensma

ABSTRACT

We explore factors determining board membership of venture capitalists (VCs) in a syndicate in privately held entrepreneurial ventures. We suggest that board membership is determined by the bargaining process between VCs and new ventures in governing those ventures. Specifically, VCs are more likely to become board members in new ventures if they are highly reputable due to the success of their prior new venture investees, whereas VCs are less likely to gain board rights in new ventures with greater bargain power from superior innovation or marketing track records. Our empirical analysis using 1,812 dyads of investment ties formed between VCs and new ventures support our predictions.

Keywords: Board rights; corporate governance; technology entrepreneurship; venture capital

INTRODUCTION

The separation of ownership and control begins when young, private firms receive funding from external investors and give up some ownership to those investors. A critical factor determining how these firms will be governed is the composition of their board of directors, whose members may exercise significant influence in shaping strategic choices that firms make (e.g., Baysinger, Kosnik, & Turk, 1991; Hillman & Dalziel, 2003; Jensen & Meckling, 1976). Board membership is particularly important to the governance of young, private firms because board members are typically more active and exercise greater influence on the outcome of these firms (Fried, Bruton, & Hisrich, 1998; Lerner, 1995).

Conventional wisdom suggests that control rights come with equity ownership (e.g., Grossman & Hart, 1986; Hart & Moore, 1990). However, factors determining board membership of external investors in young, private firms is more complex. Aghiom and Tirole (1994) predict that control rights will be allocated efficiently by determining the party whose effort will yield the greatest marginal productivity and observing the relative bargaining power of the two parties. Lerner and Merges (1998) test these predictions and find that greater financial resources lead to greater control rights in biotech R&D alliances.

We extend this line of research by examining factors determining the likelihood of particular venture capitalists (VCs) obtaining board rights in VC syndicates in new ventures. We suggest that bargaining power, stemming from signals of their marginal productivity, determines the distribution of control rights between VCs and entrepreneurs. Specifically, we argue that the reputation of VCs from facilitating the success of past venture investees increases their bargaining power to obtain board rights in their subsequent venture investees. Likewise, new ventures with superior innovation and marketing capabilities have greater bargaining power and are thus less likely to give up board rights to external investors. Using a dataset of 1,812 investment ties between 924 VCs and 508 new ventures in computer hardware, semiconductor, and wireless service sectors during the period between 1990 and 2003, we find robust support for these predictions.

This study contributes to entrepreneurship and corporate governance literature at the intersection between strategy and finance in several ways. First, although venture boards are assumed to play an important role in shaping the development of new ventures (Fried et al., 1998; Garg, 2013; Krause & Bruton, 2014; Lerner, 1995), little empirical research has explored the composition of new venture board. This study considers factors affecting the composition of new venture board. Second, this study extends the idea that entrepreneurs pay a premium to obtain funding from reputable investors (Hsu, 2004). In addition to offering valuation discounts, giving up control rights can be an important aspect of this negotiation process for entrepreneurs seeking external funding. Moreover, we find that this negotiation process is two-sided by incorporating the bargaining power of both VCs and entrepreneurs in determining the outcomes.

BACKGROUND AND HYPOTHESES

Although the proportion of new ventures receiving VC funding among all newly created businesses is not high, a significant proportion of them in highly capital and technology-intensive industries (e.g., biotech, semiconductor, telecommunications) receive VC funding (Gompers & Lerner, 2004). Indeed, many leading technology-based firms like Apple, Genentech, Google, and Intel were funded by VCs in their early days before becoming public.

In addition to providing capital funding, VCs typically play an active role in the management of their new venture investees to increase their likelihood of successful outcomes (Gompers & Lerner, 2004; Sahlman, 1990). For instance, VCs often match new ventures with resources to develop their businesses (Hsu, 2006; Lindsey, 2008), provide managerial advice (Sahlman, 1990), or help new ventures hire professional managers for growth (Hellmann & Puri, 2002). Moreover, new ventures affiliated with reputable investors can signal their quality and can more easily acquire resources elsewhere (Hochberg, Ljungqvist, & Lu, 2007; Stuart, Hoang, & Hybels, 1999) or can gain direct access to complementary assets from corporate VCs (Dushnitsky, 2006; Park & Steensma, 2012). As a result, new ventures funded by prominent VCs are more likely to succeed compared with their counterparts without VC funding or those funded by less prominent VCs (Hsu, 2006; Nahata, 2008; Sørensen, 2007).

Because external investors are critical to the outcome of new ventures, entrepreneurs seek to obtain funding from prominent VCs with successful track record. Indeed, they are willing to pay a premium, in terms of valuation discounts, to be affiliated with such VCs (Hsu, 2004). Entrepreneurs actively participate in the market for VC funding and bargain with prospective external investors to receive their support. In this process, a critical component of the negotiation between VCs and entrepreneurs involves control rights (Aghiom & Tirole, 1994; Hellmann, 1998; Kaplan & Strömberg, 2003). These rights grant the right holders to influence important governance decisions, such as appointment of top management team members and exit events. Although property rights arguments often assume that control rights come with ownership (e.g., Grossman & Hart, 1986; Hart & Moore, 1990), governance structure of modern firms is generally more complex due to separation of ownership and control (Berle & Means, 1932). Indeed, VCs almost always obtain preferred shares when they invest in young, privately held ventures and acquire additional control rights over common shareholders, such as founders and employees of those ventures (Kaplan & Strömberg, 2003).

An important aspect of control rights in new ventures concerns with the composition of board of directors. Board members may exercise significant influence in shaping strategic choices that firms make, and may access trade secrets of the ventures that they oversee (Baysinger et al., 1991; Coff, 1999; Jensen & Meckling, 1976). Because board rights grant formal power to investors to defend their own interests, external investors and entrepreneurs engage in contentious negotiations to allocate these rights. In such a process, we highlight the bargaining power of each party, that is, VCs and new ventures.

Bargaining Power between VCs and New Ventures

External investors and entrepreneurs can bring their bargaining chips to the table to obtain favorable terms that can help them fulfill their respective objectives. We argue that the reputation of VCs for facilitating new venture success can be an effective bargaining chip for VCs to gain greater control rights (Hsu, 2004; Spence, 1974). Reputable VCs can directly offer superior managerial advice to new ventures to improve their performance or indirectly enable new ventures to obtain superior resources elsewhere by providing certification or endorsement to those ventures (Hochberg et al., 2007; Hsu, 2004; Stuart et al., 1999). Moreover, reputable investors can affect decision-making calculus of a complex web of stakeholders in highly uncertain environments (Park & Steensma, 2013).

Prior studies have argued that an actor's reputation stems from his prior performance (Rindova, Williamson, Petkova, & Sever, 2005). Similarly, a VC firm's prior performance is typically determined by successful outcome of its prior investments. Those VCs that helped their prior venture investees to exit successfully is a signal of their ability to do so in the future (Nahata, 2008). New ventures seeking resources from external investors are more likely to give up control rights to those reputable VCs and obtain superior resources to increase their likelihood of success (Hochberg et al., 2007; Hsu, 2004; Stuart et al., 1999). Thus, we hypothesize the following relationship between VC firm reputation and its likelihood of obtaining board rights.

Hypothesis 1 (H1). VCs with higher reputation are more likely to become board members in their new venture investees.

New ventures are also likely to vary in their bargaining power to avoid giving up too much control to external investors. New ventures that are highly sought after by several external investors may have considerable bargaining power. We posit that those ventures with superior innovation or marketing capabilities have greater bargaining power and are thus less likely to give up board rights to VCs. Unique technology is one of the primary reasons why VCs invest in new ventures. Further, those ventures that can establish partnerships to bring their technology into the market can signal their likelihood of success (Baum, Calabrese, & Silverman, 2000). These factors can reduce their dependency from VCs to obtain resources for their entrepreneurial endeavors. For instance, new ventures with considerable innovation capability are less likely to need the help of VCs to make business deals because their technology is more likely to be desired by potential deal partners, whereas their counterparts without such a capability are more likely to need advice and external contacts provided by their VC investors for such deals. The magnitude of this dependency is likely to influence the negotiation between VCs and new ventures in drafting their contracts. More capable ventures, in terms of their innovation or marketing track records, are less likely to give up board rights to their VC investors because they could easily find alternative VCs willing to invest in those ventures without requiring the rights. Thus, we hypothesize the following relationship between a venture's innovation and marketing capabilities and its likelihood of giving up board rights to VC investors.

Hypothesis 2a (H2a). VCs that invest in new ventures with greater innovation capability are less likely to obtain board rights in their new venture investees.

Hypothesis 2b (H2b). VCs that invest in new ventures with greater marketing capability are less likely to obtain board rights in their new venture investees.

METHODS

Data and Sample

Because we are interested in the likelihood of a VC investor becoming a board member in a new venture, our unit of analysis is investor–investee dyad. We identified 2,153 materialized investment ties between 924 VC firms that invested in 508 new ventures in computer hardware (VentureXpert code = 2100), semiconductor (VentureXpert code = 3111/3112), and wireless service (VentureXpert code = 1320) sectors between 1998 and 2003. These sectors showed robust VC investment activities during this period. We excluded non-U.S. ventures to control for institutional aspects that may affect the likelihood of new ventures granting board rights to external investors. Although we used VentureXpert as our primary data source to collect information on VC firms, new ventures, and their financing deals, we also used additional data sources including linkSV (www.linksv.com), the Internet Archive service (www.archive.org), Factiva, and LexisNexis to reduce missing data problems and increase the accuracy of our data. We used the U.S. Patent and Trademark Office (USPTO) database for patent data and Security Data Corporation (SDC) database for alliance data. After eliminating 341 observations due to missing data, our final sample consisted of 1,812 realized investment ties.

Analytical Approach

Because our dependent variable is binary, we used logistic regression using characteristics of VC investors, new ventures, and dyads as explanatory variables to test our hypotheses. This model specification used the full sample of 1,812 observations.

Additionally, we used conditional fixed effects logit model (Chamberlain, 1980; Hsu, 2004) for more rigorous testing of our hypotheses. Although conditional fixed effects logit model reduces endogeneity issues in the model by controlling fixed characteristics of VC investors or new ventures that may affect the value of explanatory variables, it has the drawback of eliminating observations when there are no variations in the fixed entries. Specifically, we used two equations to examine how VC investor, new venture, and dyad characteristics influencing the likelihood of a VC investor serving as a board member in a new venture. We fixed new venture investee characteristics and examined how VC investor and dyad characteristics affected the likelihood of a VC investor becoming a board member to test H1.

$$\Pr(\textit{Board membership} = 1) = F(\textit{VC reputation, controls}) \qquad (1)$$

Likewise, we fixed VC investor characteristics and examined how new venture and dyad characteristics affected the likelihood of a new venture giving up a board seat to test H2a and H2b.

$$\begin{aligned}\Pr(\textit{Board membership} = 1) \\ = F(\textit{Innovation capability, marketing capability, controls})\end{aligned} \qquad (2)$$

Conditional fixed effects logit model drops observations in testing (1) when new ventures received funding from only one VC investor because there would be no variation in VC investor characteristics. Likewise, it drops observations in testing (2) when a VC investor invested in only one venture in our sample because there would be no variation in new venture characteristics. Our final sample for (1) consisted of 1,528 investment ties, whereas that for (2) consisted of 948 investment ties.

Variable Description

Dependent Variable
Our variable of interest is whether a VC investor obtained board membership in a new venture investee. We coded 1 for dyads of VC firms and new ventures that materialized into board membership and 0 for those that did not.

Explanatory Variables
A firm's reputation is function of its prior performance (Rindova et al., 2005). Initial public offering (IPO) is generally considered as the most successful outcome for venture investors, as it has the highest average return among all possible exit outcomes (e.g., IPO, acquisition, and so on) (Gompers & Lerner, 2004). Thus, consistent with a number of prior studies (e.g., Hsu, 2006; Nahata, 2008), we measured *VC reputation* by counting the number of previously invested ventures by a VC firm that eventually

that went public. *Innovation capability* was measured by counting the number of patent applications (that were subsequently granted) by the new venture investees prior to their first round of funding using the USPTO database. Likewise, *Marketing capability* was measured by counting the number of alliances formed by the new venture investees prior to their first round of funding using the SDC database. Because *VC reputation*, *Innovation capability*, and *Marketing capability* were highly skewed, we took the natural log of these variables to enhance normality.

Control Variables
We controlled for a number of VC investor, new venture, and dyad characteristics that may affect the likelihood of board membership. For VC investor characteristics, we controlled for *VC age* because older VC firms with greater experience may be advantageous in negotiating a deal with new ventures (Nahata, 2008). Moreover, because corporate investors have greater potential conflicts of interests with new ventures (Park & Steensma, 2013), many corporate investors are reluctant to serve as board members. Indeed, our interviews with corporate investors revealed that a number of them have explicit policies prohibiting them from serving on venture boards. Thus, we controlled for whether a VC investor was *Corporate VC* or not. Approximately 53% of all new ventures in our sample received funding from at least one corporate VC investor, whereas 14% of all investment ties involved corporate VC investors. Because the venture stage in which a VC investor joins the investment syndicate may affect its likelihood of serving on the board, we controlled for the funding round in which the VC investor joined the investment syndicate by using binary indicators for first through sixth rounds of funding.

For venture characteristics, we controlled for *Total amount of investment* that a new venture received from all investment syndicate members. We also controlled for *Number of investors*, *Number of rounds*, *Venture age*, and industry binary indicators for *Semiconductor* and *Wireless* ventures, as these factors are likely to affect the bargaining power of new ventures or availability of board seats to external investors.

We also inserted a number of dyad-level controls. Most importantly, although it is important to control for ownership percentage by a particular investor, VentureXpert database does not provide ownership information of private firms. We thus had to use a proxy. Specifically, we first calculated the total amount of funding that a particular venture received from all external investors. We then obtained *Investment percentage* by a particular VC investor from the total capital funding that a new venture

Table 1. Variable Definition and Summary Statistics (for Materialized Investment Ties.)

Variable	Definition	Mean	SD
Dependent variable			
(1) *Board membership*	One if a VC obtained board membership	0.36	0.48
VC characteristics			
(2) *VC reputation* (L)	Number of IPOs taken by focal VC prior focal investment	2.04	1.48
(3) *Corporate VC*	One if a VC is affiliated with an established firm	0.14	0.34
(4) *VC age*	Age at first participating round in a new venture	12.33	26.10
Venture characteristics			
(5) *Innovation capability* (L)	Number of patent application prior to first funding round	0.44	0.81
(6) *Marketing capability* (L)	Number of alliances established prior to first funding round	0.04	0.19
(7) *Number of funding rounds*	Number of funding rounds by a new venture	4.86	3.00
(8) *Number of investors*	Number of VCs in the investment syndicate in a new venture	8.79	5.43
(9) *Total amount of funding* (L)	Total amount of funding in $mm	3.70	1.12
(10) *New venture age*	Age of a new venture in first funding round	1.86	2.03
Industry indicators	Binary indicators for new ventures in semiconductor and wireless industries		
Dyad characteristics			
(11) *Geographical proximity*	One if VC and new venture are located within 50 miles from each other	0.36	0.48
(12) *Investment percentage*	Percentage of funding provided by a VC of total funding raised by a new venture	0.18	0.19
(13) *Number of participating rounds*	Number of participating rounds by a VC in a new venture	2.25	1.74
Market climate	Number of IPOs in the funding year reflecting hot/cold market		
Funding round in which a VC joined the syndicate	Dummy variables indicating the funding round a VC joined the syndicate (2nd, 3rd, and so on; 1st round is base)		

Note: A natural log transformation was done to enhance normality for variables indicated by (L).

Table 2. Pairwise Correlation Matrix.

	(1)	(2)	(3)	(4)	(5)	(6)	(7)	(8)	(9)	(10)	(11)	(12)	(13)
(1) Board membership	1.00												
(2) VC reputation (L)	0.14	1.00											
(3) Corporate VC	−0.19	−0.10	1.00										
(4) VC age	0.03	0.28	−0.08	1.00									
(5) Innovation capability (L)	−0.04	0.01	0.03	0.01	1.00								
(6) Marketing capability (L)	−0.06	0.02	0.04	−0.01	−0.02	1.00							
(7) Number of funding rounds	−0.03	0.07	−0.01	−0.02	−0.02	−0.12	1.00						
(8) Number of investors	−0.16	0.05	0.00	0.01	0.06	−0.07	0.67	1.00					
(9) Total amount of funding (L)	−0.05	0.11	0.02	0.02	0.08	−0.08	0.62	0.65	1.00				
(10) New venture age	−0.02	0.01	−0.01	0.00	0.20	0.15	−0.14	−0.17	−0.10	1.00			
(11) Geographical proximity	0.14	−0.06	−0.04	−0.05	−0.02	−0.05	0.03	−0.02	−0.05	−0.11	1.00		
(12) Investment percentage	0.31	0.08	−0.08	0.01	0.06	0.04	0.39	−0.57	−0.51	0.10	−0.01	1.00	
(13) Number of participating rounds	0.32	0.11	−0.13	0.02	0.00	−0.07	0.50	0.23	0.31	−0.07	0.11	−0.00	1.00

Notes: Based on 1,812 investment dyads; correlations above 0.05 or below −0.05 are significant at 5% level.

received. Although new ventures typically obtain funding using different valuations for different funding rounds and differ on how much equity share to give up to external investors, *Investment percentage* was a crude way of controlling for the ownership percentage of a particular VC investor in the investment syndicate. In our models for robustness checks, we discuss our results when we weight reputation of a particular VC investor and market climate in calculating *Investment percentage*. We also inserted *Geographical proximity*, that is, whether new ventures were located within 50 miles from VCs, and *Number of participating rounds* by a particular VC. Geographical proximity between the investor and investee is likely to increase the efficiency of the monitoring by the investors and thus increase the likelihood of a VC investor serving as a board member (Gompers & Lerner, 2004). Moreover, we included *Number of IPOs* in the year in which the VC investor made its investment in a new venture, reflecting the climate of the IPO market for that particular year that may affect the bargaining power of new ventures receiving VC funding (Lerner & Merges, 1998). Table 1 reports variable descriptions and summary statistics. Table 2 reports correlations based on all 1,812 observations.

RESULTS

Table 3 presents logistic regression results including all VC investor, new venture, and dyad characteristics using the full sample of 1,812 observations. Model 3-1 presents the effects of all control variables on the likelihood of a VC investor becoming a board member. As predicted, corporate VCs were less likely to serve as a board member ($p < 0.001$). Moreover, VC investors joining investment syndicate at later rounds were generally more likely to obtain board seats. Among venture characteristics, greater number of funding rounds ($p < 0.001$) and investors ($p < 0.01$) reduced the likelihood of a particular VC investor becoming a board member, whereas total amount of external funding received by a new venture increased it ($p < 0.01$). Further, VC investors located close to their new venture investees ($p < 0.001$), those investing a high percentage of total funding received by a new venture ($p < 0.001$), or those participating in multiple rounds ($p < 0.001$) were more likely to serve as a board member. Finally, *Number of IPOs* in a particular ($p < 0.05$) year decreased a VC investor's likelihood of becoming a board member, suggesting that new ventures generally have greater bargaining power when the IPO market is hot.

Table 3. Likelihood of VCs Becoming a Board Member Using Logistic Regression Model.

N = 1,812	3-1	3-2	3-3	3-4	3-5	3-6	3-7
VC characteristics							
H1: VC reputation (L)		0.135**		0.141**	0.120**	0.141**	0.121**
		(0.045)		(0.046)	(0.045)	(0.045)	(0.046)
Corporate VC	−1.206***	−1.176***	−1.183***	−1.155***	−1.140***	−1.146***	−1.130***
	(0.201)	(0.202)	(0.201)	(0.202)	(0.202)	(0.203)	(0.202)
VC age	0.001	−0.002	0.001	−0.003	−0.002	−0.003	−0.002
	(0.002)	(0.004)	(0.002)	(0.004)	(0.004)	(0.004)	(0.004)
Venture characteristics							
H2a: Innovation capability (L)			−0.145*	−0.144*	−0.142†	−0.145*	−0.144*
			(0.073)	(0.073)	(0.073)	(0.073)	(0.073)
H2b: Marketing capability (L)			−0.773*	−0.834*	−0.841*	−0.815*	−0.820*
			(0.348)	(0.351)	(0.352)	(0.348)	(0.348)
Number of funding rounds	−0.213***	−0.210***	−0.219***	−0.216***	−0.211***	−0.218***	−0.213***
	(0.039)	(0.040)	(0.040)	(0.040)	(0.039)	(0.040)	(0.039)
Number of investors	−0.054**	−0.056**	−0.053**	−0.056**	−0.055**	−0.056***	−0.055***
	(0.017)	(0.018)	(0.017)	(0.018)	(0.018)	(0.018)	(0.018)
Total amount of funding (L)	0.268***	0.237**	0.276***	0.243**	0.232**	0.250**	0.238**
	(0.078)	(0.079)	(0.079)	(0.080)	(0.080)	(0.080)	(0.080)
New venture age	−0.035	−0.035	−0.023	−0.022	−0.022	−0.023	−0.023
	(0.023)	(0.023)	(0.024)	(0.024)	(0.024)	(0.024)	(0.024)
Industry indicators (Semicon, Wireless)	Yes	Yes	Yes	Yes	Yes	Yes	Yes

Dyad characteristics							
Geographical proximity	0.497***	0.509***	0.492***	0.504***	0.500***	0.507***	0.502***
	(0.119)	(0.120)	(0.119)	(0.120)	(0.120)	(0.120)	(0.120)
Investment percentage[a]	3.151***	2.291***	3.168***	2.924***	2.834***	2.924***	2.849***
	(0.395)	(0.399)	(0.397)	(0.402)	(0.392)	90.391)	(0.383)
Number of participating rounds	0.541***	0.536***	0.537***	0.533***	0.529***	0.529***	0.524***
	(0.051)	(0.052)	(0.052)	(0.052)	(0.052)	(0.052)	(0.052)
Market climate	−0.001*	−0.001**	−0.001**	−0.001**	−0.001**	−0.001†	−0.001†
	(0.000)	(0.000)	(0.000)	(0.000)	(0.000)	(0.000)	(0.000)
Funding rounds in which a VC joined the syndicate	Yes	Yes	Yes	Yes	Yes	Yes	Yes
Constant	−2.151***	−2.188***	−2.100***	−2.134***	−0.242	−2.265***	−0.258
	(0.343)	(0.345)	(0.344)	(0.346)	(0.557)	(0.354)	(0.555)
Log likelihood	−938.1	−933.3	−934.6	−929.4	−931.4	−927.3	−929.3

Notes: †$p < 0.10$, *$p < 0.05$, **$p < 0.01$, ***$p < 0.001$. Two-tailed tests.
[a]Investment percentage was adjusted by VC reputation for Model 3-5, by market climate for Model 3-6, and both factors for Model 3-7.

Model 3-2 inserts the hypothesized relationship between *VC reputation* and the likelihood of a VC investor serving as a board member. As predicted, higher VC reputation increased the likelihood of a particular VC investor serving as a board member ($p < 0.01$). All signs and magnitudes of control variables remained qualitatively similar to those in Model 3-1. Thus, H1 is supported.

Model 3-3 inserts the effects of *Innovation capability* ($p < 0.05$) and *Marketing capability* ($p < 0.05$) on the likelihood of a VC investor serving as a board member. Both capabilities of new ventures reduced the likelihood of a VC investor serving as a board member at the 5% level. Thus, H2a and H2b are supported. Model 4-4 shows the results with all hypothesized variables. Signs and coefficients for all explanatory and control variables remain qualitatively consistent.

Table 4 presents the results for Eq. (1) testing H1 using conditional fixed effects logit model fixing venture characteristics. Overall, our results are consistent with those from the standard logistic regression model. Model 4-1 shows the effect of control variables on whether a VC investor becomes a board member. *Corporate VCs* ($p < 0.001$), *Investment percentage* ($p < 0.001$), and *Number of participating rounds* ($p < 0.001$) remained highly significant in predicting a VC investor's likelihood of becoming a board member. Although VC investors located in geographical proximity to new ventures were more likely to serve as a board member, its significance level decreased ($p < 0.05$ vs. $p < 0.001$ in Model 3-4). Moreover, *Market climate* was no longer significant at the 10% level. We introduced the effect of *VC reputation* in Model 4-2 and found support for H1 ($p < 0.05$).

Table 5 presents the results for Eq. (2) testing H2a and H2b using conditional fixed effects logit model fixing investor characteristics. Among venture characteristics, *Number of funding rounds* was negative and significant ($p < 0.001$). Moreover, signs and coefficients for dyad characteristics were consistent with the results from Model 4-2. *Geographical proximity* ($p < 0.05$), *Investment percentage* ($p < 0.001$), and *Number of participating rounds* ($p < 0.001$) increased a new venture's likelihood of giving up a board seat to a VC investor. Consistent with Model 4-2, *Market climate* was not significant at the 10% level. Model 5-2 introduces the effect of *Innovation capability* and *Marketing capability* of new ventures related to a new venture's likelihood of giving up board membership to a VC investor. Although the signs were consistent with the models presented in Table 3, significance levels were changed. The effect of *Innovation capability* became less strong ($p < 0.10$), whereas *Marketing capability* became stronger ($p < 0.01$).

Table 4. Likelihood of VCs Becoming a Board Member Using Conditional Fixed Effects Logit Model Controlling for New Venture Characteristics.

$N = 1,528$	4-1	4-2	4-3	4-4	4-5
VC characteristics					
H1: VC Reputation (L)		0.126*	0.131*	0.113†	0.127*
		(0.062)	(0.062)	(0.062)	(0.063)
Corporate VC	−1.369***	−1.349***	−1.329***	−1.372***	−1.351***
	(0.244)	(0.243)	(0.241)	(0.247)	(0.245)
VC age	0.001	−0.004	−0.004	−0.005	−0.004
	(0.005)	(0.005)	(0.006)	(0.006)	(0.006)
Dyad characteristics					
Geographical proximity	0.342*	0.348*	0.352*	0.326*	0.328*
	(0.156)	(0.156)	(0.156)	(0.157)	(0.157)
Investment percentage[a]	6.547***	6.620***	6.181***	6.110***	6.026***
	(0.840)	(0.837)	(0.819)	(0.793)	(0.779)
Number of participating rounds	0.675***	0.667***	0.669***	0.667***	0.668***
	(0.082)	(0.082)	(0.082)	(0.082)	(0.081)
Market climate	−0.001	0.001	0.000	0.002*	0.002*
	(0.001)	(0.001)	(0.000)	(0.001)	(0.000)
Funding rounds in which a VC joined the syndicate	Yes	Yes	Yes	Yes	Yes
Log likelihood	−429.3	−427.5	−427.8	−425.9	−425.9

Notes: †$p < 0.10$, *$p < 0.05$, **$p < 0.01$, ***$p < 0.001$. Two-tailed tests.
[a]*Investment percentage* was adjusted by VC reputation for Model 4-3, by market climate for Model 4-4, and both factors for Model 4-5.

Robustness Checks

Controlling for ownership percentage of VC investors is critical because we want to show the likelihood of VCs obtaining board membership in their new venture investees is influenced by factors other than their mere ownership percentages. Although the accuracy of our proxy for ownership percentage, *Investment percentage*, is limited, we conducted two robustness checks that could alleviate this limitation.

First, an alternative explanation could be that more reputable VCs obtain greater ownership percentage and may be more likely to obtain board membership. We therefore took into account the reputation of particular VCs in calculating our proxy for *Investment percentage*. Hsu (2004) observed that above-average reputable VCs obtained an average of 10–14% valuation discounts compared with below-average reputable VCs.

Table 5. Likelihood of VCs Becoming a Board Member Using Conditional Fixed Effects Logit Model Controlling for VC Characteristics.

N = 948	5-1	5-2	5-3	5-4	5-5
Venture characteristics					
H2a: Innovation capability (L)		−0.192† (0.107)	−0.190† (0.107)	−0.196† (0.107)	−0.194† (0.107)
H2b: Marketing capability (L)		−1.187** (0.453)	−1.190** (0.453)	−1.205** (0.454)	−1.207** (0.454)
Number of funding rounds	−0.225*** (0.055)	−0.246*** (0.056)	−0.246*** (0.056)	−0.247*** (0.056)	−0.246*** (0.056)
Number of investors	−0.006 (0.025)	−0.004 (0.025)	−0.004 (0.025)	−0.004 (0.026)	−0.003 (0.026)
Total amount of funding (L)	0.040 (0.129)	0.067 (0.132)	0.063 (0.132)	0.072 (0.133)	0.068 (0.132)
Venture age	−0.011 (0.034)	0.014 (0.036)	0.013 (0.036)	0.011 (0.037)	0.010 (0.036)
Industry indicators (semicon, wireless)	Yes	Yes	Yes	Yes	Yes
Dyad characteristics					
Geographical proximity	0.501* (0.245)	0.494* (0.248)	0.494* (0.248)	0.489* (0.248)	0.487* (0.247)
Investment percentage[a]	2.563*** (0.618)	2.569*** (0.617)	2.473*** (0.595)	2.639*** (0.599)	2.540*** (0.579)
Number of participating rounds	0.493*** (0.077)	0.497*** (0.078)	0.498*** (0.077)	0.494*** (0.078)	0.495*** (0.078)
Market climate	−0.001 (0.000)	−0.001 (0.000)	−0.001 (0.000)	−0.000 (0.000)	−0.000 (0.000)
Funding rounds in which a VC joined the syndicate	Yes	Yes	Yes	Yes	Yes
Log likelihood	−290.6	−285.9	−286.0	−284.4	−284.6

Notes: †$p < 0.10$, *$p < 0.05$, **$p < 0.01$, ***$p < 0.001$. Two-tailed tests.
[a] *Investment percentage* was adjusted by VC reputation for Model 5-3, by market climate for Model 5-4, and both factors for Model 5-5.

To be conservative, we applied a 14% premium in number of pseudo shares in calculating our proxy for *Investment percentage* for VC investors whose reputation was above median. Our results in Models 3-5, 4-3, and 5-3 show consistent results from our main ones.

Second, valuations in different funding rounds may vary according to the overall market climate and status of venture performance. Although we could not observe the development of new venture throughout their fundraising periods, we could infer the overall market climate affecting the valuation of new venture equity. We took changes in the market climate into account by measuring deviations in the NASDAQ index from that of a new venture's first round of funding and adjusted pseudo shares obtained by a particular VC in different funding rounds using this deviation. For instance, if NASDAQ index was at 2,000 in the year in which the first funding round was conducted and 2,500 in the year in which the second funding round was conducted, we applied a 25% premium in valuations for the investments in the second funding round. Our results were robust after adjusting for market climate changes in calculating ownership percentage of VC investors. Models 3-6, 4-4, and 5-4 show consistent results. Finally, Model 3-7, 4-5, and 5-5 show results combining both methodologies to check for the robustness of our results. Again, results remain qualitatively consistent.

DISCUSSION AND CONCLUSION

We explored the bargaining process between VC investors and new ventures in allocating board rights. We found that reputable VC investors were more likely to serve as a board member in their new venture investees, whereas new ventures with greater innovation or marketing capabilities were less likely to give up board rights to external VC investors. Our findings extend the idea that entrepreneurs pay a premium, in terms of giving up greater control rights, to obtain certification or endorsement from reputable external investors (Hsu, 2004). However, our study reveals that this bargaining process is two-sided. VC investors are less likely to obtain control rights when new ventures possess greater innovation or marketing capabilities in terms of their number of patents and alliances, respectively. Our results are robust using two alternative specifications after controlling for the *Investment percentage* of VC investors in new ventures proxying their ownership percentage.

Our findings document factors influencing the composition of board of directors in young, private ventures. Although other studies have provided insights on the importance of venture boards in influencing the development and performance of those ventures (e.g., Fried et al., 1998; Garg, 2013; Landau, 2014), this study provides antecedents on how those boards and corporate governance structures emerge. Indeed, because separation and ownership is not clear in young, private ventures, examining venture boards may provide new insights to the literature at the intersection between entrepreneurship and corporate governance (Garg, 2013; Krause & Bruton, 2014).

Our work also contributes to the literature on property rights by providing insights on how control rights are determined in young, private firms. The core argument of property rights theory focuses on assigning ownership or control rights to the party who can best contribute to the marginal product of an asset (Grossman & Hart, 1986; Hart & Moore, 1990). We provide evidence that greater reputation and capabilities of parties involved in young, private firms, presumably providing greater marginal benefits to their firm performance, do indeed lead to greater control rights in the entrepreneurial process above and beyond ownership percentage. Specifically, we extend the work by Aghion and Tirole (1994) and Lerner and Merges (1998) by showing how the bargaining power, stemming from signals of marginal productivity affecting venture outcomes, leads to greater control rights. These results provide insights on how entrepreneurial projects are governed and may have implications to increasing social welfare.

There are several ways to extend this study to provide greater insights on venture boards and corporate governance issues of entrepreneurial ventures. First, our data did not allow us to control for the precise ownership percentage of external investor and insiders in new ventures. Further, we did not explicitly control for other preferred shareholder rights when VCs and entrepreneurs negotiate their contracts. In addition, due to lack of time-varying, longitudinal dataset, we were not able to incorporate the evolutionary process in the staged rounds of new ventures. Interestingly, and somewhat contrary to our original speculation, VC investors joining the investor syndicate at later rounds were generally more likely to obtain board rights. One explanation could be that new ventures purposely choose to obtain funding from VC investors who can serve on their board at later rounds. Future studies using richer micro dataset on the precise ownership share of external investors, various contractual terms, and evolutionary aspects of the fundraising process could provide more accurate estimates of the magnitude and significant levels of the coefficients in this study, and explain how VCs and entrepreneurs make their tradeoffs for those terms when they negotiate investment contracts.

Second, our results from the conditional fixed effects logit model suggest that marketing capabilities of new ventures grant them greater bargaining power compared with innovation capability to retain control rights from external investors. Future studies exploring these and other factors that grant new ventures to gain bargaining power against external investors could enhance our understanding of the entrepreneurial process. This is particularly valuable because new ventures are presumed to have low status compared with external investors (Hallen, 2008; Katila, Rosenberger, & Eisenhardt, 2008), and insights to overcome this status deficit to obtain external resources may be critical for their development and success.

Third, we restricted our sample to new ventures in the U.S. to control for institutional environments. However, other stakeholders, such as creditors and government, may play a larger role in shaping the corporate governance mechanisms and structure of young, private ventures in other countries. Comparing the market for corporate control for privately held entrepreneurial ventures in different countries may bring fruitful insights to international entrepreneurship and finance.

In conclusion, venture boards may have important consequences for the development and performance of entrepreneurial ventures. We hope that this Chapter has shed some light on the initial formation of those boards.

REFERENCES

Aghion, P., & Tirole, J. (1994). The management of innovation. *Quarterly Journal of Economics*, *109*(4), 1185–1209.

Baum, J. A. C., Calabrese, T., & Silverman, B. S. (2000). Don't go it alone: Alliance networks and startup performance in Canadian biotechnology. *Strategic Management Journal*, *21*(3), 267–294.

Baysinger, B. D., Kosnik, R. D., & Turk, T. A. (1991). Effects of board and ownership structure on corporate R&D strategy. *Academy Management Journal*, *34*(2), 205–214.

Berle, A. A., & Means, G. C. (1932). *The modern corporation and private property*. New York, NY: Macmillan.

Chamberlain, G. (1980). Analysis of covariance with qualitative data. *Review of Economic Studies*, *47*(1), 225–238.

Coff, R. W. (1999). When competitive advantage doesn't lead to performance: The resource-based view and stakeholder bargaining power. *Organization Science*, *10*(2), 119–133.

Dushnitsky, G. (2006). Corporate venture capital: Past evidence and future directions. In M. Casson, B. Yeung, A. Basu, & N. Wadeson (Eds.), *Oxford handbook of entrepreneurship (Oxford handbooks in business & management)* (pp. 387–431). Oxford, UK: Oxford University Press.

Fried, V. H., Bruton, G. D., & Hisrich, R. D. (1998). Strategy and the board of directors in venture-capital backed firms. *Journal of Business Venturing*, *13*(6), 493–503.

Garg, S. (2013). Venture boards: Differences with public firm boards, and implications for monitoring and firm performance. *Academy of Management Review*, *38*(1), 90–108.

Gompers, P. A., & Lerner, J. (2004). *The venture capital cycle*. Cambridge, MA: MIT Press.

Grossman, S. J., & Hart, O. D. (1986). The costs and benefits of ownership: A theory of vertical integration. *Journal of Political Economy*, *94*, 691–719.

Hallen, B. L. (2008). The causes and consequences of the initial network positions of new organizations: From whom do entrepreneurs receive investments? *Administrative Science Quarterly*, 53(4), 685−718.

Hart, O. D., & Moore, J. (1990). Property rights and the nature of the firm. *Journal of Political Economy*, 98, 1119−1150.

Hellmann, T. (1998). The allocation of control rights in venture capital contracts. *RAND Journal of Economics*, 29(1), 57−76.

Hellmann, T., & Puri, M. (2002). Venture capital and the professionalization of start-up firms: Empirical evidence. *Journal of Finance*, 57(1), 169−197.

Hillman, A. J., & Dalziel, T. (2003). Board of directors and firm performance: Integrating agency and resource dependence perspectives. *Academy of Management Review*, 28(2), 383−396.

Hochberg, Y. A., Ljungqvist, Y., & Lu, Y. (2007). Whom you know matters: Venture capital networks and investment performance. *Journal of Finance*, 62(1), 251−301.

Hsu, D. H. (2004). What do entrepreneurs pay for venture capital affiliation? *Journal of Finance*, 59(4), 1805−1844.

Hsu, D. H. (2006). Venture capitalists and cooperative start-up commercialization strategy. *Management Science*, 52(2), 204−219.

Jensen, M. C., & Meckling, W. F. (1976). Theory of the firm: Managerial behavior, agency costs, and ownership structure. *Journal Economics of International*, 3, 305−360.

Kaplan, S. N., & Strömberg, P. (2003). Financial contracting theory meets the real world: An empirical analysis of venture capital contracts. *Review of Economic Studies*, 70, 281−315.

Katila, R., Rosenberger, J. D., & Eisenhardt, K. M. (2008). Swimming with sharks: Technology ventures, defense mechanisms and corporate relationships. *Administrative Science Quarterly*, 53(2), 295−332.

Krause, R., & Bruton, G. (2014). Agency and monitoring clarity on venture board of directors. *Academy of Management Review*, 39(1), 111−113.

Landau, C. (2014). Active involvement of private equity firms in portfolio companies and its performance effects. In B. Villalonga (Ed.), *Finance and strategy* (Vol. 31). Advances in Strategic Management. Bingley, UK: Emerald Group Publishing Limited.

Lerner, J. (1995). Venture capitalists and the oversight of private firms. *Journal of Finance*, 50(1), 301−318.

Lerner, J., & Merges, R. P. (1998). The control of technology alliances: An empirical analysis of the biotechnology industry. *Journal of Industrial Economics*, 46(2), 125−156.

Lindsey, L. (2008). Blurring firm boundaries: The role of venture capital in strategic alliances. *Journal of Finance*, 63(3), 1137−1168.

Nahata, R. (2008). Venture capital reputation and investment performance. *Journal of Financial Economics*, 90(2), 127−151.

Park, H. D., & Steensma, H. K. (2012). When does corporate venture capital add value for new ventures? *Strategic Management Journal*, 33(1), 1−22.

Park, H. D., & Steensma, H. K. (2013). The selection and nurturing effects of corporate investors on the innovativeness of new ventures. *Strategic Entrepreneurship Journal*, 7(4), 311−330.

Rindova, V. P., Williamson, I. O., Petkova, A. P., & Sever, J. M. (2005). Being good or being known: An empirical examination of the dimensions, antecedents, and consequences of organizational reputation. *Academy of Management Journal*, 48(6), 1033−1049.

Sahlman, W. A. (1990). The structure and governance of venture-capital organizations. *Journal of Financial Economics, 27*(2), 473–521.

Sørensen, M. (2007). How smart is smart money? A two-sided matching model of venture capital. *Journal of Finance, 62*(6), 2725–2762.

Spence, M. A. (1974). *Market signaling: Informational transfer in hiring and related screening processes*. Cambridge, MA: Harvard Business Press.

Stuart, T. E., Hoang, H., & Hybels, R. C. (1999). Interorganizational endorsement and the performance of entrepreneurial ventures. *Administrative Science Quarterly, 44*(2), 315–349.

OWNERSHIP EFFECTS ON UNRELATED DIVERSIFICATION: AN INSTITUTIONS' PERSPECTIVE

Nikolaos Kavadis and Xavier Castañer

ABSTRACT

Purpose — *To show that differences in the extent to which firms engage in unrelated diversification can be attributed to differences in ownership structure.*

Methodology/approach — *We draw on longitudinal data and use a panel analysis specification to test our hypotheses.*

Findings — *We find that unrelated diversification destroys value; pressure-sensitive Anglo-American owners in a firm's equity reduce unrelated diversification, whereas pressure-resistant domestic owners increase unrelated diversification; the greater the firm's free cash flow, the greater the negative effect of pressure-sensitive Anglo-American owners on unrelated diversification.*

Research limitations/implications — *We contribute to corporate governance and strategy research by bringing in owners' institutional origin as a shaper of owner preferences in particular with regards to unrelated diversification. Future research may expand our investigation to more* than one home institutional context, and theorize on institutional origin effects beyond the dichotomy between Anglo-American and non-Anglo-American (not oriented toward shareholder value maximization) owners.

Practical implications – Policy makers, financial analysts, owners, and managers may want to reflect about the implications of ownership structure, as well as promoting or joining corporations with particular ownership configurations.

Social implications – A shareholder value-destroying strategy, such as unrelated diversification has adverse consequences for society at large, in terms of opportunity costs, that is, resources could be allocated to value-creating activities instead. Promoting an ownership configuration that creates value should contribute to social welfare.

Originality/value – Owners may not be exclusively driven by shareholder value maximization, but can be influenced by normative beliefs (biases) stemming from the institutional context they originate from.

Keywords: Corporate governance; corporate strategy; institutions; ownership structure; unrelated diversification; value creation

INTRODUCTION

The central question in corporate strategy is in which business or businesses a firm ought to operate to create value (synergy) for shareholders (Porter, 1987). In institutional contexts with high market efficiency, operating in unrelated businesses is considered as a non-value creating or even value-destroying strategy (Mayer & Whittington, 2003; Palich, Cardinal, & Miller, 2000; Ramaswamy, Li, & Veliyath, 2002), often attributed to agency problems (Amihud & Lev, 1981; Eisenhardt, 1989; Jensen & Meckling, 1976). Specifically, based on the assumption of managerial risk aversion and owners' risk neutrality, a CEO is thought to favor unrelated diversification for risk reduction (e.g., Amihud & Lev, 1981), and empire-building, which allows top managers to obtain higher remuneration and status (e.g., Agrawal & Mandelker, 1987; Murphy, 1985). Unrelated diversification however is by definition devoid of economic synergies and linked to poor performance (e.g., Palich et al., 2000; Rumelt, 1974; Rumelt, 1982).[1]

In examining whether owners can prevent unrelated diversification, researchers obtained mixed findings on the role of ownership concentration, among other corporate governance devices, such as board independence and CEO incentives (Amihud & Lev, 1981; Goranova, Alessandri, Brandes, & Dharwadkar, 2007; Lane, Cannella, & Lubatkin, 1998). We identify two reasons for such inconclusive results. First, most agencies theoretic research has tended to treat owners as a homogeneous group with identical preferences. In addressing this limitation, researchers have started to examine how owners' monitoring inclination may determine their goals and hence their stance toward different strategies (e.g., Brickley, Lease, & Smith, 1988; David, O'Brien, Yashikawa, & Delios, 2010; Hoskisson, Hitt, Johnson, & Grossman, 2002). In particular, past research has focused on the role of institutional investors as more shareholder value-oriented and critical to opportunistic CEO proposals, what Brickley et al. (1988) call "pressure-resistant" owners vis-a-vis "pressure-sensitive" owners (banks, insurance companies, and non-financial corporations) who more easily give in to CEO self-interested proposals. Second, research has shown that some categories of foreign shareholders are likely to resist CEO opportunistic projects, and in particular unrelated diversification projects (Goyer, 2003; Ramaswamy et al., 2002). In that regard, we argue that the institutional origin of owners shapes their conception of corporate goals, and thus matters in determining their strategic outlook (e.g., Fiss & Zajac, 2004; Lubatkin, Lane, Collin, & Very, 2005; Ramaswamy et al., 2002).

These reasons represent a gap in our understanding, that is, whether and how owner monitoring inclination (pressure-resistant vs. pressure-sensitive) and institutional origin (normative beliefs) jointly impact unrelated diversification. It is unclear for instance the extent to which institutional investors, classified as pressure-resistant by Brickley et al. (1988), will actively advocate for strategies that are thought to promote shareholder value maximization (SVM), if they come from an institutional (country) context with different goals and expectations than SVM (e.g., Fiss & Zajac, 2004). Viceversa, it is not clear either whether pressure-sensitive owners, according to Brickley et al. (1988), will behave as such if they come from a country where SVM is considered the primary goal of a corporation.

Hence, whereas prior research has recognized the limiting assumption of owner homogeneity, little is known on whether and how owners' institutional (country of) origin, in conjunction with owners' monitoring inclination, affects firms' unrelated diversification. In this study, we draw on institutional and behavioral perspectives of corporate governance (Aguilera & Jackson, 2003; Davis, Diekmann, & Tinsley, 1994; Hambrick, v. Werder, &

Zajac, 2008; Westphal & Zajac, 2013) to develop and test the thesis that corporate owner heterogeneity in terms of monitoring inclination and institutional origin explains variation in a type of corporate strategic behavior, namely unrelated diversification. Specifically, we claim that the context from which owners stem matters for their preferences or goals. Owner preferences are "socially situated" and "socially constituted" (Westphal & Zajac, 2013), that is, shaped by the institutional context from which they originate.

Our study focuses on large, publicly-listed French firms from 2000 to 2007. France offers a suitable novel setting because it is a country where SVM has not been the sole or overriding corporate objective. France is a country where different stakeholders — the state, unions, professions, and corporations — have a significant role in the economy (e.g., Gedajlovic & Shapiro, 1998; Goyer, 2003; Katzenstein, 1985). Moreover, as of 1990s, there was increasing owner heterogeneity, mostly due to the influx of Anglo-American owners who are considered as having a SVM orientation (e.g., Clift, 2007; Davis et al., 1994; Morin, 2000). Our results show that unrelated diversification destroys value, and provide support to our thesis. Specifically, the presence of supposedly pressure-sensitive (i.e., banks and insurance companies) Anglo-American owners lead to a subsequent reduction of unrelated diversification; the presence of allegedly pressure-resistant (i.e., institutional) domestic owners subsequently increases unrelated diversification; the greater the amount of firm free cash flow (FCF), the greater the negative effect of pressure-sensitive (i.e., banks and insurance companies) Anglo-American owners on subsequent unrelated diversification.

This study contributes to research on corporate governance and strategy (Aguilera & Jackson, 2003; Hambrick et al., 2008; Westphal & Zajac, 2013), in particular with regards to the ownership determinants of unrelated diversification. We show that besides formal governance devices (e.g., Amihud & Lev, 1981; Goranova et al., 2007; Lane et al., 1998) the categorization of owners based on their monitoring inclination and, especially, institutional origin influences unrelated diversification. Our study also extends prior research as to the effect of different types of owners on a variety of corporate outcomes (e.g., Bethel & Liebeskind, 1993; Brickley et al., 1988; Fiss & Zajac, 2004; Hoskisson et al., 2002; Ramaswamy et al., 2002). Moreover, prior research classified countries' corporate governance systems (including France) assuming governance homogeneity within a country (e.g., Gedajlovic & Shapiro, 1998). We contribute to this literature by unpacking differences between firms in terms of ownership across firms headquartered in the same country, and in a much less studied institutional (country) context with a different governance tradition, as compared to the Anglo-American one.

LITERATURE REVIEW

Corporate diversification occurs when a firm operates in different industries (e.g., Montgomery, 1994). In contrast to related diversification, which refers to business segments that share resources, unrelated diversification refers to the extent to which a firm operates in industries that have different input–output configurations, and thus have little or no resources in common (e.g., Montgomery, 1982; Rumelt, 1974, 1982).

Prior research has theorized and provided evidence on a variety of factors that can impact corporate diversification in general, and unrelated diversification in particular. One main explanation of unrelated diversification is the firm's corporate governance structure. Research on the impact of corporate governance on (unrelated) diversification has mainly drawn from agency theory (Jensen & Meckling, 1976; Ross, 1973) and argued that both incentives and control should reduce that type of diversification (e.g., Amihud & Lev, 1981; Denis, Denis, & Sarin, 1997; Goranova et al., 2007), given evidence that it relates to poor subsequent performance (e.g., Palich et al., 2000; Rumelt, 1982).

Extant literature has examined different corporate governance devices, as well as used diverse corporate diversification measures and samples, making cumulativeness difficult to evaluate. Early studies focused on ownership concentration as a measure of shareholder control (Amihud & Lev, 1981), whereas recently, researchers have included other measures of control such as board independence and vigilance (Lane et al., 1998), as well as incentives such as CEO ownership and compensation (e.g., Denis et al., 1997; Goranova et al., 2007). In that regard, these most recent studies, which simultaneously analyze multiple corporate governance devices, are more informative as they provide more specified models and thus the effect or explanatory power of a corporate governance device is assessed when controlling for the others (e.g., Goranova et al., 2007).

Nevertheless, the empirical evidence on the impact of corporate governance in terms of both control and incentives on unrelated diversification is inconclusive and controversial. Specifically, the empirical evidence on the impact of control on unrelated diversification is mixed. Amihud and Lev (1981) found that, in the absence of a large blockholder (i.e., no ownership concentration), firms tend to be more diversified. Lane et al. (1998) replicated Amihud and Lev's (1981) study with their sample of 309 U.S. 1965 Fortune 500 firms that conducted acquisitions in the 1961–1970 period and found that, using Rumelt's typology of diversification strategy, ownership concentration has no significant impact on unrelated diversification. However, temporal precedence might be an issue here, as the independent variable appears to correspond to the same period than the dependent variable. Further, in a sample of 286 Fortune 500 firms that conducted acquisitions between 1980 and 1987, Lane et al. (1998) observed no significant effect of board vigilance (as the sum of the proportion of outside directors and their ownership) on unrelated diversification. Again, though, the fact that the temporal structure of their model is unknown (i.e., they do not specify when they measure board vigilance) prevents a solid (causal) interpretation and conclusion.

The extant evidence on the impact of incentives on unrelated diversification is also scant and mixed. Denis et al. (1997) investigated the effect of management ownership on diversification. However, as Lane, Cannella, and Lubatkin (1999) point out, in their measure of management ownership, Denis et al. (1997) included the ownership of both managers and directors, the latter being a measure of board vigilance and thus control rather than incentives, an operationalization which mixes and thus confounds the two types of governance devices. Recently, in their longitudinal study of 231 S&P 500 firms in the 1994–1999 period, Goranova et al. (2007) deal with both the issues of temporal precedence and separate measurement of incentives and control devices in the same model, and find no support that prior executive ownership reduces unrelated diversification over time. However, they found that chairman/CEO duality, that is, when the firm's CEO is also the chair of the board of directors, an indicator of weak board governance for agency theorists, significantly increases subsequent unrelated diversification.

In sum, the empirical evidence is rather inconclusive on the impact of different corporate governance devices on unrelated diversification, in particular as regards to the role of ownership. One reason why prior research is inconclusive as to the role of ownership may be that it did not extensively consider the potential role of heterogeneity among owners and, in particular, the potential heterogeneity of their preferences or goals. As Hambrick et al. (2008, p. 383) point out, in contrast to "the typical portrayal of a divergence between interests of *the* shareholders and *the* managers," it is likely that different types of shareholders (as well as different types of managers) have different preferences. For instance, prior corporate governance research has shown that SVM is not the overarching objective in all institutional environments (e.g., Fiss & Zajac, 2004; Jackson, 2005). In the same vein, objectives other than SVM may lead different owners to evaluate the use of corporate financial funds differently. That is, whereas in a SVM-oriented institutional context such as the U.S. FCF is expected to be paid back to the shareholders in the form of dividends or share repurchases (e.g., Lazonick & O'Sullivan, 2000; Zajac & Westphal, 2004), in other institutional environments this may not be the case.

We believe our understanding of the antecedents of unrelated diversification is incomplete. Specifically, despite some recognition by prior research of the limiting assumption of owner homogeneity, little is known on whether and how owners' institutional (country of) origin, in conjunction with owners' monitoring inclination, affects a firm's corporate unrelated diversification strategy (and the use of financial resources to this aim), given that SVM may not be the sole or overriding concern for all categories of owners. This may be especially true in institutional environments (countries), where SVM is not the dominant corporate governance principle supposed to guide corporate strategy. In this chapter, we aim to address this question.

THEORY

Researchers have proposed that different types of owners may have different preferences or goals, which will be enacted in their stance toward different strategies (e.g., Brickley et al., 1988; David et al., 2010; Hoskisson et al., 2002). For instance, Brickley et al. (1988) argued and showed that only pressure-resistant owners (institutional investors) oppose value-destroying CEO proposals, such as the adoption of anti-takeover provisions in contrast to pressure-sensitive owners (e.g., banks and insurance companies), likely to defer to the CEO. Furthermore, research has shown that some categories of foreign shareholders are likely to resist CEO opportunistic projects, and in particular unrelated diversification (Goyer, 2003; Ramaswamy et al., 2002). However, prior research has not taken into account the institutional origin of foreign owners (e.g., Douma, George, & Kabir, 2006). We argue that owners' country of origin matters in determining their preferences, that is, whether they will primarily be SVM-oriented (e.g., Fiss & Zajac, 2004; Lubatkin et al., 2005; Ramaswamy et al., 2002; Westphal & Zajac, 2013). To our knowledge, current research is rather silent about this. Each country is likely to have different beliefs and norms about corporate goals and whose preferences are to be prioritized (e.g., Fiss & Zajac, 2004; Lubatkin et al., 2005). Hence, normative beliefs about what the corporate objectives should be may differ among firm owners, if they differ in their institutional origin.

We argue that institutional origin shapes owner preferences in a lasting way. Research has elaborated on the existence of cross-national diversity in corporate governance (e.g., Aguilera & Jackson, 2003), and has contrasted the corporate governance model observed in the Anglo-American institutional environment – where the publicly traded corporation is viewed as an economic entity whose primary purpose is SVM – to the ones observed in other institutional environments – where the corporation is seen as an institution serving the interests of a variety of stakeholders (e.g., Fiss & Zajac, 2004). Such contrast draws on legal, institutional, and political differences. Specifically, the strong legal investor protection observed in the Anglo-American institutional environment is contrasted to a weaker investor protection observed in other institutional environments, such as the ones of continental Europe (La Porta, Lopez-de-Silanes, Shleifer, & Vishny, 1998). Similarly, from institutional and political standpoints, research has underscored the importance of a stakeholder-oriented model as an economically viable and competitive alternative to the Anglo-American (pro-SVM) one, under conditions of economic globalization (e.g., Hollingsworth, Schmitter, & Streeck, 1994; see also Guillén, 2000). In contrast to the Anglo-American model where the financial market plays the primary role in governing transactions, in other institutional environments there is some greater degree of centralized coordination, a formal recognition of various interest groups in having a say in economic and social policy decision-making (Murtha & Lenway, 1994). France has been considered as traditionally having such an orientation, in contrast to the Anglo-American environment (Katzenstein, 1985; Morin, 2000; Zysman, 1983).

Therefore, differences in institutional environments may imply different beliefs and norms about what the main corporate goals or objectives "ought" to be. Subsequently, differences in shared beliefs and norms are likely to impact corporate actors' preferences in terms of a corporation's strategy. Contrary to the Anglo-American, pro-SVM environment, where the primacy of the market as means of resource allocation is likely to give primacy to the interests of those that allocate resources through the stock market, that is, investors in a non-SVM context, such as France the interests of different stakeholders are expected to be weighted in.

Whether diversification is shareholder value creating or not has been the object of substantial research (e.g., Amihud & Lev, 1981; Berger & Ofek, 1995; Campa & Kedia, 2002; Villalonga, 2004). Starting in the 1980s though, the belief especially in the United States is that it destroys shareholder value (Davis et al., 1994). That said, this belief is not dominant in other countries, such as in France and Germany where unrelated diversification was a prevalent strategy well into the 1990s (e.g., Goyer, 2003). As a result, we expect Anglo-American owners to have a negative disposition toward unrelated diversification, but not owners from a non-SVM institutional context. That is, because of their institutional imprint from their originating embeddedness (e.g., Granovetter, 1985) in contexts with no historical association with SVM primacy, owners may not advocate for decisions that are considered to be shareholder value-maximizing, such as a decrease in unrelated diversification, as is the case in other countries such as the United States (Davis et al., 1994). Moreover, a strategy such as unrelated diversification might be of interest to other stakeholders, such as the state and unions, which owners are expected to take into consideration.

Our argumentation rests on that owners will carry their beliefs in the new environment because that is what they know and have been applying and honing in the past. Although not directly related to owners, Zaheer (1995) provides relevant evidence for corporate internationalization. She shows that, despite the institutional differences between Japan and the United States, U.S. companies investing in Japan first applied their home practices to their Japanese subsidiaries rather than adopting Japanese practices. The imprinting influence of home practices is stronger than the apparent need for local adaptation. In our study, we don't focus on corporate practices but on beliefs regarding corporate goals, that is, goals that in a given society are viewed as the appropriate or legitimate ones to be pursued by a corporation. While Zaheer and Mosakowski (1998) showed that, over time, U.S. companies settling in Japan adapted to the Japanese practices, we argue that it is much more difficult for owners to change their views on what the corporate goals "ought" to be, even if they have remained in a given (different than their own) country for a long time.

Based on the previously developed two dimensions of owner categorization, that is, pressure-resistance versus pressure-sensitivity, and Anglo-American, SVM orientation versus French, non-SVM orientation, we classify equity owners into four categories: (1) pressure-resistant SVM oriented (Anglo-American); (2) pressure-sensitive SVM oriented (Anglo-American); (3) pressure-resistant non-SVM oriented (French); and

Table 1. Typology of Owners Based on Monitoring Inclination (Pressure-Resistant vs. Pressure-Sensitive) and Institutional Origin (Anglo-American SVM vs. French non-SVM) and their Hypothesized Effects on Unrelated Diversification (UD).

Monitoring Inclination/Institutional Origin	Anglo-American SVM	French non-SVM
Pressure-resistant	Against UD (H1)	In favor of UD (H4)
Pressure-sensitive	Against UD (H2)	In favor of UD (H3)

(4) pressure-sensitive non-SVM oriented (French) (Table 1). Next, we develop our hypotheses as to their effects on unrelated diversification.

Our model elucidates the joint influence of potentially opposing owners' features, namely their pressure-resistant versus sensitive inclination and the institutional beliefs of their country of origin, in terms of the degree of unrelated diversification.

Hypotheses Development

Pressure-Resistant SVM Oriented (Anglo-American) Owners
Institutional investors, such as investment firms (mutual funds), investment advisors (brokerage firms), pension funds, and endowment funds, do not own shares directly, but they manage others' shares, that is, they buy, sell, and sometimes vote on behalf of third-party investors.

The presence of institutional investors in corporate equity capital has increased worldwide. In the United States for example, institutional investors' share ownership rose from 3% in the early 1950s to about 9% in 1970, to reach 40% in 1991, and 66% in 2005 (Bethel & Liebeskind, 1993; Dalton, Hitt, Certo, & Dalton, 2007). Institutional investors have been regarded as having both the ability and the motivation to exercise effective monitoring over corporate managers (Pound, 1988, 1992). That is, they have the expertise, which decreases the cost of monitoring, and the incentive to exercise monitoring, because they can aggregate ownership positions in a firm's equity capital, and can use coordination devices to increase their monitoring effectiveness. Due to their monitoring ability and motivation, institutional investors have been qualified as pressure-resistant owners, because they are likely to resist corporate managers' opportunistic initiatives, for instance, to vote more actively against anti-takeover amendments (Brickley et al., 1988). Empirical evidence from the United States suggests that institutional investors also react negatively to CEO compensation increases (David, Kochhar, & Levitas, 1998), while reacting positively to corporate R&D expenditures (Hill & Hansen, 1991) and innovation (Kochhar & David, 1996), indicating their preference to support policies that are thought to be value-creating. Regarding corporate strategy in particular, Ramaswamy et al. (2002) report that institutional investors respond negatively to unrelated diversification from Indian firms.

When those pressure-resistant owners come from an institutional environment with a strong SVM orientation, such as the Anglo-American one, where unrelated diversification is believed to stem from managerial opportunism and to result in shareholder value destruction (e.g., Davis et al., 1994; Zajac & Westphal, 2004), we expect that they will strongly oppose unrelated diversification.

Hypothesis 1 (H1). The greater the presence of pressure-resistant (i.e., institutional) Anglo-American owners in a firm's equity, the greater the subsequent reduction of unrelated diversification.

Pressure-Sensitive SVM Oriented (Anglo-American) Owners
Banks, insurance companies, and non-financial corporations are usually considered as pressure-sensitive owners (Brickley et al., 1988), that is, they are likely to defer to corporate managers. The reason is that they are often involved in important business relationships with the corporations of whom they hold equity shares, in a way that render them dependent on these corporations (e.g., Mizruchi, 1996; Pfeffer & Salancik, 1978). For instance, a bank derives interest income from their client corporations. This dependence places this kind of owners in a position of deference to corporate management when it comes to assess their strategy and proposals, including (unrelated) diversification (Ramaswamy et al., 2002).

Nevertheless, we expect their stance toward strategy in general and unrelated diversification in particular to vary depending on their institutional origin, and the associated normative beliefs about unrelated diversification. Given that in the Anglo-American institutional context, there is a normative belief against unrelated diversification (e.g., Davis et al., 1994; Useem, 1993), we expect that banks, insurance companies, and corporations that originate from that institutional context to be against that strategy. Hence, we consider that the beliefs and values of the country of origin in terms of which goals corporations should pursue will overpower the supposed pressure-sensitivity of the owner monitoring inclination. Thus, a normative belief against diversification and relatively lower dependence from the focal firm's management, may lead an Anglo-American bank, insurance company, or non-financial corporation to oppose unrelated diversification of the focal firm from which it holds shares.

Hypothesis 2 (H2). The greater the presence of pressure-sensitive (i.e., banks, insurance companies, and corporations) Anglo-American owners in a firm's equity, the greater the subsequent reduction of unrelated diversification.

Pressure-Sensitive Non-SVM Oriented (French) Owners
Pressure-sensitive owners from other countries that are less or not at all SVM-oriented than the owners from the Anglo-American institutional environment might not oppose unrelated diversification; actually, they might even promote it sometimes. This is the case for instance of France, a country that does not have a historical governance tradition related to the principle of SVM (e.g., Lubatkin et al., 2005; Morin, 2000), and where banks were nationalized in the 1980s and became instrumental in carrying state influence (Kadushin, 1995), including through ownership in large French corporations. Even after the early 1990s, with the "going public" of most French banks, they continued to occupy a central position in the economic system, by maintaining shareholdings and board seats in major large French publicly traded non-financial corporations. Their economic role has been considered as significant as an alternative funding source to (Anglo-American) institutional investors in an institutional context where financial markets traditionally played a less important role in corporate financing, as compared to banks (e.g., Kwok & Tadesse, 2006, see also Gedajlovic & Shapiro, 1998; Murtha & Lenway, 1994). French banks support the economic weight and size of French non-financial corporations as means to promote national economic interests (e.g., employment or visibility in the global competitive landscape), even if national interests may not be in line with SVM. This may imply to actively sustain the existence of large multi-business corporations, even if some of their businesses are unrelated. Indeed, as Whittington and Mayer (2000) document, unrelated diversification among large French firms increased between the mid-1980s and the mid-1990s, a period where pressure-sensitive institutions in France (specifically, domestic banks and insurance companies), had a particularly influential position in the French corporate landscape (e.g., Morin, 2000). As a result, banks from non-SVM countries such as France might have converging interests with opportunistic CEOs who are also interested in larger corporate size and diversity for self-interested reasons. For the same reason

(i.e., embeddedness in an institutional context with different prevailing beliefs than SVM about whose interests are to be prioritized when managing the firm), we expect a similar stance from other shareholding (non-financial) corporations coming from countries where SVM is not the dominant corporate goal.

Hypothesis 3 (H3). The greater the presence of pressure-sensitive (i.e., banks, insurance companies, and corporations) French owners in a firm's equity, the greater the subsequent increase of unrelated diversification.

Pressure-Resistant Non-SVM Oriented (French) Owners
The core element of our argumentation is that owner preferences are shaped by the institutional context from which they originate (Fiss & Zajac, 2004; Lubatkin et al., 2005; Ramaswamy et al., 2002). Because they originate from countries where SVM is not the dominant corporate governance ideology (Lazonick & O'Sullivan, 2000), some otherwise considered pressure-resistant owners may not oppose unrelated diversification.

In most countries, institutional investors and CEOs are likely to frequently interact and as a result establish a rather dense network of ties also due to common education, and memberships in associations, corporations, foundations, and other entities (see Mizruchi, 1996; Useem, 1984, for the U.S. case). Common educational and professional backgrounds (Maclean, Harvey, & Press, 2006) and social ties between owners and top managers are likely to impact owners' preferences, making them closer to the interests of top managers. For instance, Lubatkin et al. (2005, p. 882) mention that "senior management, directors, and shareholders of major French firms (…) are members of the same small circle of societal elites who have similar interests and expectations regarding the firm's priorities and performance." Given the corporate governance tradition of France, these priorities are likely to differ from SVM, in contrast to the Anglo-American context. As a result, we expect that pressure-resistant (institutional) owners from non-SVM countries to support corporate management in unrelated diversification. Here again, for consistency, we assume that the country of origin will have a stronger effect than the owner monitoring inclination in shaping the owners' position vis-à-vis unrelated diversification. Indeed, evidence suggests (Deutsche Bank Research, 1998) that French institutional investors have a strong fixed-income bias, and a strong "home" bias. A strong fixed-income bias may indicate risk aversion (which would contrast to the assumed risk neutrality of investors) in line with assumptions about managerial risk preferences, whereas a strong home bias implies low international portfolio diversification and great focus in investing in home assets. According to Deutsche Bank analysts, such strong home bias in the behavior of French institutional investors is peculiar to France, seemingly above and beyond the impact of regulatory constraints. These elements (i.e., fixed-income bias and home bias) corroborate our argumentation that, in contrast to their Anglo-American counterparts, domestic (French) pressure-resistant investors will not be averse to (but even favor) unrelated diversification programs.

> **Hypothesis 4 (H4).** The greater the presence of pressure-resistant (i.e., institutional) French owners in a firm's equity, the greater the subsequent increase of unrelated diversification.

The Role of FCF in SVM Oriented (Anglo-American) Owner Preferences
As mentioned, a main feature of the Anglo-American corporate governance tradition is the primacy of SVM as regards to the question of who "ought" to have control over the allocation of corporate resources, and subsequently which corporate goal should be pursued (e.g., Fiss & Zajac, 2004; Fligstein, 1990; Lazonick & O'Sullivan, 2000; Westphal & Zajac, 2013). That is, in the Anglo-American context, researchers suggest that there is a normative belief about the primacy of shareholder interests in terms of SVM. Further, there is also the belief that excess corporate financial resources (profits) should be given back to shareholders through dividends or share repurchases, instead of being allocated to projects that do not increase shareholder value. In this context, the primacy of SVM comes along with the agency-theoretic belief that CEOs, if left unmonitored, will use FCF to engage in value-destroying behavior, that is, new projects that might increase CEO utility but reduce shareholder value (e.g., Jensen, 1986). Thus, we claim that FCF is likely to accentuate the potential divergence of interests between SVM-oriented shareholders and managers over its use (Castañer & Kavadis, 2013). It is likely to further increase the inclination of Anglo-American owners to take action and oppose unrelated diversification. Therefore, we hypothesize that, when a firm's CEO has FCF at her or his disposal, Anglo-American owners (who adhere to SVM) will be further inclined to prevent the use of such funds in projects believed to be value destroying, such as unrelated diversification. That is, we hypothesize that FCF will accentuate (moderate) the behavioral bias due to the Anglo-American SVM-oriented institutional origin.

Hypothesis 5 (H5). The greater the focal firm's FCF, the greater the negative effect of Anglo-American (a) pressure-resistant (i.e., institutional) and (b) pressure-sensitive (i.e., banks, insurance companies, and corporations) owners on subsequent unrelated diversification.

METHODS

Sample and Data

The population for this study is the 100 largest French firms (headquartered in France) in terms of annual turnover for the 2000–2007 period, according to "Le Guide des Etats-Majors," an annual edition which scans the largest French companies.

France is a suitable setting to test our hypotheses for two reasons. First, it is a country where SVM is not considered as the sole or overriding corporate goal during the period under study (see also Katzenstein, 1985; Zysman, 1983, on political economic institutions). Further, French banks and insurance companies originating have an important economic role, including through corporate shareholdings even in the period considered (Clift, 2007; Gedajlovic & Shapiro, 1998; Goyer, 2003; Murtha & Lenway, 1994; Schmidt, 2003). Second, during the period under study, French publicly traded corporations witnessed a significant entry of Anglo-American owners. Specifically, during the 1990s, the previously highly concentrated ownership structure of large French firms progressively became more dispersed and, following the globalization of financial markets, foreign investors, in particular U.S.- and U.K.-based investors, became important shareholders (Morin, 2000; Schmidt, 2003). Foreign ownership of French firms increased significantly from 10% of total equity in 1985 to 35% in 1997 (Clift, 2007). These changes in French firms' ownership structure are thought to have had an effect in their strategy (e.g., Goyer, 2003; Morin, 2000).

Further, during the period considered, a norm against unrelated diversification prevailed in the United States and the United Kingdom (e.g., Davis et al., 1994; Zajac & Westphal, 2004). It was believed that firm's FCF "ought" to be given back to shareholders (through dividends or share repurchases) instead of funding other strategies, such as corporate diversification, and in particular unrelated diversification projects.

However, such belief against diversification was not prevalent in France, where publicly traded firms engaged in diversification strategies well into the 1990s (Whittington & Mayer, 2000).

From our population, we selected all publicly traded firms with available data that were independent enterprises (i.e., the majority of their shares were not owned by another operating firm). The final dataset contains 60 firms over the 2000–2007 period. To allow for temporal precedence, there is a one-year lag between the dependent variable (observed for the 2001–2007 period), and the explanatory and control variables (observed for the 2000–2006 period). The final dataset contains 414 firm/year observations.

To assess the effect of unrelated diversification on shareholder value, and hence to take into account what investors might have known about the value impact of unrelated diversification, we use the excess value measure. As per prior research (Berger & Ofek, 1995; Campa & Kedia, 2002; Villalonga, 2004), we define excess value as the log of the ratio of firm value to its imputed value, that is, the sum of the values of the firm's businesses, if each of its businesses operated as a stand-alone, single-business firm. To obtain imputed values for each business, we multiplied each business sales with the median sales multiplier of all publicly traded single-business firms available in the Thomson database in the corresponding 2-digit SIC industry, at a given year. The sales multipliers are the median of the ratio of total capital over sales for all single-business firms in the corresponding 2-digit SIC industry, at a given year. Total capital is the sum of market value of equity, long-term and short-term debt, and preferred stock (Campa & Kedia, 2002, p. 1736). A negative excess value implies that the firm destroys value (i.e., trades at a discount), while a positive excess value implies that the firm creates value (i.e., trades at a premium). In our sample, values for this measure range between −5.90 and 4.71, with a mean of 0.12. In addition to the control variables used for the unrelated diversification models, in our value analysis, we control for firm-level factors that have been shown to impact firms' value, namely *financial diversification*, that is, the extent to which a firm's operations in unrelated industries allow for revenue smoothing, given that prior research has shown that it negatively impacts firm value (Castañer & Kavadis, 2013); *related diversification* with the related component of the entropy measure (Palepu, 1985); and *CEO succession* with a dichotomous variable equaling 1 when a firm experienced a CEO succession event (and 0 if no such event occurred), given that prior research has shown that succession events can influence investors (e.g., Zajac, 1990). Because of some missing data in the excess value measure, we performed our analysis using 384 firm/year observations.

We obtained firm financial data from the Thomson database, Datastream, and MergentOnLine. We collected CEO-level and board-level data from "Le Guide des Etats-Majors." Proxinvest provided data on CEO compensation and ownership for each owner category. In the few cases where data were unavailable from these sources, corporate annual reports provided the necessary information.

Dependent Variable

Unrelated Diversification

We calculated the unrelated component of the entropy measure (UD) to capture the firm's unrelated diversification level at each given year (Jacquemin & Berry, 1979; Palepu, 1985). This measure has high construct validity (Hoskisson, Hitt, Johnson, & Moesel, 1993) and is widely used in research on business diversification (e.g., Goranova et al., 2007; Robins & Wiersema, 1995). As per prior research, we calculated it as follows:

$$UD = \sum_{i=1}^{N} Si \ln(1/Si)$$

where Si is the share of a firm's total sales in 2-digit SIC industry i and N is the number of 2-digit SIC industries in which the firm operates. Unrelated entropy equals zero for a firm operating in a single 2-digit industry and it rises with the extent of diversity. The value of this measure in our sample ranges from 0 to 1.599, with a mean of 0.485.

Independent Variables

Ownership Categories

As per prior research (e.g., Davis et al., 1994; Fiss & Zajac, 2004; Lazonick & O'Sullivan, 2000), we consider Anglo-American owners (i.e., headquartered in the United States or the United Kingdom) as SVM oriented, domestic owners (i.e., headquartered in France) as non-SVM oriented (e.g., Katzenstein, 1985; Lubatkin et al., 2005; Zysman, 1983). *Domestic bank and insurance ownership* measures the percentage of equity ownership in the focal firm of French banks and insurance companies. *Anglo-American bank and insurance ownership* captures the percentage of ownership of

U.S.- and U.K.-based banks and insurance companies in the firm's equity. *Domestic corporate ownership* measures the percentage of equity ownership of non-financial corporate owners headquartered in France. *Anglo-American corporate ownership* measures the percentage of equity ownership of U.S.- and U.K.-based non-financial corporate owners in the firm's equity. *Domestic institutional ownership* measures the percentage of the focal firm's equity owned by institutional investors headquartered in France. *Anglo-American institutional ownership* measures the percentage of ownership of U.S.- and U.K.-based institutional investors in the firm's equity.

Firm Free Cash Flow
It is measured as operating cash flow minus cash dividends minus capital expenditures (e.g., Brush, Bromiley, & Hendrickx, 2000). Operating cash flow is defined as the net cash receipts and disbursements resulting from the operations of the firm, and measured as net cash flow minus operating activities. Thus, operating cash flow is the sum of Funds from Operations, Funds From/Used for Other Operating Activities, and Extraordinary Items (as per Thomson database).

Control Variables

Firm Core Industry Conditions
Prior research has shown that conditions in a firm's core industry can impact the firm's corporate strategy (e.g., Markides, 1992; Ravenscraft & Scherer, 1991). Thus, we control for *core industry market share* and *core industry growth*, that is, the market share of the firm in its primary 2-digit SIC industry, and the annual growth rate of the firm's primary 2-digit SIC industry, respectively.

Firm Performance
Prior research documented that firm performance is related to subsequent corporate diversification (e.g., Goranova et al., 2007; Markides, 1995). We employ two measures of performance: an industry-adjusted measure of the firm's ROA for *firm accounting performance*, that is, firm ROA minus the average industry ROA, based on each firm's primary 2-digit SIC as the firm's primary industry, and *firm stock return*, measured as the firm's stock price at the end of the year minus the firm's stock price at the

beginning of that year, plus dividends, divided by the firm's stock price at the beginning of the year.

Firm Size
Research has found that firm size increases corporate diversification (e.g., Bettis, 1981; Hoskisson & Hitt, 1994; Montgomery, 1982). We measure firm size as the log of total assets.

Firm Leverage
We measure firm leverage with the debt to equity ratio (Bergh, 1997; Jensen, 1986). Highly leveraged firms are more likely to decrease their unrelated diversification level in order to reduce their leverage (debt) and the interest burden that debt generates.

CEO Finance Background
CEOs with finance, accounting, and law background have been considered as having a greater preference for unrelated diversification (Hambrick & Mason, 1984; Jensen & Zajac, 2004). This is a dichotomous variable, which equals 1 when the firm's CEO has a dominant functional experience in finance, accounting, or law and 0 otherwise.

CEO Variable Compensation
This variable measures the ratio of variable compensation over total CEO compensation for a given year, indicating the extent to which the salary of the CEO is contingent upon some measure of firm performance (e.g., Beatty & Zajac, 1994; Tosi & Gomez-Mejia, 1989).

CEO Stock Options
Due to the importance for the board to offer or not stock options to the CEO as an incentive device, we created a dichotomous measure (e.g., Beatty & Zajac, 1994), attributing 1 when the CEO had stock options in a given year, and 0 otherwise.

CEO Ownership
According to agency theory, this is thought to align CEO interests with the ones of the firm's shareholders (Fama & Jensen, 1983; Goranova et al., 2007), thus affecting a firm's corporate strategy. We measure CEO ownership as a continuous variable indicating the share of the firm's stock (in percentage) owned by the CEO in a given year.

Chairman/CEO Duality
Whether the firm's CEO also holds the position of Chairman of the board has been linked to potential agency problems (Fama & Jensen, 1983). Given that CEOs are thought to have a preference for greater (unrelated) diversification levels than shareholders, according to agency theory (e.g., Amihud & Lev, 1981; Jensen, 1986), we expect Chairman/CEO duality to increase unrelated diversification. Chairman/CEO duality is a dichotomous variable, with a value of 1 indicating duality and 0 indicating non-duality.

Outside Directors
Outside directors are directors who are not employees of the firm (e.g., Goodstein, Gautam, & Boeker, 1994; Zahra & Pearce, 1989). This is a commonly used measure of a board's monitoring propensity (e.g., Beatty & Zajac, 1994; Daily, Dalton, & Cannella, 2003; Hill & Snell, 1988; Morck, Shleifer, & Vishny, 1988). From outside directors we excluded those that concurrently serve as CEOs in other French firms, because such directors may be less inclined to intervene independently on behalf of the focal firm's shareholders due to "solidarity" with the focal CEO. This is especially true in France, where strong ties among top executives are prevalent (e.g., Lubatkin et al., 2005). We expect the presence of outside directors to reduce subsequent unrelated diversification. This measure is the ratio of outside non-CEO directors over the total number of board directors in a given year.

Ownership Concentration
Ownership concentration, that is, the share of stock owned by the largest owner, may influence the degree of monitoring and involvement of owners in the firm's strategy formulation (e.g., Denis et al., 1997). This is a continuous variable indicating the share of stock (in percentage) owned by the largest owner.

Domestic Family Ownership
This is the percentage of ownership of domestic, that is, French owner families in the firm's equity.

Foreign Family Ownership
This variable measures the percentage of equity ownership of foreign owner families.

Domestic State Ownership

The state in France traditionally has had a very important role in business through, for instance, shares (e.g., Lubatkin et al., 2005). State-owned firms tend to behave differently than firms in which the state does not own shares (e.g., Boardman & Vining, 1989; Millward & Parker, 1983; Picot & Kaulman, 1989). Public officials representing the state may defend goals other than SVM, such as local/national employment. These goals might impact corporate strategy, and in particular lead to more diversification. Therefore, we control for this possible influence over unrelated diversification with the percentage of equity owned by the French state.

Foreign State Ownership

This variable measures the percentage of ownership of foreign states in the firm's capital.

Time Parameters

We also included year-dichotomous variables in the analyses.

Data Analysis

To test the effect of unrelated diversification on excess value, we employed instrumental variables (2SLS) regression models, which account for the endogeneity of the model's predictor (Shaver, 1998). The first stage consists in regressing unrelated diversification on a set of instruments which must satisfy the conditions of relevance and exogeneity (Bascle, 2008; Hall, Rudebusch, & Wilcox, 1996; Wooldridge, 2002). We identified three instruments that meet these criteria. The first is CEO finance background, an indicator of the CEO's inclination to engage in unrelated diversification activities (e.g., Hambrick & Mason, 1984; Jensen & Zajac, 2004). The second is CEO elite education, an indicator of power of the CEO (Finkelstein, 1992), especially in the French context (e.g., Lubatkin et al., 2005). The third is CEO tenure, an indicator of power of the CEO (e.g., Ocasio, 1994), but also an indicator of the propensity of the CEO to engage in strategic change (e.g., Miller, 1991). We report the first-stage F-statistic, the Anderson statistic, which tests for the relevance of the instruments, and the Sargan statistic, which tests for the instruments' exogeneity.

To test the hypotheses relative to the antecedents of unrelated diversification, we employed the Arellano−Bond dynamic panel data estimator which enables to deal with (1) the potentially endogenous character of our models' hypothesized predictors, that is, ownership categories, (2) the extent to which our dependent variable is predicted by its prior level, and (3) the relatively short time dimension (Arellano & Bond, 1991). To test the hypotheses of this study that involve multiplicative interaction terms, we further calculated the joint effect (Friedrich, 1982) of our main predictors (i.e., ownership variables) for high values (i.e., one standard deviation above the mean) of our moderating variable (i.e., FCF).

RESULTS

Table 2 presents descriptive statistics and correlations for the full panel dataset. Table 3 presents the regression results of estimating models predicting excess value (Model 1) and unrelated diversification (Models 2, 3, and 4). In Table 3, all models are significant at $p \leq 0.001$.

In Model 1, the first-stage F-statistic and the Anderson statistic are significant at $p \leq 0.001$, indicating the relevance of the instruments employed. Further, the lack of significance for the Sargan statistic in Model 1 indicates that our instruments are exogenous. Moreover, Model 1 shows that unrelated diversification negatively impacts excess value ($p \leq 0.05$), thus revealing the value-destroying character of unrelated diversification in the French context during the period considered.

Model 2 represents the control model predicting unrelated diversification. As shown in Model 2, firm accounting performance, foreign family ownership, and foreign state ownership are significant and positively related to unrelated diversification ($p \leq 0.10$, $p \leq 0.001$, and $p \leq 0.05$, respectively). CEO ownership is significant and negatively related to unrelated diversification ($p \leq 0.10$).

Model 3 includes, in addition to the control variables, the direct effects of our predictors, namely Anglo-American and domestic (French, non-SVM) ownership variables, and FCF. In Model 3, Anglo-American bank and insurance ownership is significantly ($p \leq 0.05$) and negatively related to unrelated diversification, thus supporting Hypothesis 2. In addition, domestic (French, non-SVM) institutional ownership is significantly ($p \leq 0.10$) and positively related to unrelated diversification, thus supporting Hypothesis 4. The effects of Anglo-American institutional ownership and of domestic bank, insurance, and corporate ownership are not significant, thus not providing support to Hypothesis 1 and Hypothesis 3.

Table 2. Descriptive Statistics and Correlation Matrix.

Variable	Mean	SD	1	2	3	4	5	6	7	8	9	10	11
1. Excess value	0.12	1.19	1.00										
2. Firm unrelated diversification	0.49	0.42	−0.07	1.00									
3. Core industry market share	0.29	0.27	−0.14	−0.10	1.00								
4. Core industry growth	0.05	0.15	−0.04	0.07	0.03	1.00							
5. Firm accounting performance	0.71	5.82	0.08	−0.14	−0.06	−0.03	1.00						
6. Firm stock return	0.12	0.42	−0.03	0.02	0.06	−0.01	0.12	1.00					
7. Firm size	9.67	1.51	0.21	0.03	0.07	0.05	−0.14	−0.03	1.00				
8. Firm leverage	2.00	8.03	0.01	0.12	−0.07	0.01	−0.19	−0.05	0.11	1.00			
9. Firm financial diversification	−0.19	0.44	−0.06	−0.13	0.03	−0.07	0.02	0.11	−0.09	−0.07	1.00		
10. Firm-related diversification	0.31	0.33	0.10	−0.29	0.00	−0.10	−0.03	−0.04	0.10	−0.01	0.09	1.00	
11. CEO succession	0.12	0.32	0.01	0.03	0.00	−0.01	−0.10	−0.03	0.05	0.00	0.00	0.00	1.00
12. CEO finance background	0.53	0.50	0.12	−0.03	−0.11	0.01	−0.04	−0.09	0.09	0.01	0.06	−0.15	0.02
13. CEO variable compensation	0.38	0.27	0.04	−0.07	0.21	−0.08	0.13	0.19	0.36	0.06	0.06	−0.01	−0.02
14. CEO stock options	0.57	0.50	0.05	−0.10	0.06	−0.14	0.06	0.03	0.19	0.03	0.11	0.10	−0.01
15. CEO ownership	4.02	12.06	0.03	0.07	0.18	0.00	−0.05	0.00	−0.14	−0.03	0.07	−0.10	−0.05
16. Chairman/CEO duality	0.59	0.49	0.14	−0.03	0.01	0.08	−0.06	−0.03	0.04	0.00	0.02	0.00	−0.20
17. Outside directors	0.82	0.14	−0.04	−0.12	0.05	−0.06	−0.01	0.03	−0.16	−0.02	0.00	0.01	0.03
18. Ownership concentration	25.00	20.00	−0.04	−0.13	−0.15	−0.04	0.00	−0.04	−0.10	−0.08	−0.04	0.04	−0.02
19. Domestic family ownership	4.81	13.87	−0.23	−0.07	−0.15	−0.04	0.15	−0.04	−0.11	−0.04	−0.11	−0.09	−0.01
20. Foreign family ownership	0.27	2.12	−0.09	0.02	−0.02	−0.03	−0.17	−0.04	−0.09	−0.01	0.08	−0.10	0.07
21. Domestic state ownership	5.52	12.27	0.04	−0.09	0.13	0.01	−0.09	−0.03	0.11	−0.03	−0.12	−0.04	0.03
22. Foreign state ownership	0.36	1.91	0.02	0.02	0.04	−0.04	0.05	0.13	0.04	0.01	0.05	−0.07	0.20
23. Domestic bank and insurance Ownership	2.09	4.30	0.04	0.17	0.02	0.05	−0.15	0.00	0.05	0.06	0.04	−0.08	−0.09
24. Anglo-American bank and insurance ownership	0.40	2.63	0.05	0.00	0.03	−0.05	−0.13	−0.01	0.04	0.00	−0.11	0.01	0.01
25. Domestic corporate ownership	4.72	12.91	−0.04	0.03	−0.17	0.04	0.12	0.05	−0.18	−0.03	−0.10	−0.12	0.00
26. Anglo-American corporate ownership	0.44	2.55	−0.03	0.11	−0.07	−0.06	−0.05	−0.06	−0.01	−0.02	−0.06	0.05	0.09
27. Domestic institutional ownership	1.82	5.24	0.00	0.05	−0.12	−0.06	−0.03	0.01	−0.08	0.04	0.11	0.09	0.08
28. Anglo-American institutional ownership	2.26	5.26	0.03	−0.05	−0.05	−0.03	−0.06	0.03	−0.05	0.05	0.03	0.03	0.07
29. Firm free cash flow	1.11	3.09	−0.08	−0.17	0.05	0.08	−0.01	0.00	0.51	0.04	0.12	0.12	0.04

Table 2. (Continued)

Variable	12	13	14	15	16	17	18	19	20	21	22	23	24
12. CEO finance background	1.00												
13. CEO variable compensation	−0.02	1.00											
14. CEO stock options	−0.06	0.29	1.00										
15. CEO ownership	−0.02	−0.01	−0.14	1.00									
16. Chairman/CEO duality	0.08	−0.11	0.03	0.14	1.00								
17. Outside directors	0.06	−0.06	−0.07	−0.26	−0.46	1.00							
18. Ownership concentration	0.01	−0.32	−0.28	0.25	0.03	0.12	1.00						
19. Domestic family ownership	−0.15	−0.08	−0.07	−0.11	−0.05	0.09	0.33	1.00					
20. Foreign family ownership	0.02	−0.07	0.04	−0.04	−0.07	0.08	−0.04	−0.02	1.00				
21. Domestic state ownership	0.14	−0.13	−0.09	−0.13	0.21	−0.03	0.21	−0.12	0.00	1.00			
22. Foreign state ownership	0.06	0.09	0.07	−0.06	−0.10	−0.06	−0.09	−0.06	−0.02	0.04	1.00		
23. Domestic bank and insurance ownership	0.11	−0.01	−0.18	0.35	0.11	−0.10	−0.04	−0.12	−0.05	−0.14	−0.09	1.00	
24. Anglo-American bank and insurance Ownership	−0.03	0.00	−0.08	−0.06	0.00	−0.04	−0.09	0.04	−0.02	−0.05	0.05	0.05	1.00
25. Domestic corporate ownership	−0.01	−0.08	−0.09	−0.03	0.17	−0.07	0.03	0.17	−0.04	−0.03	0.07	−0.07	−0.03
26. Anglo-American corporate ownership	0.05	−0.08	−0.04	−0.05	−0.01	0.02	−0.03	−0.06	0.04	0.09	−0.02	−0.06	0.04
27. Domestic institutional ownership	0.00	0.04	0.03	0.06	0.04	0.04	−0.10	0.02	−0.04	−0.09	−0.06	0.04	−0.06
28. Anglo-American institutional ownership	0.00	0.13	−0.10	−0.03	−0.08	0.07	−0.11	−0.06	−0.02	−0.07	−0.03	−0.02	0.05
29. Firm free cash flow	0.14	0.17	0.09	−0.07	−0.04	−0.02	0.03	−0.09	−0.03	0.12	−0.01	0.01	0.00

Variable	25	26	27	28	29
25. Domestic corporate ownership	1.00				
26. Anglo-American corporate ownership	−0.02	1.00			
27. Domestic institutional ownership	0.01	−0.03	1.00		
28. Anglo-American institutional ownership	0.01	−0.03	0.47	1.00	
29. Firm free cash flow	−0.08	−0.03	−0.09	0.01	1.00

Notes: $N = 414$ ($N = 384$ for excess value); all correlations equal or above 0.10 are significant at $p \leq 0.05$.
$N = 414$; all correlations equal or above 0.10 are significant at $p \leq 0.05$.

Table 3. 2SLS/IV Regression of Excess Value (Model 1), Arellano–Bond Estimation of Unrelated Diversification (Models 2–4).

Variable	Model 1	Model 2	Model 3	Model 4
Constant	−3.670 (0.746)***	−0.257 (0.750)	−0.391 (0.732)	−0.203 (0.754)
Prior unrelated diversification		1.316 (0.385)***	1.294 (0.317)***	1.385 (0.345)***
Core industry market share	−1.068 (0.285)***	0.131 (0.250)	0.145 (0.250)	0.243 (0.262)
Core industry growth	−0.081 (0.403)	−0.098 (0.155)	−0.108 (0.142)	−0.050 (0.140)
Firm accounting performance	0.029 (0.010)**	0.007 (0.004)†	0.007 (0.004)†	0.007 (0.004)†
Firm stock return	−0.218 (0.173)	−0.020 (0.030)	−0.021 (0.027)	−0.036 (0.032)
Firm size	0.345 (0.053)***	0.017 (0.070)	0.026 (0.069)	0.008 (0.067)
Firm leverage	0.001 (0.007)	0.004 (0.004)	0.002 (0.005)	0.004 (0.005)
Firm financial diversification	−0.115 (0.137)			
Firm-related diversification	−0.108 (0.259)			
CEO succession	0.191 (0.178)			
CEO finance background	−0.286 (0.326)	−0.032 (0.044)	−0.030 (0.041)	−0.044 (0.044)
CEO variable compensation	0.018 (0.138)	0.166 (0.103)	0.192 (0.103)†	0.157 (0.110)
CEO stock options	1.600 (0.623)**	−0.020 (0.043)	−0.020 (0.042)	−0.042 (0.042)
CEO ownership	0.351 (0.144)*	−0.003 (0.002)†	−0.004 (0.002)*	−0.004 (0.002)†
Chairman/CEO duality	1.041 (0.523)*	0.042 (0.071)	0.056 (0.079)	0.060 (0.087)
Outside directors	−0.408 (0.366)	−0.212 (0.171)	−0.220 (0.148)	−0.228 (0.174)
Ownership concentration	−0.021 (0.005)***	−0.005 (0.013)	−0.001 (0.002)	−0.002 (0.002)
Domestic family ownership	−0.022 (0.025)	−0.004 (0.031)	−0.006 (0.029)	−0.002 (0.003)
Foreign family ownership	0.001 (0.006)	0.018 (0.005)***	0.026 (0.008)***	0.027 (0.008)***
Domestic state ownership	0.002 (0.029)	0.003 (0.002)	0.003 (0.002)	0.003 (0.002)
Foreign state ownership		0.018 (0.008)*	0.020 (0.008)*	0.022 (0.008)**
Domestic bank and insurance ownership	−0.001 (0.014)		0.002 (0.006)	0.006 (0.007)
Anglo-American bank and insurance ownership	0.037 (0.027)		−0.017 (0.008)*	−0.026 (0.007)***
Domestic corporate ownership	−0.001 (0.004)		0.002 (0.002)	0.005 (0.003)
Anglo-American corporate ownership	−0.016 (0.022)		0.005 (0.003)	0.020 (0.006)***
Domestic institutional ownership	−0.006 (0.013)		0.015 (0.008)†	0.013 (0.016)
Anglo-American institutional ownership	0.010 (0.013)		−0.008 (0.007)	−0.008 (0.007)

Table 3. (*Continued*)

Variable	Model 1	Model 2	Model 3	Model 4
Firm free cash flow (FCF)	−0.121 (0.024)***		0.015 (0.025)	0.028 (0.027)
Firm unrelated diversification	−0.966 (0.479)*			
FCF × Domestic bank and insurance ownership				0.007 (0.005)
FCF × Anglo-American bank and insurance ownership				−0.017 (0.005)***
FCF × Domestic corporate ownership				0.003 (0.003)
FCF × Anglo-American corporate ownership				0.024 (0.007)***
FCF × Domestic institutional ownership				−0.006 (0.014)
FCF × Anglo-American institutional ownership				0.004 (0.001)**
F-statistic (1st stage)	12.62***			
F-statistic	4.09***			
Anderson statistic	37.57***			
Sargan statistic	2.97			
Wald χ^2		78.74***	115.72***	266.72***

Notes: Std errors are in parentheses; year-dichotomous variables were included in all models; $N = 414$ ($N = 384$ for Model 1).
†$p \leq 0.10$; *$p \leq 0.05$; **$p \leq 0.01$; ***$p \leq 0.001$.

Model 4 represents the full model predicting unrelated diversification, which includes the interaction terms between the hypothesized ownership predictors and FCF. As shown in Model 4, the interaction of FCF with Anglo-American bank and insurance ownership is significant ($p \leq 0.001$) and negative. The interactions of FCF with Anglo-American corporate ownership and Anglo-American institutional ownership are significant ($p \leq 0.001$ and $p \leq 0.01$ respectively) and positive. However, to test our Hypotheses 5a and 5b, we calculated the joint effects of Anglo-American institutional ownership, Anglo-American bank and insurance ownership, and Anglo-American corporate ownership, respectively, under conditions of high FCF (Friedrich, 1982). When FCF is high (i.e., one standard deviation above the mean), the joint effect of Anglo-American institutional ownership and of the interaction between Anglo-American institutional ownership with FCF is not significant, thus not supporting Hypothesis 5a. However, we found that when FCF is low (i.e., one standard deviation below the mean), the joint effect of Anglo-American institutional ownership and of the interaction between Anglo-American institutional ownership with FCF is significantly ($\chi^2 = 4.13$ at $p \leq 0.05$) and negatively related to unrelated diversification.

When FCF is high (i.e., one standard deviation above the mean), the joint effect of Anglo-American bank and insurance ownership and of the interaction between Anglo-American bank and insurance ownership with FCF is significantly ($\chi^2 = 13.10$ at $p \leq 0.001$) and negatively related to unrelated diversification, thus supporting Hypothesis 5b. When FCF is high (i.e., one standard deviation above the mean), the joint effect of Anglo-American corporate ownership and of the interaction between Anglo-American corporate ownership with FCF is significantly ($\chi^2 = 12.86$ at $p \leq 0.001$) and positively related to unrelated diversification, in contrast to Hypothesis 5b.

Overall, we found support for Hypotheses 2, 4, and (partially for) 5b, but no support for Hypotheses 1, 3, and 5a.

Supplemental Analysis

Although banks and insurance companies, and (non-financial) corporate owners are different types of organizations, they are both considered as pressure-sensitive (e.g., Brickley et al., 1988). We thus further estimated their effect on subsequent unrelated diversification by combining them in one variable. The direct effect of the combined Anglo-American bank and insurance ownership with Anglo-American corporate ownership has no significant effect. That is, the effect of Anglo-American bank and insurance ownership ($p \leq 0.05$) loses its significance when combined in the same variable with Anglo-American corporate ownership. The direct effect of domestic institutional investors remains significant at the same level ($p \leq 0.10$) and positive. The interaction of FCF with the combined Anglo-American bank and insurance ownership with Anglo-American corporate ownership has no significant effect, which means that their combination cancels out the two opposing effects of Anglo-American bank and insurance ownership (negative at $p \leq 0.001$) and Anglo-American corporate ownership (positive at $p \leq 0.001$). We observed the same when calculating the joint effects of the hypothesized owner category effects, under conditions of high FCF, that is, the significant but contrasting effects of Anglo-American bank and insurance ownership, and Anglo-American corporate ownership, become non-significant when combining them in a single-owner category. The interaction between FCF and Anglo-American institutional investors remains significant at a similar level and positive. Therefore, by distinguishing between banks and insurance companies, and corporate owners, we are able to reveal the differing effects of each of these two categories of owners, despite being considered as having the same monitoring inclination (e.g., Brickley et al., 1988). We additionally tested the effects of Anglo-American owners combined in one variable (i.e., Anglo-American bank and insurance ownership, corporate ownership, and institutional investor ownership) and domestic owners combined in one variable. The results show that, while Anglo-American owners combined do not have a significant direct effect on unrelated diversification, domestic owners have a positive effect on unrelated diversification ($p \leq 0.10$), in line with our theory. Furthermore, we tested our interaction model by excluding the interaction terms for which we do not hypothesize (i.e., the interaction terms of FCF with domestic bank and insurance ownership, of FCF with domestic corporate ownership, and of FCF with domestic institutional ownership). The results remained similar. Finally, to increase our confidence in the results, we tested our models (of direct effects and of interaction effects) by excluding all control variables that were not significant in any of the three models estimating unrelated diversification, presented in Table 3. Again, the results remained the same.[2]

DISCUSSION AND CONCLUSION

In this study, we discussed that to understand the effects of corporate ownership structure on a firm's corporate strategy, one has to account for the institutional origin of owners, next to their monitoring inclination. We propose that differences in the extent to which firms engage in a type of corporate strategy, namely unrelated diversification, can be at least partially attributable to differences among owner categories in terms of their monitoring inclination – pressure resistant versus pressure sensitive – and institutional origin – Anglo-American SVM-oriented versus French non-SVM oriented. In a panel dataset from 60 French publicly-listed firms during the 2000–2007 period, we find that (1) unrelated diversification destroys value; (2) the presence of supposedly pressure-sensitive (i.e., banks and insurance companies) Anglo-American owners reduces subsequent unrelated diversification; (3) allegedly pressure-resistant (i.e., institutional) French owners increases subsequent unrelated diversification; and (4) the greater the firm's FCF, the greater the negative effect of pressure-sensitive (i.e., banks and insurance companies) Anglo-American owners on subsequent unrelated diversification. In addition, we find that when FCF is low, the presence of Anglo-American institutional owners reduces unrelated diversification. We speculate that low FCF leads Anglo-American institutional investors to promote a reduction in the firm's unrelated diversification, possibly through business divestments, so that the firm increases its financial resources available, and thus the potential for returning these resources to shareholders, in the form of dividends or share repurchases.

This study contributes to institutional and behavioral research on corporate governance (e.g., Aguilera & Jackson, 2003; Davis et al., 1994; Hambrick et al., 2008; Westphal & Zajac, 2013), and extends prior research as to the effect of different types of owners on a variety of corporate outcomes (e.g., Bethel & Liebeskind, 1993; Brickley et al., 1988; Fiss & Zajac, 2004; Hoskisson et al., 2002; Ramaswamy et al., 2002). We show that besides formal governance devices (e.g., Amihud & Lev, 1981; Goranova et al., 2007; Lane et al., 1998) the categorization of owners based on their monitoring inclination and institutional origin (thus the associated normative beliefs about governance and strategy that institutional origin is thought to proxy) is an important determinant of unrelated diversification. Overall, our findings confirm our thesis that owners' institutional (country of) origin matters. It has a stronger influence than the owners' supposed role in terms of inclination – pressure resistant versus pressure sensitive.

That is, institutional origin and the beliefs that stem from it appear to overshadow the owners' monitoring inclination as characterized by Brickley et al. (1988). We believe this is an important extension of the institutional and behavioral views on corporate governance and strategy, which to a large extent seem to contradict the primacy of owner monitoring inclination, as theorized by research that draws upon the dominant agency perspective (Brickley et al., 1988).

Moreover, prior research classified countries' corporate governance systems (including France) assuming governance homogeneity within a country (e.g., Gedajlovic & Shapiro, 1998). We contribute to this literature by unpacking differences between firms in terms of ownership across firms headquartered in the same country, and in a much less studied institutional (country) context with a different governance tradition, as compared to the Anglo-American one.

As any research, this study also has limitations. Specifically, we test our contingent model in one context (France). Future research may extend our investigation to a variety of other contexts where publicly-listed firms also exhibit ownership heterogeneity, in terms of their institutional origin. It would be interesting to test our hypotheses (for firms originating or headquartered) in other countries where SVM is not the dominant ideology, such as Germany or Japan, as well as in countries – such as the United States or the United Kingdom – where SVM is the dominant ideology. In addition, a more detailed account of foreign ownership effects besides Anglo-American ones may increase our understanding of the ownership drivers of corporate strategy. Future research can also theorize for other types of owners, such as states and families, based on their institutional origin. In our study, we find that foreign family ownership and foreign state ownership (at large) significantly impact unrelated diversification. Unpacking these categories based on their institutional origin may offer new insights as regards to owner effects on corporate strategy.

Overall, this study offers an explanation as to ownership effects on a particular type of corporate strategy, namely unrelated diversification. The owners' institutional origin (and the associated normative beliefs about governance and strategy) matters in predicting the owners' strategic outlook in regards to the pursuit or prevention of unrelated diversification by French publicly traded firms, in a period of increasing presence of Anglo-American owners in those firms. Policy makers, financial analysts, owners, and managers may want to incorporate these findings to reflect about the implications of promoting, impeding, or joining certain owner categories, as well as joining corporations with particular ownership configurations.

NOTES

1. Next to agency-theoretic explanations, transaction cost and internal cost arguments can explain whether corporate diversification has a positive or negative effect on performance. For the case of related diversification, the possibility of exploiting through contracts versus internal exploitation has to be considered (e.g., Silverman, 1999; Teece, 1980) and contracts could be more profitable than internalization. However, for the case of unrelated diversification, it is by definition not possible to create economic synergies from relatedness. We also highlight that our focus on agency explanations is due to the belief in the Anglo-American context that unrelated diversification stems from agency problems (e.g., Davis, Diekman, & Tinsley, 1994; Lazonick & O'Sullivan, 2000). We thank an anonymous reviewer for encouraging us to further clarify this point.

2. We thank the editor for these suggestions to further strengthen the robustness of our analysis.

REFERENCES

Agrawal, A., & Mandelker, G. N. (1987). Managerial incentives, corporate investment and financing decisions. *Journal of Finance, 42*(4), 823–837.

Aguilera, R. V., & Jackson, G. (2003). The cross-national diversity of corporate governance: Dimensions and determinants. *Academy of Management Review, 28*(3), 447–465.

Amihud, Y., & Lev, B. (1981). Risk reduction as a managerial motive for conglomerate mergers. *Bell Journal of Economics, 12*(2), 605–617.

Arellano, M., & Bond, S. (1991). Some tests of specification for panel data: Monte Carlo evidence and application to employment equations. *Review of Economic Studies, 58*, 277–297.

Bascle, G. (2008). Controlling for endogeneity with instrumental variables in strategic management research. *Strategic Organization, 6*, 285–327.

Beatty, R. P., & Zajac, E. J. (1994). Managerial incentives, monitoring, and risk bearing: A study of executive compensation, ownership, and board structure in initial public offerings. *Administrative Science Quarterly, 39*(2), 313–335.

Berger, P. G., & Ofek, E. (1995). Diversification's effect on firm value. *Journal of Financial Economics, 37*(1), 39–65.

Bergh, D. D. (1997). Predicting divestiture of unrelated acquisitions: An integrative model of ex ante conditions. *Strategic Management Journal, 18*(9), 715–731.

Bethel, J. E., & Liebeskind, J. (1993). The effects of ownership structure on corporate restructuring. *Strategic Management Journal, 14*(Special issue), 15–31.

Bettis, R. A. (1981). Performance differences in related and unrelated diversified firms. *Strategic Management Journal, 2*(4), 379–393.

Boardman, A., & Vining, A. (1989). Ownership and performance in competitive environments: A comparison of the performance of private, mixed, and state-owned enterprises. *Journal of Law and Economics, 32*, 1–33.

Brickley, J. A., Lease, R. C., & Smith, C. W. (1988). Ownership structure and voting on antitakeover amendments. *Journal of Financial Economics, 20*, 267–291.

Brush, T. H., Bromiley, P., & Hendrickx, M. (2000). The free cash flow hypothesis for sales growth and firm performance. *Strategic Management Journal, 21,* 455–472.

Campa, J. M., & Kedia, S. (2002). Explaining the diversification discount. *Journal of Finance, 57*(4), 1731–1762.

Castañer, X., & Kavadis, N. (2013). Does good governance prevent bad strategy? A study of corporate governance, financial diversification, and value creation by French corporations, 2000–2006. *Strategic Management Journal, 34,* 863–876.

Clift, B. (2007). French corporate governance in the new global economy: Mechanisms of change and hybridization within models of capitalism. *Political Studies, 55,* 546–567.

Daily, C. M., Dalton, D. R., & Cannella, A. A. (2003). Corporate governance: Decades of dialogue and data. *Academy of Management Review, 28*(3), 371–382.

Dalton, D., Hitt, M., Certo, T., & Dalton, C. (2007). The fundamental agency problem and its mitigation: Independence, equity and the market for corporate control. *Academy of Management Annals, 1,* 1–64.

David, P., Kochhar, R., & Levitas, E. (1998). The effects of institutional investors on the level and mix of CEO compensation. *Academy of Management Journal, 41,* 200–208.

David, P., O'Brien, J. P., Yashikawa, T., & Delios, A. (2010). Do shareholders or stakeholders appropriate the rents from corporate diversification? The influence of ownership structure. *Academy of Management Journal, 53,* 636–655.

Davis, G. F., Diekmann, K. A., & Tinsley, C. H. (1994). The decline and fall of the conglomerate firm in the 1980s: A study in the de-institutionalization of an organizational form. *American Sociological Review, 59,* 547–570.

Denis, D. J., Denis, D. K., & Sarin, A. (1997). Agency problems, equity ownership and corporate diversification. *Journal of Finance, 52*(1), 135–160.

Deutsche Bank Research. (1998, November 23). French institutional investors: A pivotal position in the euro zone. In U. Schröder (Eds.), *EMU Watch* (Vol. 61, pp. 1–16). Frankfurt am Main: Deutsche Bank.

Douma, S., George, R., & Kabir, R. (2006). Foreign and domestic ownership, business groups, and firm performance: Evidence from a large emerging market. *Strategic Management Journal, 27,* 637–657.

Eisenhardt, K. M. (1989). Agency theory: An assessment and review. *Academy of Management Review, 14*(1), 57–74.

Fama, E. F., & Jensen, M. C. (1983). Separation of ownership and control. *Journal of Law and Economics, 26,* 1–32.

Finkelstein, S. (1992). Power in top management teams: Dimensions, measurement, and validation. *Academy of Management Journal, 35*(3), 505–538.

Fiss, P. C., & Zajac, E. J. (2004). The diffusion of ideas over contested terrain: The (non)adoption of a shareholder value orientation among German firms. *Administrative Science Quarterly, 49*(4), 501–534.

Fligstein, N. (1990). *The transformation of corporate control.* Cambridge, MA: Harvard University Press.

Friedrich, R. J. (1982). In defense of multiplicative terms in multiple regression equations. *American Journal of Political Science, 26*(4), 797–833.

Gedajlovic, E. R., & Shapiro, D. M. (1998). Management and ownership effects: Evidence from five countries. *Strategic Management Journal, 19,* 533–553.

Goodstein, J., Gautam, K., & Boeker, W. (1994). The effects of board size and diversity on strategic change. *Strategic Management Journal, 15*(3), 241–250.

Goranova, M., Alessandri, T. M., Brandes, P., & Dharwadkar, R. (2007). Managerial ownership and corporate diversification: A longitudinal view. *Strategic Management Journal*, 28, 211–225.

Goyer, M. (2003). Corporate governance, employees, and the focus on core competencies in France and Germany. In C. Milhaupt (Ed.), *Global markets, domestic institutions* (pp. 183–213). New York, NY: Columbia University Press.

Granovetter, M. S. (1985). Economic action and social structure: The problem of embeddedness. *American Journal of Sociology*, 91(3), 481–510.

Guillén, M. F. (2000). Corporate governance and globalization: Is there convergence across countries? *Advances in International Comparative Management*, 13, 175–204.

Hall, A., Rudebusch, G., & Wilcox, D. (1996). Judging instrument relevance in instrumental variables' estimation. *International Economic Review*, 37, 283–298.

Hambrick, D. C., & Mason, P. A. (1984). Upper echelons: The organization as a reflection of its top managers. *Academy of Management Review*, 9(2), 193–206.

Hambrick, D. C., v. Werder, A., & Zajac, E. J. (2008). New directions in corporate governance research. *Organization Science*, 19(3), 381–385.

Hill, C. W., & Hansen, G. (1991). Are institutional investors myopic? A time-series study of four technology-driven industries. *Strategic Management Journal*, 12, 577–590.

Hill, C. W., & Snell, S. A. (1988). External control, corporate strategy, and firm performance in research intensive industries. *Strategic Management Journal*, 9(6), 577–590.

Hollingsworth, J. R., Schmitter, P. C., & Streeck, W. (1994). *Governing capitalist economies: Performance and control of economic sectors*. New York, NY: Oxford University Press.

Hoskisson, R. E., & Hitt, M. A. (1994). *Downscoping: How to tame the diversified firm*. New York, NY: Oxford University Press.

Hoskisson, R. E., Hitt, M. A., Johnson, R. A., & Grossman, W. (2002). Conflicting voices: The effects of institutional ownership heterogeneity and internal governance on corporate innovation strategies. *Academy of Management Journal*, 45(4), 697–716.

Hoskisson, R. E., Hitt, M. A., Johnson, R. A., & Moesel, D. D. (1993). Construct validity of an objective (entropy) categorical measure of diversification strategy. *Strategic Management Journal*, 14, 215–235.

Jackson, G. (2005). Stakeholders under pressure: Corporate governance and labor management in Germany and Japan. *Corporate Governance: An International Review*, 13(3), 419–428.

Jacquemin, A. P., & Berry, C. H. (1979). Entropy measure of diversification and corporate growth. *Journal of Industrial Economics*, 27(4), 359–369.

Jensen, M. C. (1986). Agency costs of free cash flow, corporate finance and takeovers. *American Economic Review*, 76(2), 323–329.

Jensen, M. C., & Meckling, W. H. (1976). Theory of the firm: Managerial behavior, agency costs and ownership structure. *Journal of Financial Economics*, 3(4), 305–360.

Jensen, M. C., & Zajac, E. J. (2004). Corporate elites and corporate strategy: How demographic preferences and structural position shape the scope of the firm. *Strategic Management Journal*, 25(6), 507–524.

Kadushin, C. (1995). Friendship among the French financial elite. *American Sociological Review*, 60, 202–221.

Katzenstein, P. J. (1985). *Small states in world markets: Industrial policy in Europe*. London: Cornell University Press.

Kochhar, R., & David, P. (1996). Institutional investors and firm innovation: A test of competing hypotheses. *Strategic Management Journal, 17*, 73–84.

Kwok, C. C. Y., & Tadesse, S. (2006). National culture and financial systems. *Journal of International Business Studies, 37*, 227–247.

La Porta, R., Lopez-de-Silanes, F., Shleifer, A., & Vishny, R. W. (1998). Law and finance. *Journal of Political Economy, 106*(6), 1113–1155.

Lane, P. J., Cannella, A. A., & Lubatkin, M. H. (1998). Agency problems as antecedents to unrelated mergers and diversification: Amihud and Lev reconsidered. *Strategic Management Journal, 19*(6), 555–578.

Lane, P. J., Cannella, A. A., & Lubatkin, M. H. (1999). Ownership structure and corporate strategy: One question viewed from two different worlds. *Strategic Management Journal, 20*, 1077–1086.

Lazonick, W., & O'Sullivan, M. (2000). Maximizing shareholder value: A new ideology for corporate governance. *Economy and Society, 29*(1), 13–35.

Lubatkin, M. H., Lane, P. J., Collin, S. O., & Very, P. (2005). Origins of corporate governance in the USA, Sweden and France. *Organization Studies, 26*(6), 867–888.

Maclean, M., Harvey, C., & Press, J. (2006). *Business elites and corporate governance in France and the UK*. Basingstoke: Palgrave Millan.

Markides, C. C. (1992). Consequences of corporate refocusing: Ex-ante evidence. *Academy of Management Journal, 35*, 398–412.

Markides, C. C. (1995). Diversification, restructuring and economic performance. *Strategic Management Journal, 16*, 101–118.

Mayer, M., & Whittington, R. (2003). Diversification in context: A cross-national and cross-temporal extension. *Strategic Management Journal, 24*(8), 773–781.

Miller, D. (1991). Stale in the saddle: CEO tenure and the match between organization and environment. *Management Science, 37*(1), 34–52.

Millward, R., & Parker, D. M. (1983). Public and private enterprise: Comparative behaviour and relative efficiency. In R. Millward, D. Parker, & L. Rosenthal (Eds.), *Public sector economics* (pp. 199–274). London: Longman.

Mizruchi, M. (1996). What do interlocks do? An analysis, critique, and assessment of research on interlocking directorates. *Annual Review of Sociology, 22*, 271–298.

Montgomery, C. A. (1982). The measurement of firm diversification: Some new empirical evidence. *Academy of Management Journal, 28*, 299–307.

Montgomery, C. A. (1994). Corporate diversification. *Journal of Economic Perspectives, 8*(3), 163–178.

Morck, R., Shleifer, A., & Vishny, R. W. (1988). Management ownership and market valuation. *Journal of Financial Economics, 20*, 293–315.

Morin, F. (2000). A transformation in the French model of shareholding and management. *Economy and Society, 29*(1), 36–53.

Murphy, K. J. (1985). Corporate performance and managerial remuneration: An empirical analysis. *Journal of Accounting and Economics, 7*, 11–42.

Murtha, T. P., & Lenway, S. A. (1994). Country capabilities and the strategic state: How political institutions affect multinational corporations' strategies. *Strategic Management Journal, 15*, 113–129.

Ocasio, W. (1994). Political dynamics and the circulation of power: CEO succession in the US industrial corporations, 1960–1990. *Administrative Science Quarterly, 39*(2), 285–312.

Palepu, K. (1985). Diversification strategy, profit performance and the entropy measure. *Strategic Management Journal, 6*(3), 239–255.

Palich, L. E., Cardinal, L. B., & Miller, C. C. (2000). Curvilinearity in the diversification-performance linkage: An examination of over three decades of research. *Strategic Management Journal, 21*(2), 155–174.

Pfeffer, J., & Salancik, G. R. (1978). *The external control of organizations: A resource dependence perspective.* New York, NY: Harper and Row.

Picot, A., & Kaulman, T. (1989). Comparative performance of government-owned and privately-owned industrial corporations. Empirical results from six countries. *Journal of Institutional and Theoretical Economics, 14*, 298–316.

Porter, M. E. (1987). From competitive advantage to corporate strategy. *Harvard Business Review, 65*, 43–59.

Pound, J. (1988). Proxy contests and the efficiency of shareholder oversight. *Journal of Financial Economics, 20*, 237–265.

Pound, J. (1992). Beyond takeovers: Politics comes to corporate control. *Harvard Business Review, 70*, 83–93.

Ramaswamy, K., Li, M., & Veliyath, R. (2002). Variation in ownership behavior and propensity to diversify: A study of the Indian context. *Strategic Management Journal, 23*, 345–358.

Ravenscraft, D. J., & Scherer, F. M. (1991). Divisional sell-off: A hazard function analysis. *Managerial and Decision Economics, 12*(6), 429–438.

Robins, J., & Wiersema, M. F. (1995). A resource-based approach to the multibusiness firm: Empirical analysis of portfolio interrelationships and corporate financial performance. *Strategic Management Journal, 16*(4), 277–299.

Ross, S. (1973). The economic theory of agency: The principal's problem. *American Economic Review, 63*, 134–139.

Rumelt, R. (1974). *Strategy, structure, and economic performance.* Boston, MA: Harvard Business School.

Rumelt, R. (1982). Diversification strategy and profitability. *Strategic Management Journal, 3*, 359–369.

Schmidt, V. A. (2003). French capitalism transformed, yet still a third variety of capitalism. *Economy and Society, 32*(4), 526–554.

Shaver, J. (1998). Accounting for endogeneity when assessing strategy performance: Does entry mode choice affect FDI survival? *Management Science, 44*, 571–585.

Silverman, B. S. (1999). Technological resources and the direction of corporate diversification: Toward an integration of the resource-based view and transaction cost economics. *Management Science, 45*(8), 1109–1124.

Teece, D. (1980). Economies of scope and the scope of the enterprise. *Journal of Economic Behavior and Organization, 1*, 223–247.

Tosi, H. L., & Gomez-Mejia, L. R. (1989). The decoupling of CEO pay and performance: An agency theory perspective. *Administrative Science Quarterly, 34*, 169–190.

Useem, M. (1984). *The inner circle: Large corporations and the rise of business political activity in the U.S. and U.K.* New York, NY: Oxford University Press.

Useem, M. (1993). *Executive defense: Shareholder power and corporate reorganization.* Cambridge, MA: Harvard University Press.

Villalonga, B. (2004). Diversification discount or premium? New evidence from the business information tracking series. *Journal of Finance, 59*(2), 479–506.

Westphal, J. D., & Zajac, E. J. (2013). A behavioral theory of corporate governance. *Academy of Management Annals, 7*(1), 605–659.
Whittington, R., & Mayer, M. C. J. (2000). *The European corporation: Strategy, structure and social science*. New York, NY: Oxford University Press.
Wooldridge, J. (2002). *Econometric analysis of cross section and panel data*. Cambridge, MA: The MIT Press.
Zaheer, S. (1995). Overcoming the liability of foreignness. *Academy of Management Journal, 38*(2), 341–363.
Zaheer, S., & Mosakowski, E. (1998). The dynamics of the liability of foreignness: A global study of survival in financial services. *Strategic Management Journal, 18*(6), 439–464.
Zahra, S. A., & Pearce, J. A. (1989). Boards of directors and corporate financial performance: A review and integrative model. *Journal of Management, 15*, 291–334.
Zajac, E. J. (1990). CEO selection, succession, compensation and firm performance: A theoretical integration and empirical analysis. *Strategic Management Journal, 11*(3), 217–230.
Zajac, E. J., & Westphal, J. D. (2004). The social construction of market value: Institutionalization and learning perspectives on stock market reactions. *American Sociological Review, 69*, 433–457.
Zysman, J. (1983). *Governments, markets and growth*. London: Cornell University Press.

PART III
HOW STRATEGY SHAPES CAPITAL AND OWNERSHIP STRUCTURES

HOW INNOVATION CAN AFFECT OWNERSHIP STRUCTURE: THE CASE OF TRANSIENT AND DEDICATED INSTITUTIONAL INVESTORS

Abdullah A. Alshwer and
Edward Levitas

ABSTRACT

This study empirically examines the relationship between institutional ownership and innovation activity in the unique setting of the clinical trials for US biopharmaceutical companies. We used multiple statistical techniques in the period from 1990 through 2006 for firms in the biopharmaceutical industry to examine this relationship. Contrary to the widely believed relationship discussed in the literature, our findings suggest that institutional investors vary in their reactions to innovative progress. Specifically, we find that institutional investors with a long-term investment horizon (i.e., dedicated owners) increase their holdings of a firm's equity as the number of the firm's products increases in phases I and II of FDA clinical trials. These findings are robust for heteroskedasticity and autocorrelation as well as for different operationalizations of the change of institutional ownership.

Keywords: Institutional investment; innovation; biopharmaceutical; ownership structure

INTRODUCTION

Previous studies argue that the relationship between institutional ownership and innovation is generally monotonic such that institutional ownership has a direct effect on innovation activities such as research and development (R&D) expenses (e.g., Hansen & Hill, 1991; Kochhar & David, 1996). In addition, some studies argue that the type of institutional investor may determine the level of activism through which the institutional investor can exercise influence in directing innovation resources (Bushee, 1998; Neubaum & Zahra, 2006) and corporate diversification decisions (Kavadis & Castañer, 2014). Nonetheless, little research has addressed the issue of a possible reverse causal relationship. Similar to Demsetz and Lehn (1985), who argue that managerial ownership is endogenously determined in models of firm activity, we contend that institutional ownership is a function of the firm's environment and the strategic choices an investee-firm makes. Such possibilities have been either overlooked or inadequately examined in the finance and strategy literatures. Yet, since investors may seek guidance from other investors (Scharfstein & Stein, 1990) or may take cues from environmental signals in making their investment decisions, recognizing how institutions respond to such stimuli is essential if we are to truly understand the activities of these investors.

In this study, we examine how institutional investors respond to the uncertainties of product development based on varying tolerances of these investors for uncertainty. Following Bushee (1998), we distinguish between *dedicated* institutions, those recognized for their long-term investment horizon as well as their active role in monitoring investees, and *transient* institutions, which have far shorter investment horizon and more frequently trade in their positions. Based on these characteristics, we make predictions about how different institutional owners will react to progress made by firms in the product development cycle. To do so, we examine this relationship in an innovation-intensive industry − the biopharmaceutical industry — and treat innovation as a process with multiple stages rather than as a one-stage, static process, which has been the tendency in the empirical literature. In doing so, we argue that institutional investors vary in their reactions to the changes during the innovation process.

The main contribution of this study is the examination of the hypothesized reverse causal relationship between institutional ownership and innovation. Specifically, we believe that strategic events such as the (lack of) progress made toward the commercialization of products can play a significant role in explaining the changes in institutional ownership. A considerable amount of work has suggested that institutions monitor and cause firm actions (e.g., Hansen & Hill, 1991), but relatively little research has examined how firm actions affect the level of institutional holdings (see Shin & Shin, 2013 for an exception). We contribute to the literature by examining how institutional holdings respond to a firm's progress in the innovation value chain. Interestingly, we find no support for the hypothesis that changes in institutional ownership affect innovative productivity. Our results indicate that, contrary to most research, institutional ownership responds to rather than causes a firm's innovative progress.

Second, we disaggregate the product development process to examine how institutions react to events at multiple stages of development. Most studies of the relationship between institutional investors and research/development focus on a single stage in the process. By disaggregating the development process into phases, we show how institutional appetites for uncertainty can change over the development cycle. We, therefore, demonstrate that institutional sentiment is not static over time.

Third, we demonstrate how different types of institutions vary in their appetite for uncertainty. A considerable amount of research has shown how institutions vary in the vigilance with which they monitor firms (Bushee, 1998; Kochhar & David, 1996). However, little research has demonstrated how product development stages can differentially impact types of institutional investors. In this study, we examine how product development stages can differentially impact various institutional investors' sentiment.

Our study proceeds as follows. First, we provide definitions of our key constructs. We then review the literature regarding institutions' effects on innovation. Next, we develop hypotheses regarding institutions' responses to innovation. We then describe our results and provide conclusions and implications of our research.

RELATED LITERATURE AND HYPOTHESIS DEVELOPMENT

Innovation

Innovation is the firm's "commitment to creating and introducing products, production processes, and organizational systems" (Zahra, 1996, p. 1715). It is, however, a process fraught with uncertainty. Innovation involves the progression of an idea from obscurity to clarity as abstract thoughts are transformed into useful products, services, and processes. Generally, innovation results from the recombination of assets and technologies to form new and potentially valuable ideas (Schumpeter, 1934). Further complicating the process is the need to transform these ideas downstream into valuable outcomes. Such transformations are contingent on a firm's possession of, or access to, complementary assets or those resources apart from the technology needed to capitalize on or profit from technology discovery (e.g., marketing, manufacturing, and legal skills; Teece, 1986). With regard to United States Food and Drug Administration (FDA)-approved clinical trials, Carpenter (2004) argues that a firm's experience in managing through the FDA regulatory process enhances the speed and likelihood of FDA approval. Inexperience with the FDA approval process and inability to file FDA submissions in a legally precise manner has been shown to decrease the likelihood of successfully completing FDA clinical trials (Czerepak & Ryser, 2008). Other competencies such as managing administrative demands of clinical trials, the ability to manufacture enough product to supply clinical trials, and the ability to fund clinical trials also seem to be keys to successfully navigating through the FDA regulatory process (e.g., Pisano, 2006). In brief, a number of nonscientific factors seem to impact the transformation of idea into innovation.

Institutional Investment

Institutional investors refer to those institutions that own and manage investment funds in the capital market with the objective to optimize the wealth of their clients. Institutional ownership of common stocks has increased significantly over the past 50 years (Chen, Harford, & Li, 2007). In fact, more than 60% of the voting equity in US public companies is owned by institutions (Brancato, 2005; Flow of Funds Account of the United States, 2004).

Moreover, institutional investors differ in their investment strategies. Generally, there are five types of institutional investors: pension funds, asset managers, insurance companies, banks, and mutual funds. Each type has been classified in the literature based on different criteria. For example, Brickley, Lease, and Smith (1988) classified institutional investors based on the ability of the institution to resist pressure exerted by the investee's management to make (amend) favorable (unfavorable) investment decisions. This classification has been broadly used in predicting the effect of institutional investors on various corporate outcomes. However, mixed results have been found that used this classification for examining the consequences of institutional ownership (e.g., Hoskisson, Hitt, Johnson, & Grossman, 2002; Kochhar & David, 1996; Neubaum & Zahra, 2006).

Alternatively, investors can differ based on investment strategies. Gaspar, Massa, and Matos (2005) show that the institutional investment horizon has an effect on corporate decisions. For the purpose of this study, we use Bushee's (1998) classification where we partition institutional investors into two groups based on their investment strategies.[1] The first group includes all institutional investors classified as *dedicated*. This group of investors is known for their long-term investment orientation, for their activism, and for the monitoring role they may exert on the investee (Bushee, 1998). The long-term orientation of such investors is partly attributable to their compensation − since these investors tend to be salaried, their compensation is not closely tied, at least in the short term, to the performance of their portfolios (Neubaum & Zahra, 2006; Zahra, 1996). Therefore, long-term institutional investors usually favor long-term investment decisions made by the investees that convey positive future cash flows.

The second group includes all institutional investors considered as *transient*. Transient investors are known for their short-term investment horizons and frequent trading (Bushee, 1998). These investors usually do not emphasize analyzing investments to find opportunities; instead, they depend on fundamental analysis that provides "snap-shot" information about the state of the firm under consideration (Bodie, Kane, & Marcus, 2005). Such strategies mean that investors can focus on information gathering and trading, choosing not to extensively and elaborately collect and analyze public and/or private data (Chen et al., 2007).[2] Therefore, such investors are generally driven by short-term profit-maximization goals. Another issue that pertains to short-term investment horizons is the reward system used to evaluate fund managers. For example, some mutual fund and investment bank managers are evaluated quarterly and are rewarded or penalized based on short-term performance (Neubaum & Zahra, 2006).

Consequently, they are pressured to invest in rapidly rising stocks for a short period of time.

Innovation and Institutional Ownership

The nature of the relationship between institutional ownership and firm innovation has not been conclusive. The majority of studies that examined the effect of institutional ownership on firm innovation suggest a positive effect of institutional ownership on the firm's innovation activities due to the activism exerted by institutional investors on the investees' management. Furthermore, other studies that examined the influence of institutional ownership on firm innovation have approached this relationship from the agency theory perspective. Because the separation of firm ownership and control creates an agency problem (Jensen & Meckling, 1976), some scholars argue that institutional ownership would reduce the agency problem by increasing the concentration of and concomitantly the monitoring by ownership (Chen et al., 2007; Schnatterly, Shaw, & Jennings, 2008; Shleifer & Vishny, 2003; Useem, 1996). Other studies also argue that institutional investors are able to more effectively monitor the investee's decisions than can individual investors because of the former's ability to gather private information about the firm.[3] Therefore, some institutional investors would invest (disinvest) in firms that show promising (unpromising) innovative projects and may also exercise pressure to direct some of those innovation activities in directions that are aligned with the institution's goals (Agrawal & Mandelker, 1990; Shleifer & Vishny, 1986).

Kochhar and David (1996) argue that institutional investors, in general, influence corporate investment decisions in innovation-related activities such as R&D expenditure. Brickley et al. (1988) argue that long-term-oriented institutional investors may exercise some pressure on the investee's management as well as resist the pressure from entrenched and risk-averse managers. Therefore, they find a positive (negative) relationship between long-term (short-term)-oriented institutional holdings and R&D intensity.

In the same vein, institutional investors with low levels of investment turnover (i.e., long-term-oriented investors using a buy-and-hold investment strategy) are less likely to have other business relationships with investees (e.g., investment banking and other services; Kochhar & David, 1996).[4] Such investors are viewed as pressure resistant since managers cannot use the threat to terminate these relationships as a way to reduce institutional activism. These investors may, therefore, attempt to push for more investment in innovation activities as they can resist the pressure from entrenched managers. Consistently, Kochhar and David (1996) find a positive relationship between such institutional holdings and R&D intensity for long-term investors.

Yet, few studies have examined how institutional ownership *responds* to the demands of a firm's contracting environment. Demsetz and Lehn (1985) argue that managerial ownership is endogenously determined in models of firm behavior, resulting from the requirements imposed by a firm's context. Shin and Shin (2013) examine how institutional ownership is affected by the technological relatedness of a firm's business units or the degree to which technological capabilities across a firm's business units are similar. Thus, Shin and Shin take a step toward examining how institutional ownership responds to a firm's contracting environment. We build on this by examining how institutional ownership reacts to progress along the firm's innovation value chain. We go beyond Shin and Shin (2013) in examining how innovative progress impacts institutional holdings by various investors. We discuss these issues next.

Hypothesis Development

Prior studies point to several stages in the successful innovation process (e.g., Hall, Jaffe, & Trajtenberg, 2005; Kelm, Narayanan, & Pinches, 1995; Matolcsy & Wyatt, 2008; Schumpeter, 1934). Specifically, during the early phases of the innovation process a firm is involved in attempts to invent and later to market new products. Such attempts are prompted by the need to find solutions to a problem or to respond to internal or external events. The firm thus will evaluate the potential of these events as either opportunities to take advantage of or threats to which it will react. This evaluation is coupled with another evaluation of the internal capabilities (strengths and weaknesses) to make appropriate strategic investment decisions. Therefore, we view innovation as a multistage process where products and services develop dynamically over time, and where each stage has different characteristics, which can impact decisions made by current and potential investors.

For the purpose of this study, the process of innovation consists of the three major clinical trial phases through which all products developed by pharmaceutical and biotechnology firms (biopharmaceuticals, thereafter) must proceed. These sequential phases are necessary for a product to receive regulatory approval for marketing. Also, the clinical trial process is significant in terms of cost, as the average research cost per product during the clinical trials is almost three times the cost spent during the preclinical trial stage (DiMasi & Grabowski, 2007).

According to the National Institutes of Health (NIH), clinical trials go through sequential phases where each phase differs in the scope of tests and subjects it covers given the level of effectiveness in the previous phase. Therefore, the NIH defines each phase as follows:

Phase I: "Researchers test a new drug or treatment in a small group of people for the first time to evaluate its safety, determine a safe dosage range, and identify side effects" (National Institutes of Health [NIH], 2010).

Phase II: "The drug or treatment is given to a larger group of people to see if it is effective and to further evaluate its safety" (NIH, 2010).

Phase III: "The drug or treatment is given to large groups of people to confirm its effectiveness, monitor side effects, compare it to commonly used treatments, and collect information that will allow the drug or treatment to be used safely" (NIH, 2010).

Generally, the degree of uncertainty regarding the viability of approving a product fluctuates as the product moves from one phase to the next and, of course, diminishes as the product is commercialized. Such a process of product development provides a unique context to study institutional ownership. At each stage, therefore, we hypothesize that institutional ownership will react differently given their investment strategy (i.e., dedicated vs. transient).

Phase I: Investment in innovation activity is a tangible effort to build and maintain innovative capabilities and firms differ in the intensity of such effort (Gamble, 2000; Kor & Mahoney, 2005). This phase can take, on average, between 12 and 20 months (DiMasi & Grabowski, 2007). During this phase, technical risk influences the timing of milestones of the feasibility of products. Risks are likely to be lower, however, for firms with greater technological capability. Therefore, a firm that has the necessary skills, knowledge, and resources to act upon opportunities will attempt to show the commitment to seize those opportunities. Long-term institutional investors may demonstrate patience in waiting for a long period of time to reap the benefit from potential innovations (Hoskisson et al., 2002). For them, a product at phase I may signal potentially positive future cash flows.

Therefore, we predict that as firms signal their commitment to innovation by filing for phase I trials, long-term institutional investors will significantly increase their investment in such firms. Put formally:

Hypothesis 1. Positive changes in the number of products in phase I will be associated with positive changes in dedicated institutional ownership levels.

As for the transient institutional investors, phase I may mean a higher level of uncertainty, more costs to incur, and less returns in the near-term future. Therefore, we expect a significant negative relationship between a product at phase I and short-term institutional ownership. Put formally:

Hypothesis 2. Positive changes in the number of products in phase I will be associated with negative changes in transient institutional ownership levels.

Phase II: At this phase, a product has met the criteria to pass phase I and can now be tested on a larger group of objects to determine its effectiveness in treating or preventing the intended disease(s). This phase could take, on average, between 26 and 29 months to complete (DiMasi & Grabowski, 2007). The level of success uncertainty is still high. In fact, phase II products experience the lowest transition probability with an average of about 44% (compared to 83% for phase I and 70% for phase III) chance to move to phase III (DiMasi & Grabowski, 2007).

Therefore, being in this phase could convey a signal about future opportunities to reap economic rents or to have the ability to advance other existing innovations (Hall et al., 2005). For dedicated institutional investors, therefore, an investment in firms with increasing numbers of products at this stage could provide the potential for long-term success. Therefore, we predict that dedicated institutional investors will increase their holdings in firms that demonstrate increases in their number of projects at phase II. Put formally:

Hypothesis 3. Positive changes in the number of products in phase II will be associated with positive changes in dedicated institutional ownership levels.

As for transient investors, results at this stage do not provide clear guidance as the fate of the product is still largely unknown (i.e., there is no guarantee that it will be commercialized). Again, given the low transition probability to advance to phase III, transient investors are expected to be much less likely to change their ownership. Hence, for transient institutional investors we predict that at phase II they will be indifferent – institutional investment activities will significantly decrease or even will not be initiated. Put formally:

Hypothesis 4. Positive changes in the number of products in phase II will not be associated with a specific pattern of ownership change for transient institutional investors.

Phase III: At this phase, the product has made a significant improvement in the process of getting approved. In fact, the transition probability to finally get approved and possibly marketed jumps to about 70%. Therefore, the level of uncertainty has diminished compared to that of phase II. Therefore, for dedicated investors, this phase can be considered a too-late-to-invest stage since their investment horizon is generally long term and with an above-average return expectation. Thus, the chance to increase investment in a firm in which they have already invested will not provide a significant return versus the investment in the previous two phases (on a risk-adjusted basis). Also, considering the fact that the managers of dedicated institutional investors are generally salaried employees and an increase in return may not necessarily indicate higher rewards (Bushee, 1998; Hoskisson et al., 2002), we expect that dedicated investors will be indifferent when products transition to phase III such that their ownership structure will not change.

This phase, however, represents a favorable context for transient investors in anticipating foreseeable events since the degree of uncertainty has decreased. Therefore, transient investors are now in a better position to evaluate the firm's future cash flows due to current innovational developments. Therefore, at this stage transient investors are expected to increase their ownership. Put formally:

Hypothesis 5. Positive changes in the number of products in phase III will be associated with positive changes in transient institutional ownership levels.

METHODS

Sample Selection

Our focus is on US institutional investors investing in US publically traded biopharmaceutical companies. Table 1 shows the definition and source of

Table 1. Variables Definition.

Variable		Definition	Source
Institutional ownership	INST_OWN	Ratio of the number of shares owned by institutional owner type to the total shares outstanding	Thomson-Reuters 13-F
Δ Institutional ownership	Δ INST_OWN	Difference in ownership by type between year t and year $t-1$	Thomson-Reuters 13-F
Δ Number of products at phase I	Δ PRODUCT_@_PHASE$_j$	Difference in number of products at phase j between year t and year $t-1$	R&D Focus database provided by IMS LifeCycle
Δ Number of products at phase II			
Δ Number of products at phase III			
Therapeutic class	THERAP_CLASS	Ratio of the total number of therapeutic classes in which the firm is engaged in to the total number of all therapeutic classes engaged by the same firm	R&D Focus database provided by IMS LifeCycle
Cumulative annual return	CUMULT_RET	Cumulative daily stock return over year t	CRSP
Analysts coverage	ANALYST	Number of analysts covering a firm	I/B/E/S
Cash holdings	CASH	Ratio of cash holdings and short-term investments to total book assets	Compustat
Leverage	LVRG	Ratio of total debt to total assets	Compustat
Firm size	SIZE	Natural log of total assets	Compustat

Table 1. (*Continued*)

Variable		Definition	Source
Tobin's Q	Q	Ratio of the market value of assets to the book value of assets, where the market value of assets is the book value of assets plus the market value of common equity less the sum of the book value of common equity and deferred taxes	Compustat
R&D intensity	RD_INT	Ratio of R&D expenditure to total sales	Compustat
Sales growth	SALES$_G$	Percentage increase/decrease in sales from year $t-1$ to year t	Compustat
Institutional investor classifications	DED	Dedicated institutional investors are long-term-oriented	Brian Bushee's institutional classification scheme data
	TRA	Transient institutional investors are short-term-oriented	

each variable used in the analyses. The sample covers the period from 1991 through 2006. Institutional ownership data are obtained from the Thomson-Reuters Institutional Holdings (13F) database. For institutional investors' classification, data are obtained from Brian Bushee's website, where he publishes and updates institutional investors' classifications. Accounting and financial data are obtained from Compustat and CRSP databases. Data on clinical trial phases are obtained from the R&D Focus database provided by IMS LifeCycle. The total sample size is 727 firm-year observations covering the period from 1990 through 2006.

Variables

We report the univariate statistics of all variables used in this study in Table 2. Correlation coefficients arealso reported in Table 3.

Measures of Institutional Ownership
Most studies use the level of ownership of institutional investors defined as the total number of shares owned by the institutional investors divided by total outstanding ordinary shares of the investees. In our study, we use the change in institutional ownership from time $t-1$ to time t, divided by the institutional ownership at time $t-1$, and then multiply the product by 100.

Table 2. Summary Statistics.

Variable	Mean	Median	Std. Dev.	Min.	Max.	N
Δ Institutional ownership (dedicated (LT))	0.38	0	5.31	−21.05	33.01	727
Δ Institutional ownership (transient (ST))	0.32	0	6.87	−25.78	33.19	727
Δ Number of products at phase I	0.21	0	3.12	−44	67	727
Δ Number of products at phase II	0.14	0	2.89	−43	44	727
Δ Number of products at phase III	0.03	0	1.50	−11	17	727
Cumulative annual return	0.28	0.06	1.12	−0.98	15.69	727
Analysts coverage	9	5	9.57	0	46	727
Cash holdings	0.48	0.57	0.28	0.01	0.74	727
Leverage	0.16	0.05	0.22	0	0.89	727
Firm size	5.53	5.14	2.12	0.34	10.41	727
Tobin's Q	4.50	3.43	3.17	0.73	24.16	727
R&D intensity	0.29	0.19	0.39	0.01	7.80	727
Sales growth	22.63	7.35	54.06	−50.86	158.02	727

Table 3. Correlation Matrix.

	1	2	3	4	5	6	7	8	9	10	11	12	13	14	15	16	17
1 Δ INST_OWN_DED																	
2 Δ INST_OWN_TRA	0.08***	1.00															
3 Δ INST_OWN_DED (t−1)	0.01	0.00	1.00														
4 Δ INST_OWN_TRA (t−1)	0.07**	−0.02	0.10	1.00													
5 Δ PRODUCT_@_PHASE 1	0.01	−0.04**	−0.01	−0.03	1.00												
6 Δ PRODUCT_@_PHASE 2	0.01	−0.05**	−0.01	−0.04	0.89	1.00											
7 Δ PRODUCT_@_PHASE 3	0.02	−0.03	−0.01	−0.05**	0.66***	0.71***	1.00										
8 Δ PRODUCT_@_PHASE 1 (t−1)	0.01	−0.01	0.01	0.00	−0.45***	−0.37***	−0.29***	1.00									
9 Δ PRODUCT_@_PHASE 2 (t−1)	0.02	−0.01	0.01	−0.02	−0.41***	−0.42***	−0.32***	0.89***	1.00								
10 Δ PRODUCT_@_PHASE 3 (t−1)	0.00	0.00	0.01	0.03	−0.32***	−0.30***	−0.41***	0.66***	0.71***	1.00							
11 SIZE	0.06**	−0.03	0.07**	−0.06*	0.09***	0.06***	0.02	0.07**	0.05	0.00	1.00						
12 CUMULT_RET (t−1)	0.09***	0.05	−0.10*	0.24***	0.01	−0.04	−0.01	−0.02	0.01	0.03	0.01	1.00					
13 Q (t−1)	0.06**	0.08***	0.04	0.12***	−0.04	−0.06**	−0.05*	−0.03	−0.03	−0.05	−0.13***	0.21***	1.00				
14 ANALYST (t−1)	0.00	−0.09***	0.01	−0.10***	0.03	0.03	0.01	0.03	0.03	0.01	0.83***	−0.02	−0.02	1.00			
15 RD_INT	−0.04	0.08***	−0.07**	0.06	−0.03	−0.03	−0.03	−0.03	−0.02	−0.01	−0.51***	0.03	0.25***	−0.35***	1.00		
16 CASH (t−1)	0.00	−0.07***	0.01	−0.04	0.00	0.00	0.00	0.00	0.00	0.00	−0.62***	−0.02	0.05*	0.13***	0.32***	1.00	
17 SALES_G (t−1)	0.02	0.02	0.06**	0.03	−0.02	0.00	0.00	−0.03	−0.04	0.00	−0.03	−0.07*	0.10***	−0.05*	0.04	0.05	1.00
18 LVRG (t−1)	0.01	0.03	0.01	−0.02	0.01	0.00	−0.01	0.02	0.01	0.00	0.10***	0.03	0.02	−0.02	0.03	−0.08***	0.04

*Significant at 10%; **significant at 5%; ***significant at 1%.
Correlation coefficients of therapeutic lasses are omitted for brevity.

Control Variables
We control for those variables that were found to affect institutional ownership. Namely, we control for *firm size, cumulative daily return, Tobin's Q, analysts coverage, therapeutic class,* and *innovation intensity*.

Firm size
Based on the assumption that smaller firms are younger and less well known, small firms should be more vulnerable to capital market imperfections. Also, prior studies (O'Brien & Bhushan, 1990) find that there is a positive relationship between firm size and institutional ownership. Therefore, we expect this positive relationship to remain.

Cumulative daily return
Cumulative daily return is a control for profitability. Therefore, we expect a positive relationship between cumulative daily return of firm stock and change in institutional ownership.

Tobin's Q
Firms with higher Q ratios can be perceived by market participants as more highly valued. Therefore, we expect a positive relationship between Tobin's Q and institutional ownership change.

Analysts coverage
Analysts coverage can provide information about firms under consideration. Institutional investors could benefit from such information when deciding on asset allocation and portfolio rebalancing (O'Brien & Bhushan, 1990).

Therapeutic class
A biopharmaceutical firm that develops new drugs may signal to outsiders its ability to survive through the phases of the clinical trial (Pisano, 2006). Therefore, we control for the ratio of the total number of number of therapeutic classes in which a drug is tested to the total number of all therapeutic classes for a given company in a given year. This classification is drawn from the European Pharmaceutical Market Research Association, which classifies drugs into 16 broad categories of therapy.

Innovation intensity
We measure innovation intensity as the ratio of R&D expenditures to total sales. Innovation intensity is a resource that could determine the number of

products at different stages which a biopharmaceutical firm has. We expect a positive relationship between innovation intensity and institutional ownership change.

RESULTS

Effect on Institutional Ownership of Changes in Products during Clinical Trials

Our analyses tested the hypothesis that changes in the number of products during the clinical trial process for the investee would have an effect on institutional ownership. That is, the relationship represents the changes in the institutional ownership as a function of the changes of the components of products during the clinical trial process. This is depicted as follows:

Δ Institutional ownership $= f\,(\Delta$ Products in clinical trials$)$

To test the abovementioned relationship, we estimate models using the change regression method as used in similar studies (e.g., Klock, Mansi, & Maxwell, 2005) to alleviate endogeneity concerns. Our specification is:

$$\begin{aligned}\Delta INST\_OWN_{i,t} = &\beta_0 + \beta_1(\Delta PRODUCT\_@\_PHASE_j)_{i,t-1} + \beta_2(SIZE)_{i,t} \\ &+ \beta_3(\Delta CUMULT\_RET)_{i,t-1} + \beta_4(Q)_{i,t-1} \\ &+ \beta_5(ANALYST)_{i,t-1} + \beta_6(THERAP\_CLASS)_{i,t-1} \\ &+ \beta_7(RD\_INT)_{i,t} + \beta_8(TIME\_DUM)_{i,t} + \varepsilon_{i,t}\end{aligned} \quad (1)$$

where $\Delta INST\_OWN_{i,t}$ denotes the change in institutional ownership in firm i at time t; $\Delta PRODUCT\_@\_PHASE_j$ denotes the change in the number of products at phase j at time t and in firm i; $SIZE$ is the firm size at time t; $\Delta CUMULT\_RET$ denotes the lagged change in firm i's daily cumulative stock return; Q is firm i's Tobin's Q at time $t-1$; $ANALYST$ is the number of analysts at time $t-1$ that follow firm i; $THERAP\_CLASS$ is the ratio of the total number of therapeutic classes in which firm i is engaged in to the total number of all therapeutic classes engaged by the same firm in year t-1 and RD_INT is firm i's innovation intensity at time $t-1$.

The results of the ordinary least-squares (OLS) regression are shown in Table 4. Six regressions are reported where three sets of two parallel regressions (one for dedicated investors and the other for transient investors) are run for each clinical trial phase. The standard errors in these regressions

Table 4. Institutional Ownership Change during Clinical Trial (OLS).

Dependent Variable									
		OLS Δ Institutional ownership
Clinical trial stage	colspan="3"	Phase I	colspan="3"	Phase II	colspan="3"	Phase III
Type of Institution	Dedicated	Transient	P-value dedicated vs. transient	Dedicated	Transient	P-value dedicated vs. transient	Dedicated	Transient	P-value dedicated vs. transient
Model	(1)	(2)		(3)	(4)		(5)	(6)	
Δ Products in the phase (t−1)	0.081** (2.01)	−0.003 (−0.25)	0.04	0.144*** (2.98)	−0.031 (−1.21)	0.03	0.042 (1.50)	0.026 (0.610)	0.75
Firm size	0.980*** (2.98)	0.540* (1.79)	0.32	1.12*** (3.50)	1.234*** (3.29)	0.82	1.010*** (3.34)	1.304*** (3.49)	0.54
Δ Cumulative rate of return (t−1)	−0.308* (−1.70)	0.875*** (2.90)	0.00	−.332* (−1.85)	0.888*** (2.97)	0.00	−0.363** (−2.06)	0.813*** (2.79)	0.00
Tobin's Q (t−1)	0.207** (2.45)	0.305*** (3.39)	0.43	0.229*** (2.89)	0.295*** (3.26)	0.58	0.212** (2.47)	0.324*** (3.65)	0.36
Number of analysts (t−1)	−0.198* (−1.67)	−0.244** (−2.56)	0.73	−0.208* (−1.81)	−0.249*** (−2.69)	0.78	−0.211* (−1.79)	−0.498*** (−3.98)	0.10
Innovation intensity (t−1)	0.587 (1.45)	0.709 (1.48)	0.85	0.724* (1.70)	0.681 (1.43)	0.95	0.588 (1.48)	0.711 (1.49)	0.84
Therapeutic class	Yes	Yes		Yes	Yes		Yes	Yes	
Constant	−1.986 (−0.59)	8.358 (0.65)	0.30	−2.336 (−0.69)	8.084 (0.61)	0.24	−1.588 (−0.40)	0.712 (0.95)	0.29
Observations	727	727		727	727		727	727	
Adj R²	0.07	0.12		0.09	0.12		0.09	0.14	
Year FE	Yes	Yes		Yes	Yes		Yes	Yes	

Robust t statistics are in parentheses. Coefficients of therapeutic classes are omitted for brevity.
* significant at 10%; ** significant at 5%; *** significant at 1%.

are robust to heteroskedasticity and autocorrelation. The lagged change in the number of products at phase I, as hypothesized, is associated with the change in the dedicated institutional ownership. The coefficient for the lagged change in the number of products shown in model 1 was positive and statistically significant at the 5% level, indicating that the addition of one product in phase I would increase dedicated ownership, on average, by 0.1% in the following year. This result supports Hypothesis 1. As for the transient investors, the coefficient for the lagged change in the number of products shown in model 2 was positive and statistically insignificant, which does not support Hypothesis 2. The t-test rejects the equality of the coefficients for the two groups (i.e., dedicated vs. transient) at the 5% level, indicating a significant difference between the change in ownership in each group of investors at phase I.

As for phase II, the result in model 3 suggests that a positive and significant (at the 1% level) association exists between the lagged change in the number of products at phase II and the change in dedicated ownership, supporting Hypothesis 3. This result indicates that the addition of one product in phase II increases dedicated ownership, on average, by 0.144% in the following year. The result in model 4 supports Hypothesis 4 in finding no relationship between the change in transient ownership and change in the number of products at phase II. The t-test rejects the equality of the coefficients for the two groups (i.e., dedicated vs. transient) at the 5% level, indicating a significant difference between the change in ownership for each investor at phase II.

As for phase III, the regression in model 6 shows the coefficient of the change in the number of products in the predicted direction (Hypothesis 5); however, it is statistically insignificant. In all models tested, control variables have their predicted sign (except cumulative rate of return for dedicated ownership).

Dynamic Panel-Data Regression

Using a dynamic panel-data method allows us to control for endogeneity issues raised by the possible reverse causality in our proposed model. That is, there could be a relationship running from institutional ownership to changes in the number of products (i.e., the reverse of our hypothesized causal direction). If such a reverse relationship exists, the OLS regressions we estimated would give inconsistent estimates. To account for this possibility, we use the Arellano–Bond technique for dynamic panel-data.[5] The

Table 5. Institutional Ownership Change during Clinical Trial (Arellano–Bond).

Dependent Variable: Arellano–Bond Dynamic Panel-Data — Δ Institutional ownership

	Phase I Dedicated (1)	Phase I Transient (2)	P-value dedicated vs. transient	Phase II Dedicated (3)	Phase II Transient (4)	P-value dedicated vs. transient	Phase III Dedicated (5)	Phase III Transient (6)	P-value dedicated vs. transient
Δ Products in the phase (t−1)	0.034 (0.61)	−0.029 (−0.58)	0.41	0.127*** (2.59)	0.020 (0.60)	0.03	0.003 (0.04)	−0.027 (−0.52)	0.79
Δ Institutional ownership (t−1)	0.259*** (5.01)	0.159** (2.01)	0.09	−0.080 (−1.29)	−0.280*** (−4.64)	0.00	0.244*** (4.62)	0.160** (2.01)	0.38
Firm size	1.786* (1.89)	1.27 (1.22)	0.71	0.864* (1.72)	1.241 (1.36)	0.72	1.89** (2.08)	1.19 (1.12)	0.62
Δ Cumulative rate of return (t−1)	−0.229 (−1.63)	0.599* (1.93)	0.02	−0.13 (−0.11)	−0.010 (−0.10)	0.94	−0.256* (−1.70)	0.624** (1.98)	0.01
Tobin's Q (t−1)	0.141 (0.80)	0.173 (0.69)	0.92	0.133 (1.06)	−0.030 (−0.18)	0.43	0.145 (0.88)	0.198 (0.80)	0.86
Number of analysts (t−1)	−0.013 (−0.60)	−0.091 (−0.19)	0.87	−0.033 (−0.18)	0.098 (0.41)	0.66	−0.037 (−0.18)	−0.064 (−0.14)	0.95
Innovation intensity (t−1)	1.109* (1.70)	−0.321 (−0.43)	0.15	0.934* (1.67)	−0.438 (−0.60)	0.13	0.985* (1.66)	−0.354 (−0.48)	0.16
Therapeutic class	**Yes**	**Yes**		**Yes**	**Yes**		**Yes**	**Yes**	
Constant	−8.437* (−1.78)	−8.991** (−2.12)	0.93	−2.228 (−0.68)	−2.026 (−1.201)	0.96	−8.904* (−1.92)	−8.985** (−2.14)	0.99
Observations	566	566		566	566		566	566	
Wald χ^2	131.27***	73.97***		46.08***	241.14***		131.53***	59.41***	
Sargan test	n.s.	n.s.		n.s.	n.s.		n.s.	n.s.	
Year FE	Yes	Yes		Yes	Yes		Yes	Yes	

Robust z statistics are in parentheses. Coefficients of therapeutic classes are omitted for brevity.
* significant at 10%; ** significant at 5%; *** significant at 1%.

results of the dynamic panel-data are reported in Table 5.[6] The results are similar to those reported in Table 4 with the exception of a lack of support for Hypothesis 1. Specifically, model 3 indicates that the addition of one product in phase II would increase dedicated ownership, on average, by 0.271% in the following year. The t-test rejects the equality of the coefficients for the two groups of institutional investors at the 5% level, indicating a significant difference between the change in ownership in each group and its association with the change in the number of products at phase II.

Additional Analysis for Causality Issues

We further investigate the issue of reverse causality through the use of a three-stage least squares (3SLS) technique. In our 3SLS estimation, we model both the change in institutional ownership and the change in the number of products at each stage as endogenous. In our 3SLS specifications, all explanatory variables are 1-year lagged. Our specification for the 3SLS procedure is the following:

$$\Delta INST\_OWN_{i,t} = \beta_0 + \beta_1(\Delta PRODUCT\_@\_PHASE_j)_{i,t-1} + \beta_2(SIZE)_{i,t} \\ + \beta_3(\Delta CUMULT\_RET)_{i,t-1} + \beta_4(Q)_{i,t-1} \\ + \beta_5(ANALYST)_{i,t-1} + \beta_6(THERAP\_CLASS)_{i,t-1} \\ + \beta_7(RD\_INT)_{i,t} + \beta_8(TIME\_DUM)_{i,t} + \varepsilon_{i,t} \quad (2)$$

$$\Delta PRODUCT\_@\_PHASE_{j,i,t} = \beta_0 + \beta_1(\Delta INST_{OWN_{i,t-1}}) + \beta_2(RD\_INT)_{i,t-1} \\ + \beta_3(CASH)_{i,t-1} + \beta_4(SALES_G)_{i,t-1} \\ + \beta_5(LVRG)_{i,t-1} + \beta_5(THERAP\_CLASS)_{i,t-1} \\ + \beta_7(RD\_INT)_{i,t} + \beta_8(TIME\_DUM)_{i,t} + \varepsilon_{i,t} \quad (3)$$

The control variables used in this estimation are drawn from the existing literature on the determinants of firm innovation (e.g., Hansen & Hill, 1991; Kelm et al., 1995; and Pisano, 2006). Specifically, we control for the firm's R&D intensity, cash holdings, sales growth, and leverage. Again, all these variables are defined in Table 1.

The 3SLS results in Table 6 show similar results to those shown in the previous tests. Hypothesis 3, in particular, is positive and statistically significant at the 1% level (model 5). At the same time, the test for Eq. (3) shows no support for the causal relationship running from changes of institutional

Table 6. Institutional Ownership Change during Clinical Trial (3SLS).

							3SLS					
Clinical Trial Stage		Phase I				Phase II				Phase III		
Type of Institution	Dedicated		Transient		Dedicated		Transient		Dedicated		Transient	
Dependent variable	Ownership	Products in phase	Ownership	Products in Phase	Ownership	Products in phase	Ownership	Products in phase	Ownership	Products in phase	Ownership	Products in phase
Model	(1)	(2)	(3)	(4)	(5)	(6)	(7)	(8)	(9)	(10)	(11)	(12)
Δ Products in the phase (t−1)	−0.015 (−0.27)		0.072 (0.82)		0.155*** (3.57)		0.078 (1.16)		0.013 (0.69)		0.076 (0.79)	
Δ Ownership (t−1)		0.110 (0.18)		0.393 (1.05)		0.008 (0.10)		0.002 (0.03)		−0.037 (−0.96)		0.001 (0.08)
Firm size	0.094* (1.81)		0.187** (2.07)		0.111* (1.92)		0.193** (2.14)		0.122** (2.07)		0.188** (2.08)	
Δ Cumulative rate of return (t−1)	0.048* (1.88)		−0.059 (−1.30)		0.070** (2.40)		−0.052 (−1.29)		0.064** (2.18)		−0.06 (−1.42)	
Tobin's Q (t−1)	0.049*** (3.82)		−0.011 (−0.52)		0.057*** (4.19)		−0.014 (−0.53)		0.056*** (4.06)		−0.010 (−0.47)	
Number of analysts (t−1)	−0.017 (−1.09)		−0.057** (−2.40)		−0.014 (−0.90)		−0.061** (−2.42)		−0.017 (−1.12)		−0.57** (−2.44)	
Innovation intensity (t−1)	0.772** (2.54)	−0.408 (−01.36)	1.862*** (4.20)	−0.419 (−1.41)	0.701** (2.34)	0.022 (0.07)	1.883*** (4.26)	0.079 (0.23)	0.766** (2.53)	−0.166 (−0.94)	1.840*** (4.14)	−0.198 (−1.13)
Cash (t−1)		−0.198 (−0.54)		−0171 (−0.46)		−0.668 (−1.55)		−0.691 (−1.60)		0.129 (0.60)		0.140 (0.64)

Table 6. (*Continued*)

	\multicolumn{4}{c	}{Phase I}	\multicolumn{4}{c	}{3SLS Phase II}	\multicolumn{4}{c}{Phase III}
Clinical Trial Stage												
Type of Institution	\multicolumn{2}{c	}{Dedicated}	\multicolumn{2}{c	}{Transient}	\multicolumn{2}{c	}{Dedicated}	\multicolumn{2}{c	}{Transient}	\multicolumn{2}{c	}{Dedicated}	\multicolumn{2}{c}{Transient}
Dependent variable	Ownership Products in phase	Ownership Products in phase	Ownership Products in Phase	Ownership Products in Phase	Ownership Products in phase	Ownership Products in phase	Ownership Products in phase	Ownership Products in phase	Ownership Products in phase	Ownership Products in phase	Ownership Products in phase	Ownership Products in phase
Model	(1)	(2)	(3)	(4)	(5)	(6)	(7)	(8)	(9)	(10)	(11)	(12)
Sales growth ($t-1$)		−0.001		−0.001		0.001		0.001		0.001		0.001
		(−1.10)		(−1.14)		(0.57)		(0.70)		(0.31)		(0.18)
Leverage ($t-1$)		−0.093		−0.094		−0.373		−0.373		−0.164		−0.163
		(−0.33)		(−0.34)		(−1.13)		(−1.13)		(−1.01)		(−0.98)
Therapeutic classes	Yes	Yes	Yes	Yes	Yes	Yes	Yes	Yes	Yes	Yes	Yes	Yes
Constant	−0.184	−0.884	−2.496	−0.911	−0.500	1.362	−3.010	1.603	−0.199	1.719	−2.824	1.766
	(−0.11)	(−0.41)	(−0.93)	(−0.43)	(−0.29)	(0.54)	(−1.11)	(0.62)	(−0.12)	(1.36)	(−1.08)	(1.39)
Observations	727	727	727	727	727	727	727	727	727	727	727	727
χ^2	59.62***	119.17***	52.51***	120.72***	73.98***	111.89***	53.40***	112.22***	64.62***	46.16**	54.05***	45.66**
Year FE	Yes	Yes	Yes	Yes	Yes	Yes	Yes	Yes	Yes	Yes	Yes	Yes

Robust z statistics are in parentheses. Coefficients of therapeutic classes are omitted for brevity.
* significant at 10%; ** significant at 5%; *** significant at 1%.

ownership to the changes in the number of products at each stage of the clinical trial process.

DISCUSSION

The results presented in this study provide evidence in contrast to many prior studies regarding the relationship between institutional ownership and innovation activity. Specifically, we show that the type of the institutional investor does matter when examining reactions to changes in the innovation process. This evidence comes after controlling for various variables over an extended period using different techniques to alleviate the endogeneity and causality issues that are present in such studies. Contrary to the wide belief in the literature regarding the effect of institutional ownership on innovation, our results show no support for such an effect. In fact, we find evidence for the reverse causal relationship (i.e., one that runs from innovation to ownership).

Our results suggest that institutions respond to advances in the innovation development chain, but may not prompt such advances. This is somewhat surprising in light of the extant financial and management research that alludes to the essential monitoring relationship played by institutions. Scholars seem to take comfort in the idea that institutions provide broad-based scrutiny of firm activities. In the absence of oversight from many investors, institutional investors' power, conferred by their large block holdings, ostensibly afford them voice in the governance process. This voice could pressure managers into disclosing information via meetings and communications that promote more efficient pricing of a firm's common equity.

Many would find it surprising and alarming if such oversight were absent in the case of innovation. To be sure, the innovation venue is one of the more uncertain contexts shareholders face when evaluating a firm's prospects. Additional oversight from sophisticated investors here is certainly beneficial and comforting in shedding light on a research-intensive firm's operations. The absence of such oversight might add to the perceived uncertainty faced by other investors.

It may be that such oversight in this context is a fleeting desire given the unpredictability of the research environment. Whereas the probability of certain investment decisions can be estimated with a reasonable degree of accuracy, probabilities of innovative success often defy robust inference.

Since it involves an idea's transformation from obscurity to clarity, innovation entails delving into domains whose outcomes cannot be envisaged beforehand but only observed once success or failure is realized (Schumpeter, 1934). Effective monitoring may be an impossibility since successful innovation often requires a "leap of faith" rather than scientific approach to capital allocation. If so, it may be that institutions simply provide mistaken comfort to investors,

Furthermore, much of what innovative researchers know resides in their minds and cannot be easily provided to external monitors. Such knowledge which is often obtained only through experimentation is tacit in that it defies easy articulation (e.g., Henderson & Cockburn, 1994). Knowledge involved in innovation is also highly complex since it involves not a single technology but a network of intertwined knowledge bases (e.g., knowledge of inorganic, organic, and biochemistries) and capabilities with supporting skills (e.g., statistical techniques), which further increases the "stickiness" of this knowledge (von Hippel, 1994). Our findings may reflect the fact that institutional investors who do not share this tacit knowledge cannot easily evaluate a research-intensive firm's operations.

An important implication of this study then is the questionable effectiveness of institutional investors in monitoring innovative activities. As such, researchers should further examine the munificence of institutional monitoring in research-intensive environments. As noted, most researchers rely on the assumption of institutional monitoring's impact. Our results cast some doubt on this assumption. Additional research should attempt to corroborate our results. If results are replicated, then researchers should address the effectiveness of other mechanisms (e.g., analysts) in monitoring the innovation process.

Of course, our results may not be generalized to most industries; however, the nature of the clinical trial data provides a unique opportunity to study the relationship between the change in firms' innovation activity and the change in institutional ownership. Changes in the product components proceeding through the clinical trial stages can be perceived differently by investors depending on their return goals, risk tolerances, investment time horizons, liquidity requirements, and other constraints they may face.[7] Therefore, it could be naive to conclude that *all* institutional investors would behave similarly in response to the same information.

Moreover, our results oppose those found in Hansen and Hill's (1991) study. They examine the issue of causality in the pharmaceutical industry (among three other "research-intensive" industries). Their results support the traditional hypothesis that institutional ownership has a positive effect on a firm's innovation activity. These contrasting results could be attributed to Hansen & Hill's focus on pharmaceutical firms without including biotechnology firms. We address this possibility after running separate regressions for pharmaceutical firms alone and other regressions for biotechnology firms. Our results generally remain intact for both subindustries. Another reason that could contribute to this disagreement is the use of a different statistical technique. Hansen & Hill estimate a generalized least-squares (GLS) model as they argue it is robust to heteroskedasticity and autocorrelation. We also eliminate this possibility as the models we used are robust for both issues as explained earlier. Therefore, a key reason that may explain the difference in our results compared to those of Hansen and Hill is the operationalization of innovation. Hansen and Hill (1991) used R&D intensity, which we controlled for in our analyses, to proxy for innovation. A major issue with such a measure is its cross-sectional nature.[8] This is in contrast to our measure of changes in product levels during the clinical trial process, which is more dynamic in nature.

From the results presented in this study, the coefficient for the change in the number of products at phase II was positive throughout and statistically significant at 5% level. This result also persists for different operationalizations for the change in the number of products during the clinical trial process. For example, we get similar results when we dummy coded the change in the number of products in phase II (i.e., if the number of products increases at time t compared to time $t-1$ it will equal 1, zero otherwise).

Therefore, the consistent results for the effect of the change of the number of product at phase II is intriguing. One reason could be the fact that phase II exhibits a sort of a "bottleneck" for biopharmaceutical products with the lowest probability of success (44%) and usually the longest average time to complete (about 29 months) among the three stages. In other words, investing in firms with more products in phase II entails potentially higher risk and return with commitment to a longer investment horizon. Such investment characteristics are less likely to fit investors who are transient but more likely to fit those who are dedicated.

CONCLUSION

In this study, we attempted to address the effect of innovation process on institutional ownership. More specifically, we addressed the nature of the relationship between institutional ownership and innovation, with a special emphasis on the reactions exhibited by different types of institutional investors to the changes in the number of biopharmaceutical products going through the clinical trial process. We demonstrated that the dedicated institutional investors' reaction to changes of a firm's product components generally differs from those of transient institutional investors.

Although prior studies have examined the relationship between institutional ownership and innovation with a consensus that institutional ownership affecting innovation, no study has examined this relationship in the unique clinical trial setting provided in the biopharmaceutical industry. To the best of our knowledge, this is the first study that documents the reverse relationship between changes in the innovation activity and institutional ownership taking into account the different investment strategies of institutional investors.

Our findings partially support the findings documented in Kelm et al. (1995) in that institutional investors react positively to changes in innovation activity. However, the Kelm et al.'s study does not account for the differences in investment strategies among institutional investors. That is, our study points to the fact that different institutional investors react differently to changes in innovation activity depending on the institution's investment strategies.

Our study points to at least two major implications. First, institutional investors that exhibit long-term investment horizons (i.e., dedicated) react differently to changes in corporate innovation activities than do institutional investors that exhibit short-term investment horizons (i.e., transient). Second, the relationship between institutional ownership and innovation activity we found opposes those identified by the majority of studies in the literature as we found that ex ante changes in innovation activity are associated with changes in long-term institutional ownership but not with short-term institutional ownership.

NOTES

1. Bushee's classification is based on the institution's past investment patterns using cluster analysis in the areas of portfolio turnover and diversification.
2. This is also known as technical analysis.
3. This does not necessarily mean that all institutional investors would get access and act upon nonpublic, material information (which is illegal in most jurisdictions).

4. This is in line with Brickley et al.'s (1988) classification of institutional investors based on the level of pressure they may exert on the investee's management.

5. We get similar results when we ran the Least Squares Dummy Variable (LSDV) dynamic regression for bias correction.

6. We ran the Sargan test, which tests for the validity of the instruments used, across the six models in Table 5. The tests cannot reject the null hypothesis that the system's instruments are uncorrelated with the error term, which indicates the validity of the instruments used.

7. The fundamental tenets of the efficient market hypothesis (EMH) are that investors are risk averse and rational who assess public information in a similar manner such that they would have similar expectations for a firm's future cash flows. Also, EMH does not distinguish between individual and institutional investors (Hansen & Hill, 1991), which is a weakness as institutional investors possess more resources when they decide for asset allocation strategies.

8. Although R&D investments have been found to be a predictor of high-tech firms' survival in some European financial markets (Vismara & Signori, 2014).

ACKNOWLEDGMENTS

We appreciate helpful comments from Maria Goranova, Scott Hsu, Richard Priem, Valeriy Sibilkov, participants at the 1st Paris Financial Management Conference, and the 2013 Academy of Management Annual Meeting. The first author would like to extend his sincere appreciation to the Deanship of Scientific Research at King Saud University for its funding this Research Group No. (RG#364).

REFERENCES

Agrawal, A., & Mandelker, G. N. (1990). Large shareholders and the monitoring of managers: The case of antitakeover chater amendments. *Journal of Financial and Quantitative Analysis, 25*, 143–161.

Bodie, Z., Kane, A., & Marcus, A. J. (2005). *Investments* (6th ed.), Boston, MA: McGraw-Hill.

Brancato, C. K. (2005). *Institutional investment report*. New York, NY: Conference Board.

Brickley, J. A., Lease, R. C., & Smith, C. W. (1988). Ownership structure and voting on antitakeover amendments. *Journal of Financial Economics, 20*, 267–291.

Bushee, B. J. (1998). The influence of institutional investors on myopic R&D investment behavior. *The Accounting Review, 73*, 305–333.

Carpenter, D. P. (2004). Protection without capture: Product approval by a politically responsive, learning regulator. *American Political Science Review, 98*, 613–631.

Chen, X., Harford, J., & Li, K. (2007). Monitoring: Which institutions matter? *Journal of Financial Economics, 86*, 279–305.

Czerepak, E. A., & Ryser, S. (2008). Drug approvals and failures: Implications for alliances. *Nature Reviews: Drug Discovery, 7*, 197, 190, 198.

Demsetz, H., & Lehn, K. (1985). The structure and consequences of corporate ownership: Causes and consequences. *Journal of Political Economy, 93*, 1155–1177.

DiMasi, J. A., & Grabowski, H. G. (2007). The cost of biopharmaceutical R&D: Is biotech different? *Managerial and Decision Economics, 28*, 469–479.

Flow of Funds Account of the United States. (2004). Board of Governors of the Federal Reserve System, Washington, DC.

Gamble, J. E. (2000). Management commitment to innovation and ESOP stock concentration. *Journal of Business Venturing, 15*(5), 433–447.

Gaspar, J. M., Massa, M., & Matos, P. (2005). Shareholder investment horizons and the market for corporate control. *Journal of Financial Economics 76*(1), 135–165.

Hall, B. H., Jaffe, A. B., & Trajtenberg, M. (2005). Market value and patent citations. *RAND Journal of Economics, 36*, 16–38.

Hansen, G. S., & Hill, C. W. L. (1991). Are institutional investors myopic? A time-series study of four technology-driven industries. *Strategic Management Journal, 12*, 1–16.

Henderson, R., & Cockburn, I. (1994). Measuring competence? Exploring firm effects in pharmaceutical research. *Strategic Management Journal, 15*(Winter Special Issue), 63–84.

Hoskisson, R. E., Hitt, M. A., Johnson, R. A., & Grossman, W. (2002). Conflicting voices: The effects of ownership heterogeneity and internal governance on corporate strategy. *Academy of Management Journal, 45*, 697–716.

Jensen, M., & Meckling, W. (1976). Theory of the firm: Managerial behavior agency, cost and ownership structure. *Journal of Financial Economics, 3*, 305–360.

Kavadis, N., & Castañer, X. (2014). Ownership effects on unrelated diversification: An institutions' perspective. In B. Villalonga (Ed.), *Finance and strategy* (Vol. 31). Advances in Strategic Management. Bingley, UK: Emerald Group Publishing Limited.

Kelm, K. M., Narayanan, V. K., & Pinches, G. E. (1995). Shareholder value creation during R&D innovation and commercialization stages. *Academy of Management Journal, 38*, 770–786.

Klock, M. S., Mansi, S. A., & Maxwell, W. F. (2005). Does corporate governance matter to bondholders? *Journal of Financial and Quantitative Analysis, 40*, 693–719.

Kochhar, R., & David, P. (1996). Institutional investors and firm innovation: A test of competing hypotheses. *Strategic Management Journal, 17*, 73–84.

Kor, Y. Y., & Mahoney, J. T. (2005). How dynamics, management, and governance of resource deployments influence firm-level performance. *Strategic Management Journal, 26*, 489–496.

Matolcsy, Z., & Wyatt, A. (2008). The association between technological conditions and the market value of equity. *The Accounting Review, 83*, 479–518.

National Institutes of Health. (2010). *Understanding clinical trials* [Internet]. What is a clinical trial. Retrieved from http://clinicaltrials.gov/ct2/info/understand. Accessed on August 29, 2010.

Neubaum, O. D., & Zahra, S. A. (2006). Institutional ownership and corporate social performance: The moderating effects of investment horizon, activism, and coordination. *Journal of Management, 32*, 108–131.

O'Brien, P., & Bhushan, R. (1990). Analyst following and institutional ownership. *Journal of Accounting Research, 28*, 55–76.

Pisano, G. (2006). *Science business: The promise, the reality and the future of biotech.* Boston, MA: Harvard Business School Press.

Scharfstein, D., & Stein, J. (1990). Herd behavior and investment. *The American Economic Review, 80*(3), 465–479.

Schnatterly, K., Shaw, K. W., & Jennings, W. W. (2008). Information advantages of large institutional owners. *Strategic Management Journal, 29,* 219–227.

Schumpeter, J. A. (1934). *The theory of economic development.* Cambridge, MA: Harvard University Press.

Shin, J., & Shin, H. (2013). Institutional ownership and technological relatedness: A test of endogeneity. *Journal of Business Research, 66,* 2279–2286.

Shleifer, A., & Vishny, R. (1986). Large shareholders and corporate control. *Journal of Political Economy, 94,* 461–488.

Shleifer, A., & Vishny, R. (2003). Stock market driven acquisitions. *Journal of Financial Economics, 70,* 295–311.

Teece, D. J. (1986). Profiting from technological innovation: Implications for integration, collaboration, licensing and public policy. *Research Policy, 15,* 285–305.

Useem, M. (1996). *Investor capitalism.* New York, NY: Basic Books.

Vismara, S., & Signori, A. (2014). How innovation shapes a firm's survival profile: Takeovers, regulatory and voluntary delistings. In B. Villalonga (Ed.), *Finance and strategy* (Vol. 31). Advances in Strategic Management. Bingley, UK: Emerald Group Publishing Limited.

von Hippel, E. (1994). "Sticky information" and the locus of problem solving: Implications for innovation. *Management Science, 40*(4), 429–439.

Zahra, S. A. (1996). Technology strategy and financial performance: Examining the moderating role of the firm's competitive environment. *Journal of Business Venturing, 11,* 189–219.

HOW INNOVATION SHAPES A FIRM'S SURVIVAL PROFILE: TAKEOVERS, REGULATORY AND VOLUNTARY DELISTINGS

Silvio Vismara and Andrea Signori

ABSTRACT

Innovation is a key driver of a firm's ability to survive in the financial market. Previous studies typically consider a firm dead once its shares are delisted from the stock exchange. Despite its negative connotation, delisting may be a strategic decision and therefore be a positive outcome for the company. We study how a firm's innovative activity, in terms of R&D investments and number of patents, shapes its survival profile, taking into account the heterogeneous nature of delistings. Using a sample of high-tech small and medium enterprises (SMEs) going public in Europe during 1998–2003, we find that more innovative firms, both in terms of patents and R&D investments, have a higher probability to be taken over. However, while firms with a rich portfolio of patents are less likely to voluntarily delist, higher R&D investments increase a firm's likelihood of being delisted due to compliance failure.

Keywords: Patents; R&D; IPOs; M&As; delistings

INTRODUCTION

Both management and finance literatures have investigated how firms increase their performance through innovation. In terms of financial performance, studies are typically based on the signaling theory or the resource-based view of the firm framework to assess the impact of innovation on operating performance, valuation, or market returns (Bonardo, Paleari, & Vismara, 2011; Heeley, Matusik, & Jain, 2007; Khurshed, Paleari, Pandè, & Vismara, 2014; Lee & Lee, 2008). Some of these studies address the question of how a firm's level of innovation impacts its survival on a stock exchange, with the number of patents increasing the likelihood of survival (Audretsch & Lehmann, 2008; Wagner & Cockburn, 2010). However, firms can delist for different, not necessarily negative, reasons (Macey, O'Hara, & Pompilio, 2008). For instance, firms can delist from a second-tier market to transfer to a main market (Vismara, Paleari, & Ritter, 2012) or be taken over due to their attractiveness as acquisition targets (Bonardo, Paleari, & Vismara, 2010). Delistings can therefore even represent a desirable outcome.

We address the heterogeneous nature of delisting by classifying takeover-driven, voluntary and regulatory (compliance failure) delistings. First, takeovers either represent good outcomes, when the acquirer values the firm more than the public market, or "fire-sales." Second, delistings can either be imposed by stock exchanges, pursuant to a rule of the market, or they can be a firm's decision. Regulatory delistings are typically due to negative reasons, because of the firm's inability to meet listing requirements. However, the failure to comply with listing standards might be, at least partly, voluntary. Third, voluntary delistings occur following the firm's own request, conditional upon the approval of a qualified majority of shareholders,[1] for a number of reasons, such as bankruptcy filings or reorganizations that imply raising more financing from private lenders. Firms can also voluntary delist when going public has turned out to be an unsuccessful strategy but their product market potential is still relevant. The delisting event is therefore more complicated than assumed by prior studies, and the impact of innovation on the probability of each type of delisting is presumably different.

Innovation as a key driver of a firm's performance is well established, and both research and development (R&D) investments and patents are perceived as information-sensitive assets, which makes them different from other tangible assets. Patents are signals of quality, bases for commercial transactions, and measures of protection from competition and imitation. It is therefore plausible that firms with a richer portfolio of patents are better equipped to survive, and when they do delist, it is a voluntary decision. Although patents are widely used by researchers and policy makers to evaluate a firm's innovative activity, they are not a perfect measure. For instance, inventions can be protected by trade secrets. A second, more general measure of innovation is R&D intensity, whose impact on a firm's survival may be substantially different from that of patents. While patents are an output measure of achieved innovation, R&D expenses quantify innovative inputs. Costs are borne immediately, but benefits are likely to be observed only after years, due to the long-term nature of this kind of investment. Moreover, they sometimes turn out to be wasteful investments yielding low returns, with no innovative outputs (Jensen, 1989). This increases a firm's level of uncertainty and, consequently, its risk of failure. A further reason to associate higher risk profiles with R&D-focused firms is related to self-selection mechanisms. Entrepreneurial firms with prototypes and substantial R&D investments are more likely to receive financing from venture capitalists, which in turn increases the incentive to take these companies public to monetize the investment, even when their quality is not yet clear. We argue, therefore, that larger R&D investments lead to higher risk of delisting due to regulation.

We test our hypotheses using the population of 382 high-tech small and medium enterprises gone public in the period 1998–2003 on the stock markets of the four largest European economies (namely, Germany, the United Kingdom, France, and Italy). We find that the number of patents significantly increases a firm's likelihood of being delisted due to takeover, while it decreases the likelihood of voluntary delisting. On the other hand, we document that more R&D-intensive firms are more likely to be delisted due to takeover, but also due to unmet regulatory requirements. Our analysis controls for a number of potential determinants of the likelihood of survival, including firm age, size, profitability, Initial Public Offering (IPO) valuation, quality and behavior of the company's upper echelons, and affiliation with venture capitalists and prestigious underwriters.

The remainder of the chapter is structured as follows. The section "Literature Review and Hypotheses Development" defines the hypotheses. In the section "Research Design," we describe the sample of IPOs, the variables, and the methodologies. The econometric results are presented in the section "Results", while the "Robustness Checks" section tests our predictions using alternative methodologies. The final section concludes.

LITERATURE REVIEW AND HYPOTHESES DEVELOPMENT

Delistings should not be unequivocally interpreted as a signal of failure. Only recent survival studies in the financial literature have started to take into account the different reasons for delistings. Vismara et al. (2012) show that approximately one-fourth of the delistings occurred among European IPOs over the past two decades are associated with an M&A, and that transfers from different markets are also frequent. Pour and Lasfer (2013) and Espenlaub, Khurshed, and Mohamed (2012) document that a significant fraction of delistings from the London's Alternative Investment Market are voluntary. Despite such an empirical relevance, the literature that investigates the impact of innovation on the survival profile of firms has neglected the heterogeneity of delistings. This is surprising, given that different delisting reasons represent dramatically different outcomes for the firm and reflect diverse theoretical motivations of the role of innovation.

Patents

Patents provide firms with a bunch of benefits, such as facilitated access to financing and legal safeguards against product market competition (Hsu & Ziedonis, 2013). As a consequence, they are publicized in IPO prospectuses by firms going public. They are perceived as credible signals about the technological value of a firm's knowledge base, as firms with larger patent portfolios are expected to embed better research capabilities and invest more in innovative activity. Patenting activity is therefore associated with firms that have already overcome the earliest and riskiest phases of the innovative process by demonstrating the ability to finalize R&D efforts and convert them in profitable assets.

A firm's investment in innovative activities is a determinant of its propensity to be involved in the market for corporate control. First, the matching theory of ownership change (Lichtenberg & Siegel, 1989) predicts that M&A dynamics allow effectively reallocating resources and facilitating the division of labor. The threat of takeover motivates managers to align their decisions with the shareholders' interests, because an acquisition by another firm would open the possibility to purge ineffective managers and correct efficiency lapses. For innovative firms, the M&A market can be useful to match new ownership and management structures that allow to enhance productivity and maximize the financial return of the human and technological capital. Therefore, takeovers may be a win-win solution for both the acquirer and the target firm, as a consequence of the division of scientific labor between entrepreneurial firms and established firms that implicitly shapes their roles as targets and acquirers.

Second, in the presence of opportunities that could be better exploited if matched with the resources of the acquirer, complementary assets are worth more if bound together under common ownership. Synergies between alliance counterparts are a well-documented reason to combine complementary assets and capabilities. Such a combination adds value over and above what the acquirer's and target's resources could create independently. Innovation-based firms tend to embed considerable technological competences, thereby increasing their attractiveness toward potential acquirers. Acquirers may get interested in these firms because of the opportunity to commercially exploit such competences, or to develop synergies in innovation activities by promoting the interaction of different knowledge sources, resulting in superadditive effects for the merged entity.

Third, the transfer of knowledge and intangible assets from the acquired to the acquiring firm may motivate takeovers. A firm with a large number of patents may be a favorable acquisition target for firms that have been competing in innovation but eventually lost the patent race. Potential bidders are primarily interested in the possibility to acquire a target's patent portfolio that may threaten the outcome of their own R&D activity, or also block their competitors' investments in innovation. Such a preemptive power is valuable to acquirers, allowing them to defend a spot in technology space around the patented invention, and to capture value from innovative activities (Grimpe & Hussinger, 2014). Therefore, while patenting initially facilitates small entrants to compete in an industry, it often leads to a transfer of the ownership of small firms' technological and intellectual property to larger incumbents.

In the financial markets, patents are also considered a reliable proxy for the firm's ability to survive in the long run. Audretsch and Lehmann (2008) document that surviving firms own a significantly larger number of patents than nonsurviving firms. Similarly, Wagner and Cockburn (2010) find that, among Internet-based firms that went public during the boom phase of the dot-com bubble, those with greater patenting activity faced lower probability of business failure during the burst period that followed. A limitation of these studies, however, resides in the fact that delistings are treated as homogeneous events. Audretsch and Lehmann (2008) do not distinguish the different motivations that lead firms to remove their shares from the stock market, while Wagner and Cockburn (2010) simply categorize delistings as takeovers or failures, without accounting for the possibility that firms can delist upon their own request. Other studies, such as Meoli, Paleari, and Vismara (2013) and Bonardo et al. (2010), relate a firm's innovative activity with the survival rate, but focusing exclusively on M&A-related delistings.

Our chapter fills this gap by disentangling the impact of patents on firm survival after taking into account the heterogeneity of delistings. Firms with larger patent portfolios are more likely to draw the attention of potential acquirers, thereby increasing the likelihood of a delisting due to takeover. Given that firms with greater patenting activity have lower probability to delist in the first years after the IPO, arguably due to the positive reasons reported above (Audretsch & Lehmann, 2008; Wagner & Cockburn, 2010), we expect these firms to have a lower likelihood of regulatory delisting. Moreover, firms that go public already having a robust portfolio of patents are presumably doing so for staying in the market. The possibility to raise debt capital using patents as collaterals (Bezant, 2003) makes the public equity market not a residual, opportunistic choice for these firms.

Based on these arguments, we formulate the following hypotheses:

Hypothesis 1a. Firms with more patents have higher probability of being taken over.

Hypothesis 1b. The number of patents held does not affect the probability of being delisted due to regulation.

Hypothesis 1c. Firms with more patents have lower probability of being voluntarily delisted.

R&D Investments

Together with patenting activity, R&D intensity is a common measure of a firm's propensity to innovate (e.g., Lefebvre, Lefebvre, & Bourgault, 1998). However, these two practices present substantial differences in the way in which costs and benefits are faced by the firm. Patents are a tangible output of achieved innovation, while R&D expenses identify the immediate firm's commitment in terms of innovative inputs, whose future outcome is affected by uncertainty. Negative cash flows are immediately borne by the firm, while positive cash flows often arise after many years. In a dynamic setting, R&D investments can be considered as options, whose value increases with the firm's risk-taking behavior.

For instance, R&D investments are subject to the influence of contingent factors. While patents, once recognized by the legal environment, provide firms with a temporary monopoly on the commercialization of an innovation, fluctuations in the general economic conditions may undermine the success of once promising investment decisions. Consequently, the impact of R&D investments on a firm's survival can be substantially different from that of patents. While raising the profile of the firm by demonstrating the possession of promising technologies, they also increase the uncertainty of its future growth prospects (Cogliati, Paleari, & Vismara, 2011). This exposes the firm to a greater risk of being delisted due to regulatory reasons.

Firms with high R&D investments suffer from information asymmetries to a larger extent than firms with a large portfolio of patents due to, among other aspects, the lack of disclosure. Therefore, these firms may encounter difficulties in raising funds. Start-up firms with substantial R&D investments find it problematic to access to debt capital compared to non-R&D-focused start-up firms (Robb & Seamans, 2014). R&D-intensive firms with no patents are characterized by larger valuation uncertainty due to the difficulty of managers to communicate the value of intangibles to outside investors (Vismara, 2014). This may exert a detrimental effect on the market valuation of the firm for two main reasons. First, Merton's (1987) investor recognition hypothesis predicts that outside investors recognize higher valuations to firms affected by a smaller extent of information asymmetry. Second, the value of an asset is inversely related to the uncertainty of the future benefits expected from that asset (Robichek & Myers, 1966). The greater information asymmetry and future uncertainty characterizing R&D-intensive firms may therefore lead to suboptimal market clearing prices. This results in a higher probability to be delisted due unmet regulatory requirements.

Finally, a further motivation for associating greater risk with companies undertaking substantial R&D investments is related to the selection mechanisms of venture capitalists. New entrants with R&D investments and promising technological capabilities are more likely to receive financing from venture capitalists. Since venture capitalists have the ultimate objective to cash out once the investment in the portfolio firm has become profitable, they may have the incentive to take these companies public even if they have not yet reached the optimal stage, and their quality has not become sufficiently clear to the market. For this reason, IPO firms with higher R&D investments may face a higher probability of failure to comply with stock market regulations.

Based on these arguments, we formulate the following hypotheses:

Hypothesis 2a. Firms with higher R&D investments have higher probability of being taken over.

Hypothesis 2b. Firms with higher R&D investments have higher probability of being delisted due to regulation.

Hypothesis 2c. The amount of R&D investments does not affect the probability of being voluntarily delisted.

RESEARCH DESIGN

Data and Sample

The sample is composed of 382 high-tech small and medium enterprises (SMEs) gone public in Europe in the period 1998–2003. SMEs are identified according to the definition of the European Commission as firms with pre-IPO sales inferior to €50 million, while to identify high-tech industries we resort to the Eurostat sectorial classification. Manufacturing industries are classified by Eurostat into high-tech, medium-tech, and low-tech according to their technological intensity (R&D expenditure/value added). Services are aggregated by Eurostat into knowledge-intensive services and less knowledge-intensive services based on the share of tertiary educated persons. Our sample is made of companies operating in sectors classified by Eurostat as high-tech manufacturing or knowledge-intensive services. We focus on the four largest economies in Europe, namely, Germany (Deutsche Börse), the United Kingdom (London Stock Exchange), France (Euronext), and Italy (Borsa Italiana). Our sample of 382 companies represents the entire population of high-tech SMEs that went public in these countries in the period 1998–2003 and accounts for 14% of the total 2,779 IPOs.

Primary sources of information are the IPO prospectuses collected from the EURIPO database, which provides the IPO prospectus as well as very detailed information on the companies and their management.[2] When firms raise equity for the first time in their life cycle, they face the big challenge of convincing a wide variety of stakeholders about their long-term potential. At this stage, the official IPO prospectus is the primary means of disclosure through which investors can consider and evaluate the opportunity to invest in the company. Since the purpose of the prospectus is to sell stocks, issuers have the incentive to include all relevant information that is able to raise the profile of the firm and certify its quality. Prospectus data are considered reliable by outside investors because owners and managers are legally accountable for the accuracy of the information reported. Indeed, such information has been extensively investigated in strategy research and, more recently, in entrepreneurship research.

Definition of Delisting

We track these IPOs until December 31, 2012, which is the truncation date. Survivors are identified as stocks of firms that continue to be traded on the same market where they went public. Firms that transfer their listing to another market (e.g., from London's Alternative Investment Market (AIM) to the Official List) are treated as "censored" survivors and their observation is truncated at the transfer date. We use the stock exchanges' websites to find the delisting date and check sample firms in DataStream to verify that these delisted firms are not listed in different markets.

Of the 382 IPOs from 1998 to 2003, 171 (44.8%) were delisted by the end of 2012. The 60-month delisting rate is 36%. Vismara et al. (2012) report similar survival rates for companies going public in Europe's second-tier markets, while Espenlaub et al. (2012) report higher delisting rates for companies going public on London's second market (AIM). As argued by Vismara et al. (2012), this is related to the nature of the companies going public (older and larger in continental Europe than in the United Kingdom) and to regulatory differences, because delistings are more expensive and require more time to be finalized in continental Europe, where they compulsorily involve a tender offer.

To identify the type of delisting, we rely on the stock exchanges' websites, which report monthly statistics on the delisted firms along with the delisting reason.[3] Voluntary delistings occur upon the firm's voluntary request. Examples of delistings following the company's request are management buy-outs, members' voluntary liquidations, schemes of restructuring, or schemes of arrangement.[4] On the other hand, delistings due to regulation are imposed by the stock exchange as a consequence of the firm's inability to meet listing requirements. Breaches of regulations include failing to comply with the minimum public holding (free float), minimum market capitalization or sales levels, or failure to pay listing fees.[5]

Table 1 provides the number of delisted firms for each type of delisting, by country. In our sample, voluntary delistings and delistings due to regulatory reasons account for 41 and 49 firms, respectively. Almost half of the delistings in our sample are due to takeover (81 firms, 47%). Germany and the United Kingdom are the most highly represented countries in the sample (51 and 75 firms, respectively) due to the larger size of the German economy and the higher activism of the market for corporate control in the United Kingdom.

Independent Variables

We investigate the impact of R&D investments and patents on the survival rate of IPO firms. R&D investments are measured as the ratio between R&D investments and sales at the last fiscal year before IPO, as reported in the offering prospectuses. The number of patents held by the firm is also obtained from IPO prospectuses, where they are disclosed in the Intellectual Property section, included in the company description chapter. We consider the number of patents to which the firm has exclusive rights at the date of public offering. Thus, the measure captures both patents issued directly to the firm and patents acquired through arrangements with other firms.

Table 1. Sample.

	Sample	France	Italy	Germany	UK
Takeovers	81	11	7	23	40
Regulatory delistings	49	11	5	17	16
Voluntary delistings	41	5	6	11	19
Delistings (total)	171	27	18	51	75

The types of delisting are identified from information available on the stock exchanges' websites. Regulatory delistings are imposed by the stock exchange as the consequence of the firm's inability to meet listing requirements, such as minimum public holding (free float), minimum market capitalization or sales levels, or failure to pay listing fees. Voluntary delistings occur upon the firm's voluntary request and include management buy-outs, members' voluntary liquidations, schemes of restructuring or schemes of arrangement, and other voluntary reasons for delisting.

All models control for a common set of variables, selected according to prior literature on IPOs and innovation, and for industry (IT and biotech), countries (Italy, Germany, and the United Kingdom) and year fixed effects.

Firm age, measured as the natural logarithm of firm age (in years) since incorporation at the IPO (Log Age + 1), proxies for the firm's ability to react to changes on the supply or demand side and to learn from these changes. The stock of learning accumulates with age (Audretsch, 1995) and is expected to positively influence its survival. Similarly, size is measured in terms of pre-IPO sales (Log Sales) as a proxy for economies of scales and is expected to increase the likelihood of survival. While less profitable firms are riskier, less efficient firms are more often targeted by other companies, according to the matching theory of ownership (Lichtenberg & Siegel, 1989). Consequently, we expect firm profitability, measured as pre-IPO return on assets, to be negatively related to the likelihood of delisting either due to takeover, as mechanisms for correcting efficiency lapses, or to regulation. Everything else equal, firms with higher valuations are more robust and, being more expensive, become less appealing targets (Vismara et al., 2012). We therefore expect the Tobin's Q ratio of market value of assets to the book value of assets, where the market value is calculated as the sum of the book value of assets and the market value of common stock less the book value of common stock, to negatively influence the probability of delisting due to takeover.

Survival chances of high-tech SMEs also depend on intangible or tacit resources, embodied in the human capital of employees and managers (Audretsch & Stephan, 1996). We refer to quality and behavior of the upper echelons, that is, the combination of the top management team and board members. Relying on the definition of upper echelons allows us to better account for differences in the design and functioning of top management teams across national borders (Meoli et al., 2013). We consider the proportion of upper echelons holding an academic degree, either doctor or professor, as proxy for the firm's human capital (Audretsch & Lehmann, 2008). Thanks to their superior advisory role, upper echelons with higher human capital are expected to ensure a longer survival time. As far as ownership allocation influences incentive schemes, ownership divestments at the IPO by upper echelons or by existing shareholders might be perceived as a negative signal (Leland & Pyle, 1977), thereby increasing agency problems after the IPO (Jensen & Meckling, 1976). If the firm is bankrupt, upper echelons lose their private benefits of control (Audretsch & Lehmann, 2006). Thus, we expect an ownership divestment, measured as shares sold at the IPO over pre-IPO stakes, to result in a higher probability of delisting. The dilution effect makes divested firms easier takeover targets.

Venture capitalists (VCs) play an important role in the life of high-tech SMEs by providing not only capital at critical stages but also monitoring and decision-support capabilities. Entrepreneurs can benefit from the industry expertise of VCs when evaluating strategic decisions for the firm. Therefore, the presence of VCs may be perceived as a mark of quality (certification) by a potential acquirer, increasing its appeal as a target. Coherently, we expect the VC dummy variable, coded one if the IPO firm is backed by venture capital and zero otherwise, to be positively (negatively) related the probability of takeover (other forms of delistings). Similar expectations hold for the affiliation with prestigious underwriters, whose reputational capital as repeat players in the IPO market would be damaged if associated with poor-quality companies. We proxy underwriter reputation by computing each underwriter's market share (Megginson & Weiss, 1991), based on the amount of capital raised in Europe during 1995–2011, as in Signori, Meoli, and Vismara (2013).

Table 2 describes the sample. High-tech SMEs going public in Europe are in median 7.5 years old, have average pre-IPO revenues of €16 million, and are profitable, with a 5.46% return on assets. On average, 9.87% of the upper echelon members hold a PhD, while upper echelon divestment is larger than that realized by existing shareholders (11.65% vs. 9.98%). More than half of our IPO sample is VC-backed. R&D investments account for 11.89% of pre-IPO annual sales on average, and firms hold 14.71 patents at their arrival on the market. Table 3 provides the correlation matrix for the independent variables. Multicollinearity is not a major concern because none of the variance inflation factors exceed 3, which is below the critical cut-off of 10.

Models

Since takeover-driven, regulatory, and voluntary delistings are mutually exclusive, competing events, we use a competing risks model that allows to directly assess the covariate effects on the cumulative incidence function. We perform a test for the proportionality assumption behind competing-risks regression modeling time-varying coefficient. Such test consists of introducing in the model specification interaction terms between covariates and the time variable, as confirming that a coefficient is time invariant is a way to check the proportional-subhazards assumption. Proportional

Table 2. Descriptive Statistics.

Average Values	IPOs	Delistings	Takeover	Regulatory	Voluntary
Patents (no.)	14.71	13.83	13.17	15.35	13.32
R&D investments (%)	11.89	13.91	13.77	15.67	12.06
Age (years, median)	7.5	7	7	6	6
Size (sales, € million)	16.41	14.27	14.34	15.82	11.85
Profitability (%, median)	5.46	4.11	4.16	3.88	4.22
Tobin's Q (median)	3.65	3.34	3.15	2.98	3.65
PhD in the upper echelon (%)	9.87	10.53	10.56	10.63	10.35
Upper echelon divestment (%)	11.65	12.88	13.54	12.69	11.81
Ownership divestment (%)	8.98	10.62	11.49	10.35	9.21
Venture capital (% of firms)	54.65	48.5	48.1	53.1	43.9
Underwriter reputation	29.58	24.44	28.10	19.32	23.33
No. of observations	382	171	81	49	41

The table presents the average values of each variable for the original population of IPOs and for delistings, classified by type. R&D investments are measured as the pre-IPO ratio between R&D investments and sales, as reported in the offering prospectuses; the number of patents held by the firm is obtained from IPO prospectuses; firm age is measured in years since incorporation at the IPO; size is pre-IPO sales; profitability is measured by return on assets at the IPO; Tobin's Q is the ratio of the market value of assets to the book value of assets, where the market value is calculated as the sum of the book value of assets and the market value of common stock less the book value of common stock; PhD in the upper echelon is the proportion of upper echelons (board members plus Top Management Team members) holding an academic degree; upper echelon divestment (ownership divestment) is measured as shares sold at listing over pre-IPO stakes by upper echelons (substantial shareholders); VC-backed firms are identified from the EURIPO database; and underwriter reputation is computed as market share based on the amount of capital raised in Europe during 1995–2011.

subhazards imply that the relative subhazard is fixed over time, and this assumption holds if these interactions turn to be non-statistically significant. The results indicate that this assumption has not been violated, confirming the appropriateness of the selected method.

As a robustness check, we implement three Cox proportional hazard models where the dependent variable is the probability of delisting per unit time (month), conditional on the event not having occurred yet. This model allows us to take into account not just binary information on whether a stock survives for a specified period or until a specified point in time, but also the length of survival time. We run three Cox models where the failure event is delisting due to (1) takeover, (2) regulation, and (3) for other voluntary reasons. In our study, observations are "right-censored" if they are still listed on the same market of their IPO by the end of the study period (December 31, 2012), or if they transferred to another market, in which

Table 3. Correlation Matrix.

Variables	1	2	3	4	5	6	7	8	9	10	11
1. Patents (no.)	1.000										
2. R&D investments (%)	0.034	1.000									
3. Age (years, median)	0.065	−0.026	1.000								
4. Size (sales, € million)	0.124*	0.081	0.123*	1.000							
5. Profitability (%, median)	0.016	−0.038	−0.025	0.021	1.000						
6. Market to book (median)	0.107	0.011	−0.239*	−0.129*	0.141*	1.000					
7. PhD in the upper echelon (%)	0.132*	0.098	−0.004	−0.025	0.083	0.105	1.000				
8. Upper echelon divestment (%)	−0.031	0.054	−0.093	0.045	−0.048	0.070	−0.025	1.000			
9. Ownership divestment (%)	0.042	−0.062	−0.007	0.061	0.054	0.052	0.052	0.103	1.000		
10. Venture capital (% of firms)	0.082	0.031	0.016	−0.043	0.022	0.115	0.089	0.036	−0.082	1.000	
11. Underwriter reputation	0.120*	0.104	−0.008	0.131*	−0.103	0.093	0.012	−0.023	−0.112	0.022	1.000

***1% significance level; **5% significance level; *10% significance level of the correlation coefficients.

case they are truncated at the transfer date. In the Cox models, delistings for different reasons are also treated as censored observations. For instance, regulatory and voluntary delistings are treated as censored in Model 1, where the failure event is takeover-driven delisting.

RESULTS

Table 4 provides the results of the competing risks model in which the dependent variable takes different values for each of the delisting motivations (i.e., takeover, regulatory, voluntary). Concerning the role of patents, the coefficient of the number of patents variable is significantly positive for takeover-related delistings, consistent with Hypothesis 1a.

Table 4. Competing Risks Model.

	(1) Takeover	(2) Regulatory Delisting	(3) Voluntary Delisting
Patents	1.54**	0.34	−1.53**
R&D investments	1.94*	2.16**	0.67
Age	0.22	−0.23	−0.01
Size	−0.42*	−0.02	−0.21
Profitability	1.86**	0.15	0.30
Tobin's Q	−0.42**	0.022**	0.21**
PhD in the upper echelon	0.30	−0.20	−0.15
Upper echelon divestment	1.23**	0.67**	1.13**
Ownership divestment	0.73*	0.13	0.45
Venture capital	0.42**	0.02	−0.21**
Underwriter reputation	1.22*	−1.72***	−0.11
IT	0.25	1.31*	−0.10
Pharma	1.23*	0.42	0.32
Italy	−0.11	−0.27	−0.14
UK	0.65	0.64	1.78***
Germany	0.011	−0.31	−0.38
Log pseudo likelihood	−586.06***	−354.96***	−395.81***

Competing risks model estimated by maximizing the likelihood function of the competing risk hazard model of takeovers, regulatory delistings, and other voluntary reasons for delisting. The sample is made of 382 high-tech SMEs that went public in Europe in the period 1998–2003. Significance levels of the log pseudo likelihood is based on the Wald χ^2-test for significance of the regression. Standard errors have been adjusted for clustering.
***1% significance level; **5% significance level; *10% significance level.

This documents that the size of a firm's patent portfolio is an effective mechanism to attract potential acquirers. As predicted by Hypothesis 1b, we find no significant effect of patents on the likelihood of being delisted due to regulation. Consistent with Hypothesis 1c, firms with more patents have a lower probability to voluntarily delist, confirming the role of patents as credible signals about the firm's ability to take advantage from its innovative activity.

As for the impact of R&D investments on a firm's survival, we find that more R&D-intensive firms are more likely to be delisted due to takeover, as predicted by Hypothesis 2a, although statistical evidence is weak. Consistent with Hypothesis 2b, the amount of R&D investments significantly increases a firm's likelihood of being delisted due to unmet regulatory requirements because of the riskier nature of R&D-intensive firms. Finally, R&D investments do not affect the probability to voluntarily delist.

ROBUSTNESS CHECKS

Table 5 reports the results of the three Cox proportional hazard models where the dependent variable is the probability of delisting per unit time (month), conditional on delisting not having occurred yet. The coefficients of the patent variable are positive for takeovers, not significant for regulatory delistings, and negative for voluntary delistings. This is consistent with our hypotheses, and coherent with the evidence provided by the competing risk model previously discussed. Also, the coefficients of the R&D investments variable are consistent with our hypotheses and provide robustness to our previous evidence, as the amount of R&D investments significantly increases the likelihood of delisting due to takeover and unmet regulation, while it does not influence the likelihood of voluntary delisting.

CONCLUSION

Previous literature has documented the positive impact of innovation on a firm's survival in a stock market (Audretsch & Lehmann, 2008; Wagner & Cockburn, 2010). However, delistings occur for different reasons that may not always be negative. Firms can voluntarily delist, be taken over because

Table 5. Robustness Checks.

	(1) Takeover	(2) Regulatory Delisting	(3) Voluntary Delisting
Patents	0.89*	0.02	−1.12**
R&D investments	1.97*	2.42**	0.84
Age	0.14	−0.15	−0.12
Size	−0.61*	−0.24	−0.08
Profitability	−0.32*	−0.23	−0.21
Tobin's Q	−0.82**	−0.93**	−0.08
PhD in the upper echelon	0.21	0.50	−0.59
Upper echelon divestment	1.30**	1.29**	1.09*
Ownership divestment	0.98*	0.79	0.68
Venture capital	1.56**	−0.43	−1.74***
Underwriter reputation	1.48*	−2.74***	−0.02
IT	0.30	1.19*	−0.29
Pharma	1.56**	0.35	0.29
Italy	−0.09	−0.31	−0.19
UK	0.71*	0.66	1.87***
Germany	0.09	−0.35	−0.75
Log pseudo likelihood	−293.12***	−109.21***	−107.45***

Cox model where the dependent variable is, in Model 1, equal to 1 if the firm is delisted due to takeover; in Model 2, equal to 1 if the firm is delisted due to unmet regulatory requirements; and, in Model 3, equal to 1 if the firm is delisted for other voluntary reasons. The time variable measures the time elapsing between IPO and delisting. The sample is made of 382 high-tech SMEs that went public in Europe in the period 1998–2006. Wald χ^2-test is used for significance of the regression.
*** 1% significance level; ** 5% significance level; * 10% significance level.

of their superior attractiveness, or be delisted due to their inability to meet ongoing listing requirements. The heterogeneity in delisting reasons carries profoundly different implications that should not be neglected by studies on the survival profile of IPOs. In this chapter, we develop a fine-grained classification of delisting by distinguishing takeover-related delistings caused by the firm being acquired, voluntary delistings occurring upon the firm's direct request, and regulatory delistings imposed by the stock exchange due to unmet listing requirements. This is a new, valuable contribution to the literature.

Using a sample of 382 high-tech SMEs going public in Europe during 1998–2003, we investigate how a firm's innovative activity shapes its survival profile. We disentangle the effect of corporate innovation by investigating the influence of a firm's number of patents and amount of R&D

investments. While patents are an output measure of achieved innovation, R&D expenses quantify innovative inputs, so that their effect on the survival rate may be substantially different. This chapter investigates for the first time in the literature the substantially different effects that corporate innovation can exert on a firm's survival depending on the way in which innovation is measured, that is, whether it captures the firm's commitment in innovative input, as in the case of R&D investments, or the firm's already achieved output, as in the case of the size of patent portfolios. Specifically, we find that firms with richer patent portfolios are more likely to delist due to takeover and are less likely to voluntarily delist. Greater patenting not only draws the attention of potential acquirers but also ensures an increased ability of the firm to meet ongoing listing requirements. R&D-intensive firms not only face a higher probability of being delisted due to takeover but also a higher probability of being delisted due to regulation, arguably because the considerable uncertainty of R&D projects raises the firms' risk profile.

By investigating the role of innovation in shaping the survival probability while distinguishing the different delisting motivations, this chapter contributes to the literature on the relationship between corporate innovation and performance. Perhaps more importantly, the question of how long an IPO survives on a stock exchange carries important implications for a firm's stakeholders. The interests of stakeholders such as investors, directors, and managers are clearly linked to the survival profile of firms. Furthermore, underwriters who want to preserve their reputational capital should be cautious in taking public companies that may not be able to survive in the long term. Failure to do so would undermine their credibility as certifying agents about the quality of the firm taken public, resulting in a progressive loss of market share. Regulators can also use a firm's survival as one of the benchmarks to measure the success of the rules they impose on firms that plan a listing. Finally, the different delisting motivations need to be considered by policy makers interested in the long-run impact of innovation.

Our study is obviously not exempt from limitations. We treat patents and R&D investments as two distinct variables and we study their linear effects on the probability of delisting. The investigation of the interaction effects between R&D investments and patents, as well as the existence of nonlinear relationships, is a promising topic worth further research. Lastly, this study sheds light on the effects of innovation on delistings, taking into account the heterogeneous nature of the latters. However, further insights can be delivered by investigating the performance of firms prior to delisting, distinguishing good from bad performers.

NOTES

1. For instance, companies listed on the London Stock Exchange need to get not less than 75% of votes cast by their shareholders.
2. See Vismara et al. (2012) for a detailed description of the database.
3. For instance, the London Stock Exchange website provides the list of all delisted companies on a monthly basis (see Companies and Issuers section at www.londonstockexchange.com/statistics/companies-and-issuers/companies-and-issuers.htm) and the delisting reason in the corresponding corporate event notice.
4. Since companies are not obliged to motivate their voluntary request, sometimes the only information available is "voluntary agreement." Another voluntary reason that is however unobservable to the researcher is the firm's choice not to comply with regulatory requirements even when it could. This may lead to some voluntary delistings being erroneously classified as regulatory delistings. We acknowledge this limitation to our study.
5. Listing requirements vary across stock exchanges and stock markets. For a description of listing requirements in Europe, see Vismara et al. (2012), Table 4.

REFERENCES

Audretsch, D. B. (1995). Innovation, growth and survival. *International Journal of Industrial Organization*, 13, 441–457.

Audretsch, D. B., & Lehmann, E. E. (2006). Do locational spillovers pay? Empirical evidence from German IPO data. *Economics of Innovation and New Technology*, 15, 71–81.

Audretsch, D. B., & Lehmann, E. E. (2008). The Neuer Markt as an institution of creation and destruction. *International Entrepreneurship and Management Journal*, 4, 419–429.

Audretsch, D. B., & Stephan, P. E. (1996). Company-scientist locational links: The case of biotechnology. *American Economic Review*, 86, 641–652.

Bezant, M. (2003). The use of intellectual property as security for debt finance. *Journal of Knowledge Management*, 1, 237–263.

Bonardo, D., Paleari, S., & Vismara, S. (2010). The M&A dynamics of European science-based entrepreneurial firms. *Journal of Technology Transfer*, 35, 141–180.

Bonardo, D., Paleari, S., & Vismara, S. (2011). Valuing university-based firms: The effects of academic affiliation on IPO performance. *Entrepreneurship Theory and Practice*, 35, 755–776.

Cogliati, G. M., Paleari, S., & Vismara, S. (2011). IPO pricing: Growth rates implied in offer prices. *Annals of Finance*, 7, 53–82.

Espenlaub, S., Khurshed, A., & Mohamed, A. (2012). IPO survival in a reputational market. *Journal of Business Finance & Accounting*, 39, 427–463.

Grimpe, C., & Hussinger, K. (2014). Resource complementarity and value capture in firm acquisitions: The role of intellectual property rights. *Strategic Management Journal*. (forthcoming).

Heeley, M. B., Matusik, S. F., & Jain, N. (2007). Innovation, appropriability, and the underpricing of initial public offerings. *Academy of Management Journal*, 50, 209–225.

Hsu, D. H., & Ziedonis, R. H. (2013). Resources as dual sources of advantage: Implications for valuing entrepreneurial-firm patents. *Strategic Management Journal, 34*, 761–781.

Jensen, M. C. (1989). The eclipse of the public corporation. *Harvard Business Review, 67*, 61–74.

Jensen, M. C., & Meckling, W. H. (1976). Theory of the firm: Managerial behavior, agency costs and ownership structure. *Journal of Financial Economics, 3*, 305–360.

Khurshed, A., Paleari, S., Pandè, A., & Vismara, S. (2014). Grading, transparent books and initial public offerings. *Journal of Financial Markets, 19*, 154–169.

Lee, Y. J., & Lee, J. D. (2008). Strategy of start-ups for IPO timing across high technology industries. *Applied Economics Letters, 15*, 869–877.

Lefebvre, É., Lefebvre, L., & Bourgault, M. (1998). R&D-related capabilities as determinants of export performance. *Small Business Economics, 10*, 365–377.

Leland, H., & Pyle, D. (1977). Informational asymmetries, financial structure and financial intermediations. *Journal of Finance, 32*, 317–387.

Lichtenberg, F. R., & Siegel, D. (1989). The effects of leveraged buyouts on productivity and related aspects on firms' behaviour. *Journal of Financial Economics, 27*, 165–194.

Macey, J., O'Hara, M., & Pompilio, D. (2008). Down and out in the stock market: The law and economics of the delisting process. *Journal of Law and Economics, 51*, 683–713.

Megginson, W. L., & Weiss, K. (1991). Venture capitalist certification in initial public offerings. *Journal of Finance, 46*, 879–903.

Meoli, M., Paleari, S., & Vismara, S. (2013). Completing the technology transfer process: M&As of science-based IPOs. *Small Business Economics, 40*(2), 227–248.

Merton, R. C. (1987). A simple model of capital market equilibrium with incomplete information. *Journal of Finance, 42*, 483–510.

Pour, E. K., & Lasfer, M. (2013). Why do companies delist voluntarily from the stock market? *Journal of Banking & Finance, 37*, 4850–4860.

Robb, A., & Seamans, R. (2014). The role of R&D in entrepreneurial finance and performance. *Advances in Strategic Management*. (forthcoming).

Robichek, A. A., & Myers, S. C. (1966). Valuation of the firm: Effects of uncertainty in a market context. *Journal of Finance, 21*, 215–227.

Signori, A., Meoli, M., & Vismara S., M. (2013). Short covering and price stabilization of IPOs. *Applied Economics Letters, 20*, 931–937.

Vismara, S. (2014). Patents, R&D investments and post-IPO strategies. *Review of Managerial Science, 8*, 419–435.

Vismara, S., Paleari, S., & Ritter, J. R. (2012). Europe's second markets for small companies. *European Financial Management, 18*, 352–388.

Wagner, S., & Cockburn, I. (2010). Patents and the survival of internet-related IPOs. *Research Policy, 39*, 214–228.

THE ROLE OF R&D IN ENTREPRENEURIAL FINANCE AND PERFORMANCE

Alicia Robb and Robert Seamans

ABSTRACT

We extend theories of the firm to the entrepreneurial finance setting and argue that R&D-focused start-up firms will have a greater likelihood of financing themselves with equity rather than debt. We argue that mechanisms which reduce information asymmetry, including owner work experience and financier reputation, will increase the probability of funding with more debt. We also argue that start-ups that correctly align their financing mix to their R&D focus will perform better than firms that are misaligned. We study these ideas using a large nationally representative dataset on start-up firms in the United States.

Keywords: Entrepreneurship; entrepreneurial finance; information asymmetry; firm performance; research and development; transaction cost economics

INTRODUCTION

In this chapter, we draw from entrepreneurship, finance, and strategy literatures to hypothesize on the relationship between the type of finance obtained by a start-up firm and underlying firm characteristics. In particular, we investigate how information asymmetry affects the capital structure of research and development (R&D)-focused start-up firms. Information asymmetry is particularly acute in such settings (Goldfarb, Kirsch, & Shen, 2012), and so we expect that equity is more likely to be used than debt (Leland & Pyle, 1977; Williamson, 1988). However, we also expect that firms in such settings will be able to mitigate information asymmetry via different mechanisms, at least in part. We study two such mechanisms: founder experience and firm reputation gained through equity financing from venture capitalists (VCs) and/or angel investors. Finally, we expect performance to be positively correlated with alignment between the firm's R&D focus and its financing mix. We test these ideas using the *Kauffman Firm Survey* (KFS), a representative sample of nearly 5,000 start-up firms in the United States.

Our chapter contributes to existing literature in several ways. First, we draw on a broad literature on founder and funder characteristics to describe mechanisms that can alleviate the information asymmetry problem for R&D-focused start-ups. One finding from this literature is that founders' prior affiliations and experiences reduce frictions that entrepreneurs face when trying to finance new ventures (e.g., Gompers, Kovner, Lerner, & Scharfstein, 2005; Kaplan & Strömberg, 2004; Kotha & George, 2012; Stuart, Hoang, & Hybels, 1999). We also study the extent to which funder characteristics can alleviate information asymmetry. Existing literature shows that reputational benefits can "spill over" to closely linked firms (e.g., Bengtsson & Sensoy, 2011; Hochberg, Ljungqvist, & Lu, 2007). Moreover, entrepreneurs are willing to take worse terms from more reputable VCs (Hsu, 2004), arguably in part to benefit from reputational spillovers. In our setting, we explore the extent to which founder work experience and relationships with VCs or angel investors allow start-ups to overcome information asymmetries and rely more on debt financing, even when financing R&D activity.

Second, we extend the Transaction Cost Economics (TCE) theory in Williamson (1988) by studying its applicability in a boundary condition — the entrepreneurial firm context — and by linking TCE to a broader finance literature that studies the role of information asymmetry in financing choices (Leland & Pyle, 1977; Ueda, 2004). While working from a microanalytic, project-based point of view, Williamson's focus is on mature firms in an equilibrium state (1988, p. 582). Start-up firms, on the other hand, are neither mature nor in equilibrium, but instead face large barriers to survival (Aldrich & Auster, 1986; Stinchcombe, 1965). Indeed, as highlighted in the entrepreneurial finance literature (e.g., Cosh, Cumming, & Hughes, 2009; Goldfarb et al., 2012; Winston-Smith, 2012), due to the informational opaqueness of new and young firms, access to finance is one crucial barrier (Berger & Udell, 1998).

Finally, we contribute to literature on new firm performance (e.g., Arend, Patel, & Park, 2014; Chaddad & Reuer, 2009) by describing how alignment between a firm's R&D focus and its choice of financing can affect survival. To do this, we attempt to link our "first-stage" results to "second stage" performance outcomes, using an instrumental variables (IV) approach to address the endogeneity of a firm's choice of financing. Our approach also complements a broader literature that links performance to the alignment between firm characteristics and its governance structure (e.g., Mayer & Nickerson, 2005; Nickerson & Silverman, 2003; Sampson, 2004).

The chapter proceeds as follows. In the next section, we outline our theory and hypotheses, linking our work to prior entrepreneurship, finance, and strategy literatures. We then describe our data and methods, followed by discussion of our results and conclusion.

THEORY AND HYPOTHESES

In situations characterized by information asymmetry, lenders find it difficult to evaluate firms (Berger & Udell, 1998; Diamond, 1989). The relationship between entrepreneurs and lenders is thus one that is characterized by information asymmetry: in many cases, the lender has little information about the potential for the entrepreneur's idea to succeed. This information asymmetry is exacerbated for R&D-focused firms due to the lack of tangible assets and concurrent reliance on knowledge assets. Therefore, in the absence of contractual safeguards, traditional bank lenders are less likely to lend to R&D-focused firms because of the difficulty in determining the value of the firm's resources (Chaddad & Reuer, 2009; Diamond, 1989; Junkunc & Eckhardt, 2009; Leland & Pyle, 1977; Robb & Winston-Smith, 2013; Vismara & Signori, 2014). In addition, banks face greater liquidity constraints than VCs, resulting in preferences for collateral, transparent valuation, and low-risk sectors (Berger & Udell, 1998; Ueda, 2004; Winton & Yerramilli, 2008).

The entrepreneurial finance literature has identified several contractual safeguards that financiers can use to mitigate information asymmetry. On the debt side, information asymmetry increases the likelihood that lenders will charge higher interest rates and write more covenants into the loan contract. However, banks often ration capital rather than raise the interest rate because of the increased risk arising from moral hazard and adverse selection that can come with higher interest rates (Berger & Udell, 1998; Stiglitz & Weiss, 1981). Empirical studies suggest that banks do not favor the use of complicated contractual safeguards (Cole, 2008; Cosh et al., 2009). Thus, for some firms, traditional bank financing will not be an option at any interest rate. Hellmann, Lindsey, and Puri (2008), however, find that in some cases banks use strategic equity investments to gather "soft" information, which is used to mitigate information asymmetry and inform subsequent lending relationships.

Even in cases where banks do not ration capital and offer debt financing at high interest rates, the cost of debt financing may be too expensive for the entrepreneur relative to equity. In such cases, the entrepreneur will instead use equity financing from an investor, who then takes partial ownership of the company so as to gain more information about and exercise more control over how the technologies are being used. Kaplan and Strömberg (2003) find that cash flow rights and control rights are allocated separately in contracts between VCs and portfolio companies, and are made contingent upon observable performance measures. In a separate paper, they further associate specific risks with particular contractual terms (Kaplan & Strömberg, 2004) and find that VCs are given greater control rights under conditions of high information uncertainty between the entrepreneur and the investor. In summary, existing finance literature argues that entrepreneurs are more likely to finance their companies with equity rather than debt when information asymmetry between the entrepreneur and potential lenders is high.

TCE focuses on the governance of contractual relations and asks which transactions are better managed in the firm than in the market (e.g., Williamson, 1975, 1985, 1988). According to TCE, market governance is lower cost for transactions between trading partners that rely on generic, nonspecific assets. As the assets become more specialized and less easily redeployed, transaction costs may increase. Individuals who are party to a transaction may engage in opportunistic behavior when the stakes are high and take advantage of their trading partners to claim a more favorable distribution of the rents accruing from the transaction. To mitigate these hazards, the supplier and the buyer can be organized under unified ownership within the firm, where fiat and authority supplement renegotiation to resolve conflict. Moving the transaction from the market into the firm involves trading off the benefits of incentives (found in markets) for the benefits of coordinated adaptation (found in firms). The central prediction is that as asset specificity increases, vertical integration becomes more likely, all else equal (Williamson, 1975, 1985).[1]

Using a TCE framework, Williamson (1988, 2002) argues that established firms with projects using nongeneric assets will be more likely to use equity instead of debt financing. Debt is a simple, cheap governance structure better suited than equity for projects that use generic technology (Myers & Majluf, 1984; Shyam-Sunder & Myers, 1999). If things go poorly, the lender can repossess the technology and redeploy it in alternative ways with little loss of productive value. If a project instead uses less-generic technology, the debt holder will impose more restrictions. In general, as we move from generic to more specialized technologies, the restrictions imposed by debt become more onerous, and debt becomes exceedingly expensive. At some point, it will cost less for the firm to finance the technology using equity instead of debt. Williamson (1988) argues that equity is an appropriate governance structure in this case. It provides many safeguards that debt does not. In particular, the residual claimant status to the firm and the power to replace management through the shareholder-elected board of directors align management's incentives and allow for monitoring and oversight.

The central prediction from Williamson (1988) is that the debt ratio (the ratio of debt to debt plus equity) decreases as the asset specificity of the technology underlying the project increases. One of the ways in which the concept of asset specificity has been operationalized in empirical studies is by the presence of R&D employees or R&D spending. Existing empirical work in the TCE literature studying the link between R&D and firm financing focuses primarily on large established firms (e.g., Balakrishnan & Fox, 1993; David, O'Brien, & Yoshikawa, 2008; Titman & Wessels, 1988; Vicente-Lorente, 2001). The results are generally supportive of the predictions, but counterexamples exist (e.g., Harris, 1994). Large firms, however, are engaged in multiple projects at once, each of which may require different financing needs; also, large firms often cross-subsidize their businesses (Kuppuswamy & Villalonga, 2012), or invest in R&D via corporate venture capital (e.g., Dushnitsky & Lenox, 2005; Dushnitsky & Shapira, 2010), R&D alliances (e.g., Ahuja, 2000; Mowery, Oxley, & Silverman, 1996), and

R&D consortia (e.g., Joshi & Nerkar, 2011; Seamans, 2013). Hence, the link between the nature of R&D involved in each project and the financing mix for the firm as a whole is unclear in the case of large firms; the link is clearer in the case of a small start-up. To the extent that Williamson (1988) can be extended to the entrepreneurial firm context, we believe the project finance nature of our setting provides a more direct test of Williamson's theory.

Building off of TCE and finance literature, we expect that lenders will be more willing to lend to start-ups that do not engage in R&D compared with start-ups that do engage in R&D. In the case of a non-R&D-focused start-up, any technologies used to bring the start-up's service or product to the market are likely to be nonspecific and therefore easily resold on a secondary market if the entrepreneur's project fails. Such technology therefore can be used as collateral to obtain debt. On the other hand, in the case of an R&D-focused start-up, any technologies used to bring the start-up's service or product to the market are likely to be highly specific, which poses two problems. First, building on the TCE literature, any technologies in this case may be highly specific to the entrepreneur's project and thus harder to resell on a secondary market if the project fails, all else being equal. Second, building on finance literature, information asymmetry is likely to be higher between the entrepreneur and the potential financier. For these reasons, we expect that R&D-focused firms are more likely to be funded with relatively more equity than debt.

Hypothesis 1. An R&D-focused start-up will have a lower debt ratio than a start-up that is not R&D-focused.

Mechanisms to Mitigate Information Asymmetries

There is evidence that the choice of financial contract evolves with experience (e.g., Kaplan, Martel, & Strömberg, 2007; Kotha & George, 2012). Numerous academic studies have found that personal relationships help alleviate information asymmetries and facilitate financial intermediation. For example, "who you know" matters in the venture capital industry, in which entrepreneurs pay more to associate with more networked VCs (Hsu, 2004) and better-networked VCs achieve better outcomes (Bengtsson & Sensoy, 2011; Hochberg et al., 2007). As an entrepreneur gains more experience, he or she gains legitimacy from stakeholders (Aldrich, 1990) and grows his or her professional network, both of which should lead to a decrease in information asymmetry. Thus, to the extent that an entrepreneur engaging in R&D activities faces barriers to debt financing, this should be somewhat alleviated for entrepreneurs with more experience. Moreover, more experienced entrepreneurs understand the industry better (Bhide, 2000; Carroll & Hannan, 2000), and experience has been associated with better business outcomes in some cases (Bosma, Van Praag, Thurik, & De Wit, 2004; Cooper, Gimeno-Gascon, & Woo, 1994; Pennings, Lee, & Van Witteloostuijn, 1998; Taylor, 1999), which should give them a track record that puts them in a better bargaining position vis-à-vis lenders, and thereby allow them to negotiate more control rights (Cumming, 2008). Thus, we expect that R&D-focused start-ups with owners that have high amounts of prior industry work experience will have a higher debt ratio than R&D-focused start-ups that do not.

Hypothesis 2. An R&D-focused start-up with more owner experience will have a higher debt ratio than an R&D-focused start-up with less owner experience.

Existing research suggests that VC firms provide reputational benefits to their portfolio firms (Hellmann & Puri, 2002; Hsu, 2007). Robb and Robinson (2014) found that firms with VC backing had much higher levels of bank financing, in addition to higher levels of equity. Hellmann et al. (2008) provide evidence that some banks first provide VC financing and then subsequently engage in lending to start-ups. In addition, it appears that firms receiving funding from angels also receive such benefits. Kerr, Lerner, and Schoar (2014) use a regression discontinuity design to document that start-ups receiving angel funding do better than those that do not. We therefore expect that the reputational benefits from VCs and/or angel investors also will accrue to R&D-focused firms by easing the information asymmetry between the firm and potential lenders. Thus, we expect that R&D-focused start-ups that are backed by VCs and/or angel investors will have a higher debt ratio than R&D-focused start-ups that are not.

Hypothesis 3. An R&D-focused start-up with angel or VC backing will have a higher debt ratio than an R&D-focused start-up with no angel or VC backing.

Performance Consequences of Entrepreneurial Finance Alignment

As per Hypothesis 1, we expect that, *on average*, the new firm's debt ratio will decrease as the R&D underlying its business increases. However, we do not expect this relationship to necessarily hold for all firms. There may be many reasons for the firm to deviate from the optimal capital structure (Moskowitz & Vissing-Jorgensen, 2002). For example, the entrepreneur may have preferences for certain types of risk or a certain amount of control over the firm, which leads the firm to adopt a certain mix of equity and debt financing (Cassar, 2004; Coleman & Robb, 2012). As another example, discrimination may hinder access to certain types of credit (Chatterji & Seamans, 2012; Fairlie & Robb, 2008). As a result of these idiosyncratic forces, there may be firms in which the actual mix of debt and equity financing differs from the predicted mix.

In a related paper, David et al. (2008) draw a distinction between relational debt, which has characteristics similar to equity, and transactional debt, and show that publicly traded Japanese firms with higher levels of R&D and relational debt perform well. That is, performance improves as the firms in their sample align their R&D with their financing mix. While specific to R&D, their finding mirrors a broader finding in the literature that the failure to correctly align governance structure with asset specificity has adverse consequences for the firm. Nickerson and Silverman (2003) study the trucking industry and show that firms with a suboptimal governance structure for their core technology suffer lower profits than their optimally governed counterparts. Sampson (2004) studies R&D alliances in the telecommunications industry and shows that patent counts are lower when the alliance contract is misaligned with the underlying asset attributes of the project. Mayer and Nickerson (2005) study 190 IT projects and show that the firm is more likely to use in-house employees as asset specificity increases. They also show that failure to appropriately align contract governance with underlying asset specificity has a negative effect on profitability.

In our setting, two types of misalignment can occur: (i) too much equity for projects that do not involve R&D and (ii) too much debt for projects with R&D. Misalignment in either case can occur for a variety of reasons, including discrimination (Chatterji & Seamans, 2012) or preference (Cassar, 2004). Whatever the reason, misalignment (alignment) can negatively (positively) affect performance. For example, if the entrepreneur has a project that does not involve R&D, he or she should have a high debt ratio. If instead he or she has a low debt ratio, he or she eschews the high-powered incentives of debt (Williamson, 1988) and may need to spend added time interacting with equity holders who want to monitor the new firm's progress and less time on the business itself. This extra burden may cause the entrepreneur to react slowly to changing market conditions and perform worse than peers without the extra burden. As another example, if the entrepreneur has a project that involves R&D he or she should have a low debt ratio. If he or she instead has a high debt ratio and the business suffers temporary setbacks due to idiosyncratic shocks, debt holders may foreclose on the entrepreneur. In short, misalignment increases the costs to a new firm, and we therefore expect misalignment to result in negative performance consequences for the firm. Misalignment arises when non-R&D-focused start-ups are financed primarily with equity, so we expect such start-ups to do better when financed primarily with debt; similarly, misalignment arises when R&D-focused start-ups are financed primarily with debt, so we expect such start-ups to do worse when financed primarily with debt. We state this with the following hypothesis:

Hypothesis 4. Start-ups with misalignment between their R&D focus and debt ratio will experience worse performance than start-ups with alignment between their R&D focus and debt ratio.

DATA AND METHODS

Data

We test the hypotheses using data from the KFS microdata. KFS data contain detailed information on firms and their owners for a cohort of almost 5,000 firms that began operations in 2004. Importantly, firms in the KFS are sampled in the year of founding, which helps avoid the left-censoring problem in much entrepreneurial research (Eckhardt, Shane, & Delmar, 2006). KFS data contain detailed information on firms and their owners. For more information on the KFS design and methodology, see Robb et al. (2009). Total financial capital can come from the owner, other insiders (friends and family), and outsiders (banks, VCs, etc.), and, in each case, can be in the form of equity or debt. We therefore construct measures of *insider equity$_i$*, *outsider equity$_i$*, *insider debt$_i$* and *outsider debt$_i$*, as well as *total equity$_i$* (the sum of the first two) and *total debt$_i$* (the sum of the last two) for each firm i. We calculate the continuous variable *debt ratio$_i$* for each firm i as the ratio of *outsider debt$_i$* to *total equity$_i$* plus *total debt$_i$*. We follow the standard practice of grouping inside debt with equity, as inside debt often has equity-like features (Fama, 1985). Following Robb and Robinson (2014), we winsorize at the 99 percent level to remove observations that have outlier values for any of the financial variables.

The first hypothesis studies the relationship between a firm's R&D activity and its *debt ratio$_i$*. We create a binary variable *R&D$_i$*, which equals one if the firm spent any money on R&D and zero otherwise.[2] The second set of hypotheses studies the moderating effect of experience and external reputation on the relationship between a firm's R&D activity and its *debt ratio$_i$*. We use the average number of years of the owners' industry *work experience$_i$* to measure experience. We create a dummy variable indicating whether the firm *i* has received any funding from angels or VCs, called *angel VC funding$_i$*, to indicate external reputation. We acknowledge that this dummy variable is a rather coarse measure of the financier's relationship to the firm. One limitation of the data is that we do not know the contract terms under which the angel or VC firm provides funding, yet from prior literature we know that contract terms can vary widely (Bengtsson, 2011; Hsu, 2004).

Our final hypothesis studies the effect on performance of a firm's alignment or misalignment between *R&D$_i$* activity and *debt ratio$_i$*. We follow other entrepreneurship literature (e.g., Sarkar, Echambadi, Agarwal, & Sen, 2006) and study survival to assess performance. The variable *survives until 2011$_i$* equals one if the firm does not exit the sample before 2011 (the last year of the *KFS* panel) and zero otherwise. For use in robustness checks described below, we also construct the variables *survives until 2007$_i$*, which equals one if the firm does not exit the sample before 2007 and zero otherwise; *ln revenue in 2011$_i$*; and *ln revenue in 2004$_i$*. While we are able to replicate the results using revenue, we prefer survival as a measure of performance. Projects that require substantial R&D often experience a significant lag between the initial investment and the monetization of that investment (Herath & Park, 1999; Vismara & Signori, 2014).[3]

The ideal experiment to assess our final hypothesis would involve randomly assigning debt ratios to firms with and without R&D, then assessing the effect of alignment between R&D and financing on performance. We of course are unable to run such an experiment, and forward-looking firms likely choose debt ratios to fit their R&D focus, as we hope to show in our first hypothesis. Hence, any regression of performance on debt ratio will suffer from endogeneity (Hamilton & Nickerson, 2003). We therefore use an IV approach to assess performance.[4] We use housing supply *elasticity$_i$* at the Metropolitan Statistical Area (MSA) level, obtained from Saiz (2010), as an instrument for *debt ratio$_i$* and *elasticity$_i$*R&D$_i$* as an instrument for *debt ratio$_i$*R&D$_i$*. Saiz (2010) uses exogenous variation in geographical and regulatory constraints to construct the MSA-level housing supply elasticity.[5] Robb and Robinson (2014) show that entrepreneurs in areas with high housing supply elasticity are better able to use their homes as collateral and therefore rely more on bank loans for capital needs. A similar instrument has been used by several finance papers (e.g., Adelino, Schoar, & Severino, 2012; Chaney, Sraer, & Thesmar, 2012; Mian & Sufi, 2011).

For the instrument to be valid, we need it to satisfy two conditions. First, *elasticity$_i$* needs to directly affect *debt ratio$_i$*, which we verify in our "first-stage" regressions below. Second, *elasticity$_i$* cannot directly affect a firm's performance, but only affect it indirectly through its effect on *debt ratio$_i$*, conditional on the other independent variables. While we believe this is a reasonable assumption in our case, the validity of the second condition, the so-called exclusion restriction, cannot be tested (Angrist & Pischke, 2009). We believe the most plausible story for how housing supply elasticity might directly affect survival is if areas with high housing supply elasticity were differently affected by the recession that began in late 2007. To rule out any story contingent on the 2007−2008 recession, we also run robustness checks that use the variable *survives until 2007$_i$* to study the effect of debt ratio on survival prior to the start of the recession.

Finally, we recognize that many factors influence both an entrepreneur's choice of financing and the entrepreneur's chance of success (Shane, 2008), so we include a large number of control variables in all the regressions. The set of control variables include indicators for *product$_i$* based firm, *home based$_i$* firm, *incorporation$_i$*, *multiple owners$_i$*, *high tech$_i$*, *black$_i$*, *other nonwhite$_i$*, *female$_i$*, *college$_i$* or *graduate$_i$* degrees, and *same business$_i$*, which indicates previous start-up experience in the same industry; we also include a categorical variable for *credit score$_i$* provided to the KFS by Dun & Bradstreet. We collect information on *owner age$_i$* but, because of high correlation with *work experience$_i$*, we only use *owner age$_i$* in a robustness test.

For some of the regressions, we include a number of state-level controls. From Cerqueiro and Penas (2013), we collect information on *homestead exemptions$_i$* at the state level. Homestead exemption limits indicate the amount of home equity that a homeowner in the state can exempt when filing for personal bankruptcy protection. Recent studies have linked homestead exemption limits with entrepreneurship (Cerqueiro & Penas, 2013) and innovation (Cerqueiro, Hegde, Penas, & Seamans, 2014). We use bank deposit data from the Federal Deposit Insurance Corporation's (FDIC) *Summary of Deposits* dataset to construct a state-level Herfindahl index of bank concentration, *bank HHI$_i$*. Recent studies have linked banking concentration to entrepreneurship (Kerr & Nanda, 2009) and innovation (Chava, Oettl, Subramanian, & Subramanian, 2013). From the U.S.

Census, we collect state-level information on *population density$_i$*, *gross state product$_i$*, and *median income$_i$*. We obtain a state-level *house price index$_i$* from the Federal Housing Finance Agency. Following Mian and Sufi (2011), we use data from the Federal Reserve Bank of New York (FRBNY) and the Internal Revenue Service (IRS) to construct an MSA level *debt—income ratio$_i$*.[6] Mian and Sufi use this ratio to identify areas that had too much debt relative to income, and hence were harder hit by the 2007—2008 financial crisis. Because of high correlation with other state-level variables, we use *house price index$_i$* and *debt—income ratio$_i$* in robustness tests described below. We also include nine industry dummies (at the two-digit North American Industry Classification System (NAICS) level) to control for systematic differences in financing requirements across industries and state or regional dummies to control for differences in employment opportunities and regulatory or other institutional differences

Table 1. Summary Statistics.

Variable	Mean	Std. Dev.
Debt ratio	0.197	0.312
Total equity	66,666.430	329,559.900
Outside equity	27,038.930	300,866.800
Inside equity	2,310.601	22,997.080
Total debt	68,151.810	301,842.300
Outside debt	55,203.470	278,625.200
Inside debt	7,342.022	57,275.700
R&D	0.224	0.417
Elasticity	1.778	0.955
Work experience	12.496	10.741
Angel or VC funding	0.041	0.198
Survives to 2011	0.474	0.499
Survives to 2007	0.604	0.489
Revenue in 2011	719,999.8	1,834,696
Revenue in 2004	130,911.2	711,259.6
Age of owners	45.186	11.047
Black	0.087	0.281
Other non-white	0.112	0.316
Female	0.261	0.439
College degree	0.310	0.462
Graduate degree	0.204	0.403
Same business	0.178	0.383
Credit score	3.266	0.780
Product	0.528	0.499

Table 1. (*Continued*)

Variable	Mean	Std. Dev.
Home based	0.503	0.500
Incorporated	0.616	0.486
High tech	0.135	0.342
Homestead exemptions ($100,000s)	2.345	3.744
Bank HHI	0.152	0.067
Population density (pop/sq mile)	216.787	223.901
Gross state product ($billion)	455.370	391.659
Median income ($1,000s)	44.998	5.296
House price index	166.282	23.051
Debt–income ratio	1.968	0.636

Notes: Data from *Kauffman Firm Survey* of 3,544 start-ups founded in 2004. KFS data on maximum and minimum values are not disclosed for confidentiality. See text for source of demographic and other variables.

across geographic areas.[7] Summary statistics of the variables are provided in Table 1 and selected correlations are provided in the appendix.

Methods

To assess the relationship between R&D and entrepreneurial finance in Hypothesis 1, we run ordinary least-squares (OLS) regressions of the following form:

$$debt\ ratio_i = \beta_1 R\&D_i + \mathbf{X}_{1i} + \varepsilon_i \quad (1)$$

where *debt ratio*$_i$ and *R&D*$_i$ are described above and $\mathbf{X}_{1i}$ is a vector of control variables. Hypothesis 1 predicts that $\beta_1 < 0$. Note that *debt ratio*$_i$ is a ratio that combines different types of inside and outside equity and debt. In addition to providing results on the hypothesized relationship between *debt ratio*$_i$ and *R&D*$_i$, we also provide separate results on the relationship between *R&D*$_i$ and each type of finance.

To assess the relationship between R&D, owner work experience, or angel or VC backing and entrepreneurial finance in Hypotheses 2 and 3, we run OLS regressions of the following form:

$$debt\ ratio_i = \beta_1 R\&D_i + \beta_2\ work\ experience_i + \beta_3 R\&D * work\ experience_i + \mathbf{X}_{1i} + \varepsilon_i \quad (2)$$

$$\text{debt ratio}_i = \gamma_1 R\&D_i + \gamma_2 \text{ angel VC funding}_i + \gamma_3 R\&D * \text{angel VC funding}_i + \mathbf{X}_{1i} + \varepsilon_i \tag{3}$$

where *debt ratio*$_i$, *R&D*$_i$, *work experience*$_i$, *angel VC funding*$_i$ and $\mathbf{X}_{1i}$ are described above. Hypothesis 2 predicts that $\beta_3 > 0$. Hypothesis 3 predicts that $\gamma_3 > 0$.

Finally, we run a series of OLS and IV regressions to assess the performance consequences of entrepreneurial finance alignment in the "second stage" (Hypothesis 4). We first focus on the entire sample, interact *debt ratio*$_i$ and *R&D*$_i$, and run regressions of the following type:

$$\text{performance}_i = \theta_1 \text{debt ratio}_i + \theta_2 R\&D_i + \theta_3 \text{debt ratio}_i * R\&D_i + \mathbf{X}_{2i} + \varepsilon_i \tag{4}$$

where *performance*$_i$ is one of the survival measures described above, $\mathbf{X}_{2i}$ is a vector of control variables, *debt ratio*$_i$ is instrumented using *elasticity*$_i$ and *debt ratio*$_i$**R&D*$_i$ is instrumented using *elasticity*$_i$**R&D*$_i$, as described above, when running IV models.

Hypothesis 4 predicts that start-ups with misalignment between their R&D focus and debt ratio will experience worse performance than start-ups with alignment between their R&D focus and debt ratio. There are two types of firms, those with R&D and those without R&D. Firms with no R&D (i.e., $R\&D_i = 0$) should have a high debt ratio. We therefore expect that $\theta_1 > 0$, indicating that as debt ratio increases performance increases. Firms with R&D (i.e., $R\&D_i = 1$) should have a low debt ratio. We therefore expect that $\theta_3 < 0$, indicating that as debt ratio increases for these firms performance decreases.

To better understand what is driving the results, we then separate the sample into firms with and without R&D and run OLS and IV regressions of the following form:

For the subsample of firms that do not engage in R&D (i.e., $R\&D_i = 0$):

$$\text{performance}_i = \theta_1 \text{debt ratio}_i + \mathbf{X}_{2i} + \varepsilon_i \tag{5A}$$

For the subsample of firms that do engage in R&D (i.e., $R\&D_i = 1$):

$$\text{performance}_i = \delta_1 \text{debt ratio}_i + \mathbf{X}_{2i} + \varepsilon_i \tag{5B}$$

where *performance*$_i$ is one of the survival measures described above, X_{2i} is a vector of control variables, and *debt ratio*$_i$ is instrumented using *elasticity*$_i$, as described above, when running IV models. As before, we predict that $\theta_1 > 0$ and that $\delta_1 < 0$.

RESULTS

Relationship Between R&D Activity and Entrepreneurial Finance

Table 2 provides the results of our analyses assessing Hypothesis 1. All results include state and industry dummies and a full set of controls, though we do not report the coefficients on these variables for space considerations. Column (1) reports the results of OLS regressions of *debt ratio*$_i$ on *R&D*$_i$. The coefficient on *R&D*$_i$ is negative and significant at the 1 percent level.[8] In the remaining columns of the table, we provide results separately for each type of finance: *total equity*$_i$, *outside equity*$_i$, *inside equity*$_i$, *total debt*$_i$, *outside debt*$_i$, and *inside debt*$_i$. For space considerations, we describe only the findings of particular interest. Column (2) reports the results of OLS regressions of *total equity*$_i$ on *R&D*$_i$. The coefficient is positive and significant at the 5 percent level. Taken together, the results from Table 2 provide evidence in support of Hypothesis 1: firms that engage in R&D have lower debt ratios, on average. Moreover, the lower debt ratio appears to be driven by higher levels of equity. It also is interesting to note the positive coefficients on *angel VC funding*$_i$ in Columns (2) and (5), which regress *total equity*$_i$ and *total debt*$_i$, respectively, on the full set of covariates. These results indicate that firms which receive angel or VC funding have not only higher amounts of equity, as would be expected, but also higher levels of debt.

We next investigate the role played by previous industry work experience. To do this, we rerun the set of regressions reported in Table 2, but interact *work experience*$_i$ with *R&D*$_i$. The results are reported in Table 3. Column (1) reports the results of OLS regressions of *debt ratio*$_i$ on *R&D*$_i$, *work experience*$_i$, and *R&D*work experience*$_i$. The coefficient on *R&D*$_i$ is negative and significant at the 1 percent level and the coefficient on *R&D*work experience*$_i$ is positive and significant at the 5 percent level. The results in Column (1) provide evidence in support of Hypothesis 2: firms that engage in R&D and have experienced owners have higher debt ratios than firms that engage in R&D and do not have experienced owners. However, while the coefficients on *R&D*work experience*$_i$ are positive in

Table 2. Effect of R&D on Entrepreneurial Finance.

Dependent Variable	(1) Debt Ratio	(2) Total Equity	(3) Outside Equity	(4) Inside Equity	(5) Total Debt	(6) Outside Debt	(7) Inside Debt
R&D	−0.050***	25,836.393**	13,222.729	−579.435	−5,318.239	−11,480.718	3,366.361
	[0.014]	[12,068.338]	[10,311.926]	[911.974]	[17,964.979]	[15,444.939]	[3,969.962]
Work experience	−0.001	232.184	−32.557	−50.720	341.592	302.451	−1.413
	[0.001]	[413.518]	[336.423]	[35.272]	[647.926]	[588.055]	[107.566]
Angel or VC funding	−0.054*	378,635.015***	338,602.441***	3357.678	186,558.928**	178,654.173**	−39.288
	[0.030]	[80,842.762]	[75,694.260]	[2,908.444]	[84,387.906]	[82,727.146]	[4,046.851]
Constant	0.349***	45,959.286*	5,622.166	−30.488	109,108.242***	88,975.345***	10,738.260
	[0.070]	[26,596.904]	[22,475.162]	[3,382.027]	[34,594.662]	[31,633.523]	[7,652.353]
Controls	Y	Y	Y	Y	Y	Y	Y
Industry dummies	Y	Y	Y	Y	Y	Y	Y
State dummies	Y	Y	Y	Y	Y	Y	Y
Observations	3,544	3,544	3,544	3,544	3,544	3,544	3,544
R-squared	0.078	0.136	0.111	0.028	0.079	0.073	0.028

Notes: Results from OLS regressions. Controls include black, other non-white, female, college, graduate, same business, credit score, product, home based, incorporation, and high tech dummy. Standard errors are in brackets.
* significant at 10%, ** significant at 5%, *** significant at 1%.

Table 3. Effect of R&D and Work Experience on Entrepreneurial Finance.

Dependent Variable	(1) Debt Ratio	(2) Total Equity	(3) Outside Equity	(4) Inside Equity	(5) Total Debt	(6) Outside Debt	(7) Inside Debt
R&D	-0.087***	192.812	-1,094.669	-276.921	-41,287.028**	-39,750.610**	-5,063.378
	[0.020]	[17,694.819]	[15,164.445]	[1,396.197]	[18,200.233]	[16,312.224]	[4,009.830]
R&D*Work Experience	0.003**	2,294.771	1,281.223	-27.071	3,218.745	2,529.792	754.353
	[0.001]	[1,503.421]	[1,276.530]	[69.011]	[2,318.114]	[1,843.810]	[565.638]
Work experience	-0.001*	-132.206	-236.004	-46.422	-169.517	-99.259	-121.198
	[0.001]	[403.580]	[329.288]	[39.023]	[692.225]	[644.605]	[95.876]
Angel or VC funding	-0.057*	376,946.957***	337,659.960***	3,377.592	184,191.186**	176,793.232**	-594.198
	[0.030]	[80,636.044]	[75,565.469]	[2,915.078]	[84,373.425]	[82,666.735]	[4,134.447]
Constant	0.354***	49,614.774*	7,663.109	-73.611	114,235.586***	93,005.212***	11,939.918
	[0.070]	[26,078.152]	[21,827.934]	[3,369.554]	[35,877.012]	[32,441.752]	[8,024.403]
Controls	Y	Y	Y	Y	Y	Y	Y
Industry dummies	Y	Y	Y	Y	Y	Y	Y
State dummies	Y	Y	Y	Y	Y	Y	Y
Observations	3,544	3,544	3,544	3,544	3,544	3,544	3,544
R-squared	0.08	0.137	0.112	0.028	0.08	0.074	0.031

Notes: Results from OLS regressions. Controls include black, other non-white, female, college, graduate, same business, credit score, product, home based, incorporation, and high-tech dummy. Standard errors are in brackets.
* significant at 10%, ** significant at 5%, *** significant at 1%.

Table 4. Effect of R&D and Angel or VC Funding on Entrepreneurial Finance.

Dependent Variable	(1) Debt Ratio	(2) Total Equity	(3) Outside Equity	(4) Inside Equity	(5) Total Debt	(6) Outside Debt	(7) Inside Debt
R&D	-0.047***	-274.285	-11,427.673**	-434.340	1,893.449	-4,336.003	3,231.920
	[0.014]	[7,873.438]	[5,805.686]	[923.472]	[16,689.421]	[13,848.966]	[4,064.513]
R&D*Angel or VC	-0.053	516,029.776**	487,170.093**	-2,867.536	-142,525.821	-141,202.226	2,656.970
	[0.055]	[205,489.926]	[194,611.683]	[4,992.140]	[152,557.773]	[150,436.624]	[9,079.072]
Angel or VC funding	-0.037	205,763.806***	175,399.295***	4,318.310	234,305.419*	225,957.257*	-929.380
	[0.040]	[74,183.308]	[66,643.345]	[4,147.687]	[123,561.743]	[121,120.456]	[4,185.444]
Work experience	-0.001	107.827	-149.959	-50.029	375.939	336.479	-2.053
	[0.001]	[415.717]	[342.747]	[35.541]	[640.283]	[578.491]	[107.747]
Constant	0.348***	56,146.377**	15,239.530	-87.096	106,294.599***	86,187.831***	10,790.712
	[0.070]	[23,996.754]	[19,595.966]	[3,360.595]	[34,301.430]	[31,374.251]	[7,625.222]
Controls	Y	Y	Y	Y	Y	Y	Y
Industry dummies	Y	Y	Y	Y	Y	Y	Y
State dummies	Y	Y	Y	Y	Y	Y	Y
Observations	3,544	3,544	3,544	3,544	3,544	3,544	3,544
R-squared	0.078	0.168	0.147	0.028	0.08	0.075	0.028

Notes: Results from OLS regressions. Controls include black, other non-white, female, college, graduate, same business, credit score, product, home based, incorporation, and high-tech dummy. Standard errors are in brackets.
* significant at 10%, ** significant at 5%, *** significant at 1%.

Columns (5)–(7), which investigate the role of different types of debt, none are significant. Hence, it is not clear whether the positive coefficient on *debt ratio$_i$* is driven by more inside or more outside debt.

We next investigate the role played by angels and VCs. To do this, we rerun the set of regressions reported in Table 2, but interact *angel VC funding$_i$* with *R&D$_i$*. The results are reported in Table 4. Column (1) reports the results of OLS regressions of *debt ratio$_i$* on *R&D$_i$*, *angel VC funding$_i$*, and *R&D*angel VC funding$_i$*. The coefficient on *R&D$_i$* is negative and significant at the 1 percent level. The coefficients on *angel VC funding$_i$* and *R&D*angel VC funding$_i$* are both negative, but not significant. Thus, the results in Column (1) do not provide any evidence in support of Hypothesis 3. There are other interesting results in the table. As in Table 2, the coefficients on *angel VC funding$_i$* are positive and significant for both *total equity$_i$* and *total debt$_i$*, indicating that firms that receive angel or VC funding have not only higher amounts of equity but also higher amounts of debt. The coefficients on *RD*angel VC funding$_i$* are positive and statistically significant for *total equity$_i$* and *outside equity$_i$*, but negative (though not statistically significant) for *total debt$_i$*. Thus, firms that engage in R&D and receive angel or VC funding receive large amounts of outside equity, but do not appear to receive additional debt. It is possible that the presence of angel and VC funding is providing a signal of quality to lenders that helps relieve the informational asymmetries between lenders and entrepreneurs, as speculated in prior literature, including Marx (1998) and Hall and Lerner (2010). However, there may be a limit to the signal provided by angel and VC funding, as start-ups that engage in R&D do not seem to raise more debt.

In the appendix, we replicate the results from Column (1) of Tables 2–4 using alternate specifications. First, we show that the results are robust to the inclusion of owner's age, which had been omitted due to high correlation with *work experience$_i$*. We also show that the results are robust to models that use alternate specifications of the dependent variable. Recall that we run OLS models on *debt ratio$_i$*. By construction, *debt ratio$_i$* is bounded below by 0 and above by 1, yet the OLS model does not account for this. Hence, we show that our results are robust to common "fixes" to this problem, including the log-odds and arcsine transformations of *debt ratio$_i$* as well as a two-sided Tobit model (Bartlett, 1947; Maddala, 1983).

Performance Consequences of Entrepreneurial Finance Alignment

We finally turn to performance. Recall that we will use MSA-level variation in housing supply elasticity as an instrument. Due to the limited amount of variation within each state, we no longer use state dummies but instead use regional dummies and state-level controls. In the appendix we show that our "first-stage" results from Table 2 are unchanged when removing the state-level dummies and including regional dummies and other state-level controls. We also document a positive and significant correlation between $elasticity_i$ and $debt\ ratio_i$. The direction of the coefficient is as we would expect given prior literature: entrepreneurs in areas with high housing supply elasticity are better able to use their homes as collateral and therefore rely more on bank loans for capital needs (Robb & Robinson, 2014).

Table 5 provides the results of our analyses assessing Hypothesis 4 using the dependent variable $survives\ to\ 2011_i$. In Column (1) we run an OLS regression on $debt\ ratio_i$, $R\&D_i$, and $R\&D_i*debt\ ratio_i$. The coefficient on $debt\ ratio_i$ is positive and significant at the 5 percent level. The coefficient on $R\&D_i*debt\ ratio_i$ is negative but not statistically significant. The signs of these two coefficients are in the direction hypothesized, though only statistically significant in one case. In Columns (2) and (3) we split the sample into cases where $R\&D_i = 0$ and $R\&D_i = 1$ to better understand what is driving the results. When $R\&D_i = 0$, we again find a positive and statistically significant coefficient on $debt\ ratio_i$ as predicted. However, when $R\&D_i = 1$ we find no statistically significant coefficient on $debt\ ratio_i$; indeed, the sign has switched from negative, as predicted, to positive.

The OLS results in Columns (1)–(3) indicate limited support for Hypothesis 4 — firms that do not engage in R&D and that have a high debt ratio experience better performance, but performance does not seem to suffer for firms that engage in R&D and have a high debt ratio. Of course, these are OLS regressions and potentially suffer from endogeneity. We therefore instrument for $debt\ ratio_i$ and $R\&D_i*debt\ ratio_i$ using $elasticity_i$ and $R\&D_i*elasticity_i$, and present the results in Columns (4)–(6). In Column (4), the sign on $debt\ ratio_i$ (instrumented using $elasticity_i$) remains positive and significant at the 10 percent level. The sign on $R\&D_i*debt\ ratio_i$ (instrumented using $R\&D_i*elasticity_i$) is positive but not statistically significant. Moreover, the F-statistic associated with the instruments (1.2) is low relative to standard thresholds (Stock, Wright, & Yogo, 2002). In Column (5), when $R\&D_i = 0$, we again find a positive and statistically significant coefficient on $debt\ ratio_i$ (instrumented using $elasticity_i$) as predicted. In addition, the F-statistic associated with the instrument (9.1) is at standard thresholds (Stock et al., 2002). However, when $R\&D_i = 1$ we do not find the coefficient on $debt\ ratio_i$ to be statistically significant (instrumented using $elasticity_i$).

Table 5. Effect of Debt Ratio and R&D on Entrepreneurial Performance.

Method	(1) OLS Full	(2) OLS R&D = 0	(3) OLS R&D = 1	(4) IV Full	(5) IV R&D = 0	(6) IV R&D = 1
Subsample						
Dependent variable	Survives to 2011			Survives to 2011		
Debt ratio	0.067**	0.060**	0.058	2.267*	1.839**	16.415
	[0.030]	[0.030]	[0.066]	[1.256]	[0.785]	[73.492]
R&D	0.013			−0.546		
	[0.024]			[0.769]		
R&D*Debt Ratio	−0.046			3.900		
	[0.070]			[4.810]		
Work experience	0.004***	0.004***	0.001	0.004*	0.007***	−0.025
	[0.001]	[0.001]	[0.002]	[0.002]	[0.002]	[0.120]
Angel or VC funding	−0.056	−0.056	−0.028	0.264	0.055	1.633
	[0.043]	[0.057]	[0.068]	[0.251]	[0.098]	[7.487]
Homestead exemptions	−0.003	−0.002	−0.004	0.005	0.001	0.089
	[0.004]	[0.004]	[0.009]	[0.010]	[0.006]	[0.425]
Bank HHI	0.201	0.214	0.111	−0.335	−0.122	−2.193
	[0.144]	[0.158]	[0.355]	[0.453]	[0.279]	[10.827]
Population density	0.000	0.000	0.000	0.000	0.000	0.000
	[0.000]	[0.000]	[0.000]	[0.000]	[0.000]	[0.003]
Gross state product	0.000	0.000	0.000	0.000	0.000	−0.001
	[0.000]	[0.000]	[0.000]	[0.000]	[0.000]	[0.004]
Median income	0.002	0.005	−0.006	0.007	0.005	0.045
	[0.002]	[0.003]	[0.006]	[0.007]	[0.004]	[0.239]
Constant	0.462***	0.372**	0.951***	−0.510	−0.230	−5.216
	[0.142]	[0.161]	[0.328]	[0.660]	[0.358]	[27.860]
Controls	Y	Y	Y	Y	Y	Y
Industry dummies	Y	Y	Y	Y	Y	Y
Regional dummies	Y	Y	Y	Y	Y	Y
Observations	3,544	2,752	792	3,544	2,752	792
R-squared	0.046	0.05	0.073			
F-statistic				1.2	9.1	0.1

Notes: Results from OLS and IV regressions, as indicated. Debt ratio and R&D*debt ratio are instrumented using elasticity and R&D*elasticity, respectively, in IV regressions. Controls include black, other non-white, female, college, graduate, same business, credit score, product, home based, incorporation, and high-tech dummy. Standard errors are in parentheses.
* significant at 10%, ** significant at 5%, *** significant at 1%.

We provide a number of robustness tests in the appendix. We first show that the results in Table 5 are robust to the exclusion of outlier areas that have high or low (top or bottom 5 percent) debt−income ratios or house price index values. We next replicate the analyses performed in Columns

(5) and (6) of Table 5 using a different dependent variable, *survives to 2007$_i$*, and obtain similar results. We also replicate the analyses in Table 5 using *ln revenue in 2011$_i$*, while also including *ln revenue in 2004$_i$* as a control, and obtain similar results. Thus, across the results presented in Table 5 and in the appendix, we find partial support for Hypothesis 4.

CONCLUSION

We provide four sets of findings. First, R&D-focused start-up firms have a lower debt ratio than non-R&D-focused start-ups. Much of this effect appears to be driven by the larger amount of equity, particularly outside equity, used by firms that engage in R&D activities. Second, start-up firms that receive angel or VC funding have higher levels of both equity and debt. However, this result does not appear to be driven by R&D-focused start-ups, as we had hypothesized. Third, firms whose owners have more work experience rely more on debt and less on equity, on average. As a result, R&D-focused start-ups that have owners with more previous industry work experience have higher debt ratios than R&D-focused start-ups that do not. Finally, we present some mixed findings on the link between R&D financing alignment and performance. In the case of firms that do not engage in R&D, we find some evidence that alignment helps performance, but in the case of R&D-focused start-ups, the link between alignment and performance is too noisy to make any definitive statements.

While the findings presented herein should be of interest to both researchers and practitioners, we note that our findings do not "prove" any of the hypotheses (Bettis, 2012). Similarly, the lack of support for one of our predictions does not mean the hypothesized relationship does not exist (Miller & Tsang, 2011). In any case, "non-results" findings should still be useful for other researchers (Bettis, 2012), especially given our large nationally representative sample of start-ups from a wide variety of industries located throughout the United States. We find it particularly interesting that R&D-focused start-ups with high debt ratios do not seem to perform worse than similar R&D-focused start-ups with low debt ratios. This suggests that one avenue for future research is to explore the extent to which the link between alignment and performance is systematically stronger for firms with low levels of R&D, as we find here.

Our results have implications for new firms. To better create and capture value, a new firm should arrange financing in alignment with its underlying technological assets. Our study shows that, in many cases, appropriate financial structure increases a new firm's chance of survival. The results suggest that policy makers should work to ensure that many types of financing are available without hindrance to new firms. New firms that have ready access to both debt and equity financing will be able to use the appropriate mix of financing for their ventures, and in turn will have better performance prospects.

NOTES

1. As reported by Macher and Richman (2008), the central prediction of TCE has been empirically documented in research across fields including industrial organization, marketing, finance, accounting, and law.
2. From 2004 to 2006, the KFS only collected information on whether a firm spent money on R&D, not the amount. Starting in 2007, the KFS also collected information on the amount of R&D spending.
3. The KFS provides revenues reported by firms. When a firm reports that it is in business but reports no revenues, we assume it has zero revenues.
4. Debt ratio is a continuous variable so we use an IV approach rather than the Heckman selection correction suggested by Hamilton and Nickerson (2003), which assumes a binary endogenous variable.
5. Firms in our sample not in an MSA are assigned the average elasticity across MSAs in the state.
6. From the FRBNY we obtain 2006 information on per capita auto, credit card, and mortgage debt at the county level. We add these together and multiply by county population to get the total debt at the county level. We then sum these numbers across all the counties in the MSA. From the IRS we get total wages and salaries for each zip code in the United States in 2006. We then sum these numbers across all zip codes in the MSA. We then construct an MSA-level ratio of debt to income. For observations not assigned to an MSA, we use the median value of debt to income across MSAs in the state.
7. We assign each state to one of the nine mutually exclusive regions, using the U.S. Census definition of a region.
8. We use two-tailed tests of significance in all cases.

ACKNOWLEDGMENTS

Juan Carlos Suarez Serrato provided excellent research assistance. We thank Belen Villalonga and two referees for comments and suggestions that greatly improved the chapter. We also thank Rajshree Agarwal, Janet Bercovitz, Gavin Cassar, Waverly Ding, Jon Eckhardt, Ha Hoang,

Georgia Kosmopoulou, Jenny Kuan, Sharon Matusik, Joanne Oxley, Kaye Schoonhoven, Jennifer Walske, Oliver Williamson, Arvids Ziedonis, Rosemarie Ziedonis, and seminar participants at numerous conferences for their valuable comments. All errors are the authors' responsibility. Certain data included herein are derived from the *Kauffman Firm Survey* release 4.0. Any opinions, findings, and conclusions or recommendations expressed in this material are those of the author(s) and do not necessarily reflect the views of the Ewing Marion Kauffman Foundation.

REFERENCES

Adelino, M., Schoar, A., & Severino, F. (2012). *Credit supply and house prices: Evidence from mortgage market segmentation.* Working Paper 17832. National Bureau of Economic Research.

Ahuja, G. (2000). The duality of collaboration. *Strategic Management Journal, 21*(3), 317–343.

Aldrich, H. (1990). Using an ecological perspective to study organizational founding rates. *Entrepreneurship Theory and Practice, 14*(3), 7–24.

Aldrich, H., & Auster, E. R. (1986). Even dwarfs started small: Liabilities of age and size and their strategic implications. *Research in Organizational Behavior, 8*, 165–198.

Angrist, J. D., & Pischke, J. (2009). *Mostly harmless econometrics: An empiricist's companion.* Princeton, NJ: Princeton University Press.

Arend, R. J., Patel, P. C., & Park, H. D. (2014). Explaining post-IPO venture performance through a knowledge-based view typology. *Strategic Management Journal, 35*(3), 376–397.

Balakrishnan, S., & Fox, I. (1993). Asset specificity, firm heterogeneity and capital structure. *Strategic Management Journal, 14*(1), 3–16.

Bartlett, M. S. (1947). The use of transformations. *Biometrics, 3*, 39–52.

Bengtsson, O. (2011). Covenants in venture capital contracts. *Management Science, 57*(11), 1926–1943.

Bengtsson, O., & Sensoy, B. (2011). Investor abilities and financial contracting: Evidence from venture capital. *Journal of Financial Intermediation, 20*(4), 477–502.

Berger, A., & Udell, G. (1998). The economics of small business finance: The roles of private equity and debt markets in the financial growth cycle. *Journal of Banking & Finance, 22*(6), 613–673.

Bettis, R. A. (2012). The search for asterisks: Compromised statistical tests and flawed theories. *Strategic Management Journal, 33*, 108–113.

Bhide, A. (2000). *The origin and evolution of new businesses.* Oxford, UK: Oxford University Press.

Bosma, N., Van Praag, M., Thurik, R., & De Wit, G. (2004). The value of human and social capital investments for the business performance of startups. *Small Business Economics, 23*(3), 227–236.

Carroll, G., & Hannan, M. (2000). *The demography of corporations and industries.* Princeton, NJ: Princeton University Press.

Cassar, G. (2004). The financing of business start-ups. *Journal of Business Venturing, 19*, 261–283.

Cerqueiro, G., Hegde, D., Penas, F., & Seamans, R. (2014). *Debtor rights, creditor supply and innovation.* Working Paper, Stern School of Business, New York University.

Cerqueiro, G., & Penas, F. (2013). *How does personal bankruptcy law affect start-ups?* Working Paper, Tilburg University.

Chaddad, F. R., & Reuer, J. J. (2009). Investment dynamics and financial constraints in IPO firms. *Strategic Entrepreneurship Journal, 3*, 39–45.

Chaney, T., Sraer, D., & Thesmar, D. (2012). The collateral channel: How real estate shocks affect corporate investment. *American Economic Review, 102*(6), 2381–2409.

Chatterji, A., & Seamans, R. (2012). Entrepreneurship, credit cards and race. *Journal of Financial Economics, 106*(1), 182–195.

Chava, S., Oettl, A., Subramanian, A., & Subramanian, K. (2013). Banking deregulation and innovation. *Journal of Financial Economics, 109*(3), 759–774.

Cole, R. A. (2008). *Who needs credit and who gets credit? Evidence from the surveys of small business finances.* Stanford, CA: Mimeo, DePaul University.

Coleman, S., & Robb, A. (2012). *A rising tide: Financing strategies for women-owned firms.* Stanford, CA: Stanford University Press.

Cooper, A., Gimeno-Gascon, J., & Woo, C. (1994). Initial human and financial capital as predictors of new venture performance. *Journal of Business Venturing, 9*(5), 371–395.

Cosh, A., Cumming, D., & Hughes, A. (2009). Outside entrepreneurial capital. *The Economic Journal, 119*, 1494–1533.

Cumming, D. (2008). Contracts and exits in venture capital finance. *Review of Financial Studies, 21*(5), 1947–1982.

David, P., O'Brien, J. P., & Yoshikawa, T. (2008). The implications of debt heterogeneity for R&D investment and firm performance. *Academy of Management Journal, 51*, 165–181.

Diamond, D. (1989). Reputation acquisition in debt markets. *Journal of Political Economy*, 828–862.

Dushnitsky, G., & Lenox, M. (2005). When do firms undertake R&D by investing in new ventures? *Strategic Management Journal, 26*(10), 947–965.

Dushnitsky, G., & Shapira, Z. (2010). Entrepreneurial finance meets organizational reality: Comparing investment practices and performance of corporate and independent venture capitalists. *Strategic Management Journal, 31*(9), 990–1017.

Eckhardt, J. T., Shane, S., & Delmar, F. (2006). Multistage selection and the financing of new ventures. *Management Science, 52*(2), 220–232.

Fairlie, R. W., & Robb, A. M. (2008). *Race and entrepreneurial success: Black-, Asian-, and white-owned businesses in the United States.* Cambridge, MA: MIT Press.

Fama, E. F. (1985). What's different about banks? *Journal of Monetary Economics, 15*(1), 29–39.

Goldfarb, B., Kirsch, D., & Shen, A. (2012). Finance of new industries. In D. Cumming (Ed.), *Oxford handbook of entrepreneurial finance.* Oxford, UK: Oxford University Press.

Gompers, P., Kovner, A., Lerner, J., & Scharfstein, D. (2005). Venture capital investment cycles: The role of experience and specialization. *Journal of Financial Economics.*

Hall, B. H., & Lerner, J. (2010). The financing of R&D and innovation. In B. H. Hall & N. Rosenberg (Eds.), *Elsevier handbook of the economics of innovation.* North Holland, Amsterdam: Elsevier.

Hamilton, B., & Nickerson, J. (2003). Correcting for endogeneity in strategic management research. *Strategic Organization, 1*(1), 53–80.
Harris, F. (1994). Asset specificity, capital intensity and capital structure: An empirical test. *Managerial and Decision Economics, 15,* 563–576.
Hellmann, T., Lindsey, L., & Puri, M. (2008). Building relationships early: Banks in venture capital. *Review of Financial Studies, 21*(2), 513–541.
Hellmann, T., & Puri, M. (2002). Venture capital and the professionalization of start-up firms: Empirical evidence. *Journal of Finance, 57*(1), 169–197.
Herath, H. B., & Park, C. S. (1999). Economic analysis of R&D projects: An option approach. *Engineering Economist, 44,* 1–35.
Hochberg, Y., Ljungqvist, A., & Lu, Y. (2007). Whom you know matters: Venture capital networks and investment performance. *Journal of Finance, 62,* 251–301.
Hsu, D. (2004). What do entrepreneurs pay for venture capital affiliation? *The Journal of Finance, 59,* 1805–1844.
Hsu, D. (2007). Experienced entrepreneurial founders, organizational capital, and venture capital funding. *Research Policy, 36*(5), 722–741.
Joshi, A. M., & Nerkar, A. (2011). When do strategic alliances inhibit innovation by firms? Evidence from patent pools in the global optical disc industry. *Strategic Management Journal, 32*(11), 1139–1160.
Junkunc, M. T., & Eckhardt, J. T. (2009). Technical specialized knowledge and secondary shares in initial public offerings. *Management Science, 55*(10), 1670–1687.
Kaplan, S., Martel, F., & Strömberg, P. (2007). How do legal differences and experience affect financial contracts? *Journal of Financial Intermediation, 16*(3), 273–311.
Kaplan, S. N., & Strömberg, P. (2003). Financial contracting theory meets the real world: An empirical analysis of venture capital contracts. *The Review of Economic Studies, 70*(2), 281–315.
Kaplan, S. N., & Strömberg, P. (2004). Characteristics, contracts, and actions: Evidence from venture capitalist analyses. *The Journal of Finance, 59*(5), 2177–2210.
Kerr, W., Lerner, J., & Schoar, A. (2014). The consequences of entrepreneurial finance: Evidence from angel financings. *Review of Financial Studies, 27*(1), 20–55.
Kerr, W., & Nanda, R. (2009). Democratizing entry: Banking deregulations, financing constraints, and entrepreneurship. *Journal of Financial Economics, 94,* 124–149.
Kotha, R., & George, G. (2012). Friends, family, or fools: Entrepreneur experience and its implications for equity distribution and resource mobilization. *Journal of Business Venturing, 27*(5), 525–543.
Kuppuswamy, V., & Villalonga, B. (2012). *Does diversification create value in the presence of external financing constraints? Evidence from the 2007–2009 financial crisis.* Working Paper, Stern School of Business, New York University.
Leland, H. E., & Pyle, D. H. (1977). Informational asymmetries, financial structure, and financial intermediation. *The Journal of Finance, 32*(2), 371–387.
Macher, J., & Richman, B. (2008). Transaction cost economics: An assessment of empirical research in the social sciences. *Business and Politics, 10,* 1.
Maddala, G. S. (1983). *Limited dependent and qualitative variables in econometrics.* Cambridge, UK: Cambridge University Press.
Marx, L. M. (1998). Efficient venture capital financing combining debt and equity. *Review of Economic Design, 3*(4), 371–387.

Mayer, K. J., & Nickerson, J. A. (2005). Antecedents and performance implications of contracting for knowledge workers: Evidence from information technology services. *Organization Science, 16*(3), 225–242.

Mian, A., & Sufi, A. (2011). House prices, home equity based borrowing, and the U.S. household leverage crisis. *American Economic Review, 101,* 2132–2156.

Miller, K. D., & Tsang, E. W. K. (2011). Testing management theories: Critical realist philosophy and research methods. *Strategic Management Journal, 32,* 139–158.

Moskowitz, T., & Vissing-Jorgensen, A. (2002). The private equity puzzle. *American Economic Review, 92,* 745–778.

Mowery, D. C., Oxley, J. E., & Silverman, B. S. (1996). Strategic alliances and interfirm knowledge transfer. *Strategic Management Journal, 17,* 77–91.

Myers, S., & Majluf, N. (1984). Corporate financing and investment decisions when firms have information that investors do not have. *Journal of Financial Economics, 13*(2), 187–221.

Nickerson, J. A., & Silverman, B. (2003). Why firms want to organize efficiently and what keeps them from doing so: Inappropriate governance, performance, and adaptation in a deregulated industry. *Administrative Science Quarterly, 48*(3), 433–465.

Pennings, J., Lee, K., & Van Witteloostuijn, A. (1998). Human capital, social capital, and firm dissolution. *Academy of Management Journal, 41*(4), 425–440.

Robb, A., Ballou, J., DesRoches, D., Potter, F., Zhao, A., & Reedy, E. J. (2009). *An overview of the Kauffman firm survey: Results from the 2004–2007 data.* Working Paper, Ewing Marion Kauffman Foundation.

Robb, A., & Robinson, D. (2014). The capital structure decisions of new firms. *Review of Financial Studies, 27*(1), 153–179.

Robb, A., & Winston-Smith, S. (2013). *Implications of demand for and access to financial capital by young firms in the current economic crisis.* Working Paper, Ewing Marion Kauffman Foundation.

Saiz, A. (2010). The geographic determinants of housing supply. *Quarterly Journal of Economics, 125,* 1253–1296.

Sampson, R. C. (2004). The cost of misaligned governance in R&D alliances. *Journal of Law, Economics, & Organization, 20*(2), 484–526.

Sarkar, M. B., Echambadi, R., Agarwal, R., & Sen, B. (2006). The effect of the innovative environment on the exit of entrepreneurial firms. *Strategic Management Journal, 27,* 519–539.

Seamans, R. (2013). Threat of entry, asymmetric information, and pricing. *Strategic Management Journal, 34,* 426–444.

Shane, S. (2008). *The illusions of entrepreneurship.* New Haven, CT: Yale University Press.

Shyam-Sunder, L., & Myers, S. C. (1999). Testing static tradeoff against pecking order models of capital structure. *Journal of Financial Economics, 51*(2), 219–244.

Stiglitz, J., & Weiss, A. (1981). Credit rationing in markets with imperfect information. *The American Economic Review, 71*(3), 393–410.

Stinchcombe, A. L. (1965). Social structure and organizations. In J. G. March (Ed.), *Handbook of organizations* (pp. 142–193). Chicago, IL: Rand McNally.

Stock, J. H., Wright, J. H., & Yogo, M. (2002). A survey of weak instruments and weak identification in generalized method of moments. *Journal of Business & Economic Statistics, 20*(4), 518–529.

Stuart, T., Hoang, H., & Hybels, R. (1999). Interorganizational endorsements and the performance of entrepreneurial ventures. *Administrative Science Quarterly, 44,* 315–349.

Taylor, M. P. (1999). Survival of the fittest? An analysis of self-employment duration in Britain. *The Economic Journal, 109*, C140–155.
Titman, S., & Wessels, R. (1988). The determinants of capital structure choice. *The Journal of Finance, 43*, 1–19.
Ueda, M. (2004). Banks versus venture capital: Project evaluation, screening, and expropriation. *The Journal of Finance, 59*, 2.
Vicente-Lorente, J. D. (2001). Specificity and opacity as resource-based determinants of capital structure: Evidence for Spanish manufacturing firms. *Strategic Management Journal, 22*, 157–177.
Vismara, S., & Signori, A. (2014). How innovation shapes a firm's survival profile: Takeovers, regulatory and voluntary delistings. In B. Villalonga (Ed.), *Finance and strategy* (Vol. 31). Advances in Strategic Management. Bingley, UK: Emerald Group Publishing Limited.
Williamson, O. E. (1975). *Markets and hierarchies: Analysis and antitrust implications*. New York, NY: The Free Press.
Williamson, O. E. (1985). *The economic institutions of capitalism*. New York, NY: The Free Press.
Williamson, O. E. (1988). Corporate finance and corporate governance. *Journal of Finance, 43*(3), 567–591.
Williamson, O. E. (2002). The theory of the firm as governance structure: From choice to contract. *Journal of Economic Perspectives, 16*(Summer), 171–195.
Winston-Smith, S. (2012). New firm financing and performance. In D. Cumming (Ed.), *Oxford handbook of entrepreneurial finance*. Oxford, UK: Oxford University Press.
Winton, A., & Yerramilli, V. (2008). Entrepreneurial finance: Banks versus venture capital. *Journal of Financial Economics, 88*(1), 51–79.

APPENDIX

Table A1. Selected Pairwise Correlations.

	Variable	1	2	3	4	5	6	7	8	9	10	11	12	13	14	15	16	17	18	19	20
1	Debt Ratio	1.00																			
2	Total Equity	−0.02	1.00																		
3	Outside Equity	−0.02	0.95	1.00																	
4	Inside Equity	−0.01	0.09	0.01	1.00																
5	Total Debt	0.33	0.23	0.15	0.07	1.00															
6	Outside Debt	0.35	0.22	0.15	0.03	0.97	1.00														
7	Inside Debt	0.01	0.08	0.06	0.19	0.36	0.18	1.00													
8	R&D	−0.06	0.11	0.09	0.01	0.03	0.02	0.04	1.00												
9	Elasticity	0.08	−0.03	−0.03	−0.02	0.00	0.01	−0.02	−0.03	1.00											
10	Work Experience	−0.02	0.03	0.01	−0.02	0.02	0.02	0.00	0.02	0.00	1.00										
11	Angel or VC Funding	−0.02	0.33	0.32	0.07	0.14	0.13	0.06	0.11	0.00	0.00	1.00									
12	Survives to 2011	0.04	−0.02	−0.02	0.00	0.02	0.02	−0.01	0.03	0.04	0.10	−0.01	1.00								
13	Survives to 2007	0.02	−0.01	−0.01	−0.01	−0.01	0.00	−0.03	0.03	0.07	0.09	−0.02	0.77	1.00							
14	Age of Owners	0.03	0.07	0.04	−0.04	0.06	0.07	−0.02	0.01	0.01	0.38	0.02	0.03	0.06	1.00						
15	Homestead Exemptions	−0.01	−0.01	−0.01	0.02	0.03	0.02	0.03	−0.02	0.19	−0.02	0.01	−0.03	−0.05	0.00	1.00					
16	Bank HHI	0.04	−0.02	−0.02	−0.02	0.01	0.01	0.00	−0.01	0.22	−0.01	−0.01	0.00	0.00	0.00	−0.02	1.00				
17	Population Density	−0.03	0.05	0.04	0.02	−0.01	−0.01	0.01	0.03	−0.25	0.05	0.00	0.05	0.04	0.00	−0.09	−0.35	1.00			
18	Gross State Product	−0.04	0.03	0.03	0.02	0.00	−0.01	0.02	0.08	−0.39	−0.04	0.01	−0.01	−0.03	−0.04	0.12	−0.23	0.14	1.00		
19	Median Income	−0.03	0.04	0.04	0.00	−0.03	−0.03	0.01	0.04	−0.38	0.03	−0.01	0.05	0.03	0.00	−0.31	−0.18	0.43	0.16	1.00	
20	House Price Index	−0.06	0.06	0.05	0.04	−0.04	−0.05	0.00	0.07	−0.54	0.00	−0.01	0.02	−0.01	−0.03	−0.08	−0.21	0.42	0.62	0.56	1.00
21	Debt–Income Ratio	−0.06	0.01	0.00	0.01	−0.03	−0.03	0.00	0.05	−0.45	−0.02	−0.01	−0.05	−0.07	−0.03	−0.15	0.00	−0.13	0.45	0.29	0.50

Table A2. Effect of R&D on Entrepreneurial Finance, Alternative Specifications.

Model	(1) OLS	(2) OLS	(3) OLS	(4) OLS	(5) Two-Sided Tobit
Dependent Variable	Debt Ratio	Debt Ratio	Log-Odds Debt Ratio	Arcsin Debt Ratio	Debt Ratio
R&D	−0.084***	−0.083***	−0.812***	−0.106***	−0.170***
	[0.020]	[0.021]	[0.248]	[0.030]	[0.050]
R&D*Work Experience	0.003**	0.003**	0.037**	0.005***	0.008***
	[0.001]	[0.001]	[0.015]	[0.002]	[0.003]
R&D*Angel or VC	−0.060	−0.052	−0.649	−0.083	−0.137
	[0.055]	[0.055]	[0.654]	[0.078]	[0.130]
Work Experience	−0.001*	−0.002**	−0.018**	−0.002***	−0.004***
	[0.001]	[0.001]	[0.007]	[0.001]	[0.001]
Angel or VC Funding	−0.037	−0.049	−0.624	−0.080	−0.096
	[0.040]	[0.040]	[0.433]	[0.052]	[0.083]
Age of Owners		0.001**			
		[0.001]			
Constant	0.353***	0.303***	−1.271*	0.629***	0.377***
	[0.070]	[0.074]	[0.693]	[0.083]	[0.134]
Controls	Y	Y	Y	Y	Y
Industry Dummies	Y	Y	Y	Y	Y
State Dummies	Y	Y	Y	Y	Y
Observations	3,544	3,525	3,544	3,544	3,544
R-squared	0.08	0.08	0.08	0.08	

Notes: Results from OLS and Tobit regressions, as indicated. Additional controls include black, other non-white, female, college, graduate, same business, credit score, product, home based, incorporation, and high tech, state, and industry dummies. Standard errors are in brackets.
* significant at 10%, ** significant at 5%, *** significant at 1%.

Table A3. Effect of R&D, Elasticity on Entrepreneurial Finance, with Regional Controls.

Dependent Variable	(1) Debt Ratio	(2) Debt Ratio	(3) Debt Ratio	(4) Debt Ratio
R&D	−0.050***	−0.051***	−0.051***	−0.051***
	[0.014]	[0.014]	[0.014]	[0.014]
Work Experience	−0.001	−0.001	−0.001	−0.001
	[0.001]	[0.001]	[0.001]	[0.001]
Angel or VC Funding	−0.055*	−0.055*	−0.057*	−0.057*
	[0.030]	[0.030]	[0.030]	[0.030]
Homestead Exemptions			−0.003	−0.002
			[0.003]	[0.003]
Bank HHI			0.145	0.133
			[0.109]	[0.110]
Population Density			0.000	0.000
			[0.000]	[0.000]
Gross State Product			0.000	0.000
			[0.000]	[0.000]
Median Income			0.000	0.000
			[0.000]	[0.000]
Elasticity				0.022**
				[0.009]
Constant	0.348***	0.310***	0.308***	0.205*
	[0.070]	[0.052]	[0.106]	[0.113]
Controls	Y	Y	Y	Y
Industry Dummies	Y	Y	Y	Y
State Dummies	Y	N	N	N
Regional Dummies	N	Y	Y	Y
Observations	3,544	3,544	3,544	3,544
R-squared	0.077	0.063	0.065	0.067

Notes: Results from OLS regressions. Additional controls include black, other non-white, female, college, graduate, same business, credit score, product, home based, incorporation, and high tech, state or regional, and industry dummies. Standard errors are in brackets.
* significant at 10%, ** significant at 5%, *** significant at 1%.

Table A4. Effect of Debt Ratio, R&D on Entrepreneurial Performance: Robustness Tests.

Subsample	(1) R&D = 0	(2) R&D = 1	(3) R&D = 0	(4) R&D = 1	(5) R&D = 0	(6) R&D = 1
Removal of Outliers Using Dependent Variable	Debt–Income Ratio Survives to 2011		House Price Index Survives to 2011		Survives to 2007	
Debt Ratio	1.424**	58.603	1.555**	8.727	2.794***	12.317
	[0.644]	[893.967]	[0.735]	[24.812]	[1.045]	[55.407]
Work Experience	0.007***	−0.11	0.007***	−0.014	0.008***	−0.019
	[0.002]	[1.687]	[0.002]	[0.042]	[0.002]	[0.090]
Angel or VC Funding	0.025	4.260	0.051	0.878	0.112	1.256
	[0.095]	[66.180]	[0.095]	[2.642]	[0.130]	[5.645]
Homestead Exemptions	−0.006	0.348	−0.003	0.052	−0.005	0.065
	[0.006]	[5.446]	[0.006]	[0.172]	[0.008]	[0.320]
Bank HHI	−0.095	−6.758	−0.113	−1.020	−0.459	−1.497
	[0.255]	[105.415]	[0.263]	[3.371]	[0.372]	[8.162]
Population Density	0.000	−0.003	0.000	0.000	0.000	0.000
	[0.000]	[0.047]	[0.000]	[0.002]	[0.000]	[0.002]
Gross State Product	0.000	−0.002	0.000	−0.001	0.000	−0.001
	[0.000]	[0.033]	[0.000]	[0.003]	[0.000]	[0.003]
Median Income	0.002	0.241	0.004	0.021	0.004	0.033
	[0.004]	[3.800]	[0.004]	[0.090]	[0.006]	[0.180]
Constant	0.200	−28.711	0.063	−2.812	−0.246	−3.779
	[0.318]	[457.097]	[0.355]	[11.716]	[0.477]	[21.005]
Controls	Y	Y	Y	Y	Y	Y
Industry Dummies	Y	Y	Y	Y	Y	Y
Regional Dummies	Y	Y	Y	Y	Y	Y
Observations	2,419	647	2,385	628	2,752	792
F-statistic	10.4	0.0	8.7	0.1	9.1	0.1

Notes: Results from IV regressions. Debt ratio is instrumented using elasticity. Columns (1)–(4) remove outliers that are in the top or bottom 5% of the sample. No outliers are removed in Columns (5)–(6). Additional controls include black, other non-white, female, college, graduate, same business, credit score, product, home based, incorporation, and high tech dummy.
Standard errors in parentheses; * significant at 10%; ** significant at 5%; *** significant at 1%.

Table A5. Effect of Debt Ratio, R&D on Entrepreneurial Performance: Revenues.

Method	(1) OLS	(2) OLS	(3) OLS	(4) IV	(5) IV	(6) IV
Subsample	Full	R&D=0	R&D=1	Full	R&D=0	R&D=1
Dependent Variable	Ln Revenue 2011			Ln Revenue 2011		
Debt Ratio	0.855**	0.793**	0.702	23.044*	19.602**	125.434
	[0.353]	[0.354]	[0.788]	[11.840]	[8.868]	[574.896]
R&D	−0.186			−3.008		
	[0.282]			[7.107]		
R&D*Debt Ratio	−0.507			21.418		
	[0.815]			[44.244]		
Ln Revenue 2004	0.135***	0.140***	0.126***	0.008	0.063	−0.490
	[0.019]	[0.022]	[0.041]	[0.097]	[0.048]	[2.849]
Work Experience	0.035***	0.044***	−0.002	0.049**	0.073***	−0.207
	[0.010]	[0.011]	[0.023]	[0.022]	[0.021]	[0.952]
Angel or VC Funding	−0.638	−0.828	−0.157	1.915	0.388	11.809
	[0.501]	[0.659]	[0.811]	[2.323]	[1.096]	[55.341]
Homestead Exemptions	−0.083*	−0.062	−0.167	−0.020	−0.030	0.514
	[0.043]	[0.047]	[0.107]	[0.089]	[0.069]	[3.201]
Bank HHI	1.033	0.333	4.491	−3.884	−3.262	−11.969
	[1.681]	[1.841]	[4.252]	[4.191]	[3.113]	[79.647]
Population Density	0.000	0.000	0.001	−0.001	−0.001	−0.003
	[0.001]	[0.001]	[0.002]	[0.002]	[0.001]	[0.021]
Gross State Product	0.000	0.000	0.001	0.000	0.000	−0.007
	[0.000]	[0.000]	[0.001]	[0.001]	[0.001]	[0.033]
Median Income	0.034	0.040	0.023	0.068	0.048	0.449
	[0.029]	[0.032]	[0.070]	[0.062]	[0.046]	[2.005]
Constant	5.020***	4.649**	6.514*	−2.656	−0.909	−37.713
	[1.674]	[1.884]	[3.934]	[5.463]	[3.741]	[205.068]
Controls	Y	Y	Y	Y	Y	Y
Industry Dummies	Y	Y	Y	Y	Y	Y
Regional Dummies	Y	Y	Y	Y	Y	Y
Observations	3,544	2,752	792	3,544	2,752	792
R-squared	0.074	0.078	0.094	−1.859	−0.883	−29.997
F-Statistic				1.1	8.7	0.1

Notes: Results from OLS and IV regressions. Debt ratio and R&D*debt ratio are instrumented using elasticity and R&D*elasticity, respectively, in IV regressions. Controls include black, other non-white, female, college, graduate, same business, credit score, product, home based, incorporation, and high tech dummy. Standard errors are in parentheses.
* significant at 10%, ** significant at 5%, *** significant at 1%.